Legalization and World Politics

LEGALIZATION AND WORLD POLITICS

edited by
Judith Goldstein, Miles Kahler, Robert O. Keohane,
and Anne-Marie Slaughter

The MIT Press

Cambridge, Massachusetts and London, England

Library of Congress Cataloging-in-Publication Data

Legalization and world politics / edited by Judith Goldstein ... [et al.].
   p.   cm.
  Includes bibliographical references.
  ISBN 0-262-57151-X (pbk. : alk. paper)
  1. Law and politics. 2. World politics. 3. International relations. 4. Legalization. I. Goldstein, Judith.
K487.P65 L34 2001
341.3—dc21   00-051117

10 9 8 7 6 5 4 3 2 1

Contents

Legalization in Three Issue Areas

Conclusion

Contributors

Frederick M. Abbott is Edward Ball Eminent Scholar Chair in International Law at Florida State University College of Law, and Visiting Professor of Law, University of California at Berkeley School of Law. He can be reached at fabbott@law.fsu.edu.

Kenneth W. Abbott is Elizabeth Froehling Horner Professor of Law and Commerce at Northwestern University, Chicago, Illinois. He can be reached at k-abbott@northwestern.edu.

Karen J. Alter is Assistant Professor of Government, Northwestern University, Chicago, Illinois. She can be reached at kalter@northwestern.edu.

Judith Goldstein is Professor of Political Science at Stanford University, Stanford, California. She can be reached at judy@leland.stanford.edu.

Miles Kahler is Rohr Professor of Pacific International Relations at the Graduate School of International Relations and Pacific Studies (IR/PS), University of California, San Diego. He can be reached at mkahler@ucsd.edu.

Robert O. Keohane is James B. Duke Professor of Political Science at Duke University, Durham, North Carolina. He can be reached at rkeohane@duke.edu.

Ellen L. Lutz is an attorney with the firm of Buckalew & Lutz in Westborough, Massachusetts, and an adjunct faculty member at the Fletcher School of Diplomacy at Tufts University in Medford, Massachusetts. She can be reached at elutz@ma.ultranet.com.

Lisa L. Martin is Professor of Government at Harvard University, Cambridge, Massachusetts. She can be reached at llmartin@fas.harvard.edu.

Andrew Moravcsik is Professor of Government at Harvard University, Cambridge, Massachusetts. He can be reached at moravcs@fas.harvard.edu.

Kathryn Sikkink is Professor of Political Science at the University of Minnesota, Minneapolis, Minn. She can be reached at ksikkink@polisci.umn.edu.

Beth A. Simmons is Associate Professor of Government at the University of California, Berkeley. She can be reached at bsimmons@socrates.berkeley.edu.

Anne-Marie Slaughter is J. Sinclair Armstrong Professor of International, Foreign, and Comparative Law at Harvard University, Cambridge, Massachusetts. She can be reached at slaughtr@law.harvard.edu.

Duncan Snidal is Associate Professor of Political Science and Public Policy at the University of Chicago, Chicago, Illinois. He can be reached at snidal@uchicago.edu.

Abstracts

The Concept of Legalization
by Kenneth W. Abbott, Robert O. Keohane, Andrew Moravcsik, Anne-Marie Slaughter, and Duncan Snidal

We develop an empirically based conception of international legalization to show how law and politics are intertwined across a wide range of institutional forms and to frame the analytic and empirical articles that follow in this volume. International legalization is a form of institutionalization characterized by three dimensions: obligation, precision, and delegation. Obligation means that states are legally bound by rules or commitments and therefore subject to the general rules and procedures of international law. Precision means that the rules are definite, unambiguously defining the conduct they require, authorize, or proscribe. Delegation grants authority to third parties for the implementation of rules, including their interpretation and application, dispute settlement, and (possibly) further rule making. These dimensions are conceptually independent, and each is a matter of degree and gradation. Their various combinations produce a remarkable variety of international legalization. We illustrate a continuum ranging from "hard" legalization (characteristically associated with domestic legal systems) through various forms of "soft" legalization to situations where law is largely absent. Most international legalization lies between the extremes, where actors combine and invoke varying degrees of obligation, precision, and delegation to create subtle blends of politics and law.

Hard and Soft Law in International Governance
by Kenneth W. Abbot and Duncan Snidal

We examine why international actors—including states, firms, and activists—seek different types of legalized arrangements to solve political and substantive problems. We show how particular forms of legalization provide superior institutional solutions in different circumstances. We begin by examining the baseline advantages of "hard" legalization (that is, precise, legally binding obligations with appropriate third-party delegation). We emphasize, however, that actors often prefer softer forms of legalization (that is, various combinations of reduced precision, less stringent obligation, and weaker delegation). Soft legalization has a number of significant advantages, including that it is easier to achieve, provides strategies for dealing with uncertainty, infringes less on sovereignty, and facilitates compromise among differentiated actors.

Although our approach is largely interest-based, we explicitly incorporate the normative elements that are central in law and in recent international relations theorizing. We also consider the important role of nonstate actors who, along with states, are central participants in contemporary international legalization. We illustrate the advantages of various forms of international legal arrangements with examples drawn from articles in this special issue and elsewhere.

Legalized Dispute Resolution: Interstate and Transnational
by Robert O. Keohane, Andrew Moravcsik, and Anne-Marie Slaughter

We identify two ideal types of international third-party dispute resolution: interstate and transnational. Under interstate dispute resolution, states closely control selection of, access to, and compliance with international courts and tribunals. Under transnational dispute resolution, by contrast, individuals and nongovernmental entities have significant influence over selection, access, and implementation. This distinction helps to explain the politics of international legalization—in particular, the initiation of cases, the tendency of courts to challenge national governments, the extent of compliance with judgments, and the long-term evolution of norms within legalized international regimes. By reducing the transaction costs of setting the process in motion and establishing new constituencies, transnational dispute resolution is more likely than interstate dispute resolution to generate a large number of cases. The types of cases brought under transnational dispute resolution lead more readily to challenges of state actions by international courts. Transnational dispute resolution tends to be associated with greater compliance with international legal judgments, particularly when autonomous domestic institutions such as the judiciary mediate between individuals and the international institutions. Overall, transnational dispute resolution enhances the prospects for long-term deepening and widening of international legalization.

The European Union's Legal System and Domestic Policy: Spillover or Backlash?
by Karen J. Alter

Under what conditions do domestic actors use international legal mechanisms to influence domestic policy? Drawing on the European case, where legalization has progressed the furthest, I develop a generalizable framework for explaining variation in the use of the European Union's legal system by domestic actors to influence national policy. Four steps are involved in using the European legal process to pressure for policy change: (1) there must be a point of European law that creates legal standing and promotes the litigant's objectives; (2) litigants must embrace this law, adopting a litigation strategy; (3) a national court must refer the case to the European Court of Justice or apply ECJ jurisprudence; and (4) domestic actors must follow through on the legal victory to pressure national governments. Different factors influence each step, creating cross-national and cross-issue variation in the influence of EU law on national policy. Raising a significant challenge to neofunctionalist theory, I argue that negative interactive effects across the four steps and backlash created by the success of integration can stop or even reverse the expansionary dynamic of the legal process. I conclude by exploring the generalizability of this framework to other international contexts.

NAFTA and the Legalization of World Politics: A Case Study
by Frederick M. Abbott

I examine the trend toward using hard legal instruments in international trade governance and explain this trend in the context of the North American Free Trade Agreement (NAFTA). I suggest that hard law (1) reduces intergovernmental transaction costs, (2) reduces private risk premiums associated with trade and investment, (3) promotes transparency and provides corollary participation benefits, (4) tends to restrain strategic political behaviors, and (5) may increase the range of integration effects by encouraging private actors to enforce intergovernmental obligations. I compare the legalization model of NAFTA with those of the European Union (EU) and the Asia-Pacific Economic Cooperation (APEC) forum.

Legalization as Strategy: The Asia-Pacific Case
by Miles Kahler

The Asia-Pacific region offers an example of low legalization of regional institutions and perhaps an explicit aversion to legalization. An examination of three key regional institutions—ASEAN (Association of Southeast Asian Nations), APEC (Asia-Pacific Economic Cooperation), and the ARF (ASEAN Regional Forum)—confirms a regional process of institution building without legalization. Recent developments in these institutions permit some discrimination among competing explanations for low legalization. On the one hand, ASEAN has embraced a legalized dispute-settlement mechanism; Asian governments have also employed legalized global institutions. On the other hand, the ARF and APEC continue to resist clear-cut legal obligations and third-party dispute resolution. This pattern suggests that legalization is best viewed as driven by the demands of economic integration and as a strategic response by governments in particular institutional settings. These explanations undermine alternatives based on domestic legal culture and uniformly high sovereignty costs. The Asian economic crisis has reopened a debate over regional institutions, which may fix on legalization as part of a new regional institutional design.

The Legalization of International Monetary Affairs
by Beth A. Simmons

For the first time in history, international monetary relations were institutionalized after World War II as a set of legal obligations. The Articles of Agreement that formed the International Monetary Fund contain international legal obligations of the rules of good conduct for IMF members. Members were required to maintain a par value for their currency (until 1977), to use a single unified exchange-rate system, and to keep their current account free from restrictions. In this article I explore why governments committed themselves to these rules and the conditions under which they complied with their commitments. The evidence suggests that governments tended to make and keep commitments if other countries in their region did so as well. Governments also complied with their international legal commitments if the regime placed a high value on the rule of law domestically. One inference is that reputational concerns have a lot to do with international legal commitments and compliance. Countries that have invested in a strong reputation for protecting property rights are more reluctant to see it jeopardized by international law violations. Violation is more likely, however, in the face of widespread noncompliance, suggesting that compliance behavior should be understood in its regional context.

Legalization, Trade Liberalization, and Domestic Politics: A Cautionary Note
by Judith Goldstein and Lisa L. Martin

If the purpose of legalization is to enhance international cooperation, more may not always be better. Achieving the optimal level of legalization requires finding a balance between reducing the risks of opportunism and reducing the potential negative effects of legalization on domestic political processes. The global trade regime, which aims to liberalize trade, has become increasingly legalized over time. Increased legalization has changed the information environment and the nature of government obligations, which in turn have affected the pattern of mobilization of domestic interest groups on trade. From the perspective of encouraging the future expansion of liberal trade, we suggest some possible negative consequences of legalization, arguing that these consequences must be weighed against the positive effects of legalization on increasing national compliance. Since the weakly legalized GATT institution proved sufficient to sustain widespread liberalization, the case for further legalization must be strong to justify far-reaching change in the global trade regime.

International Human Rights Law and Practice in Latin America
by Ellen L. Lutz and Kathryn Sikkink

Human rights practices have improved significantly throughout Latin America during the 1990s, but different degrees of legalization are not the main explanation for these changes. We examine state compliance with three primary norms of international human rights law: the prohibition against torture, the prohibition against disappearance, and the right to democratic governance. Although these norms vary in their degree of obligation, precision, and delegation, states have improved their practices in all three issue-areas. The least amount of change has occurred in the most highly legalized issue-area—the prohibition against torture. We argue that a broad regional norm shift—a "norms cascade"—has led to increased regional and international consensus with respect to an interconnected bundle of human rights norms, including the three discussed in this article. These norms are reinforced by diverse legal and political enforcement mechanisms that help to implement and ensure compliance with them.

Conclusion: The Causes and Consequences of Legalization
by Miles Kahler

The intersection of law and politics provides tentative answers for two questions: First, why, among the variety of institutional forms available to governments, are legalized institutions preferred in some contexts and not in others? Second, what are the consequences of legalization? Explanations for variation in legalization are directed to the supply of legalized institutions, grounded in the preferences of the most powerful states. Those preferences are shaped, in turn, by domestic political demands for legalization as well as unanticipated domestic political dynamics that can increase legalization over time. Domestic political demands for legalization have increased as a result of international economic integration; the effects of democratization have been more ambiguous. Outside the industrialized democracies, the intersection of supply and demand is often different: supply of legalized institutions is lower and sovereignty costs are often higher. The authors in this special issue examine three important consequences of legalization: its effects on government compliance with international agreements, its impact on the evolution of international norms, and the conditions under which it will harden and spread. In each case, domestic political links are central to the effects of legalization. International agreements and institutions that are legalized, compared with those that are not, seem to be more deeply rooted in domestic politics: their existence often draws on both anticipated and unanticipated actions by domestic actors; their consequences are shaped by domestic characteristics and constituencies.

Preface

Judith Goldstein, Miles Kahler,
Robert O. Keohane, and Anne-Marie Slaughter

A collective work such as this one depends on a genuine community of scholars, and as Aristotle says, community depends on friendship (*Politics* Book IV, chapter xi, paragraph 7). All four editors have been friends for some time, and the origins of this special issue arise from these friendships.

Anne-Marie Slaughter and Bob Keohane began in the spring of 1993 seriously to discuss a joint article that they had first imagined during a conference on another joint project: a conference at Stanford on ideas and foreign policy, organized by Judy Goldstein and Bob Keohane in January 1990. Their notions were somewhat inchoate, but had to do with how domestic courts might strengthen the credibility of international commitments. The specific origins of this volume, however, began with a visit by Bob Keohane to Stanford in early 1994, during which Judy Goldstein suggested putting together a working group on domestic politics and international law. She then took the first concrete step, by applying to the National Science Foundation program in law and society for a conference grant. For crucial funding for this project, we are particularly grateful to the National Science Foundation, and to the Institute on Global Conflict and Cooperation (IGCC) of the University of California.

The four of us first got together to discuss the project at Provence restaurant in New York City, at the American Political Science Association convention, September 1994, and decided to do this project. We then wrote in early 1995 to a number of colleagues inviting them to a preliminary conference on "domestic politics and international law." We asked not for papers but for short memos with ideas about themes. The Center for International Affairs at Harvard generously supported this conference, and the Center for European Studies offered its magnificent facilities for our meeting, which took place 2–4 November 1995.

At that meeting, we began to discuss the concept of "legalization," although our definition of this concept was quite rough and vague. The Harvard meeting, however, was decisive in turning our attention in this direction, and in solidifying our collective view that this was a topic worthy of our sustained attention. A number of eventual contributors to this volume attended that meeting, including Kenneth Abbott,

International Organization 54, 3, Summer 2000, pp. xiii–xv

Lisa Martin, Andrew Moravcsik, Kathryn Sikkink, Beth Simmons, and Duncan Snidal. We are also grateful to the other participants, some of whom we unsuccessfully sought as authors of articles for this project. These participants included Abram Chayes, Stanley Hoffmann, Benedict Kingsbury, Stephen D. Krasner, Charles Lipson, Kal Raustiala, Jeremy Rabkin, John Setear, Martin Shefter, Alec Stone Sweet, Frank Upham, Ruth Wedgwood, and Barry Weingast.

After the Harvard meeting, we continued to write on this subject and communicate with one another. Judy Goldstein, Anne-Marie Slaughter, and Kathryn Sikkink presented papers for a roundtable on international law and domestic politics at the American Political Science Association convention in August 1996, in which other members of our group also participated. Several participants in the Harvard conference reconvened for a small meeting on international institutions at Duke in September 1996, and further discussed aspects of legalization. Most significantly, Judy Goldstein and Miles Kahler began to organize a full-scale conference on domestic politics and international law at the Harvest Inn, St. Helena, California, 4–7 June 1997. At this conference, papers were presented. The "descendants" of some of those papers appear in this special issue. In addition to the contributors to this volume (all of whom attended the St. Helena conference), we are grateful to the following participants, whose comments were valuable in shaping the volume to result: William Alford, David Caron, Benjamin Cohen, Kurt Gaubatz, Peter Gourevitch, Stephan Haggard, Benedict Kingsbury, David Lake, Kal Raustiala, Amy Searight, John Setear, Christina Sevilla, Martin Shapiro, and Frank Upham.

The most significant accomplishment of the St. Helena conference was an agreement that the focus of the volume would be "legalization and world politics." This agreement required consensus on the core of the concept of "legalization," which is discussed in Abbott et al. in this volume. Elements of previously separate papers by Kenneth Abbott and Duncan Snidal, on the one hand, and Bob Keohane, Andrew Moravcsik, and Anne-Marie Slaughter, on the other, were merged to produce this five-author concepts paper. We editors are particularly grateful to Kenneth Abbott, who played a leading role in developing and explicating the concept of legalization around which this volume revolves.

It became clear at the St. Helena conference that some of the papers overlapped and others conflicted; some were quite strong, but many were in need of extensive revision. To promote discussion, Judy Goldstein had organized a roundtable on "domestic politics and international law" at the American Political Science Association convention in August 1997, in which Karen Alter, Judy Goldstein, Miles Kahler, Stephen D. Krasner, Lisa Martin, and Beth Simmons participated. A flurry of email correspondence followed over the summer and fall. By mid-December, we had devised a proposed outline for the volume, which bears a fairly close resemblance to the volume that you have in your hands. By this time, the editors had sent to all authors detailed and often extensive suggestions for changes in their papers. As the only international lawyer in our group, Anne-Marie Slaughter's guidance to authors, and her co-editors, was invaluable to whatever success this project has as an interdisciplinary venture.

Our suggestions were sufficiently extensive that the authors needed their summers to work on them. Between July and November 1998, the revised chapters flowed in. After further revisions had been made, we were ready to send some of the draft papers to *International Organization* in April 1999. Meanwhile, Miles Kahler produced a conclusion, synthesizing many of the insights of the papers, and articulating a set of themes. By late August, the editors of *IO*, Peter Gourevitch and David Lake, had received reviews from the two referees. Professors Gourevitch and Lake contributed extensive and perceptive comments and detailed instructions, which we received in September. Responding to these comments, the special issue editors communicated again (for at least the third time) with each paper author, with guidance for revisions. The results of this process included a new introduction; in addition, every paper in the volume was thoroughly revised.

The review process was extraordinary, yielding approximately eighty single-spaced pages of comments. One of the referees, whom we now know to be Professor Richard Steinberg of UCLA Law School, wrote the most brilliant and meticulously detailed comments that we have ever seen—on every paper. Professor Steinberg is truly our "shadow editor." We are extraordinarily grateful to him, to the anonymous referee, and to the editors of *IO*, for contributions that were far and above the "call of duty," and without which our volume would have been much inferior to what you have in your hands. We would also like to thank Lynne Bush and Joni Harlan for their extraordinary efforts in producing this volume.

Collective projects entail collective action, which can retard progress. With four editors, responsibility for taking initiatives was not always well-defined. As long as it was not clear that the volume would succeed, authors were naturally reluctant to give it the highest priority in their own work schedules. During the period between August 1997 and April 1999, Bob Keohane played the role of principal organizer, cheerleader, and "arm-twister," seeking to maintain momentum and morale. In the spring of 1999, when the papers were submitted to *IO*, Miles Kahler took over the chief responsibility for organizing the editorial process. When the volume was conditionally accepted for publication in September 1999, we all pushed aside other projects to put *Legalization and World Politics* on the "front burner." As a result, all papers were back to *IO* before the end of 1999. Subject to some last-minute revisions, completed in February, the editors put us on the "fast track" for publication in the summer of 2000.

The long gestation period of this project has been accompanied by some "mood swings," with periods both of exhilaration and malaise. But the editors' friendship has survived, and has even become more robust. Friendship is a stimulus to frankness but an antidote to irritation. A shared ironic sense of humor also helps. In the end, we hope that our friendship will have made a contribution to the scholarly community of which we are only a small part.

Introduction: Legalization and World Politics

Judith Goldstein, Miles Kahler,
Robert O. Keohane, and Anne-Marie Slaughter

In many issue-areas, the world is witnessing a move to law. As the century turned, governments and individuals faced the following international legal actions. The European Court of Human Rights ruled that Britain's ban on homosexuals in the armed forces violates the right to privacy, contravening Article 8 of the European Convention on Human Rights.[1] The International Criminal Tribunal for the Former Yugoslavia indicted Yugoslav president Slobodan Milosevic during a NATO bombing campaign to force Yugoslav forces out of Kosovo.[2] Milosevic remains in place in Belgrade, but Austrian police, bearing a secret indictment from the International Criminal Tribunal, arrested a Bosnian Serb general who was attending a conference in Vienna.[3] In economic affairs the World Trade Organization (WTO) Appellate Body found in favor of the United States and against the European Union (EU) regarding European discrimination against certain Latin American banana exporters.[4] A U.S. district court upheld the constitutionality of the North American Free Trade Agreement (NAFTA) against claims that its dispute-resolution provisions violated U. S. sovereignty.[5] In a notable environmental judgment, the new Law of the Sea Tribunal ordered the Japanese to cease all fishing for southern bluefin tuna for the rest of the year.[6]

1. See *Lustig-Prean and Beckett v. The United Kingdom,* App. Nos. 31417/96 and 32377/96 (27 Sept. 1999); *Smith and Grady v. The United Kingdom,* App. Nos. 33985/96 and 33986/96 (Eur. Ct. H.R.) (27 Sept. 1999) (available at <http://www.echr.coe.int/eng/Judgments.htm>).
2. See Roger Cohen, Warrants Served for Serbs' Leader and 4 Assistants, *New York Times,* 28 May 1999, A1; and Raymond Bonner, Despite Indictment, Politicians and Diplomats Control Milosevic's Future, *New York Times,* 28 May 1999, A13.
3. See Marlise Simons, Top Bosnian Officer Arrested for U.N. Tribunal, *New York Times,* 26 August 1999, A10.
4. See European Communities—Regime for the Importation, Sale, and Distribution of Bananas— Recourse to Arbitration by the European Communities Under Article 22.6 of the DSU, Decision by the Arbitrators, WTO Doc. WT/DS27/ARB (9 Apr. 1999) (available at <http://www.wto.org/wto/dispute/distab.htm>).
5. See *Made in the USA Foundation v. United States,* 56 F. Supp. 2d 1226 (n.d. Ala. 1999).
6. See Southern Bluefin Tuna Cases (*New Zealand v. Japan; Australia v. Japan*) (order of 27 August 1999) (Int'l Trib. for the Law of the Sea) (available at <http://www.un.org/Depts/los/ITLOS/Order-tuna34.htm>).

International Organization 54, 3, Summer 2000, pp. 1–15

These actions, taken in the course of a single year, were representative of a longer term trend: some international institutions are becoming increasingly legalized. The discourse and institutions normally associated with domestic legal systems have become common in world politics. This move to law is not limited to the actions of international tribunals. Legally binding environmental treaties have proliferated in recent years. These agreements often trace their lineage to hortatory political pronouncements but often become closer to hard law over time. The Montreal Protocol on Substances Depleting the Ozone Layer, for instance, is now a legally binding and precise agreement with a related system of implementation review involving third parties.[7] Arms control agreements display increasing precision and elaboration in their commitments and in the scale of their implementing bureaucracies. The proliferation of nuclear weapons and the possession and deployment of entire classes of other weapons (among them chemical weapons and landmines) are now subject to detailed legal conventions.

Despite these prominent examples, however, the move to law is hardly uniform. Compliance with the judgments of international tribunals and WTO panels remains uneven. Military intervention, both unilateral and multilateral, continues to occur without clear international legal authority. The NATO bombing of Serbia in 1999 was only one recent example of a decline in the precision of rules governing armed intervention, as challenges to the old norms of territorial sovereignty have mounted. Major arms control treaties are stalled by domestic political opposition. Neither exchange rates nor the provision of multilateral financial aid are subject to precise legal rules. An important environmental initiative, the Framework Convention on Climate Change, imposes only vague obligations, although the recent Kyoto Protocol has substantially increased the density of the norms in this regime. Other regimes, such as that for international whaling, have maintained the same degree of legalization over several decades. Many Asian nations have explicitly rejected legalized institutions, preferring a model that eschews formal legal obligations. Latin American nations have been similarly cautious about pooling sovereignty in independent institutions such as those that characterize the EU, despite repeated efforts to promote economic integration of various parts of the continent.

The goal of this special issue of *IO* is a better understanding of this variation in the use and consequences of law in international politics. Legalization, a particular form of institutionalization, represents the decision in different issue-areas to impose international legal constraints on governments. This issue of *IO* defines legalization and elaborates different types of legalization. It charts the extent of legalization and its variation across issue-areas and regions. It explains why actors choose to create legalized institutions. It investigates the consequences of legalization on participants, on political and legal processes, and on the international system. Finally, it explores how international politics within legalized institutions differs from politics in non-legalized institutions.

---

7. Victor 1998.

By developing a framework for the study of legaliz
perspectives developed by political scientists and inte
engage in a genuinely collaborative venture. We view
politics: affected by political interests, power, and ir
international lawyers and political scientists have obse
be understood in isolation from politics.[8] Converse
political processes and political outcomes. The relationship betw__
is reciprocal, mediated by institutions.

In this introduction we map the way in which legalization, its causes, and its
consequences will be assessed. We provide a summary of the definition of legalization adopted in this issue and as developed in the article by Kenneth Abbott, Robert
O. Keohane, Andrew Moravcsik, Anne-Marie Slaughter, and Duncan Snidal. We
describe the different perspectives on legalization coming from international law and
political science and outline the theoretical puzzles that legalization poses for international relations theory. Finally, we summarize the articles in the context of the
broader research problems faced by each of the contributors to this special issue.

Legalization and International Institutions

International institutions—enduring sets of rules, norms, and decision-making procedures that shape the expectations, interests, and behavior of actors—vary on many
dimensions. The WTO and the international regime for the protection of polar bears
are both institutions, but they differ according to the scope of their rules, the resources available to the formal organizations, and their degree of bureaucratic differentiation. In general, greater institutionalization implies that institutional rules govern more of the behavior of important actors—more in the sense that behavior
previously outside the scope of particular rules is now within that scope or that
behavior that was previously regulated is now more deeply regulated.

Substantial institutionalization can be demonstrated to exist in world politics, but
legalization represents a specific set of dimensions along which institutions vary. The
definition of legalization adopted in this issue contains three criteria: the degree to
which rules are obligatory, the precision of those rules, and the delegation of some
functions of interpretation, monitoring, and implementation to a third party. Fully
legalized institutions bind states through law: their behavior is subject to scrutiny
under the general rules, procedures, and discourse of international law and, often,
domestic law. Legalized institutions also demonstrate a high degree of precision,
meaning that their rules unambiguously define the conduct they require, authorize, or
proscribe. Finally, legal agreements delegate broad authority to a neutral entity for
implementation of the agreed rules, including their interpretation, dispute settlement,
and (possibly) further rule making.

---

8. See Henkin 1979; Schacter 1991; and Claude 1966.

these three dimensions can vary from high to low, and each can vary dently of the others. Abbott, Keohane, Moravcsik, Slaughter, and Snidal con- a typology of legalized institutions that varies from an ideal-type of complete alization in which all three properties are high through various forms of partial egalization to institutions without legalization. Abbott and Snidal, in their article, elaborate this typology along a spectrum from hard to soft law, and develop a rich and innovative set of candidate explanations for this variation. They draw on a wide range of actual examples of more or less legalized regimes within the categories set forth by the typology.

This definition does not portray legalization as a superior form of institutionalization. Nor do the contributors to this special issue adopt a teleological view that increased legalization in international relations is natural or inevitable. In using the concept of legalization to guide our collective analysis, we consider softer variants (lower legalization) to be of equal interest to hard law. Why actors move from one form of legalized institution to another is also central. Such moves include the formalization of an informal understanding or customary practice, the adoption of systematic rules to crystallize and codify practices as they evolve, and the strengthening of delegation to increasingly independent and powerful third-party tribunals.

The Uneven Expansion of Legalization

Legalization has expanded in contemporary world politics, but that expansion is uneven. In this section we review the approach of recent international legal scholarship, which has chronicled and categorized this "move to law" but has largely failed to evaluate or challenge it. Approaches from political science should be more helpful in explaining the puzzle of uneven legalization; the remainder of the section describes the insights and shortcomings of the political science literature.

Variation in Legalization

The revival of the use of law in international politics has not gone unnoticed, although legal scholarship has analyzed it through different lenses. The actual or arguable power of law and courts has been one central perspective in the study of the EU and the WTO, for example. Many specialists in law accept that European economic integration has depended on the construction of an effective EU legal system. The European Court of Justice (ECJ) is depicted as a central player in this process, propounding the legally binding character of both the Treaty of Rome and EU directives and ensuring that EU law was enforceable through third-party adjudication, often initiated by private individuals and firms.[9] Recently, political scientists and lawyers have challenged this canonical narrative, emphasizing congruence between ECJ judg-

---

9. See Stein 1981; Weiler 1991; and Burley and Mattli 1993.

ments and state interests and variation in the relationship between the ECJ and different national courts.[10]

In the legal literature, these debates now fall under the larger rubric of the "constitutionalization" of the Treaty of Rome,[11] a view that emphasizes the role of courts in a unique effort to construct a supranational European polity rather than the legalization of an intergovernmental regime. Constitutional rhetoric and an emphasis on a growing role for law and third-party adjudication also figure in research on the evolution of the world trading system, now increasingly understood as the emergence of an international economic constitution.[12] Constitutionalization, however, is a very broad brush, sweeping in foundational problems of social order. More narrowly focused studies of trade regimes and of the commercial arbitration agreements that facilitate foreign direct investment instead describe the phenomenon of "judicialization" of dispute-settlement processes, essentially emphasizing our third variable: delegation.[13]

Many scholars have analyzed the judicialization of the General Agreement on Tariffs and Trade (GATT) dispute-settlement system, chronicling the long-running struggle between trade "legalists," those seeking third-party adjudication of trade disputes under clear legal rules, and trade "pragmatists," those supporting nonbinding forms of dispute resolution that allowed more scope for power and diplomacy.[14] The evolution of GATT dispute-settlement procedures in the direction of a more legalized regime under the WTO represents a victory for the legalists. Contemporary WTO panels are conducted in accord with legal norms. Lawyers present detailed legal arguments that require a response from all parties; panel members construct their decisions with the assistance of a legal secretariat that helps them to resolve legal issues rather than broker a political compromise.[15] International commercial arbitration has experienced a similar evolution, as arbitrators become more like judges and arbitration procedure becomes more like judicial procedure.[16]

An emphasis on courts as both creators and guarantors of an international rule of law extends beyond economic regimes. International lawyers have drawn attention to the proliferation of international and supranational tribunals in such issue-areas as human rights, the law of the sea, intellectual property, and international environmental protection.[17] These tribunals range from courts with direct jurisdiction over individual claims and enforcement powers over national governments to much less ambitious "noncompliance bodies" designed to oversee implementation of various environmental agreements.[18] An entire subspecialty has developed in international

---

10. See Garrett and Weingast 1993; Garrett, Kelemen, and Schulz 1998; Slaughter, Stone Sweet, and Weiler 1998; and Alter 1998a,b.

11. See Weiler 1999; and Stone Sweet 1998.

12. See Jackson 1998; and Petersmann 1991.

13. See Hudec 1992; and Stone Sweet 1999 and 2000.

14. See Trimble 1985; Jackson, Louis, and Matsushita 1984; and Jackson and Davey 1986.

15. Hudec 1992 and 1999.

16. See Lillich and Brower 1994; and Stone Sweet 1999.

17. Romano 1999.

18. Ibid.

criminal law, driven by the creation of international war crimes tribunals, such as the Bosnia and Rwanda tribunals, proposed hybrid arrangements involving both national and international judges in Cambodia and possibly East Timor, and a nascent International Criminal Court.[19]

The legal literature typically describes these tribunals, analyzes and evaluates their decisions, and theorizes their relationship to one another in terms of a global legal system.[20] A growing number of scholars also seek to evaluate their effectiveness based on a set of criteria developed across issue-areas.[21] What the legal literature omits—and what this special issue includes—is an explanation for government decisions to establish such tribunals. Somewhat paradoxically, legal scholars also often fail to analyze courts in the larger context of legalization.

The broader definition of legalization that informs this special issue includes judicialization, but it also emphasizes the importance of rule precision and degree of obligation. For example, certain international agreements, including in part the UN Conference on the Law of the Sea Convention, are expressly designed as instruments of codification. Other agreements, such as the transformation of voluntary guidelines of the UN Food and Agricultural Organization and the UN Environment Program regarding hazardous pesticides and chemicals into legally binding treaties are changes in the obligatory rather than the formal qualities of law.[22] The rules themselves can become more specific, highly elaborated, and technical, qualities captured in the concept of "juridification" in some areas of domestic law.[23]

Legalization as defined here also allows capture of a wider range of variation in international institutions. A singular focus on high-profile international tribunals can obscure a broader spectrum of delegation. The World Bank, for example, under its general mandate to promote development, has developed operational standards for environmental impact assessment, treatment of indigenous peoples, and participation of nongovernmental organizations in project planning. These policies become legally binding on borrower states when incorporated in loan documents, and they are enforced by the World Bank's Inspection Panel. In other instances, states avoid such delegation. Merit Janow notes, for example, that "even the most legalistic of APEC's members [the United States, Canada, and Australia] have not called for the creation of an expanded APEC bureaucracy or the development of a new supra-national authority to administer or develop APEC-wide rules."[24] Even within particular treaty regimes, levels of delegation can vary. NAFTA contains a wide variety of dispute-settlement mechanisms: binational panels that produce resolutions enforceable through national courts, transgovernmental commissions appointed to oversee specific issue-areas, and interstate bargaining with a nonbinding panel decision as a focal point.[25]

19. See Bassiouni 1999; Morris and Scharf 1995 and 1998; and Ratner and Abrams 1997.
20. See Romano 1999; and Charney 1999.
21. See Helfer and Slaughter 1997; Romano 1999; Pan 1999; Noyes 1998; Knox 1999; and Helfer 1998.
22. Mekouar 1998.
23. Teubner 1987.
24. Janow 1996/1997.
25. Morales 1997.

Just as many existing treatments of the move to law have concentrated on the dimension of delegation and the creation of new judicial or quasi-judicial tribunals, so examination of the consequences of legalization has emphasized its effects on domestic legal institutions. NAFTA's domestic legal effects have varied to the same degree as its legalization. The binational panels established under NAFTA Chapter 19 have changed U.S. administrative behavior in the determination of unfair trading practices that warrant the imposition of countervailing duties.[26] Gilbert Winham describes the NAFTA Chapter 19 achievement as the possible "beginning of an internationalized form of administrative law."[27] A Mexican legal scholar argues that increased competition from international tribunals promotes domestic judicial reform in Mexico.[28] On the other hand, NAFTA's transgovernmental Commission on Environmental Cooperation "is too weak to create the pressures necessary to cause substantial redrafting of environmental legislation" and is useful largely as a device for disseminating information about effective domestic environmental law.[29] What is again often missing in these accounts is an exploration of the wider political context.

Explaining Legalization

The expansion of legalization into new domains and the unevenness of that expansion raise theoretical puzzles that have remained largely unexplored. Why and when do states choose legalized institutional forms when their autonomy would be less constrained by avoiding legalization? How do legalized constraints operate to change government behavior, if they do? Are efforts to legalize certain issue-areas in world politics realistic attempts to facilitate cooperation or misguided attempts to construct a stable order on the basis of fragile norms rather than the realities of power politics? Although contemporary theoretical perspectives in international relations can suggest tentative answers to these puzzles (or at least suggest where to look for the answers), in recent decades few international relations scholars have directly tackled the question of legalization and its consequences.

Realist arguments regard international legal constraints as either nonexistent or weak. For those propounding an anarchic international politics based on national self-help, the central puzzles are why states devote so much attention to constructing legalized institutions that are bound to have so little effect and why states accept as credible pledges to obey legal rules that could effectively bind them to act in ways that might be antithetical to their interests. To the degree that legalization represents rules that do bind at least some governments, the realist explanation is clear: legal rules emanate from dominant powers and represent their interests. Legal rules that "work" bind the weaker members of the system; enforcement of those rules ultimately depends on a willingness by stronger powers to bear the costs of enforcement.

26. Goldstein 1996.
27. Winham 1998.
28. Fix-Fierro and Lopes-Ayllon 1997.
29. Raustiala 1996.

Normatively, realist political scientists have been skeptical of the value of international legal advances. E. H. Carr famously criticized legalism divorced from power and politics;[30] George F. Kennan attacked what he saw as the "legalism-moralism" of U.S. foreign policy.[31] Legalism as an approach to world politics—if not legalization as defined here—provides comforting and delusional justification for policies that are inconsistent with the realities of interest and power. Those policies are likely to collapse under pressure, often with catastrophic consequences. In this view, legalism may constrain intelligent diplomatic accommodation.

Institutionalist theory offers a different, though only partial, answer to these puzzles. Functionalist theories of international institutions, which stress the role of institutions in reducing uncertainty and transaction costs, have seldom dealt directly with the distinction between legalized and nonlegalized agreements.[32] In certain respects the study of international institutions in political science has been directed to demonstrating that informal institutions—not legalized and lacking any centralized enforcement—could still be effective. On the basis of institutionalist theory one should expect frequent informal agreements, some formal rules, and loopholes that provide flexibility in response to political exigencies. Institutionalist theory accommodates such antilegalist realities as the neglect of dispute-settlement mechanisms in GATT during the 1970s, at the same time that voluntary export restraints and other "gray-area" measures proliferated outside the GATT legal structure. Institutionalist theory has explained how cooperation endures without legalization, but it has not explained legalization. Abbott and Snidal extend institutionalist reasoning to an explanation of legalization and its variations in their article in this issue.

Although liberal approaches to world politics have been most closely associated with a promotion of international law and legalized institutions (for example, the International Court of Justice), liberalism's theoretical contribution to the investigation of legalization lies more in its emphasis on the importance of domestic politics: the preferences of domestic groups and their mobilization and representation in domestic and transnational political institutions. The attention paid by liberal theorists to the relationship between domestic politics and international institutions produces hypotheses regarding the causes and consequences of legalization. Certain forms of international legalization—in particular those that fall under the category that Keohane, Moravcsik, and Slaughter term "transnational legalization"—may be designed to grant domestic actors direct access to international tribunals. This de facto shift in the institutional representation for social actors provides a unique form of representation for many social actors—one that reduces the cost of political action, thereby increasing the flow of internationally directed legal action and hence the likelihood of further development of legal rules.

---

30. Carr 1939.
31. Kennan 1984.
32. Charles Lipson's research on informal agreements is a partial exception, emphasizing that informal agreements can promote cooperation and seeking to explain how decentralized systems of incentives can help to make agreements effective without a formal legal system. Lipson 1991.

Governments and domestic groups may also deliberately employ international legalization as a means to bind themselves or their successors in the future. In other words, international legalization may have the aim of imposing constraints on domestic political behavior. Finally, liberal theory suggests that the primary site for the enforcement of international law is ultimately domestic. International legal norms are most effectively enforced when they are embedded in autonomous domestic "rule of law" legal systems through legal incorporation, judicial acceptance, or acceptance by lawyers and litigants. The more important incentives for compliance are ultimately domestic.[33]

Constructivists have called attention to the basis for international identities and institutions in shared norms and beliefs, but they have not explained the distinctiveness of legal norms or why actors sometimes prefer to reinforce normative consensus with legalized institutions. Some constructivist scholars explicitly integrate their approach with the study of law.[34] Others emphasize the particular role that law can play as the "crystallization of state expectations," suggesting a dynamic process of "hardening" norms over time.[35] Within legal scholarship, Thomas Franck's theory of legal legitimacy, which explains the "compliance pull" of legal norms through their determinacy, pedigree, adherence, and coherence, also fits easily within a constructivist frame of analysis.[36] Overall, constructivist explanations of legalization are likely to hinge less on functionalist and interest-driven accounts and more on historically contingent narratives regarding the emergence of a particular legal understanding.[37]

If legal scholars have provided a rich and valuable account of one dimension of contemporary international legalization—increasing delegation to judicial and quasi-judicial institutions—international relations theorists have pointed to several alternative explanations for the variable appearance of legalization and likely sites for examining the consequences of legalization. Each of these approaches finds expression in this special issue, as a more detailed description of the articles will demonstrate.

Organization of the Special Issue

The first three articles present a theoretical frame that each of the subsequent articles deploys. Abbott, Keohane, Moravcsik, Slaughter, and Snidal set forth and elaborate the definition of legalization. A typology of legalization, presented in Table 1 of their article, provides a classificatory structure for comparative analysis. The case studies in the remaining articles (except the article by Abbott and Snidal) can be located and compared with one another in the terms set by this table.

Abbott and Snidal develop the spectrum of hard and soft legal arrangements. They provide explanations for decisions to make agreements "harder" or "softer" on one

33. See Slaughter 1995a; and Mattli and Slaughter 1998b.
34. Finnemore 1996, 139–43.
35. Finnemore and Sikkink 1998.
36. Franck 1990.
37. Finnemore and Sikkink 1998.

or more dimensions that focus on contracting and transaction costs theory as well as normative considerations. In their view legalization can help states and other actors resolve the commitment problems that are pervasive in international politics, reduce transaction costs, and expand the grounds for compromise. These benefits stem from both interest-based and norm-based processes, and they accrue to interest-based and norm-based agreements. But legalization also entails contracting costs of its own, as well as imposing constraints on government action (autonomy costs). Under different conditions, including different levels of uncertainty and different time horizons among actors, hard and soft law will imply different ratios of costs and benefits. Hence, it should be possible, Abbott and Snidal argue, to account for variations in legalization by identifying how institutional arrangements involving greater or lesser degrees of obligation, precision, and delegation generate particular patterns of costs and benefits. Their approach to legalization can be deployed to explain government behavior as well as the behavior of groups that evaluate their interests for or against legalization.

Keohane, Moravcsik, and Slaughter introduce an explanatory variable that ties legalization to domestic politics more directly: whether individuals have direct access to the dispute-resolution process (transnational dispute resolution) or whether those processes are limited formally to governments (interstate dispute resolution). They describe the different politics that surround these two types of dispute resolution and argue that the two have very different results for the expansion of legalization. Since members of civil society may assess the autonomy costs of legalization very differently than governments, transnational legalization has much greater potential for expansion than traditional interstate legalization.

The remaining contributors examine specific institutional arrangements, arrayed by region (Karen Alter; Frederick Abbott; and Miles Kahler) and by issue-area (Beth Simmons; Judith Goldstein and Lisa Martin; and Ellen L. Lutz and Kathryn Sikkink). These contributors evaluate the extent of legalization in each case, providing explanations for the pattern of legalization and what effect legalization has had on participants and policies.

Alter concentrates on the effects of high legalization in the EU on EU policies. She discovers, in accord with the model of transnational dispute resolution presented by Keohane, Moravcsik, and Slaughter, that the politics surrounding European law and legal institutions are different from a strictly interstate model. However, she also argues that the effects of this highly legalized system are highly dependent on mediation by domestic political and judicial institutions. The dynamic of increasing legalization is far from automatic or inevitable. She suggests conditions under which that dynamic is likely to be more or less powerful, or to be reversed in the face of national backlash.

Frederick Abbott describes another, less legalized regional agreement, NAFTA, that embodies a high degree of obligation and precision but a much lower degree of delegation than one finds in the EU. NAFTA's design ensures that political leaders will continue to make key decisions. Nevertheless, where delegation has occurred, such as the delegation of midlevel decisions to binational panels, the degree of implementation of these decisions has been very high. In assessing NAFTA's implementation, Abbott notes that the agreement has not been tested in hard times: political commitment to implementation on the part of member governments has been high. Whether the constraints of NAFTA are binding in the longer term will only be revealed when a member government is dissatisfied with major provisions of the agreement.

The case of regionalism in the Asia-Pacific region, examined by Kahler in his article, is the principal example of an explicit choice in favor of low legalization. Kahler demonstrates this choice on the part of Asian governments in a comparison of three different regional organizations: the Association of Southeast Asian Nations (ASEAN), the ASEAN Regional Forum, and Asia-Pacific Economic Cooperation (APEC). Kahler presents institutionalization in the near-absence of legalization. Recent differentiation among these regional organizations, however, suggests not only that the level of legalization could change in the future, but that it is explained by the strategic choice of governments in the face of a changing international and regional environment.

The final three articles examine legalization in three key issue-areas: international monetary affairs, trade, and human rights. Simmons explains both the willingness of governments to accept binding legal obligations in international monetary affairs and their compliance with those commitments. In an international regime that has demonstrated wide swings in legalization over time, she concentrates on Article VIII of the International Monetary Fund Articles of Agreement, which requires members to keep current account transactions free from exchange restrictions. Her analysis illuminates both international and domestic explanations for these choices in favor of legalized commitments. Most provocatively, she calls into question any easy connection between democracy and the choice for legalization (or compliance with legal obligations).

Goldstein and Martin analyze legalization of the international trade regime, usually accepted as one of the most legalized global economic regimes. Despite the regime's relatively high level of legalization, Goldstein and Martin emphasize that legalization operates through politics, by changing processes of decision making, interpretation, and implementation. However, their assessment of the domestic political effects of legalization under GATT and the WTO leads to skepticism regarding the positive effects of legalization on national compliance and international cooperation. Overall, the impact of legalization on trade liberalization will depend on its effects on the incentives for political mobilization at home.

Lutz and Sikkink examine human rights law in Latin America through the evolution of norms and international legal obligations regarding democratization and two human rights abuses, torture and disappearance. Levels of legalization vary considerably in these three issue-areas, but all three demonstrated marked improvement in the 1980s and 1990s. Lutz and Sikkink propose an alternative explanation based on transnational politics and the evolution of international norms to explain improved compliance in the absence (in some cases) of higher legalization.

Kahler, in his conclusion to the special issue, couples the authors' empirical findings with the theoretical frameworks presented in the first three articles. He emphasizes that variation found in the pattern of legalization across issue-area and region can be explained only through understanding both interstate strategic calculations (will other governments accept legal obligations and higher levels of delegation?) and the domestic politics of participating states. The domestic politics of legalization, in turn, involve both choices for or against legalization by domestic groups and the often unforeseen consequences of legalization on the structure and processes of domestic politics.

Legalization and World Politics: Common Assumptions
and Working Hypotheses

The contributors to this special issue have different disciplinary perspectives and investigate cases that vary by region and issue-area. Nevertheless, they share a common set of assumptions and working hypotheses.

Legalization is a specific form of institutionalization. The contributors to this issue all adopt the conceptualization of legalization set forth in "The Concept of Legalization" by Abbott, Keohane, Moravcsik, Slaughter, and Snidal: a fully legalized institution is one with high levels of obligation, precision, and delegation. Moving away from this ideal-type of "hard law," institutions can be identified as partially legalized and legalized on one or more of these dimensions. Although the form of legalization may vary, as represented in Table 1 of the article by Abbott et al., throughout the special issue legalization is understood as a particular and distinctive form of institutionalization. All legalized regimes are institutionalized (they have durable rules); but not all institutionalized regimes are legalized. Legalized institutions incorporate relatively precise substantive rules or obligations, though they may also contain the procedural rules and largely hortatory obligations that are characteristic of nonlegalized international institutions. With respect to international agreements that are not highly legalized, the interpretation of rules occurs in national capitals; legal institutions, on the other hand, delegate this function to third parties.

Legalized institutions can be explained in terms of their functional value, the preferences and incentives of domestic political actors, and the embodiment of particular international norms. In addition to describing variation in legalized institutions, the authors offer explanations for the choice of a legal form of interstate cooperation. The special issue is not committed to the view that legalized institutions are a "better" or more efficient form of organization. Rather, the authors aim to explain why actors choose legalized forms. The explanations advanced cluster into three broad categories.

The first group of explanations is based on the anticipated consequences of a "legal" agreement. The incentive for nations to agree to more, rather than less, legalized accords derives from the functions performed by "harder" agreements. Using this mode of explanation, Abbott and Snidal emphasize in particular the benefits of legalization in forging credible commitments and reducing transactions costs. Those benefits, however, may be wholly or partially offset by negotiating costs and the added constraints that legalization imposes on government decision-making autonomy. In this functional view legalized institutions provide a different set of prospective benefits than nonlegalized institutions.

The second group of explanations modifies this model of calculation by unitary actors by adding the calculations of domestic political actors. These influential constituencies will have diverse preferences over the move to legalization. The simplest modification of the first explanatory model finds the source of government preferences in the aggregated preferences of influential groups. Individuals and groups will favor or oppose legalization based on their assessments of whether the outcomes will further their interests. More complexity is added, however, when those domestic political actors make strategic calculations designed to constrain not only other governments in their international behavior but also domestic actors, including their own government. In the eyes of some domestic actors, estimates of the relevant consequences of legalization are not only international but also domestic. Since prospective agreements differentially affect domestic actors, they change domestic politics by mobilizing some actors and giving them greater access to policymaking. In particular, precise agreements with binding arbitration introduce new actors into politics, such as domestic courts and lawyers, and they also change the venues in which disputes are handled, away from national capitals and into court-like forums.

A third explanation for the choice of more legalization lies in normative evolution. Legalization can change domestic normative discourse regarding the efficacy of the rule of law. Some actors favor law not only because it serves their interests but also because they believe decisions taken according to legal precepts are superior to other forms of governance. Belief in law as a "good" is not evenly distributed in the population or across regions. Certainly, lawyers more often believe in the use of law than other occupational groups, though it is hard to separate the normative from the material basis of their support. "Rule of law" societies, given a precise definition by Simmons, appear to have a different record of compliance with legal obligations than other societies. Understanding the interaction of norms and legalization is a challenge for social science. In this special issue, only Lutz and Sikkink explicitly take up the task. However, other contributors also suggest an interaction between an interest-based and a norms-based explanation for regime creation.

A key consequence of legalization for international cooperation lies in its effects on compliance with international obligations.   Many of the contributors examine the relationship between legalization and compliance. Without legalization, compliance is a difficult concept to define or measure, since no authoritative body exists to interpret its meaning or apply it to particular cases.[38] Legalization has its principal effect on compliance and international cooperation through the mobilization of indi-

---

38. Simmons 1998, 78.

viduals and groups in domestic politics—the compliance (or noncompliance) constituencies discussed in Kahler's conclusion. As Keohane, Moravcsik, and Slaughter argue, these compliance constituencies can have a transnational as well as a national character. Different forms of legalization, particularly interstate and transnational legalization, generate a different political dynamic, leading to variation in compliance with international obligations.

All of the contributors agree that legalization has led to some behavior change, although the magnitude and direction of these effects on compliance and international cooperation vary. Perhaps the most prominent cases are provided by the EU and the WTO, in which delegation to courts and quasi-judicial bodies has led to more fundamental changes in the locus of decision making.

Compliance with obligations, institutional effectiveness, and increased international cooperation may not coincide, in part because of the domestic effects of legalization. The contributors do not base their investigations on any assumption that legalization, as compared to other forms of institutionalization, will necessarily enhance international cooperation. The increased certainty produced by legalization could, in principle, reduce the risks of agreement and therefore enhance cooperation.[39] For the functional reasons already stated, legalized agreements and institutions may induce more long-lasting agreements. The changes in domestic politics generated by legalization may also reinforce the position of interests that favor enhanced international cooperation. On the other hand, because of their increased certainty and precision, legal agreements engender high negotiating costs, both across societies and within them: *ex ante* bargaining is likely therefore to be more prolonged and difficult.[40] As Goldstein and Martin argue, clarity of obligation in an agreement may reduce interest in the agreement itself, since its anticipated distributional consequences are clarified as well. A systematic evaluation of the net effects of legalization on cooperation is beyond the reach of this special issue. It would require both valid measures of cooperation in particular domains and an ability to distinguish the effects of legalization from other causal variables, such as increases in economic integration, shifts in domestic interests, and normative evolution. Since legalization, like institutionalization, is to some extent endogenous to such factors, such an assessment would be daunting.[41]

The effects of legalization on world politics in the long run will depend on its continuing uneven spread. Its spread will depend on the evolution of international norms, its consequences for domestic and transnational politics, and its perceived benefits for key actors. It is possible that legalization at the end of the century will be remembered as a temporary aberration, as it was in the 1920s. The

---

39. Bilder 1981.
40. Fearon 1998.
41. Keohane and Martin 1999.

articles that follow suggest at least three ways in which legalization could have longer lasting effects on international politics.

First, legalization may have a direct effect on the evolution of international norms. Legalization is more explicitly principled than specific diplomatic bargains, even if those bargains implicitly incorporate norms. The strengthening of norms helps explain patterns of compliance and the expansion of legalized forms into new issue-areas; that is, beliefs can be self-reinforcing. Second, legalization may permanently change the nature of domestic and transnational politics in participating countries. International law can become internalized.[42] Differential access by groups, the expansion of the role of the courts, and the delegation of authority to third parties could lead domestic actors to change their expectations and behavior and promote an expansion of legalization. Legalization could also create transnational communities of support for legalized agreements in specific issue-areas. This pro-law epistemic EU would protect international agreements from retrenchment, and its members would serve as transnational advocates for its expansion. Finally, the more often legal agreements are signed and reap cooperative outcomes, the more often actors will return to this institutional form as a model for future agreements. International cooperation is difficult. Actors rely on focal points, not only for the distribution of gains from cooperation but also for models of organization to assure joint gains. Whatever the reasons for success, success may well become associated with legalized forms. (Just as the failure of some legalized institutions in the interwar decades provoked a negative reaction.) Success or failure, whether due to the institutional form or not, may be the most important determinant of whether the "hard" law model becomes more widespread across regions and issue-areas.

Legalization and World Politics: Aims and Expectations

The editors and authors of this special issue do not claim to have provided a coherent new theory to explain the differentiated phenomenon that we have defined as legalization. Our interest is principally to open some conceptual and analytical doors to a more sustained and explicitly theoretical analysis of the connections between law and politics in contemporary world politics. Overall, the authors express considerable skepticism about the significance and contingency of the international and domestic effects of legalization. No assumption is made that legalization is a wave of the future. We did not begin with a normative stance, and we make few hard predictions about the future. Interstate legalization, as reflected in the jurisprudence of the International Court of Justice, has not transformed world politics. Likewise, although significant changes have occurred in such areas as trade and human rights, not all of these changes may be causally associated with legalization. We write neither to praise nor to bury legalization, but to analyze its dimensions, its sources, and its current and prospective effects.

42. Koh 1998.

The Concept of Legalization

Kenneth W. Abbott, Robert O. Keohane,
Andrew Moravcsik, Anne-Marie Slaughter,
and Duncan Snidal

The subject of this volume is "legalization and world politics." "World politics" in this formulation needs no clarification, but "legalization"—the real focus of the volume—must be more clearly defined, if only because of its relative unfamiliarity to students of international relations. In the introduction the editors have briefly previewed the concept of legalization used throughout the volume, a concept developed collaboratively by the authors of this article. We understand legalization as a particular form of institutionalization characterized by three components: obligation, precision, and delegation. In this article, we introduce these three characteristics, explore their variability and the range of institutional forms produced by combining them, and explicate the elements of legalization in greater detail.

The Elements of Legalization

"Legalization" refers to a particular set of characteristics that institutions may (or may not) possess. These characteristics are defined along three dimensions: obligation, precision, and delegation. *Obligation* means that states or other actors are bound by a rule or commitment or by a set of rules or commitments. Specifically, it means that they are *legally* bound by a rule or commitment in the sense that their behavior thereunder is subject to scrutiny under the general rules, procedures, and discourse of international law, and often of domestic law as well. *Precision* means that rules unambiguously define the conduct they require, authorize, or proscribe. *Delegation* means that third parties have been granted authority to implement, interpret, and apply the rules; to resolve disputes; and (possibly) to make further rules.

Each of these dimensions is a matter of degree and gradation, not a rigid dichotomy, and each can vary independently. Consequently, the concept of legalization encompasses a multidimensional continuum, ranging from the "ideal type" of legal-

International Organization 54, 3, Summer 2000, pp. 17–35
© 2000 by The IO Foundation and the Massachusetts Institute of Technology

ization, where all three properties are maximized; to "hard" legalization, where all three (or at least obligation and delegation) are high; through multiple forms of partial or "soft" legalization involving different combinations of attributes; and finally to the complete absence of legalization, another ideal type. None of these dimensions—far less the full spectrum of legalization—can be fully operationalized. We do, however, consider in the section entitled "The Dimensions of Legalization" a number of techniques by which actors manipulate the elements of legalization; we also suggest several corresponding indicators of the strength or weakness of legal arrangements.

Statutes or regulations in highly developed national legal systems are generally taken as prototypical of hard legalization. For example, a congressional statute setting a cap on emissions of a particular pollutant is (subject to any special exceptions) legally binding on U.S. residents (obligation), unambiguous in its requirements (precision), and subject to judicial interpretation and application as well as administrative elaboration and enforcement (delegation). But even domestic enactments vary widely in their degree of legalization, both across states—witness the vague "proclamations" and restrictions on judicial review imposed by authoritarian regimes—and across issue areas within states—compare U.S. tax law to "political questions" under the Constitution. Moreover, the degree of obligation, precision, or delegation in formal institutions can be obscured in practice by political pressure, informal norms, and other factors. International legalization exhibits similar variation; on the whole, however, international institutions are less highly legalized than institutions in democratic rule-of-law states.

Note that we have defined legalization in terms of key characteristics of rules and procedures, not in terms of effects. For instance, although our definition includes delegation of legal authority (to domestic courts or agencies as well as equivalent international bodies), it does not include the degree to which rules are actually implemented domestically or to which states comply with them. To do so would be to conflate delegation with effective action by the agent and would make it impossible to inquire whether legalization increases rule implementation or compliance. Nor does our definition extend to the substantive content of rules or their degree of stringency. We regard substantive content and legalization as distinct characteristics. A conference declaration or other international document that is explicitly not legally binding could have exactly the same substantive content as a binding treaty, or even a domestic statute, but they would be very different instruments in terms of legalization, the subject of this volume.

Our conception of legalization creates common ground for political scientists and lawyers by moving away from a narrow view of law as requiring enforcement by a coercive sovereign. This criterion has underlain much international relations thinking on the topic. Since virtually no international institution passes this standard, it has led to a widespread disregard of the importance of international law. But theoretical work in international relations has increasingly shifted attention away from the need for centralized enforcement toward other institutionalized ways of promoting cooperation.[1] In addition, the forms of legalization we observe at the turn of the millennium are flourishing in the absence of centralized coercion.

Any definition is ultimately arbitrary at the margins. Yet definitions should strive to meet certain criteria. They should be broadly consistent with ordinary language, but more precise. To achieve precision, definitions should turn on a coherent set of identifiable attributes. These should be sufficiently few that situations can be readily characterized within a small number of categories, and sufficiently important that changes in their values will influence the processes being studied. Defining legalization in terms of obligation, precision, and delegation provides us with identifiable dimensions of variation whose effects on international behavior can be empirically explored.

Our concept of legalization is a working definition, intended to frame the analytic and empirical articles that follow in this volume as well as future research. Empiricist in origin, it is tailored to the phenomena we observe in international relations. We are not proposing a definitive definition or seeking to resolve age-old debates regarding the nature of law or whether international law is "really" law. Highly legalized arrangements under our conception will typically fall within the standard international lawyer's definition of international law. But many international commitments that to a lawyer entail binding legal obligations lack significant levels of precision or delegation and are thus partial or soft under our definition.

We acknowledge a particular debt to H. L. A. Hart's *The Concept of Law*.[2] Hart defined a legal system as the conjunction of primary and secondary rules. Primary rules are rules of obligation bearing directly on individuals or entities requiring them "to do or abstain from certain actions." Secondary rules, by contrast, are "rules about rules"—that is, rules that do not "impose obligations," but instead "confer powers" to create, extinguish, modify, and apply primary rules.[3] Again, we do not seek to define "law" or to equate our conception of legalization with a definition of a legal system. Yet Hart's concepts of primary and secondary rules are useful in helping to pinpoint the distinctive characteristics of the phenomena we observe in international relations. The attributes of obligation and precision refer to international rules that regulate behavior; these closely resemble Hart's primary rules of obligation. But when we define obligation as an attribute that incorporates general rules, procedures, and discourse of international law, we are referring to features of the international system analogous to Hart's three main types of secondary rules: recognition, change, and adjudication. And the criterion of delegation necessarily implicates all three of these categories.[4]

---

1. See the debate between the "managerial" perspective that emphasizes centralization but not enforcement, Chayes and Chayes 1995, and the "compliance" perspective that emphasizes enforcement but sees it as decentralized, Downs, Rocke, and Barsoom 1996.
2. Hart 1961.
3. Hart 1961, 79.
4. Hart, of course, observed that in form, though not in substance, international law resembled a primitive legal system consisting only of primary rules. We sidestep that debate, noting only that the characteristics we observe in international legalization leave us comfortable in applying Hart's terms by analogy. We also observe that the international legal framework has evolved considerably in the decades since Hart

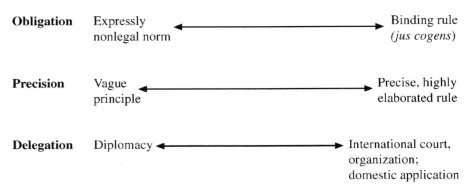

FIGURE 1. *The dimensions of legalization*

The Variability of Legalization

A central feature of our conception of legalization is the variability of each of its three dimensions, and therefore of the overall legalization of international norms, agreements, and regimes. This feature is illustrated in Figure 1. In Figure 1 each element of the definition appears as a continuum, ranging from the weakest form (the absence of legal obligation, precision, or delegation, except as provided by the background operation of the international legal system) at the left to the strongest or "hardest" form at the right.[5] Figure 1 also highlights the independence of these dimensions from each other: conceptually, at least, the authors of a legal instrument can combine any level of obligation, precision, and delegation to produce an institution exactly suited to their specific needs. (In practice, as we shall explain, certain combinations are employed more frequently than others.)

It would be inappropriate to equate the right-hand end points of these dimensions with "law" and the left-hand end points with "politics," for politics continues (albeit in different forms) even where there is law. Nor should one equate the left-hand end points with the absence of norms or institutions; as the designations in Figure 1 suggest, both norms (such as ethical principles and rules of practice) and institutions (such as diplomacy and balance of power) can exist beyond these dimensions. Figure 1 simply represents the components of legal institutions.

Using the format of Figure 1, one can plot where a particular arrangement falls on the three dimensions of legalization. For example, the Agreement on Trade-Related Aspects of Intellectual Property (TRIPs), administered by the World Trade Organization (WTO), is strong on all three elements. The 1963 Treaty Banning Nuclear Weapons Tests in the Atmosphere, in Outer Space, and Under Water is legally binding and

---

wrote. Franck reviews these changes and argues that international law has developed a general rule of recognition tied to membership in the international community. Franck 1990, 183–207.

5. On the "obligation" dimension, *jus cogens* refers to an international legal rule—generally one of customary law, though perhaps one codified in treaty form—that creates an especially strong legal obligation, such that it cannot be overridden even by explicit agreement among states.

quite precise, but it delegates almost no legal authority. And the 1975 Final Act of the Helsinki Conference on Security and Cooperation in Europe was explicitly not legally binding and delegated little authority, though it was moderately precise.

The format of Figure 1 can also be used to depict variations in the degree of legalization between portions of an international instrument (John King Gamble, Jr. has made a similar internal analysis of the UN Convention on the Law of the Sea[6]) and within a given instrument or regime over time. The Universal Declaration of Human Rights, for example, was only minimally legalized (it was explicitly aspirational, not overly precise, and weakly institutionalized), but the human rights regime has evolved into harder forms over time. The International Covenant on Civil and Political Rights imposes binding legal obligations, spells out concepts only adumbrated in the declaration, and creates (modest) implementing institutions.[7]

Table 1 further illustrates the remarkable variety of international legalization. Here, for concise presentation, we characterize obligation, precision, and delegation as either high or low. The eight possible combinations of these values are shown in Table 1; rows are arranged roughly in order of decreasing legalization, with legal obligation, a peculiarly important facet of legalization, weighted most heavily, delegation next, and precision given the least weight. A binary characterization sacrifices the continuous nature of the dimensions of legalization as shown in Figure 1 and makes it difficult to depict intermediate forms. Yet the table usefully demonstrates the range of institutional possibilities encompassed by the concept of legalization, provides a valuable shorthand for frequently used clusters of elements, and highlights the tradeoffs involved in weakening (or strengthening) particular elements.

Row I on this table corresponds to situations near the ideal type of full legalization, as in highly developed domestic legal systems. Much of European Community (EC) law belongs here. In addition, the WTO administers a remarkably detailed set of legally binding international agreements; it also operates a dispute settlement mechanism, including an appellate tribunal with significant—if still not fully proven—authority to interpret and apply those agreements in the course of resolving particular disputes.

Rows II–III represent situations in which the character of law remains quite hard, with high legal obligation and one of the other two elements coded as "high." Because the combination of relatively imprecise rules and strong delegation is a common and effective institutional response to uncertainty, even in domestic legal systems (the Sherman Antitrust Act in the United States is a prime example), many regimes in row II should be considered virtually equal in terms of legalization to those in row I. Like the Sherman Act, for example, the original European Economic Community (EEC) rules of competition law (Articles 85 and 86 of the Treaty of Rome) were for the most part quite imprecise. Over time, however, the exercise of

---

6. Gamble 1985.
7. The declaration has also contributed to the evolution of customary international law, which can be applied by national courts as well as international organs, and has been incorporated into a number of national constitutions.

TABLE 1. *Forms of international legalization*

Type	Obligation	Precision	Delegation	Examples
Ideal type:				
Hard law				
I	High	High	High	EC; WTO—TRIPs; European human rights convention; International Criminal Court
II	High	Low	High	EEC Antitrust, Art. 85-6; WTO—national treatment
III	High	High	Low	U.S.–Soviet arms control treaties; Montreal Protocol
IV	Low	High	High (moderate)	UN Committee on Sustainable Development (Agenda 21)
V	High	Low	Low	Vienna Ozone Convention; European Framework Convention on National Minorities
VI	Low	Low	High (moderate)	UN specialized agencies; World Bank; OSCE High Commissioner on National Minorities
VII	Low	High	Low	Helsinki Final Act; Nonbinding Forest Principles; technical standards
VIII	Low	Low	Low	Group of 7; spheres of influence; balance of power
Ideal type: Anarchy				

interpretive authority by the European courts and the promulgation of regulations by the Commission and Council produced a rich body of law. The 1987 Montreal Protocol on Substances that Deplete the Ozone Layer (row III), in contrast, created a quite precise and elaborate set of legally binding rules but did not delegate any significant degree of authority for implementing them. Because third-party interpretation and application of rules is so central to legal institutions, we consider this arrangement less highly legalized than those previously discussed.

As we move further down the table, the difficulties of dichotomizing and ordering our three dimensions become more apparent. For example, it is not instructive to say that arrangements in row IV are necessarily more legalized than those in row V; this judgment requires a more detailed specification of the forms of obligation, precision, and delegation used in each case. In some settings a strong legal obligation (such as the original Vienna Ozone Convention, row V) might be more legalized than a weaker obligation (such as Agenda 21, row IV), even if the latter were more precise and entailed stronger delegation. Furthermore, the relative significance of delegation vis-à-vis other dimensions becomes less clear at lower levels, since truly "high" delegation, including judicial or quasi-judicial authority, almost never exists together with low levels of legal obligation. The kinds of delegation typically seen in rows IV and VI are administrative or operational in nature (we describe this as "moderate" delegation in Table 1). Thus one might reasonably regard a precise but nonobligatory agreement (such as the Helsinki Final Act, row VII) as more highly legalized than an imprecise and nonobligatory agreement accompanied by modest administrative delegation (such as the High Commissioner on National Minorities of the Organization for Security and Cooperation in Europe, row VI).[8] The general point is that Table 1 should be read indicatively, not as a strict ordering.

The middle rows of Table 1 suggest a wide range of "soft" or intermediate forms of legalization. Here norms may exist, but they are difficult to apply as law in a strict sense. The 1985 Vienna Convention for the Protection of the Ozone Layer (row V), for example, imposed binding treaty obligations, but most of its substantive commitments were expressed in general, even hortatory language and were not connected to an institutional framework with independent authority. Agenda 21, adopted at the 1992 Rio Conference on Environment and Development (row IV), spells out highly elaborated norms on numerous issues but was clearly intended not to be legally binding and is implemented by relatively weak UN agencies. Arrangements like these are often used in settings where norms are contested and concerns for sovereign autonomy are strong, making higher levels of obligation, precision, or delegation unacceptable.

Rows VI and VII include situations where rules are not legally obligatory, but where states either accept precise normative formulations or delegate authority for implementing broad principles. States often delegate discretionary authority where judgments that combine concern for professional standards with implicit political criteria are required, as with the International Monetary Fund (IMF), the World Bank, and the other international organizations in row VI. Arrangements such as those in row VII are sometimes used to administer coordination standards, which actors have incentives to follow provided they expect others to do so, as well as in areas where legally obligatory actions would be politically infeasible.

Examples of rule systems entailing the very low levels of legalization in row VIII include "balances of power" and "spheres of influence." These are not legal institutions in any real sense. The balance of power was characterized by rules of practice[9] and by arrangements for diplomacy, as in the Concert of Europe. Spheres of influence during the Cold War were imprecise, obligations were partly expressed in treaties but largely tacit, and little institutional framework existed to oversee them.

Finally, at the bottom of the table, we approach the ideal type of anarchy prominent in international relations theory. "Anarchy" is an easily misunderstood term of art, since even situations taken as extreme forms of international anarchy are in fact structured by rules—most notably rules defining national sovereignty—with legal or pre-legal characteristics. Hedley Bull writes of "the anarchical society" as characterized by institutions like sovereignty and international law as well as diplomacy and

---

8. Interestingly, however, while the formal mandate of the OSCE High Commissioner on National Minorities related solely to conflict prevention and did not entail authority to implement legal (or nonlegal) norms, in practice the High Commissioner has actively promoted respect for both hard and soft legal norms. Ratner 2000.

9. Kaplan 1957.

the balance of power.[10] Even conceptually, moreover, there is a wide gap between the weakest forms of legalization and the complete absence of norms and institutions.

Given the range of possibilities, we do not take the position that greater legalization, or any particular form of legalization, is inherently superior.[11] As Kenneth Abbott and Duncan Snidal argue in "Hard and Soft Law in International Governance" (this volume), institutional arrangements in the middle or lower reaches of Table 1 may best accommodate the diverse interests of concerned actors. A concrete example is the argument made by Judith Goldstein and Lisa Martin in their article "Legalization, Trade Liberalization, and Domestic Politics: A Cautionary Note": more highly legalized trade rules can be problematic for liberal trade policy.

On a related set of issues—whether international legalization is increasing, or likely to increase, over time—we take no position. The comparative statics approach that informs this volume is not suitable for analyzing such dynamic phenomena. Yet the issues are important and intriguing. We undoubtedly witness increasing legalization in many issue areas. The ozone depletion regime, for example, began in 1985 with a binding but otherwise weakly legalized convention (row V). It was augmented two years later by the more precise and highly elaborated Montreal Protocol (row III). Since then, through practice and subsequent revisions, the regime has developed a "system for implementation review," with a noncompliance procedure that still falls short of third-party dispute resolution but appears to have had some impact on behavior.[12] In other issue areas, like the whaling regime described by John K. Setear, the level of legalization appears to remain largely constant over time, even as the substance of the regime changes.[13] And in still others, legalization seems to decline, as in the move from fixed to floating exchange rates. Exploration of legal dynamics would be the logical next step in the research program that this volume seeks to inaugurate.

In the remainder of this article we turn to a more detailed explication of the three dimensions of legalization. We summarize the discussion in each section with a table listing several indicators of stronger or weaker legalization along the relevant dimension, with delegation subdivided into judicial and legislative/administrative components.

The Dimensions of Legalization

Obligation

Legal rules and commitments impose a particular type of binding obligation on states and other subjects (such as international organizations). Legal obligations are different in kind from obligations resulting from coercion, comity, or morality alone. As

10. Bull 1977.
11. Compare Goldstein, Kahler, Keohane, and Slaughter, this issue.
12. Victor, Raustalia, and Skolnikoff 1998, especially chap. 4.
13. Setear 1999.

discussed earlier, legal obligations bring into play the established norms, procedures, and forms of discourse of the international legal system.[14]

The fundamental international legal principle of *pacta sunt servanda* means that the rules and commitments contained in legalized international agreements are regarded as obligatory, subject to various defenses or exceptions, and not to be disregarded as preferences change. They must be performed in good faith regardless of inconsistent provisions of domestic law. International law also provides principles for the interpretation of agreements and a variety of technical rules on such matters as formation, reservation, and amendments. Breach of a legal obligation is understood to create "legal responsibility," which does not require a showing of intent on the part of specific state organs.

The international legal system also contains accepted procedures and remedies for breaches of legal commitments. Only states injured by a breach have standing to complain; and the complaining state or its citizens must exhaust any domestic remedies within the breaching state before making an international claim. States may then pursue their claims diplomatically or through any formal dispute procedure they have accepted. International law also prescribes certain defenses, which include consent, self-defense, and necessity, as well as the broad doctrine called *rebus sic stantibus*: an agreement may lose its binding character if important conditions change materially. These doctrines automatically inject a degree of flexibility into legal commitments; by defining particular exceptions, though, they reinforce legal obligations in other circumstances.

When breach leads to injury, legal responsibility entails an obligation to make reparation, preferably through restitution. If this is not possible, the alternative in the event of material harm is a monetary indemnity; in the event of psychological harm, "satisfaction" in the form of an apology. Since achieving such remedies is often problematic, international law authorizes self-help measures, including reprisals, reciprocal measures (such as the withdrawal of equivalent concessions in the WTO), and retorsions (such as suspending foreign aid). Self-help is limited, though, by the doctrine of proportionality and other legal conditions, including restrictions on the unilateral use of force.

Finally, establishing a commitment as a legal rule invokes a particular form of discourse. Although actors may disagree about the interpretation or applicability of a set of rules, discussion of issues purely in terms of interests or power is no longer legitimate. Legalization of rules implies a discourse primarily in terms of the text, purpose, and history of the rules, their interpretation, admissible exceptions, applicability to classes of situations, and particular facts. The rhetoric of law is highly devel-

---

14. In linking obligation to the broader legal system, we are positing the existence of international law as itself imposing a body of accepted and thereby legitimized obligations on states. If the ultimate foundation of a legal system is its acceptance as such by its subjects, through a Kelsenian *Grundnorm* or an ultimate rule of recognition, then we are positing the existence of that acceptance by states with regard to the existing international legal system. The degree of obligation that we seek to measure refers instead to acceptance by subject states of a particular rule as a legal rule or not, that is, as binding or not binding as a matter of international law.

TABLE 2. *Indicators of obligation*

High
  Unconditional obligation; language and other indicia of intent to be legally bound
  Political treaty: implicit conditions on obligation
  National reservations on specific obligations; contingent obligations and escape clauses
  Hortatory obligations
  Norms adopted without law-making authority; recommendations and guidelines
  Explicit negation of intent to be legally bound
Low

oped, and the community of legal experts—whose members normally participate in legal rule-making and dispute settlement—is highly socialized to apply it. Thus the possibilities and limits of this discourse are normally part and parcel of legalized commitments.

Commitments can vary widely along the continuum of obligation, as summarized in Table 2. An example of a hard legal rule is Article 24 of the Vienna Convention on Diplomatic Relations, which reads in its entirety: "The archives and documents of the mission shall be inviolable at any time and wherever they may be." As a whole, this treaty reflects the intent of the parties to create legally binding obligations governed by international law. It uses the language of obligation; calls for the traditional legal formalities of signature, ratification, and entry into force; requires that the agreement and national ratification documents be registered with the UN; is styled a "Convention;" and states its relationship to preexisting rules of customary international law.[15] Article 24 itself imposes an unconditional obligation in formal, even "legalistic" terms.

At the other end of the spectrum are instruments that explicitly negate any intent to create legal obligations. The best-known example is the 1975 Helsinki Final Act. By specifying that this accord could not be registered with the UN, the parties signified that it was not an "agreement . . . governed by international law." Other instruments are even more explicit: witness the 1992 "Non-Legally Binding Authoritative Statement of Principles for a Global Consensus" on sustainable management of forests. Many working agreements among national government agencies are explicitly nonbinding.[16] Instruments framed as "recommendations" or "guidelines"—like the

15. Under accepted legal principles, many of which are codified in the Vienna Convention on the Law of Treaties, the intent of the parties to an agreement determines whether that instrument creates obligations that are legally binding, not merely personal or political in effect, and that are governed by international law, rather than the law of some nation. Intent is sometimes explicitly stated; otherwise it must be discerned from the overall context of an agreement, its negotiating history, the nature of its commitments, and its form. As a practical matter, however, legalization is the default position: significant agreements between states are assumed to be legally binding and governed by international law unless the parties indicate otherwise. U.S. practice on this score is summarized in the State Department's *Foreign Relations Manual*, pt. 181.

16. Zaring 1998.

OECD Guidelines on Multinational Enterprises—are normally intended not to create legally binding obligations.[17]

These contrasting legal forms have distinctive implications. Under legally binding agreements like the Vienna Convention, states may assert legal claims (under *pacta sunt servanda,* state responsibility and other doctrines of international law), engage in legal discourse, invoke legal procedures, and resort to legal remedies. Under non-binding instruments like the Forest Principles states may do none of these things, although they may make normative claims, engage in normative discourse, and resort to political remedies. Further theorizing and empirical investigation are needed to determine whether these distinctions—at least in the absence of strong delegation—lead to substantial differences in practice. The care with which states frame agreements, however, suggests a belief that they do.

Actors utilize many techniques to vary legal obligation between these two extremes, often creating surprising contrasts between form and substance. On the one hand, it is widely accepted that states expect some formally binding "political treaties" not to be observed if interests or circumstances change.[18] More frequently, provisions of legally binding agreements are worded to circumscribe their obligatory force. One common softening device is the contingent obligation: the 1994 Framework Convention on Climate Change, for example, requires parties to take various actions to limit greenhouse gas emissions, but only after considering "their specific national and regional development priorities, objectives, and circumstances."

Another widely used device is the escape clause.[19] The European Convention for the Protection of Human Rights and Fundamental Freedoms, for example, authorizes states to interfere with certain civil rights in the interest of national security and the prevention of disorder "when necessary in a democratic society," and more broadly during war "or other public emergency threatening the life of the nation."[20] Most arms control agreements include the following clause, repeated verbatim from the Limited Test Ban Treaty: "Each party shall in exercising its national sovereignty have the right to withdraw from [this agreement] if it decides that extraordinary events, related to the subject matter of [this agreement], have jeopardized the supreme interests of its country."[21] Many instruments, from the Outer Space Treaty to the Convention on the Settlement of Investment Disputes, simply allow for withdrawal after a specified notice period.

17. Although precise obligations are generally an attribute of hard legalization, these instruments use precise language to avoid legally binding character.

18. See Baxter 1980; and Schachter 1977.

19. In addition to the explicit escape clauses considered here, states are often able to escape from the strictures of particular provisions by filing reservations, declarations, and other unilateral conditions after an agreement has been negotiated.

20. These avenues of escape are quite precisely drafted and are supervised by the European Commission and Court of Human Rights, limiting the ability of states to evade their substantive obligations.

21. In contrast to the European Convention on Human Rights, this withdrawal clause is self-judging, increasing its softening effect. Nonetheless, the clause was originally inserted to impose some constraints on what might otherwise have been seen as an unconditional right to withdraw.

Other formally binding commitments are hortatory, creating at best weak legal obligations. Article IV of the IMF Articles of Agreement, for example, requires parties only to "endeavor" to adopt specified domestic economic policies and to "seek to promote" economic stability, "with due regard to [their] circumstances." The International Covenant on Economic, Social, and Cultural Rights requires parties only "to take steps . . . with a view to achieving progressively the full realization of the rights recognized in the . . . Covenant."[22]

On the other hand, a large number of instruments state seemingly unconditional obligations even though the institutions or procedures through which they were created have no direct law-creating authority! Many UN General Assembly declarations, for example, enunciate legal norms, though the assembly has no formal legislative power.[23] Instruments like the 1992 Rio Declaration on Environment and Development and the 1995 Beijing Declaration on Women's Rights are approved at UN conferences with no agreed law-making power.[24]

Instruments like these should not be troublesome in legal terms, since they do not conform to the established "rules of recognition" of international law. In fact, though, they are highly problematic. Over time, even nonbinding declarations can shape the practices of states and other actors and their expectations of appropriate conduct, leading to the emergence of customary law or the adoption of harder agreements. Soft commitments may also implicate the legal principle of good faith compliance, weakening objections to subsequent developments. In many issue areas the legal implications of soft instruments are hotly contested. Supporters argue for immediate and universal legal effect under traditional doctrines (for example, that an instrument codifies existing customary law or interprets an organizational charter) and innovative ones (for example, that an instrument reflects an international "consensus" or "instant custom"). As acts of international governance, then, soft normative instruments have a finely wrought ambiguity.[25]

Precision

A precise rule specifies clearly and unambiguously what is expected of a state or other actor (in terms of both the intended objective and the means of achieving it) in a particular set of circumstances. In other words, precision narrows the scope for reasonable interpretation.[26] In Thomas Franck's terms, such rules are

---

22. Some agreements authorize particular conduct rather than requiring or prohibiting it. Such provisions are usually couched as rights, using the word *may*. Gamble 1985.

23. See Chinkin 1989; and Gruchalla-Wesierski 1984.

24. This discussion also applies to instruments adopted by organizations with law-making competency but outside prescribed procedures. A significant example is the European Social Charter, adopted by all members of the EC Council except the United Kingdom. These states bypassed a unanimity requirement to avoid a U.K. veto, adopting a softer instrument to guide subsequent legislative action.

25. Palmer 1992.

26. A precise rule is not necessarily more constraining than a more general one. Its actual impact on behavior depends on many factors, including subjective interpretation by the subjects of the rule. Thus, a rule saying "drive slowly" might yield slower driving than a rule prescribing a speed limit of 55 miles per hour if the drivers in question would normally drive 50 miles per hour and understand "slowly" to mean

"determinate."[27] For a set of rules, precision implies not just that each rule in the set is unambiguous, but that the rules are related to one another in a noncontradictory way, creating a framework within which case-by-case interpretation can be coherently carried out.[28] Precise sets of rules are often, though by no means always, highly elaborated or dense, detailing conditions of application, spelling out required or proscribed behavior in numerous situations, and so on.

Precision is an important characteristic in many theories of law. It is essential to a rationalist view of law as a coordinating device, as in James D. Morrow's account of the laws of war.[29] It is also important to positivist visions of law as rules to be applied, whether through a centralized agency or through reciprocity.[30] Franck argues that precision increases the legitimacy of rules and thus their normative "compliance pull." Lon L. Fuller, like other liberals, emphasizes the social and moral virtues of certainty and predictability for individual actors.[31] In each case, clarity is essential to the force of law.

In highly developed legal systems, normative directives are often formulated as relatively precise "rules" ("do not drive faster than 50 miles per hour"), but many important directives are also formulated as relatively general "standards" ("do not drive recklessly").[32] The more "rule-like" a normative prescription, the more a community decides *ex ante* which categories of behavior are unacceptable; such decisions are typically made by legislative bodies. The more "standard-like" a prescription, the more a community makes this determination *ex post,* in relation to specific sets of facts; such decisions are usually entrusted to courts. Standards allow courts to take into account equitable factors relating to particular actors or situations, albeit at the sacrifice of some *ex ante* clarity.[33] Domestic legal systems are able to use standards like "due care" or the Sherman Act's prohibition on "conspiracies in restraint of trade" because they include well-established courts and agencies able to interpret and apply them (high delegation), developing increasingly precise bodies of precedent.

In some international regimes, the institutional context is sufficiently thick to make similar approaches feasible. In framing the EEC's common competition policy, for example, the drafters of the Treaty of Rome utilized both rules and stan-

---

10 miles per hour slower than normal. (We are indebted to Fred Schauer for both the general point and the example.) In addition, precision can be used to define limits, exceptions, and loopholes that reduce the impact of a rule. Nevertheless, for most rules requiring or prohibiting particular conduct—and in the absence of precise delegation—generality is likely to provide an opportunity for deliberate self-interested interpretation, reducing the impact, or at least the potential for enforceable impact, on behavior.

27. Franck 1990.

28. Franck labels this collective property "coherence." We use the singular notion of precision to capture both the precision of a rule in isolation and its precision within a rule system.

29. Morrow 1997 and 1998.

30. Simma and Paulus 1999.

31. Fuller 1964.

32. The standard regime definition encompasses three levels of precision: "principles," "norms," and "rules." Krasner 1983. This formulation reflects the fact that societies typically translate broad normative values into increasingly concrete formulations that decision-makers can apply in specific situations.

33. Kennedy 1976.

dards.[34] Where they could identify disfavored conduct in advance, they specified it for reasons of clarity and notice: Article 85, for example, prohibits agreements between firms "that . . . fix purchase or selling prices." Because they could not anticipate all problematic conduct, though, the drafters also authorized the European Court to apply a general standard, prohibiting "agreements . . . which have as their object or effect the . . . distortion of competition within the common market."

In most areas of international relations, judicial, quasi-judicial, and administrative authorities are less highly developed and infrequently used. In this thin institutional context, imprecise norms are, in practice, most often interpreted and applied by the very actors whose conduct they are intended to govern. In addition, since most international norms are created through the direct consent or practice of states, there is no centralized legislature to overturn inappropriate, self-serving interpretations. Thus, precision and elaboration are especially significant hallmarks of legalization at the international level.

Much of international law is in fact quite precise, and precision and elaboration appear to be increasing dramatically, as exemplified by the WTO trade agreements, environmental agreements like the Montreal (ozone) and Kyoto (climate change) Protocols, and the arms control treaties produced during the Strategic Arms Limitation Talks (SALT) and subsequent negotiations. Indeed, many modern treaties are explicitly designed to increase determinacy and narrow issues of interpretation through the "codification" and "progressive development" of customary law. Leading examples include the Vienna Conventions on the Law of Treaties and on Diplomatic Relations, and important aspects of the UN Convention on the Law of the Sea. Even many nonbinding instruments, like the Rio Declaration on Environment and Development and Agenda 21, are remarkably precise and dense, presumably because proponents believe that these characteristics enhance their normative and political value.

Still, many treaty commitments are vague and general, in the ways suggested by Table 3.[35] The North American Free Trade Agreement side agreement on labor, for example, requires the parties to "provide for high labor standards." Article VI of the Treaty on the Non-proliferation of Nuclear Weapons calls on the parties "to pursue negotiations in good faith on effective measures relating to cessation of the nuclear arms race . . . and to nuclear disarmament." Commercial treaties typically require states to create "favorable conditions" for investment and avoid "unreasonable" regulations. Numerous agreements call on states to "negotiate" or "consult," without specifying particular procedures. All these provisions create broad areas of discretion for the affected actors; indeed, many provisions are so general that one cannot meaningfully assess compliance, casting doubt on their legal force.[36] As Abbott and

---

34. Similarly, agreements administered by the WTO can, with similar legitimacy and effectiveness, specify detailed rules on the valuation of imports for customs purposes and rely on broad standards like "national treatment."

35. Operationalizing the relative precision of different formulations is difficult, except in a gross sense. Gamble, for example, purports to apply a four-point scale of "concreteness" but does not characterize these points. Gamble 1985.

36. The State Department's *Foreign Relations Manual* states that undertakings couched in vague or very general terms with no criteria for performance frequently reflect an intent not to be legally bound.

TABLE 3. *Indicators of precision*

High
 Determinate rules: only narrow issues of interpretation
 Substantial but limited issues of interpretation
 Broad areas of discretion
 "Standards": only meaningful with reference to specific situations
 Impossible to determine whether conduct complies
Low

Snidal emphasize in their article,[37] such imprecision is not generally the result of a failure of legal draftsmanship, but a deliberate choice given the circumstances of domestic and international politics.

Imprecision is not synonymous with state discretion, however, when it occurs within a delegation of authority and therefore grants to an international body wider authority to determine its meaning. The charters of international organizations provide important examples. In these instruments, generality frequently produces a broader delegation of authority, although member states almost always retain many levers of influence. A recent example makes the point clearly. At the 1998 Rome conference that approved a charter for an international criminal court, the United States sought to avoid any broad delegation of authority. Its proposal accordingly emphasized the need for "clear, precise, and specific definitions of each offense" within the jurisdiction of the court.[38]

Delegation

The third dimension of legalization is the extent to which states and other actors delegate authority to designated third parties—including courts, arbitrators, and administrative organizations—to implement agreements. The characteristic forms of legal delegation are third-party dispute settlement mechanisms authorized to interpret rules and apply them to particular facts (and therefore in effect to make new rules, at least interstitially) under established doctrines of international law. Dispute settlement mechanisms are most highly legalized when the parties agree to binding third-party decisions on the basis of clear and generally applicable rules; they are least legalized when the process involves political bargaining between parties who can accept or reject proposals without legal justification.[39]

---

37. Abbott and Snidal, this issue.

38. U.S. Releases Proposal on Elements of Crimes at the Rome Conference on the Establishment of an International Criminal Court, statement by James P. Rubin, U.S. State Department spokesperson, 22 June 1998, <secretary.state.gov/www/briefings/statements/1998/ps980622b.html>, accessed 16 February 1999.

39. Law remains relevant even here. The UN Charter makes peaceful resolution of disputes a legal obligation, and general international law requires good faith in the conduct of negotiations. In addition, resolution of disputes by agreement can contribute to the growth of customary international law.

TABLE 4. *Indicators of delegation*

a. Dispute resolution
 High
   Courts: binding third-party decisions; general jurisdiction; direct private access; can interpret
   and supplement rules; domestic courts have jurisdiction
   Courts: jurisdiction, access or normative authority limited or consensual
   Binding arbitration
   Nonbinding arbitration
   Conciliation, mediation
   Institutionalized bargaining
   Pure political bargaining
 Low

b. Rule making and implementation
 High
   Binding regulations; centralized enforcement
   Binding regulations with consent or opt-out
   Binding internal policies; legitimation of decentralized enforcement
   Coordination standards
   Draft conventions; monitoring and publicity
   Recommendations; confidential monitoring
   Normative statements
   Forum for negotiations
 Low

In practice, as reflected in Table 4a, dispute-settlement mechanisms cover an extremely broad range: from no delegation (as in traditional political decision making); through institutionalized forms of bargaining, including mechanisms to facilitate agreement, such as mediation (available within the WTO) and conciliation (an option under the Law of the Sea Convention); nonbinding arbitration (essentially the mechanism of the old GATT); binding arbitration (as in the U.S.-Iran Claims Tribunal); and finally to actual adjudication (exemplified by the European Court of Justice and Court of Human Rights, and the international criminal tribunals for Rwanda and the former Yugoslavia).

Another significant variable—the extent to which individuals and private groups can initiate a legal proceeding—is explored by Robert O. Keohane, Andrew Moravcsik, and Anne-Marie Slaughter in "Legalized Dispute Resolution" (this volume). Private actors can influence governmental behavior even in settings where access is limited to states (such as the WTO and the International Court of Justice). Increasingly, though, private actors are being granted access to legalized dispute settlement mechanisms, either indirectly (through national courts, as in the EC, or a supranational body like the European Commission on Human Rights) or directly (as will shortly be the case for the European Court of Human Rights). As Keohane, Moravcsik, and Slaughter argue, private access appears to increase the expansiveness of legal institutions.

As one moves up the delegation continuum, the actions of decision-makers are increasingly governed, and legitimated, by rules. (Willingness to delegate often depends on the extent to which these rules are thought capable of constraining the delegated authority.) Thus, this form of legal delegation typically achieves the union of primary and secondary rules that Hart deemed necessary for the establishment of a legal system. Delegation to third-party adjudicators is virtually certain to be accompanied by the adoption of rules of adjudication. The adjudicative body may then find it necessary to identify or develop rules of recognition and change, as it sorts out conflicts between rules or reviews the validity of rules that are the subject of dispute.

Delegation of legal authority is not confined to dispute resolution. As Table 4b indicates, a range of institutions—from simple consultative arrangements to full-fledged international bureaucracies—helps to elaborate imprecise legal norms, implement agreed rules, and facilitate enforcement.

Like domestic administrative agencies, international organizations are often authorized to elaborate agreed norms (though almost always in softer ways than their domestic counterparts), especially where it is infeasible to draft precise rules in advance and where special expertise is required. The EU Commission drafts extensive regulations, though they usually become binding only with the assent of member states. Specialized agencies like the International Civil Aviation Organization and the Codex Alimentarius Commission promulgate technical rules—often framed as recommendations—in coordination situations. In cases like these, the grant of rule-making authority typically contains (in Hart's terms) the rule of recognition; the governing bodies or secretariats of international organizations may subsequently develop rules of change. At lower levels of delegation, bodies like the International Labor Organization and the World Intellectual Property Organization draft proposed international conventions and promulgate a variety of nonbinding rules, some for use by private actors. International organizations also support interstate negotiations.

Many operational activities serve to implement legal norms.[40] Virtually all international organizations gather and disseminate information relevant to implementation; many also generate new information. Most engage in educational activities, such as the WTO's training programs for developing country officials. Agencies like the World Health Organization, the World Bank, and the UN Environment Program have much more extensive operations. These activities implement (and thus give meaning to) the norms and goals enunciated in the agencies' charters and other agreements they administer. Although most international organizations are highly constrained by member states, the imprecision of their governing instruments frequently leaves them considerable discretion, exercised implicitly as well as through formal interpretations and operating policies. The World Bank, for example, has issued detailed policies on matters such as environmental impact assessment and treatment of indigenous peoples; these become legally binding when incorporated in loan agreements.[41] The World Bank's innovative Inspection Panel supervises compliance, often as the result of private complaints.[42]

---

40. Abbott and Snidal 1998.
41. Boisson de Chazournes 1998.
42. Shihata 1994.

In Austinian approaches, centralized enforcement is the sine qua non of law. Yet even domestically, many areas of law are not closely tied to enforcement; so too, much international legalization is significant in spite of a lack of centralized enforcement. And international law can draw on some centralized powers of enforcement. The UN Security Council, for example, imposed programs of inspection, weapons destruction, and compensation on Iraq for violations of international law; it also created ad hoc tribunals for Rwanda and the former Yugoslavia that have convicted national officials of genocide, crimes against humanity, and other international crimes. As in domestic legal systems, moreover, some international agencies can enforce norms through their power to confer or deny benefits: international financial institutions have the greatest leverage, but other organizations can deny technical assistance or rights of participation to violators. (These actions presuppose powers akin to rule interpretation and adjudication.) Further, international organizations from the Security Council to the WTO legitimate (and constrain) decentralized sanctioning by states. Many also monitor state behavior and disseminate information on rule observance, creating implicit sanctions for states that wish to be seen as trustworthy members of an international community.

Legalized delegation, especially in its harder forms, introduces new actors and new forms of politics into interstate relations. As other articles in this volume discuss, actors with delegated legal authority have their own interests, the pursuit of which may be more or less successfully constrained by conditions on the grant of authority and concomitant surveillance by member states. Transnational coalitions of nonstate actors also pursue their interests through influence or direct participation at the supranational level, often producing greater divergence from member state concerns. Deciding disputes, adapting or developing new rules, implementing agreed norms, and responding to rule violations all engender their own type of politics, which helps to restructure traditional interstate politics.

Conclusion

Highly legalized institutions are those in which rules are obligatory on parties through links to the established rules and principles of international law, in which rules are precise (or can be made precise through the exercise of delegated authority), and in which authority to interpret and apply the rules has been delegated to third parties acting under the constraint of rules. There is, however, no bright line dividing legalized from nonlegalized institutions. Instead, there is an identifiable continuum from hard law through varied forms of soft law, each with its individual mix of characteristics, to situations of negligible legalization.

This continuum presupposes that legalized institutions are to some degree differentiated from other types of international institutions, a differentiation that may have methodological, procedural, cultural, and informational dimensions.[43] Although me-

---

43. Schauer and Wise 1997.

diators may, for example, be free to broker a bargain based on the "naked preferences" of the parties,[44] legal processes involve a discourse framed in terms of reason, interpretation, technical knowledge, and argument, often followed by deliberation and judgment by impartial parties. Different actors have access to the process, and they are constrained to make arguments different from those they would make in a nonlegal context. Legal decisions, too, must be based on reasons applicable to all similarly situated litigants, not merely the parties to the immediate dispute.

On the whole, however, our conception of legalization reflects a general theme of this volume: the rejection of a rigid dichotomy between "legalization" and "world politics." Law and politics are intertwined at all levels of legalization. One result of this interrelationship, reflected in many of the articles in this volume, is considerable difficulty in identifying the causal effects of legalization. Compliance with rules occurs for many reasons other than their legal status. Concern about reciprocity, reputation, and damage to valuable state institutions, as well as other normative and material considerations, all play a role. Yet it is reasonable to assume that most of the time, legal and political considerations combine to influence behavior.

At one extreme, even "pure" political bargaining is shaped by rules of sovereignty and other background legal norms. At the other extreme, even international adjudication takes place in the "shadow of politics": interested parties help shape the agenda and initiate the proceedings; judges are typically alert to the political implications of possible decisions, seeking to anticipate the reactions of political authorities. Between these extremes, where most international legalization lies, actors combine and invoke varying degrees of obligation, precision, and delegation to create subtle blends of politics and law. In all these settings, to paraphrase Clausewitz, "law is a continuation of political intercourse, with the addition of other means."

44. Sunstein 1986.

Hard and Soft Law
in International Governance

Kenneth W. Abbott and Duncan Snidal

Contemporary international relations are legalized to an impressive extent, yet international legalization displays great variety. A few international institutions and issue-areas approach the theoretical ideal of hard legalization, but most international law is "soft" in distinctive ways. Here we explore the reasons for the widespread legalization of international governance and for this great variety in the degrees and forms of legalization.[1] We argue that international actors choose to order their relations through international law and design treaties and other legal arrangements to solve specific substantive and political problems. We further argue that international actors choose softer forms of legalized governance when those forms offer superior institutional solutions. We analyze the benefits and costs of different types of legalization and suggest hypotheses regarding the circumstances that lead actors to select specific forms. We do not purport to develop a full theory of law. Nonetheless, examining these political choices in the spare institutional context of international relations may contribute to a better understanding of the uses of law more generally.

We begin by examining the advantages of hard legalization. The term *hard law* as used in this special issue refers to legally binding obligations that are precise (or can be made precise through adjudication or the issuance of detailed regulations) and that delegate authority for interpreting and implementing the law.[2] Although hard law is not the typical international legal arrangement, a close look at this institutional form provides a baseline for understanding the benefits and costs of all types of legaliza-

For helpful comments as we developed this article, we thank participants in the conferences leading up to this special issue; our discussant Alexander Thompson and other participants at the Program on International Politics, Economics, and Security Workshop at the University of Chicago; and participants at the "half-baked lunch" discussion at Northwestern University Law School. We also thank the editors of this special issue, especially Judith Goldstein and Robert Keohane, and the editors and referees of *International Organization* for valuable comments.

1. We have profited from the insights in Keohane, Moravcsik, and Slaughter 1997, which was prepared in connection with this project.
2. For an extensive discussion of these three dimensions, which guide the articles in this issue, see Abbott, Keohane, Moravcsik, Slaughter, and Snidal, this issue.

International Organization 54, 3, Summer 2000, pp. 37–72
© 2000 by The IO Foundation and the Massachusetts Institute of Technology

tion. By using hard law to order their relations, international actors reduce transactions costs, strengthen the credibility of their commitments, expand their available political strategies, and resolve problems of incomplete contracting. Doing so, however, also entails significant costs: hard law restricts actors' behavior and even their sovereignty.

While we emphasize the benefits and costs of legalization from a rational perspective focused on interests, law simultaneously engages normative considerations. In addition to requiring commitment to a background set of legal norms[3]—including engagement in established legal processes and discourse—legalization provides actors with a means to instantiate normative values. Legalization has effect through normative standards and processes as well as self-interested calculation, and both interests and values are constraints on the success of law. We consider law as both "contract" and "covenant" to capture these distinct but not incompatible characteristics. Indeed, we reject vigorously the insistence of many international relations specialists that one type of understanding is antithetical to the other.[4]

The realm of "soft law" begins once legal arrangements are weakened along one or more of the dimensions of obligation, precision, and delegation. This softening can occur in varying degrees along each dimension and in different combinations across dimensions. We use the shorthand term *soft law* to distinguish this broad class of deviations from hard law—and, at the other extreme, from purely political arrangements in which legalization is largely absent. But bear in mind that soft law comes in many varieties: the choice between hard law and soft law is not a binary one.

Soft law has been widely criticized and even dismissed as a factor in international affairs. Realists, of course, focus on the absence of an independent judiciary with supporting enforcement powers to conclude that all international law is soft—and is therefore only window dressing.[5] But some international lawyers dismiss soft international law from a more normative perspective. Prosper Weil, for example, argues that increasing use of soft law "might destabilize the whole international normative system and turn it into an instrument that can no longer serve its purpose."[6] Others justify soft law only as an interim step toward harder and therefore more satisfactory

---

3. The international legal system has developed over several centuries. International law includes secondary norms prescribing how primary rules are to be made, interpreted, and applied, as well as institutions through which both kinds of rules are implemented. The background legal system shapes many international interactions—indeed, it helps define the very notion of an international actor.

4. To be sure, there may be irreconcilable paradigmatic differences between interest-based and normative approaches at the level of grand theory. On the ground, however, either approach can be improved by carefully incorporating the arguments made by the other, with appropriate adaptation. One can profitably employ both a hammer and a wrench without declaring one tool better for all problems and without resolving whether carpenters or plumbers are the better handymen. This is especially true when analyzing law, which inherently combines both trades.

5. This perspective is so deeply held among neorealists that they rarely discuss international law at all. Classical realists such as Hans Morgenthau recognized that states generally obeyed international law but took the lack of enforcement to mean that law did not cover the significant issues of international affairs. A modern reprise of this theme is offered by Downs and his colleagues, who critique much international cooperation for consisting of agreements that reflect what states would have done on their own and so do not change behavior. Downs, Rocke, and Barsoom 1996.

6. Weil 1983, 423.

legalization. The implication is that soft law—law that "falls short" on one or more of the three dimensions of legalization—is a failure.

We argue, in contrast, that international actors often deliberately choose softer forms of legalization as superior institutional arrangements. To be sure, soft law is sometimes designed as a way station to harder legalization, but often it is preferable on its own terms. Soft law offers many of the advantages of hard law, avoids some of the costs of hard law, and has certain independent advantages of its own.[7] Importantly, because one or more of the elements of legalization can be relaxed, softer legalization is often easier to achieve than hard legalization. This is especially true when the actors are states that are jealous of their autonomy and when the issues at hand challenge state sovereignty. Soft legalization also provides certain benefits not available under hard legalization. It offers more effective ways to deal with uncertainty, especially when it initiates processes that allow actors to learn about the impact of agreements over time.[8] In addition, soft law facilitates compromise, and thus mutually beneficial cooperation, between actors with different interests and values, different time horizons and discount rates, and different degrees of power.

The specific forms of soft law chosen reflect the particular problems actors are trying to solve. While our analysis focuses on softness in general, different forms of softness may be more acceptable or more efficacious in different circumstances. We suggest a number of variables—including transactions costs, uncertainty, implications for national sovereignty, divergence of preferences, and power differentials—that influence which forms of soft law, which combinations of obligation, precision and delegation, are likely to be selected in specific circumstances.

This article is largely an exercise in comparative statics; we ask why particular situational features lead actors to adopt specific institutional arrangements at given points in time. Soft law is frequently dynamic, however, in the sense that it initiates a process and a discourse that may involve learning and other changes over time. We incorporate these considerations in our analysis by examining how actors (imperfectly) evaluate the dynamic consequences of current soft law commitments.

For ease of exposition, and because states are essential actors in international legalization, we frame our initial discussions in terms of states and the problems they face. We recognize, however, that firms, activist organizations, and other nonstate groups operating at both the domestic and international levels are increasingly key actors in the development of international legalization, and of soft law in particular. In the final section of the article we compare alternative accounts of the role of nonstate actors to examine why such groups press for different forms of legalization. The need to deal with the competing interests and values of nonstate actors also adds to the reasons states have for pursuing soft law strategies.

We employ a range of examples, including some elaborated by other articles in this issue, to illustrate the wide variety of international legal arrangements. Although

---

7. For a related discussion of the benefits and costs of informal agreements, see Lipson 1991.

8. We draw on Koremenos's insightful work on how states structure treaties to enable mutual learning. Koremenos 1999.

these examples do not provide a true empirical test of our arguments, they do provide evidence for their plausibility. To characterize our examples economically along the hard law/soft law continuum, we use the notation {O,P,D}. The elements of each triplet refer to the level of obligation, precision, and delegation, respectively. Variations along each dimension are indicated by capital letters for high levels (for example, O), small letters for moderate levels (for example, o), and dashes for low levels (-). Thus {O,P,D} indicates an arrangement that is highly legalized on all three dimensions and therefore constitutes "hard law"; {o,P,-} indicates an issue that has a moderate level of legal obligation coupled with high precision but very limited delegation; and {O,-,-} indicates an issue with high legal obligation but very low precision and very limited delegation. Although this tripartite categorization remains somewhat coarse, it suggests the continuous gradations of hardness and softness that are blurred when the hard law/soft law distinction is incorrectly taken as binary.[9]

Contracts and Covenants: Rationales for Hard Law

Introduction

"Contracts" and "covenants" refer to two distinct though not incompatible understandings of international agreements. States enter into "contracts" to further interests; they enter into "covenants" to manifest normative commitments. In international legal scholarship, interest- and norm-based agreements are essentially interchangeable;[10] but international relations scholarship (like other analyses of law[11]) often seeks to distinguish between them: contracts and covenants correspond to the rationalist and constructivist perspectives, respectively, on international institutions, approaches that are usually seen as contrasting, if not mutually exclusive.[12]

In the stereotypical view, rationalists (1) see the relevant actors (usually states) as motivated largely by material interests; (2) view international agreements as "contracts" created to resolve problems of coordination, collaboration, or domestic politics; and (3) understand contracts as operating by changing incentives or other material features of interactions, such as iteration, reciprocity, information, or the influence

9. Because our examples are illustrative, we do not develop formalized coding criteria. Note that a dash (-) indicates a low level of a property, not its absence. Low delegation, for example, would include an international consultative body that facilitates political bargaining among member states. Where an international institution handles more extensive administrative functions—such as substantial information gathering, monitoring, and nonbinding arbitration—we would code delegation as *d*. Finally, where an institution includes strong adjudicative capacity or independent administrative power, we would code delegation as *D*. The dimensions of obligation and precision pose similar problems and possibilities. A more fine-grained discussion of these dimensions is contained in Abbott et al., this issue; and Abbott and Snidal 1997. The eight rows of Table 1 in Abbott et al., which reflect only high and low values of the three elements of legalization, correspond to combinations of capital letters and dashes in our notation (that is, {O,P,D},{O,-,D} . . . {O,-,-},{-,-,-}).

10. Some agreements with strong normative content are entitled "covenants," most notably the covenants on civil and political and on economic, social, and cultural rights. But this usage is not widespread. Many human rights agreements, for example, are simply entitled "treaty" or "convention."

11. Tyler 1990.

12. Katzenstein, Keohane, and Krasner 1998.

of particular interest groups, or through enforcement.[13] Constructivist or normative scholars, on the other hand, (1) focus on nonstate and intragovernmental actors,[14] often motivated by moral or social concerns, as the source of international norms; (2) view international agreements as "covenants" embodying shared norms and understandings; and (3) understand covenants as operating through persuasion, imitation, and internalization to modify intersubjective understandings of appropriate behavior, interests, and even identities.[15]

In studying international legalization, this sharp bifurcation is clearly misplaced. In its origins and operation, law is both an interest-based and a normative enterprise:

1. States and other actors look to law to achieve their ends whether they are pursuing interests or values. In fact, these goals are normally deeply intertwined. Business groups and states seeking rules to protect intellectual property, for example, are committed to norms of property and fairness as well as self-interest; nongovernmental organizations (NGOs) and states supporting rules to promote democracy are concerned with security and trade as well as participatory values.

2. Actors utilize both normative and interest-based strategies to create legal arrangements. Business groups and Western states supporting liberal economic rules appeal to norms of individual choice as well as economic interests; NGOs and governments seeking strong human rights rules cite material benefits—and mobilize economic leverage—along with humanitarian values.[16] Most international agreements are simultaneously contract and covenant.

3. Legal rules and institutions operate both by changing material incentives and by modifying understandings, standards of behavior, and identities. In particular, they invoke doctrines and institutions that facilitate enforcement as well as social norms of obedience to law. Concerned actors strive to bring all these effects to bear, through techniques ranging from litigation and sanctions to persuasion, normative appeals, and shaming.[17]

In the remainder of this section we explore why states seek to order their relations through hard law: institutional arrangements generally characterized as $\{O,P,D\}$ or $\{O,p,D\}$.[18] Since states most often create international legal rules and institutions by negotiation and agreement,[19] we employ contracting theory to organize our analysis,

---

13. Martin and Simmons 1998.

14. In this they follow modern liberal theorists. Moravcsik 1997.

15. See Finnemore 1996; Keck and Sikkink 1998. Recent years have witnessed some convergence. Rationalists increasingly recognize that interests require explanation and that institutions do much to shape them. Keohane 1988. Constructivists stress that norm entrepreneurs pursue their goals rationally, even strategically, seeking to modify the utility functions of others to accord with preferred norms. Finnemore and Sikkink 1998.

16. Klotz 1995.

17. See Klotz 1995; Keck and Sikkink 1998; and Koh 1996.

18. As noted earlier, the first and second sections of this article focus on states and the third section on nonstate actors. Even in the first and second sections, however, some arguments turn on actions by and effects on nonstate actors, often in domestic politics.

19. Our emphasis, then, is on treaties, especially multilateral regulatory treaties. Chayes and Chayes 1995. Customary law is also an important element of the international legal system, but we do not address

incorporating normative considerations as well as the interest-based factors that dominate the contracting literature.

Credible Commitments

The difficulty states have in credibly committing themselves to future behavior is widely viewed as a characteristic feature of international "anarchy" and an impediment to welfare-enhancing cooperation. In contracting theory, credible commitments are crucial when one party to an agreement must carry out its side of the bargain before other parties are required to perform, or more generally when some parties must make relation-specific investments in reliance on future performance by others.[20] In game theory, similarly, credible commitments are essential whenever some parties to a strategic interaction demand "assurance" from others, as in situations modeled by games such as Assurance, Chicken, or Prisoners' Dilemma and when parties seek to ensure that they arrive at the same coordination point.

Other assurance issues appear when one begins to disaggregate the state. For one thing, relation-specific investments can be political as well as material: a government offering economic or political concessions in return for human rights pledges, for example, would suffer domestic political costs if the other party reneged; it would therefore demand credible assurances. The government making those pledges might also wish to enhance credibility for internal purposes: to bind its successors in office or other branches of government, or to strengthen its citizens' incentives to adjust their practices and attitudes.

Legal commitments can speak to private parties abroad as well as at home. As Frederick Abbott notes in this issue, the Mexican government sought to legalize the North American Free Trade Agreement (NAFTA) in part to increase the credibility of its increasingly liberal economic policies in the eyes of foreign investors. Reversing longstanding national policy, it even accepted significant international delegation, allowing investors from NAFTA countries to take disputes to binding arbitration.

In domestic societies, legal commitments are credible because aggrieved parties can enforce them, with the power of the state if necessary. Even "hard" international law falls short of this standard: international regimes do not even attempt to establish legal obligations centrally enforceable against states.[21] Yet it is erroneous to conclude that the "formal legal status" of international agreements is therefore meaningless. Legalization is one of the principal methods by which states can increase the credibility of their commitments.[22]

---

it systematically here. Our impression, though, is that much customary law today is the result of conscious political action by states and other actors, rather than the gradual accretion of state practice. To the extent this is correct, much of our analysis will also apply to custom.

20. Williamson 1989.

21. Keohane 1984, 88–89.

22. A more extreme way to address commitment problems, analogous to the merger of firms in business relationships that raise assurance problems, is to integrate separate sovereignties into a single political unit, such as a federal state. Integration can be partial as well as complete, as the EU illustrates. Even full integration, though, cannot solve commitment and other contracting problems among the many political, economic, and other interests within and across societies.

One way legalization enhances credibility is by constraining self-serving auto-interpretation. Precision of individual commitments, coherence between individual commitments and broader legal principles, and accepted modes of legal discourse and argument all help limit such opportunistic behavior. Granting interpretive authority to courts or other legal institutions further constrains auto-interpretation.[23] Another way legalization enhances credibility is by increasing the costs of reneging. Regime scholars argue that agreements are strengthened when they are linked to a broader regime: violating an agreement that is part of a regime entails disproportionate costs, because the reputational costs of reneging apply throughout the regime. Legal commitments benefit from similar effects, but they involve international law as a whole in addition to any specific regime.

When a commitment is cast as hard law, the reputational effects of a violation can be generalized to all agreements subject to international law, that is, to most international agreements.[24] There are few alternatives to legalization when states wish to identify undertakings as reliable commitments. Alternatives like bonding and escrow are much more costly. In addition, international law provides the very foundations of statehood: principles of sovereignty, recognition, territorial competence, nonintervention, and so on. Violations weaken the international legal system and are self-defeating, at least over time.

More concretely, legalization enhances (albeit modestly) the capacity for enforcement. First, hard legal commitments, $[O,P,D]$ or $[O,p,D]$, are interpreted and applied by arbitral or judicial institutions, like those associated with the European Union (EU), the European human rights regime or the World Trade Organization (WTO). (Softer commitments may be invoked in political institutions.) Because legal review allows allegations and defenses to be tested under accepted standards and procedures, it increases reputational costs if a violation is found. The EU may currently be experiencing such aggravated costs as a result of the repeated negative legal rulings by WTO dispute settlement bodies in litigation over European restrictions on imports of hormone-treated beef (for which the EU was unable to demonstrate a legitimate scientific justification) and bananas.

Second, the law of state responsibility fixes consequences for legal violations. In particular, like some legalized regimes (such as the WTO), it authorizes proportional "countermeasures" where other remedies are unavailable. This legitimizes retaliation and clarifies its intent, reducing the costs and risks of self-help. Third, even international law can draw on some forms of centralized enforcement, through institutions like the UN Security Council and the international financial institutions.

Other interest-based costs of legal violations arise because international legal commitments often become part of domestic law. As John K. Setear points out, for ex-

---

23. Deconstructionists, of course, would contest these statements. In practice, however, even observers of this bent see law as constraining interpretation. Koskenniemi 1999.

24. Keohane observes that states can reduce the force of reputational effects by distinguishing the circumstances of a violation from those surrounding other agreements. Keohane 1995. In the nineteenth century, the United States sought in this way to distinguish its treaties with "savage" Indian tribes, which it frequently violated, from agreements with European countries. The effort devoted to making this distinction, however, suggests that reputational effects would otherwise have spread across all legal agreements.

ample, Congress has provided that violations of the Whaling Convention and the Convention on International Trade in Endangered Species (CITES) constitute violations of U.S. law, carrying criminal penalties.[25] Ellen L. Lutz and Kathryn Sikkink in their article in this issue further describe how international rules condemning torture and other atrocities have been characterized as customary international law and applied by U.S. courts.[26] When international commitments are incorporated into domestic law, the level of delegation associated with them rises dramatically (though it evokes weaker concern for national sovereignty): the commitments can now be applied by well-established systems of courts and administrative agencies; private actors can often initiate legal proceedings; and lawyers have incentives to invoke the rules. When supranational bodies like the European Court of Justice (ECJ) have also been granted legal authority, they can nurture "partnerships" with their domestic counterparts, strengthening both institutions.[27]

Domesticated commitments can more easily be enforced against private persons and their assets. A striking example is the recent litigation against General Pinochet, which was initiated by a Spanish magistrate enforcing international conventions banning torture and other atrocities that had become part of Spanish law. Although the British House of Lords ruled that Pinochet could not be held responsible for most of the charges against him, it did hold him answerable for acts committed after the torture convention had been incorporated into British law.

Legal commitments mobilize legally oriented interest and advocacy groups, such as the organized bar, and legitimize their participation in domestic decision making. They also expand the role of legal bureaucracies within foreign offices and other government agencies. Finally, so long as domestic actors understand legal agreements to be serious undertakings, they will modify their plans and actions in reliance on such commitments, increasing the audience costs of violations.

Legalization also increases the costs of violation through normative channels. Violation of a legal commitment entails reputational costs—again generalizable to all legal commitments—that reflect distaste for breaking the law. International law reinforces this effect through its strong emphasis on compliance (*pacta sunt servanda* and the principle of good faith).[28] To the extent that states (or certain states) see themselves as members of an international society structured by international law, reputational effects may be even broader.[29] Law observance is even more highly valued in most domestic societies; efforts to justify international violations thus create cognitive dissonance and increase domestic audience costs.

Legal obligations are widely perceived as having particular legitimacy. In Thomas Franck's words, legitimacy creates an independent "compliance pull."[30] Individuals,

---

25. Setear 1999.
26. Lutz and Sikkink, this issue.
27. See Burley and Mattli 1993; and Helfer and Slaughter 1997.
28. The rule of *pacta sunt servanda* is to some extent weakened by exceptions and defenses, notably the broad change-of-circumstances defense known as *rebus sic stantibus*. Yet these doctrines introduce needed flexibility; when they are found inapplicable, the normative force of the basic rule is enhanced.
29. See Wight 1977; Bull 1977; Hurrell 1993; and Buzan 1993.
30. Franck 1990.

government agencies, and other organizations internalize rules so that the advantages and disadvantages of compliance need not be recalculated each time they are invoked. Franck argues that the legitimacy of rules varies according to certain substantive qualities—determinacy and coherence, among other properties—and the procedures by which they were approved. Legal rules are often strong on these dimensions: relatively precise, internally consistent, and adopted through formalized and often elaborate procedures.

Legalization entails a specific form of discourse, requiring justification and persuasion in terms of applicable rules and pertinent facts, and emphasizing factors such as text, precedents, analogies, and practice. Legal discourse largely disqualifies arguments based solely on interests and preferences. The nature of this discourse affords legal professionals a prominent role. When authority is delegated to adjudicative institutions, proceedings can be highly formalized. Even without strong delegation, however, this discourse imposes some constraint on state action: governments will incur reputational costs within the legal community, and often beyond, if they act without a defensible position or without reasonable efforts to justify their conduct in legal terms.

Certain hypotheses regarding the independent variables that lead states to use hard law can be distilled from this analysis. First, states should use hard legal commitments as assurance devices when the benefits of cooperation are great but the potential for opportunism and its costs are high. These conditions are most likely in "contracts," such as trade or investment agreements, that include reciprocal commitments and nonsimultaneous performance. But they may also appear in "covenants"—such as environmental or labor agreements—when violations would impose significant externalities on others. Opportunism is less significant in coordination situations, where agreements are largely self-enforcing.[31] Indeed, international coordination standards are often voluntary, $[-,P,d]$, and are created through institutions in which private actors have a significant role. Opportunism, and thus international legalization, is also less significant in settings where national actions have few external effects.[32]

Second, states should use hard legalization to increase the credibility of commitments when noncompliance is difficult to detect, as in most arms control situations. Legal arrangements often include centralized or decentralized monitoring provisions as an aspect of delegation. Even apart from these, however, legal commitments compensate in part for the reduced likelihood of detection by increasing the costs of detected violations.

Third, states should find hard law of special value when forming "clubs" of sincerely committed states, like the EU and NATO. Here legalization functions as an *ex ante* sorting device: because hard legal commitments impose greater costs on violators, a willingness to make them identifies one as having a low propensity to defect. Conversely, hard legalization is less significant in looser groupings like the Asia-

---

31. Coordination agreements may not be self-enforcing when the benefits of moving the group to a new equilibrium are high. In these situations, especially when the gains to certain parties are large enough to make such attempts feasible, hard law may be useful as an assurance device.

32. Abbott and Snidal 2000.

Pacific Economic Cooperation forum (APEC), described by Miles Kahler in this issue, that are not pursuing deep cooperation and thus do not require *ex ante* evidence of a sincere commitment from members.[33]

Fourth, looking within the state, executive officials should look to hard international law to commit other domestic agencies (especially legislatures) or political groups when those officials are able to make international agreements with little interference or control, and when their preferences differ significantly from those of competing power centers. In this perspective, domestic politics and constitutional law are significant explanatory variables.

Finally, as a secondary hypothesis, legal commitments should be more credible when made by states with particular characteristics. Externally, participation in other international legal regimes should enhance credibility: it exposes states to greater reputational costs and makes them more vulnerable to countermeasures. Internally, strong domestic legal institutions and traditions should enhance credibility. Many of the special costs of violating legal commitments stem from these characteristics.

Reducing Transactions Costs

On balance, at least, hard legalization reduces the transactions costs of subsequent interactions.[34] Two types of interactions are especially relevant: one is the "managerial" process of applying and elaborating agreed rules; the other is the more adversarial process of enforcing commitments. The role of international regimes in reducing transactions costs—especially the costs of negotiating supplementary agreements—has been extensively analyzed.[35] That literature has not, however, distinguished legalization from other institutional forms.[36]

Consider the need to "manage" the application and evolution of agreements. With virtually all agreements, even those that are quite precise, provisions must be interpreted, applied to specific fact situations, and elaborated to resolve ambiguities and address new and related issues. Delegation to courts and other legal institutions is one important way states address these problems; we discuss delegation later in connection with incomplete contracts. Even where delegation is weak—for example, $[O,p,d]$ or $[O,p,-]$—legalization facilitates interpretation, application, and elaboration by setting relatively clear bounds on dispute resolution and negotiation. Substantively, legalization implies that proposals for resolving disputes and for new or expanded rules must be integrated with existing norms. They should be compatible with settled rules if possible, so that bargains need not be reopened. In any case they should be compatible with the basic principles of the relevant regime, so that legal coherence is maintained.

Procedurally, hard law constrains the techniques of dispute settlement and negotiation. Even when delegation is relatively low, legalization implies that most disputes

---

33. Kahler, this issue.
34. As discussed later, the costs of reaching a fully legalized agreement are often relatively high, leading actors to adopt softer forms of legalization.
35. Keohane 1984.
36. Compare Abbott and Snidal 1998.

and questions of interpretation should be addressed through specialized procedures, operated primarily by legal professionals using professional modes of discourse. Even when directly negotiated solutions are permitted, the existence of legal institutions means that states will bargain "in the shadow" of anticipated legal decisions. When legal rules are in effect, moreover, unauthorized coercive behavior is generally seen as illegitimate. It is no coincidence that legalization in the WTO was explicitly tied to a requirement that member states resolve their trade disputes through the new dispute settlement procedures, not through unilateral determinations and responses—a provision aimed directly at the coercive tactics of the United States under Section 301. Even hard international law is not foolproof, of course; the principles discussed here may be ignored in practice, especially by powerful states. Nonetheless, on the whole legalization remains an effective device for organizing ongoing interactions.

Consider next the need to "enforce" commitments. The previous section examined how legalization helps states increase the credibility of their own commitments. But legalization is also significant from the perspective of the states (and other actors) that have worked to obtain commitments from others, often in the face of strong resistance. We refer to such parties as "demandeurs." Whenever there are incentives for noncompliance with international commitments, demandeurs will seek ways to forestall or respond to violations by others.

As discussed earlier, hard legalization offers a rich assortment of international and domestic institutions and procedures and normative and reputational arguments for actors in this position. Compared to alternatives like frequent renegotiation, persuasion, or coercion, it materially reduces the costs of enforcement. Other things being equal, assuming in particular that the substance of an agreement is acceptable, demandeurs should prefer hard legalization, especially in the form $[O,P,D]$.[37] Of course, other things being equal, states that resist agreement or desire greater flexibility should resist hard legalization, or at least strive for $[O,p,D]$ commitments, for these very reasons. The compromises and tradeoffs that result are discussed in the following section.

Many of the hypotheses in the previous subsection can be reformulated from the demandeur's perspective. Demandeurs should seek hard legalization (1) when the likelihood of opportunism and its costs are high, and noncompliance is difficult to detect; (2) when they wish to limit participation to those strongly committed to an agreement; and (3) when executive officials in other states have preferences compatible with those of the demandeurs, but other elites within those states have divergent preferences. Finally, demandeurs should place greatest reliance on commitments by states that participate actively in legal regimes and have strong legal institutions, professions, and traditions.

Modifying Political Strategies

As proponents of legal process theory make clear, hard legalization allows states (and other actors) to pursue different political strategies as they work to extend and

---

37. We consider later the specific forms of legalization preferred by powerful and weak states.

enforce (or to weaken or escape) international agreements.[38] Indeed, those strategies are often unavoidable. Both demandeurs and resisters may be as concerned with these tactical attributes as with the strategic issues of credibility and enforceability.

As defined in this issue, hard law includes specialized legal institutions. Regimes of the form $[O,P,D]$ and $[O,p,D]$ include judicial or arbitral organs that offer the specialized procedures and techniques of litigation as a supplement or alternative to more overtly political techniques for addressing disputes, questions of interpretation, and instances of noncompliance. Nonjudicial institutions, as in $[O,p,d]$ regimes, are often authorized to interpret governing instruments, issue regulations or recommendations, draft proposed conventions, and the like. These fora combine the politics and rhetoric of law with ordinary politics.

Legal institutions often require even more subtle strategies. In some, for example, states may not even initiate proceedings. Thus, although the International Criminal Tribunal for the Former Yugoslavia (ICTY) is a valuable tool of humanitarian and interest-based politics, decisions to prosecute (or not to prosecute) are made by ICTY officials. NATO governments (and private groups) must therefore pursue such tactics as lobbying for the appointment of acceptable ICTY officials, gathering evidence, encouraging prosecutors to bring cases—as the United States did in pressing for the indictment of Slobodan Milosevic—and arranging for the arrest of potential defendants, while using the threat of prosecution to pressure the Serbian government.

Hard legal commitments are sometimes incorporated directly into the internal law of participating states; even more frequently international agreements require states to enact implementing legislation, and sometimes to establish particular implementing institutions. Domestic litigation then becomes part of the international toolkit. There may, however, be jurisdictional obstacles to litigation by state claimants. In those situations, states must engage in the subtle process of identifying, encouraging, and supporting private litigants who will advance their interests.[39] Recent scholarship analyzes the strategies that supranational judges pursue to encourage actions by private litigants and national courts that will strengthen international law.[40] National governments presumably follow parallel strategies. Karen Alter's article in this issue explores the complex strategies pursued by this range of public and private actors in the highly legalized institutions of the EU.[41]

We hypothesize broadly that states will be more likely to seek hard legalization when the political strategies it offers are advantageous to them. Mundane issues such as the availability of resources and trained personnel can be quite significant: the United States and other advanced industrial nations with large legal staffs should be more amenable to legalization than countries with few trained specialists. States

---

38. Koh 1997.

39. This reverses the process associated with more traditional institutions like the Iran–U.S. Claims Tribunal, where private actors encourage governments to initiate proceedings and provide support and encouragement to government litigators.

40. See Burley and Mattli 1993; Helfer and Slaughter 1997; Alter 1998b; Garrett, Kelemen, and Schulz 1998; and Mattli and Slaughter 1998b.

41. Alter, this issue.

should also favor hard legalization when they can be confident that agreements will track their preferences, for legal procedures will allow them to implement those preferences efficiently and at low political cost. This suggests that powerful states have a significant and often overlooked stake in hard legalization. And states that seek to minimize political conflict in relations with other states or in particular issue-areas should favor hard legalization, for it sublimates such conflict into legal argument.

Handling Problems of Incomplete Contracting

States sometimes attempt to write detailed agreements to constrain auto-interpretation, reduce transactions costs, and increase enforceability. But though precision has great value, it also has several problems. It may be wasteful, forcing states to plan for highly unlikely events; it may be counterproductive, introducing opaque and inconsistent provisions; it may lead to undesirable rigidity; and it may prevent agreement altogether.

In any case, writing complete contracts is extremely difficult.[42] The principal-agent literature demonstrates that asymmetric information typically makes it impossible to write an optimal contract if the agent is risk-averse. Yet even this literature assumes that one could in principle write a contract complete with respect to all possible future states of the world. In fact, given bounded rationality and the pervasive uncertainty in which states operate, they can never construct agreements that anticipate every contingency. This problem invites opportunistic behavior and discourages both relation-specific investments and value-enhancing agreements.

Delegation is often the best way to deal with incomplete contracting problems. Regimes of the form $[O,p,D]$ are clearly designed with this purpose in mind: they utilize administrative and judicial institutions to interpret and extend broad legal principles. The Treaty of Rome, for example, authorizes the ECJ and the European Community's legislative institutions to elaborate and apply general principles of competition law, such as "concerted practices" and "distortion of competition," through individual cases and general regulations. Even $[O,P,D]$ regimes grant significant powers to administrative organs and judicial or arbitral bodies. Although many provisions of the European Convention on Human Rights, for example, are quite detailed, the European Court of Human Rights must still apply general standards—such as "inhuman and degrading treatment" and "respect for . . . private and family life"—in situations that could not have been anticipated when the convention was drafted.

Softer regimes often include nonjudicial procedures for filling out incomplete contracts, though these normally require state consent. Hard legal regimes, in contrast, grant greater independence to judicial or arbitral bodies but require them to follow agreed upon principles and to act only on specific disputes and requests. This combination of attributes, along with the background rules and expectations of interna-

---

42. Incomplete contracting problems arise when any agreement is negotiated under conditions of incomplete or asymmetric information, risk, and uncertainty. For a recent overview, see Hart 1995.

tional law, simultaneously constrains and legitimates delegated authority. One can hypothesize that states will grant such authority when the anticipated gains from cooperation are large and there is reasonable consensus on general principles, but specific applications are difficult to anticipate.

The Advantages of Soft Legalization

Hard law facilitates international interactions in the many ways already discussed, but it has significant costs and limitations. In this section, we explore how softer forms of legalization provide alternative and often more desirable means to manage many interactions by providing some of the benefits of hard law at lower cost. We emphasize both rationalist concerns, such as contracting costs, and the special role soft legal rules and institutions play in promoting learning and normative processes.

Contracting Costs

A major advantage of softer forms of legalization is their lower contracting costs. Hard legalization reduces the post-agreement costs of managing and enforcing commitments, but adoption of a highly legalized agreement entails significant contracting costs.[43] Any agreement entails some negotiating costs—coming together, learning about the issue, bargaining, and so forth—especially when issues are unfamiliar or complex. But these costs are greater for legalized agreements. States normally exercise special care in negotiating and drafting legal agreements, since the costs of violation are higher. Legal specialists must be consulted; bureaucratic reviews are often lengthy. Different legal traditions across states complicate the exercise. Approval and ratification processes, typically involving legislative authorization, are more complex than for purely political agreements.

Two examples suggest the impact of contracting costs on forms of legalization. First, the costs and risks of national ratification procedures led the International Labor Organization (ILO) to modify its legalization strategy.[44] Throughout its history, the ILO has acted primarily by adopting draft conventions. In recent decades, however, states have been ratifying ILO conventions at a low and declining rate. Believing that this phenomenon was damaging the prestige of the organization, two successive directors-general called for the ILO to emphasize nonlegally binding instruments, such as recommendations and codes of conduct, at the expense of binding treaties in order to reduce the costs of national ratification. Although labor representatives resisted this change, the ILO has begun to adopt some new rules in softer legal form.

Second, contracting costs were used as a delaying tactic in the negotiations that led to the 1997 Organization for Economic Cooperation and Development (OECD) con-

---

43. The regimes literature does not always distinguish between the costs of transacting *within* regimes and the costs of *creating* regimes. In early work, regimes are seen as the legacy of hegemony, so that their creation is not directly addressed.
44. Maupain 1998.

vention restricting foreign bribery in international business transactions. In those discussions, the United States hoped to reduce the commercial disadvantage created by its Foreign Corrupt Practices Act by supporting a legally binding treaty, $[O,P,d]$, requiring all OECD members to adopt equivalent regulatory limits. As negotiations proceeded, however, the very states that had resisted any action on the issue came out in favor of a binding treaty! These nations hoped to use the high contracting costs of hard legalization to impede agreement. The United States responded by supporting a nonlegally binding OECD recommendation, $[-,P,d]$. The two sides eventually compromised by setting a short deadline for treaty negotiations and agreeing to adopt a recommendation if the deadline was not met.

The costs of hard legalization are magnified by the circumstances of international politics. States, jealous of their sovereign autonomy, are reluctant to limit it through legalized commitments. Security concerns intensify the distributional issues that accompany any agreement, especially ones of greater magnitude or involving greater uncertainty. Negotiations are often multilateral. The scope of bargaining is often not clearly delimited, since the issues themselves are ill defined (for example, is free trade in magazines an economic issue or a cultural one?). Finally, the thinness of the international institutional context (including the low prevailing level of legalization) does little to lower the costs of agreement.

Soft legalization mitigates these costs as well. For example, states can dampen security and distributional concerns by opting for escape clauses, $[o,P,d]$; imprecise commitments, $[O,p,d]$; or "political" forms of delegation that allow them to maintain future control if adverse circumstances arise, $[O,p,-]$. These institutional devices protect state sovereignty and reduce the costs and risks of agreement while providing some of the advantages of legalization. Furthermore, soft legalization offers states an opportunity to learn about the consequences of their agreement. In many cases such learning processes will lower the perceived costs of subsequent moves to harder legalization.

The international nuclear regime illustrates these advantages.[45] Although fundamental nonproliferation obligations are set out in the Nuclear Non-Proliferation Treaty and other legally binding agreements, $[O,P,d]$, many sensitive issues—such as the protection of nuclear materials—are regulated predominantly through recommendations from the International Atomic Energy Agency (IAEA), $[-,P,d]$. Recommendations deal with technical matters, such as inventory control and transportation, at a level of detail that would be intractable in treaty negotiations. They also address issues of domestic policy, such as the organization of national regulatory agencies and the supervision of private actors, that states might regard as too sensitive for treaty regulation. When a high level of consensus forms around an IAEA recommendation, member states may incorporate its provisions into a binding treaty—as occurred with rules on the management of spent nuclear fuel and radioactive waste—but even these treaties must usually be supplemented by recommendations on technical issues.

45. Kellman 1998.

The international trade regime also illustrates the advantages of soft law in costly contracting environments. The proposed charter of the International Trade Organization contemplated legally binding commitments with constraints on the right of withdrawal and significant institutionalization, $[O,P,d]$; it also covered a wide range of economic issues. Such an instrument was very difficult to negotiate and draft; its institutional strength also provoked political resistance within the United States.[46] Because of these problems, the participating states adopted the 1947 General Agreement on Tariffs and Trade (GATT) as a low-cost, interim framework for tariff reductions. Compared to the draft charter of the International Trade Organization, GATT 1947 was relatively soft: it was adopted only "provisionally," included a lenient withdrawal clause, and created only skeletal institutions, $[o,p,-]$. Over time, GATT developed into the WTO as states learned the advantages of harder legalization in governing international trade. But the history of the regime—from its earliest days through the November 1999 ministerial meeting—demonstrates clearly that achieving harder legalization is a sensitive and protracted process.

In sum, we argue that states face tradeoffs in choosing levels of legalization. Hard agreements reduce the costs of operating within a legal framework—by strengthening commitments, reducing transactions costs, and the like—but they are hard to reach. Soft agreements cannot yield all these benefits, but they lower the costs of achieving (some) legalization in the first place. Choices along this continuum of tradeoffs determine the "hardness" of legalization, both initially and over time.

In general, we hypothesize that softer forms of legalization will be more attractive to states as contracting costs increase. This proposition should be true both for relatively mechanical costs—such as those created by large numbers of actors and rigorous national ratification procedures—and for more intensely political costs like those prevailing in negotiations with potentially strong distributional effects. In the remainder of this section, we explore the hard law/soft law tradeoff in terms of several key independent variables, each of which increases the costs of international agreement. These variables include sovereignty costs, uncertainty, divergence among national preferences, differences in time horizons and discount rates, and power differentials among major actors.

Sovereignty Costs

The nature of sovereignty costs.   Accepting a binding legal obligation, especially when it entails delegating authority to a supranational body, is costly to states. The costs involved can range from simple differences in outcome on particular issues, to loss of authority over decision making in an issue-area, to more fundamental encroachments on state sovereignty. While we recognize that the concept of "sovereignty" is broad and highly contested,[47] we use "sovereignty costs" as a covering term for all

---

46. Diebold 1952.

47. Krasner offers four meanings or categories of sovereignty: *domestic* sovereignty (the organization of authority and control within the state), *interdependence* sovereignty (the ability to control flows across borders), international *legal* sovereignty (establishing the status of a political entity in the international

three categories of costs to emphasize the high stakes states often face in accepting international agreements. The potential for inferior outcomes, loss of authority, and diminution of sovereignty makes states reluctant to accept hard legalization—especially when it includes significant levels of delegation.

Sovereignty costs are relatively low when states simply make international legal commitments that limit their behavior in particular circumstances. States typically accept these costs in order to achieve better collective outcomes—as illustrated by solutions to Prisoners' Dilemma and collective action problems that limit individual choices. Such agreements are undoubtedly exercises of legal sovereignty. Nevertheless, even they may limit the ability of states to regulate their borders (for example, by requiring them to allow goods, capital, or people to pass freely) and to implement important domestic policies (as when free trade impinges on labor, safety, or environmental regulations), thus encroaching on other aspects of sovereignty.

Greater sovereignty costs emerge when states accept external authority over significant decisions. International agreements may implicitly or explicitly insert international actors (who are neither elected nor otherwise subject to domestic scrutiny) into national decision procedures. These arrangements may limit the ability of states to govern whole classes of issues—such as social subsidies or industrial policy—or require states to change domestic laws or governance structures. Their significance is reflected in European concerns over the "democratic deficit" and complaints of American activists regarding the "faceless bureaucrats" in the WTO. Nevertheless, the impact of such arrangements is tempered by states' ability to withdraw from international agreements—although processes of enmeshment may make it increasingly costly for them to do so.

Sovereignty costs are at their highest when international arrangements impinge on the relations between a state and its citizens or territory, the traditional hallmarks of (Westphalian) sovereignty. Of course, ordinary restrictions on domestic policies can have such effects in contemporary welfare states, but these are heightened and generalized when, for example, an international human rights regime circumscribes a state's ability to regulate its citizens. Similarly, the United States has correctly been concerned that an International Criminal Court might claim jurisdiction over U.S. soldiers participating in international peacekeeping activities or other foreign endeavors. Agreements such as the Law of the Sea Convention both redefine national territory (for example, by delineating jurisdiction over a territorial sea, exclusive economic

---

system), and *Westphalian* sovereignty (preventing external actors from influencing or determining domestic authority structures). Krasner 1999. These categories overlap and do not covary in any necessary pattern.

Krasner argues that sovereignty has never been immutable, although legal sovereignty has tended to be more respected than Westphalian or other types of sovereignty. Indeed, some legal purists see sovereignty as a fundamental and inviolable legal concept relating to state supremacy in making and withdrawing from international treaties. But recent legal theorists argue that such a view is untenable given ongoing developments in international legalization; they conclude that "it is time to slowly ease the term out of polite language in international relations, surely in law." See Henkin et al. 1993, 19. We skirt these conceptual debates, focusing instead on the fact that states often perceive international legalization as infringing on their sovereignty, broadly construed.

zone, and continental shelf) and limit the capacity of states to restrict its use (for example, by establishing rights of innocent passage). Here, too, individual states retain the capacity to withdraw, but doing so may actually diminish their (legal) sovereignty, risking loss of recognition as members in good standing of the international community.

Legalization can lead to further, often unanticipated sovereignty costs over time. Even if rules are written precisely to narrow their range, or softened by including escape clauses or limiting delegation, states cannot anticipate or limit all of their possible effects.

Delegation provides the greatest source of unanticipated sovereignty costs. As Charles Lindblom points out, a grant of "authority always becomes to a degree uncontrollable."[48] The best example is the ECJ. As Karen Alter describes in this issue, ECJ rulings transformed the preliminary ruling procedure of Article 177 of the Treaty of Rome from a check on supranational power into a device through which private litigants can challenge national policies as inconsistent with European law. Similarly, while France and Canada have consistently sought to minimize the impact of expanding trade legalization on their autonomous cultural policies, they have nevertheless seen that autonomy slowly trimmed back by decisions in the WTO and NAFTA. Even nonjudicial organizations like the IMF or World Bank exert their independence in ways that go beyond the initial intentions or anticipations of the contracting states.[49]

The delegation of legal authority to independent domestic courts and agencies can create similar unexpected consequences. However, states generally feel they have ultimate control over domestic courts—they appoint the judges and control the justice departments that bring criminal actions—and so they find, in general, that domestic delegation has lower sovereignty costs.

Even the most powerful states recognize that legalization will circumscribe their autonomy. U.S. opposition to autonomous international institutions, whether the Enterprise in the Law of the Sea Convention, the International Criminal Court, or the UN more generally, reflects the special concern that delegation raises.[50] Even in NAFTA, where its political influence is paramount, the United States resisted delegating authority to supranational dispute settlement bodies for interstate disputes; only the Chapter 19 procedure for reviewing antidumping and countervailing duty rulings creates significant delegated authority. Congress also explicitly provided that the agreement would not be self-executing in domestic law, limiting delegation to national courts.[51] More recently, concern that highly legalized WTO dispute settlement institutions might expand the meaning of the Uruguay Round agreements led Con-

48. Lindblom 1977, 24.
49. Abbott and Snidal 1998.
50. Shapiro takes the extreme view that such developments are an inevitable part of the development of any legal system. Shapiro 1981. Our view is that the advantages of legalization exert a powerful pull in this direction but that sovereignty costs provide significant resistance; we should expect a mixed level of international legalization according to the characteristics of issues and states, at least in the foreseeable future.
51. F. Abbott, this issue.

gress to provide for an early review of the costs and benefits of WTO membership, including the results of legal proceedings, tied to a fast-track procedure for withdrawal from the organization. Conversely, the willingness of the United States and other countries to subscribe to more constrained institutions indicates that their benefits outweigh their sovereignty costs—at least up to a point.

The notion of sovereignty costs is more complicated when competing domestic and transnational interests affect the development of international legalization. Certain domestic groups may perceive negative sovereignty costs from international agreements that provide them with more favorable outcomes than national policy. Examples include free-trade coalitions that prefer their states' trade policies to be bound by WTO rulings rather than open to the vagaries of individual legislatures, and environmental groups that believe they can gain more from an international accord than from domestic politics. For similar reasons, although a government that anticipates staying in power may be reluctant to limit its control over an issue, a government less certain of its longevity may seek to bind its successors through international legal commitments.[52] We discuss such domestic variations in the following section.

Sovereignty costs may also be negative for external reasons, as where participation in international arrangements enhances a state's international and domestic position.[53] Key aspects of sovereignty have been codified in a variety of legal instruments, including the 1933 Montevideo Convention on the Rights and Duties of States, Article 2 of the UN Charter, and the UN General Assembly Declaration on Principles of International Law Concerning Friendly Relations Among States. Regional legal arrangements like the Organization of American States (OAS) provide much-needed support for state sovereignty. Chapter IV of the OAS Charter promotes the independence and sovereign equality of member states regardless of power differentials and protects internal sovereignty through principles of nonintervention.

Although negative sovereignty costs are an important exception, positive sovereignty costs are the more standard (and more difficult) case for international legalization. Hard legalization—especially the classic legal model with centralized judicial institutions capable of amplifying the terms of agreements in the course of resolving disputes—imposes high sovereignty costs. Thus states face tradeoffs between the benefits and sovereignty costs of different forms of legalization.

States can limit sovereignty costs through arrangements that are nonbinding or imprecise or do not delegate extensive powers. Most often, states protect themselves by adopting less precise rules and weaker legal institutions, as in the Council of Europe's framework Convention for the Protection of National Minorities, [O,p,d]. They frequently provide that member states must adhere to a special treaty protocol before a court or quasi-judicial body can assert jurisdiction over them, as in the

---

52. Colombatto and Macey offer a related view in arguing that governmental agencies seek international legalization in order to protect their administrative positions at a cost to domestic groups. Colombatto and Macey 1996.

53. In Krasner's terminology, these constitute international legal and Westphalian sovereignty, respectively.

inter-American human rights system, or that all parties to a particular dispute must consent before the case can be litigated. Still weaker forms of delegation—such as the consultation arrangements characteristic of arms control agreements, {O,P,-}— limit sovereignty costs even more, coupling legal obligations with political mechanisms of control and defense. Thus soft legalization offers a variety of means—none of them perfect—by which states can limit sovereignty costs.

The international money-laundering regime provides a good example.[54] Beginning in the 1980s, the United States led an effort to control the international laundering of criminal profits. Many nations resisted efforts to criminalize money laundering or to require greater scrutiny of financial transactions, fearing interference with legitimate business dealings and with the division of domestic authority between prudential regulators and prosecutors. To address these concerns, in 1989 the OECD created the Financial Action Task Force of financial experts. The task force has issued policy recommendations, administers a system of peer review, and can even impose mild sanctions. Its guidelines are not as tightly constraining as hard legal commitments and are more difficult to "enforce." Yet they provide a common basis for domestic implementation (with enough flexibility to accommodate national differences), guide behavior, and create expectations that violations will bring political costs. Task force guidelines legitimize participation in national decisions by international actors and by concerned domestic bureaucracies and NGOs. They invoke a form of legal discourse and some principles of international law. In its decade of operation, the task force has fostered a significant degree of convergence around the principles contained in its guidelines.

As this example demonstrates, soft law provides a means to lessen sovereignty costs by expanding the range of available institutional arrangements along a more extensive and finely differentiated tradeoff curve. How states evaluate these tradeoffs—and thus determine their preferences for different forms of legalization— depends on their own characteristics and the circumstances of particular issue-areas.

Sovereignty costs and issue type.   Viewing constraints on national autonomy and sovereignty as costs that vary across issues, we hypothesize that states will prefer different forms of legalization in different issue-areas. At one extreme, sovereignty costs are especially high in areas related to national security. Adversaries are extremely sensitive to unanticipated risks of agreement for the standard reasons advanced by realists, including relative gains. Even allies facing common external threats are reluctant to surrender autonomy over their security affairs. Therefore it is unsurprising that even in NATO, the most institutionalized alliance ever, delegation is moderate, {O,p,d}, or that security arrangements have lagged behind other institutional developments in the EU. Similarly, bilateral arms control agreements like SALT can be very precise in specifying missile numbers and types and are unquestionably legally binding but are only minimally institutionalized, {O,P,-}.

---

54. Simmons 2000a.

Political economy issues display a wide range of sovereignty costs and hence of legalization. At one extreme lie technical matters on which state interests are closely aligned, such as international transportation or food standards. Here sovereignty costs are low and the incidence of legalized agreements is correspondingly high. One even sees a significant level of delegation—including to organizations in which private actors play major roles, such as the International Organization for Standardization (ISO)—where sovereignty costs are low and technical complexity makes it hard to adapt agreements rapidly without some coordinating authority. Political economy issues like investment policy, money laundering, and security-related export controls, however, remain sensitive and have not been legalized to nearly the same extent. Similarly, tax policy, which lies at the core of all state functions but increasingly requires international coordination, is characterized by many bilateral treaties but displays little overall institutionalization.

Trade issues range between these extremes—sovereignty costs are significant but are frequently outweighed by the perceived benefits of legalized agreements. This is due partly to lesser conflicts of interest among states and partly to strong domestic support from beneficiaries of legalization. Consequently, even on a given issue, sovereignty costs can vary across states and over time. For example, the sovereignty costs of agricultural agreements are typically greater for less-developed states where the sector is larger and politically central; they have gradually decreased in OECD countries along with the relative importance of agriculture.

Finally, the most highly institutionalized arrangements, such as the EU, occur where there is a strong commitment to reducing sovereignty, or where a long process of legalized cooperation has led to institutionalization even against state resistance. The history of trade institutionalization is again instructive. In many respects, the WTO today is a stronger institution than the proposed International Trade Organization. Continued success in expanding trade under GATT changed domestic political balances and lowered the costs of further legalization. Moreover, states "learned" that harder legalization (such as a stronger dispute settlement mechanism) can produce greater benefits; they may also have been reassured regarding the dangers of enmeshment. Nevertheless, vigorous continuing disputes over the future of the WTO reflect states' continued wariness of sacrificing autonomy.

Uncertainty

Many international issues are new and complex. The underlying problems may not be well understood, so states cannot anticipate all possible consequences of a legalized arrangement. One way to deal with such problems is to delegate authority to a central party (for example, a court or international organization) to implement, interpret, and adapt the agreement as circumstances unfold. This approach avoids the costs of having no agreement, or of having to (re)negotiate continuously, but it typically entails unacceptably high sovereignty costs. Soft legalization provides a number of more attractive alternatives for dealing with uncertainty.

First, states can reduce the precision of their commitments: $[O,p,d]$. Of course, if they do not know the relevant contingencies, they cannot achieve the precision of hard law even if they wish to do so, except as to better-understood aspects of the problem. Thus an arms control agreement can precisely control known technologies and can even limit research into technologies whose results can reasonably be anticipated (such as testing antiballistic missile systems). But it cannot govern technologies whose military impact cannot be foreseen. And blanket limitations on all research with potential military implications would unacceptably impair the development of beneficial civilian technologies.

But uncertainty makes precision less desirable as well as less attainable. The classic distinction between risk and uncertainty is significant here.[55] When risk is the central concern—that is, when actors cannot predict the outcome of an agreement but know the probability distribution of possible outcomes, conditional on agreement terms—precise agreements offer a way to manage and optimize risk-sharing.[56] But when circumstances are fundamentally uncertain—that is, when even the range and/or distribution of possible outcomes is unknown—a more precise agreement may not be desirable. In particular, if actors are "ambiguity-averse,"[57] they will prefer to leave agreements imprecise rather than face the possibility of being caught in unfavorable commitments. Unfamiliar environmental conditions like global warming provide good illustrations: because the nature, the severity, even the very existence of these threats—as well as the costs of responding to them—are highly uncertain, the imprecise commitments found in environmental "framework" agreements may be the optimal response.

A second way to deal with uncertainty is through arrangements that are precise but not legally binding, such as Agenda 21, the Forest Principles, and other hortatory instruments adopted at the 1992 Rio Conference on Environment and Development, $[-,P,-]$. These allow states to see the impact of rules in practice and to gain their benefits, while retaining flexibility to avoid any unpleasant surprises the rules might hold. Sometimes precision is actually used to limit the binding character of obligations, as with carefully drawn exceptions or escape clauses. These also protect the parties in case the agreement turns out to have hidden costs or unforeseen contingencies, so that states are not locked into commitments they regret.

Third, although strong delegation can aggravate the uncertainty of agreements, moderate delegation—typically involving political and administrative bodies where

---

55. See Knight 1921; and Ellsberg 1963.

56. More precise agreements might, for example, contain renegotiation provisions so that states can modify the agreement as events unfold. See Koremenos 1999. This case for greater precision assumes risk-averse states; risk seekers would gamble on imprecise, binding agreements. Finally, optimization of the agreement will be second-best when it is constrained by asymmetries of information exemplified in standard principal-agent models.

57. Ambiguity aversion means that actors prefer known outcomes (including the status quo) to unknown ones. When actors know the possible outcomes but do not know which of two alternative probability distributions governs them, Ellsberg characterizes ambiguity aversion as assuming that an act leads to the minimum possible expected outcome. Ellsberg 1963. In this case, agents prefer incomplete to complete contracts even at zero contracting costs. See Mukerji 1998.

states retain significant control—provides another way to manage uncertainty. UN specialized agencies and other international organizations, {-,*p*,*d*}, play restricted administrative roles across a wide variety of issues, and a small number of (mainly financial) organizations have more significant autonomy.[58] These organizations have the capacity to provide information (and thus reduce uncertainty) and some capacity to modify and adapt rules or to initiate standards.[59] In general, however, even this level of delegation appears only in areas with low sovereignty costs, such as technical coordination. More fundamental elaboration of arrangements is typically accomplished through direct political processes. Thus arms control agreements are precise and binding but limit delegation to forums that promote political bargaining, not independent third-party decision making, {O,P,-}.

Viewed dynamically, these forms of soft legalization offer strategies for individual and collective learning.[60] Consider the case where states are legally bound but in an imprecise way, as under the original Vienna Ozone Convention, {O,*p*,-}. These obligations offer flexibility and protection for states to work out problems over time through negotiations shaped by normative guidelines, rather than constrained by precise rules. Hortatory rules, for example, {-,*p*,*d*}, similarly provide general standards against which behavior can be assessed and support learning processes that reduce uncertainty over time. Some emerging arrangements on the rights of women and children fit this model. Agreements that are precise but nonbinding, like the Helsinki Final Act, {-,*P*,*d*}, often include institutional devices such as conferences and review sessions where states can potentially deepen their commitments as they resolve uncertainties about the issue.

Indeed, moderate delegation—including international organizations that provide support for decentralized bargaining, expertise, and capacities for collecting information—may be more appropriate than adjudicative procedures (domestic or international) for adapting rules as circumstances are better understood. Examples include the numerous international agencies that recommend (often in conjunction with private actors) international standards on a range of issues, including technology, transportation, and health. Although not binding, their recommendations provide precise and compelling coordination points to which states and private actors usually adhere. In other cases, consultative committees or formal international organizations may be empowered to make rules more precise as learning occurs. Effective institutions of this sort require a certain autonomy that states may be reluctant to grant over truly important issues.

The learning processes described here are illustrated by the joint Food and Agriculture Organization–UN Environment Program (FAO-UNEP) regime requiring prior informed consent to international transfers of hazardous chemicals and pesticides.[61]

---

58. Abbott and Snidal 1998.

59. Gold 1983.

60. For a rational approach to learning, see Morrow 1994; and Koremenos 1999. For a more constructivist approach, see Finnemore 1996. Our view is that both learning as acquiring information and learning as changing preferences or identity are relevant (and compatible) aspects of legalization.

61. Mekouar 1998.

The FAO adopted a "code of conduct" on the distribution and use of pesticides in 1985; UNEP adopted "guidelines" on the exchange of information on internationally traded chemicals in 1987. Because of continued concern over exports of restricted substances to developing countries, the two organizations coordinated the amendment of their respective soft law instruments in 1989 to add a requirement for prior informed consent for international transfers of hazardous substances and a procedure for handling consents. This procedure was managed by the FAO and UNEP. Both organizations sponsored extensive consultations with expert groups from government and industry and provided technical assistance. The consent system, then, involved low obligation, relatively high precision, and moderate, largely administrative and technical, delegation, [-,P,d]. At the 1992 Rio conference, supporters attempted to "harden" the consent system through a binding treaty, but this effort failed. The FAO and UNEP continued to administer the existing system, however, and a few years later the member states of both organizations authorized formal treaty negotiations. The convention approved in September 1998 tracked the FAO-UNEP system almost exactly, [O,P,d].

In this section we have argued that soft legalization provides a rational adaptation to uncertainty. It allows states to capture the "easy" gains they can recognize with incomplete knowledge, without allowing differences or uncertainties about the situation to impede completion of the bargain. Soft legalization further provides a framework within which states can adapt their arrangement as circumstances change and can pursue "harder" gains through further negotiation. Soft law avoids the sovereignty costs associated with centralized adjudication or other strong delegation and is less costly than repeated renegotiation in light of new information.

Our discussion also suggests hypotheses as to when different forms of legalization are most likely to be used. Consider the four possible high/low combinations of uncertainty and sovereignty costs, two of the major independent variables in our analysis. Where both variables are low, states will be inclined toward hard legal arrangements to efficiently manage their interactions, [O,P,D]. When sovereignty costs are high and uncertainty is low, states will be reluctant to delegate but will remain open to precise and/or binding arrangements, [O,P,-]. Conversely, if sovereignty costs are low and uncertainty is high, states will be willing to accept binding obligations and at least moderate delegation but will resist precise rules, [O,p,d]. Finally, when both uncertainty and sovereignty costs are high, legalization will focus on the statement of flexible or hortatory obligations that are neither precise nor highly institutionalized, [o,p,-] or [-,p,-]. In all these cases, legalization provides a framework within which states can work to resolve their uncertainty, making harder legalization more attractive.

Soft Law as a Tool of Compromise

Compromise at a point in time. Soft law can ease bargaining problems among states even as it opens up opportunities for achieving mutually preferred compromises. Negotiating a hard, highly elaborated agreement among heterogeneous states is a costly and protracted process. It is often more practical to negotiate a softer agreement that establishes general goals but with less precision and perhaps with limited delegation.

Soft legalization allows states to adapt their commitments to their particular situations rather than trying to accommodate divergent national circumstances within a single text. This provides for flexibility in implementation, helping states deal with the domestic political and economic consequences of an agreement and thus increasing the efficiency with which it is carried out. Accordingly, soft law should be attractive in proportion to the degree of divergence among the preferences and capacities of states, a condition that increases almost automatically as one moves from bilateral through regional to multilateral negotiations.

Flexibility is especially important when uncertainty or one sticky problem threatens to upset a larger "package deal." Rather than hold up the overall agreement, states can incorporate hortatory or imprecise provisions to deal with the difficult issues, allowing them to proceed with the rest of the bargain. The labor and environmental side agreements to NAFTA are suggestive on this point.

Softness also accommodates states with different degrees of readiness for legalization. Those whose institutions, laws, and personnel permit them to carry out hard commitments can enter agreements of that kind; those whose weaknesses in these areas prevent them from implementing hard legal commitments can accept softer forms of agreement, perhaps through exceptions, reservations, or phase-in periods. Many treaties make such special provisions for developing countries, transitional economies, and other categories of states. States may prefer such an arrangement to either a softer agreement among all or a harder agreement with limited membership. Over time, if the soft arrangements are successful and without adverse consequences, the initially reluctant states may accept harder legalization.

The 1996 Wassenaar Arrangement for national controls on exports of conventional weapons and dual-use technologies illustrates the use of soft legalization to facilitate compromise.[62] Wassenaar is a successor to the Coordinating Committee for Multilateral Export Controls, the informal institution through which the West coordinated controls on exports to the Soviet bloc. The United States pressed for a new institution to address post–Cold War security threats like terrorism, regional conflicts, and arms buildups by rogue nations like Iraq. But it faced several barriers to agreement: nearly twice as many nations would have to take part; the "common enemy" of the Cold War no longer existed; the participating nations had very different attitudes toward particular countries and conflicts; the economic costs of export controls would fall unevenly across countries; and some states were more technically prepared than others to operate a sophisticated export control system.

The nonbinding "arrangement" overcame these barriers by incorporating substantial flexibility in all three elements of legalization, $[-,p,-]$. The core of the arrangement is the exchange of information on past exports of agreed upon products to buyers in agreed target markets. This information alerts members to suspicious acquisition patterns and focuses peer pressure against commercial undercutting. The arrange-

---

62. Dursht 1997.

ment operates by consensus, and member countries implement its requirements in domestic law. The United States yielded on a number of issues, such as prior approval of export sales. In return, however, it obtained inclusion of both conventional arms and dual-use goods, specific lists of controlled items, designation of some specific target nations, and a degree of transparency that allows it to respond in serious cases.

These advantages of flexibility do not come without cost. Soft law compromises make it harder to determine whether a state is living up to its commitments and therefore create opportunities to shirk. They also weaken the ability of governments to commit themselves to policies by invoking firm international commitments and therefore make it easier for domestic groups, including other branches of government, to undo the agreement. Again, states face a tradeoff between the advantages of flexibility in achieving agreement and its disadvantages in ensuring performance.

States can design different elements of an agreement with different combinations of hardness to fine-tune this tradeoff on different issues. Alternative forms of delegation can be used to limit the tendencies to shirk. In some cases, international reporting requirements may be sufficient to determine whether states are meeting their commitments. Elsewhere, requirements for domestic implementation, including domestic legalization, may empower private actors like firms or NGOs to enforce the agreement.

Compromise over time. Because even soft legal agreements commit states to characteristic forms of discourse and procedure, soft law provides a way of achieving compromise over time. Consider a patient state (low discount rate) that is seeking a concession but is unwilling to offer enough immediately (for example, in linkage to other issues) to induce an impatient state to offer the concession. The patient state may nevertheless be willing to make a (smaller) current payoff in return for a soft legal agreement that has some prospect of enmeshing the impatient state in a process that will deliver the concession down the road. Insofar as states find it progressively costly to extricate themselves from legal processes, soft law helps remedy the commitment problem that looms large in international relations.

The Helsinki process is a dramatic illustration of this form of compromise. The Soviet Union (the impatient party) had an immediate need to stabilize military and political relations with Western Europe and the United States so that economic relations could develop more rapidly. The West (the more patient party) was not prepared to recognize Soviet dominance in Eastern and Central Europe on a legally binding basis, but it was willing to do so in less precise and explicitly nonlegally binding terms—if in return the Soviets would accept a soft human rights framework that turned out to have an unexpectedly significant bite over the longer term.

The Soviets surely underestimated the long-run effects of Basket III, but their tenacious bargaining (including efforts to obscure the provisions with "nonintervention" terminology) shows that they took these concessions very seriously.[63] Thus the

---

63. Maresca 1985. U.S. negotiators and the American public also underestimated the long-term significance of these arrangements.

Soviet leadership addressed its pressing problems with soft commitments that deferred the costs to its successors. The subsequent inability of the Soviet regime to contain the Basket III arrangements, either domestically or internationally, illustrates the subtle strength of soft law over time.

The longer-term consequences of soft law, including processes of learning, do not mean that legal agreements have an inevitable life cycle from softer toward harder legalization. Hard law is probably more likely to evolve from soft law than from (utopian) plans to create hard law full-blown. But this does not imply that all soft legalization is a way station to hard(er) legalization, or that hard legalization is the optimal form. The contracting difficulties noted earlier may never be resolved in some issue-areas; here, the attainable soft legalization will be superior to hard law that cannot be achieved. In these cases, continuing movement toward greater legalization is neither inevitable nor necessarily desirable.

The Helsinki experience and the "backlash" against ECJ activism described by Alter in this issue suggest a further limitation on the evolution of soft law: states may learn from experience that even soft forms of legalization can have powerful effects over time. As states internalize this lesson, they will be more alert to the possibilities of enmeshment and evolutionary growth in other negotiations. It would not be surprising, for example, if the Helsinki experience were still informing China's position on (even soft) human rights commitments. Impatient states may be forced to accept soft legalization in order to obtain current payoffs, but they may demand a higher price.

Compromise between the weak and the strong.   Soft legalization facilitates compromise between weak and powerful states. The traditional legal view is that law operates as a shield for the weak, whereas the traditional international relations view is that law acts as an instrument of the powerful. These seemingly contradictory views can be reconciled by understanding how (soft) law helps both types of states achieve their differing goals.

Whatever their views on soft law, traditional legal scholars generally agree that legalization aids weak states. Weil, a severe critic of soft law, writes that "it is [hard] law with its rigor that comes between the weak and the mighty to protect and deliver."[64] Michael Reisman, more favorable toward soft law, agrees that law advantages the weak.[65] These views echo analyses of constitutionalism as a movement to create a government of laws, not of men (or states), in order to constrain the powerful.[66] At the international level, rules ranging from general principles of nonintervention to agreements like the Nuclear Non-Proliferation Treaty can be seen as bounding the struggle for power.

For just these reasons, small and dependent states often seek hard legalization. To the extent it is effective, hard law offers protection and reduces uncertainty by demar-

64. Weil 1983, 442.
65. Reisman 1988, 377.
66. Lindblom 1977.

cating the likely behavior of powerful states. Lutz and Sikkink argue in this issue that Latin American states have long seen international law as providing them with exactly this type of protection from the United States.[67] Since they have less direct control over their own fates, small states also incur lower sovereignty costs from hard legalization. Indeed hard law may entail negative sovereignty costs, enhancing international standing and offering at least formal equality. Widespread African support for postcolonial boundaries, which make little sense on ethnic, political, or economic grounds, provides a striking illustration of the value of legal arrangements to weak states.

In contrast, many international relations scholars (and some critical legal scholars) hold the more skeptical view that international law is wholly beholden to international power. Powerful states have greater control over international outcomes, are less in need of protection, and face higher sovereignty costs. They have less need for legalization and more reason to resist it, even though their adherence is crucial to its success.

For these reasons, realists see international law largely as epiphenomenal, merely reflecting the distribution of power. Institutionalists also treat power (for example, hegemony and/or a capacity for decentralized retaliation) as a primary source of order and rules in the international system. Unlike realists, however, they argue that institutions have real effects, resulting in a disjuncture between the distribution of power and benefits in the system.

These perspectives can to some extent be reconciled by understanding legalization, especially soft legalization, as furthering the goals of both classes of states. Most importantly, legally binding and relatively precise rules allow strong and weak states to regularize their asymmetric relations. Because the continual, overt exercise of power is costly, powerful states gain by embodying their advantage in settled rules. Because weaker states are at a constant disadvantage in bargaining, they benefit from the certainty and credibility of legalized commitments. The result is not unlike an insurance contract, where a weaker party gladly pays a premium to a stronger one in return for the latter bearing, or in this case reducing, certain risks. In addition, both sides benefit by reducing the transactions costs of continual bargaining.

Of course, stronger states have disproportionate influence over the substance of agreed upon rules. But even the most powerful states cannot simply dictate the outcome of every negotiation because of the high costs of coercion. Instead, strong states must typically make the substantive content of legalized arrangements (just) attractive enough to encourage broad participation at an acceptable cost. Reduced bargaining costs normally provide ample room for such concessions.

Powerful states are most concerned with delegation, the major source of unanticipated sovereignty costs. As a result, forms of legalization that involve limited delegation, for example, $[O,p,-]$ or $[O,p,d]$, provide the crucial basis for cooperation between the weak and the strong. Lower levels of delegation prevent unexpected intrusions

67. Lutz and Sikkink, this issue.

into the sovereign preserves of powerful countries while allowing them significant influence over decision making. Delegation to administrative bodies rather than judicial organs allows powerful states to retain control over ongoing issue management. The structure and decision-making rules of those bodies, including formal voting procedures, provide further means of balancing members' interests.[68]

Soft legalization provides other important grounds for cooperation as well. We described earlier how legalization helps states solve commitment problems. This point becomes relevant when powerful states want small states to take actions that would leave them vulnerable. Powerful states can induce cooperation in such cases by agreeing to operate within a framework of legally binding rules and procedures, credibly constraining themselves from opportunistic behavior; with low levels of delegation, though, they can maintain predominant influence over decision making. For example, the United States ran its Gulf War operation through the UN Security Council, $[O,p,d]$, even though doing so was burdensome, because this helped it to mobilize valuable support from weaker states, including bases in Saudi Arabia and financing from Japan. Involving the Security Council also allowed the supporting states to monitor and influence the scope of U.S. activities, notwithstanding the U.S. veto.[69]

Finally, even without an external commitment problem, governments of weak states may find it domestically costly to be perceived as following the dictates of a powerful state. Organizing international arrangements in a legalized way, and delegating modest supervisory authority to international agencies, can mitigate these costs without unduly interfering with the outcomes desired by the powerful state. We have elsewhere described the role of formal international organizations as vehicles for this type of "laundering."[70]

Two examples illustrate how softness facilitates bargains between stronger and weaker states. The Law of the Sea Convention expanded the territorial sovereignty of littoral states, gave less developed countries a role in the exploitation of ocean resources, and protected such rights as military passage for powerful states. Obligation and precision are high in most parts of the agreement, but delegation is limited—

---

68. Where power is very asymmetric, dominant states may prefer bilateral bargaining. Thus Doremus finds that the United States pursued legalized arrangements through the patent regime for biotechnology where bargaining power was relatively equal among states, used the more political mechanism of bilateral reciprocity for semiconductors where the United States was most powerful, and used its unilateral power to enforce the copyright regime for software where its power advantage was moderate. Doremus 1996. Doremus also argues that legalization will be more likely during stages of the product cycle in which no country has a strong market advantage.

69. The legalization of the Eastern bloc during the Cold War provides another intriguing example. The Soviet Union was coercively preponderant within its sphere of influence throughout the period, but it learned early on that rule by stick was not as efficient as more balanced relations. Beginning in the mid-1950s, it transformed the Council for Mutual Economic Assistance (CMEA) from an instrument of unilateral control into an arrangement that offered Eastern European states the carrot of subsidized and secure supplies of fuel and raw materials in exchange for acquiescence to Soviet control. See Marreese 1986. The level of legalization in the CMEA was low, $[o,p,-]$, and the Soviet Union could readily have reverted to a coercive strategy, as it did in Czechoslovakia in 1968. Still, the CMEA promoted continuing cooperation among the Eastern bloc states.

70. Abbott and Snidal 1998.

although the convention creates a special tribunal it has handled very few disputes— and the operation of the Enterprise remains to be worked out in practice.

The Nuclear Non-Proliferation Treaty reflected an explicit bargain: weaker states accepted the existing nuclear oligopoly; powerful states agreed to pursue weapons restraints and technology transfer. Obligation was high, though limited by escape clauses and the twenty-five-year renegotiation clause. Precision was high in limiting the transfer of military technology, but lower with regards to commercial technology transfers. Delegation to the IAEA has been largely controlled by the major powers (who monopolize the necessary expertise).

An understanding of soft legalization helps reconcile the seemingly contradictory views of the effect of law. Viewed as a process, legalization is a form of political bargaining where powerful states are advantaged. However, the efficiency gains of legalization for the powerful—cynically, providing an efficient means to extract benefits from the weak—depend on their offering the weak sufficiently satisfactory terms to induce their participation. Viewed as an outcome, legalization appears less political, since even powerful states must accept the constraints of legal principles and discourse to take advantage of legalized arrangements. Yet powerful states have the greatest influence on the substantive legal rules, and the institutions associated with (soft) international legalization are frequently constructed to ensure them a leading voice.

The Role of Private Actors

In many issue-areas, from trade and investment to human rights and the environment, individuals and private groups are the actors most responsible for new international agreements—and for resisting new agreements in favor of the status quo. A flurry of research has documented the growing role of nonstate actors, including traditional interest groups, epistemic communities based on causal knowledge and professional disciplines,[71] and NGOs committed to normative values.[72] International conferences and organizations have become more accessible to private groups, allowing them to act internationally as well as domestically. Transnational advocacy coalitions have emerged congruent with the scope of international issues and fora.[73] At the same time, individual governmental units have increasingly engaged in transnational rule making. These trends have inspired the systematic reformulation of international relations theory from a "liberal" perspective[74] and its application to issues of international law.[75]

The same developments lead us to consider the role of nonstate actors in international legalization. Our discussion thus far, while focused on states, has been consis-

---

71. Haas 1992.
72. See Slaughter 1997a; Risse-Kappen 1995a; and Raustiala 1997.
73. Keck and Sikkink 1998.
74. Moravcsik 1997.
75. Slaughter 1997b and 1995a,b.

tent with the liberal assumption that government actions reflect balances of domestic interests; much of that discussion also applies to agreements among governmental units. In this section, though, we explicitly examine why nonstate actors pursue different forms of legalization. We consider three theoretical perspectives: a pluralist account in which interactions among private groups determine national preferences and international outcomes; a public choice account in which government officials pursue private rewards; and a statist account in which (partially) autonomous national governments interact with private actors.

Pluralist Interactions

In Andrew Moravcsik's pure liberal account, individuals and groups operating within (and across) states are the fundamental actors in international politics.[76] They "organize exchange and collective action" to further their interests and values. National governments merely ratify these private bargains, acting internationally—as unitary entities or through individual units—to implement the resulting national preferences.

This view implies that variations in domestic politics will produce national preferences that diverge more widely than rationalist models normally assume. For example, wide domestic variations almost certainly characterized the negotiations on Agenda 21, $\{-,P,-\}$, and the framework Convention on National Minorities, $\{O,p,-\}$. Divergent preferences increase transaction costs, uncertainty, and bargaining problems, making soft legalization even more valuable.

Fundamentally, however, Moravcsik's account is pluralist, viewing international outcomes as resulting directly from interactions among private individuals and groups. These interactions can be understood as political bargains between demandeur groups seeking new redistributive or normative arrangements and resister groups working to block or weaken them.

As with states, private demandeurs will normally press for hard law, other things being equal, to raise the costs of violation for other parties and to facilitate enforcement against resister groups and governments, including their own. Thus business groups in Mexico favored a legalized NAFTA and high technology firms favored a legalized WTO Agreement on Trade-Related Aspects of Intellectual Property Rights (TRIPs), while worker representatives in the ILO resisted proposals to emphasize recommendations over binding conventions. Activist groups seek international legalization to gain leverage in domestic politics, a process Margaret E. Keck and Kathryn Sikkink call the "boomerang effect."[77] Here, too, the demand for hard law should be especially strong when the risks of opportunism are high and compliance is difficult to monitor.

Hard legalization also provides new strategies for nonstate actors. First, as Robert O. Keohane, Andrew Moravcsik, and Anne-Marie Slaughter discuss in this issue, a growing number of international dispute settlement institutions are open to private

76. Moravcsik 1997.
77. Keck and Sikkink 1998, 12–13.

claimants, substantially altering political dynamics.[78] Second, when international legal rules are incorporated into national law, private actors can invoke them in national courts and agencies. Multinational firms, advocacy coalitions, and other transnational groups are best suited to pursue this strategy, at least if they have sufficient resources. Finally, legal rules present new strategies even when private litigation is restricted. Private groups can, for example, urge governments to espouse their legal claims, as foreign investors have long done; the WTO Appellate Body has recently determined that dispute settlement panels can accept friend-of-the-court briefs from NGOs.

When resister groups are able to blunt or defer demands for international action, soft legalization offers a prime instrument of compromise, just as in interstate interactions. In these situations demandeurs will seek the particular forms of legalization they are best equipped to utilize, whereas resister groups, by the same logic, oppose those elements that would be most costly for them. If demandeurs are well situated to conduct national litigation, for example, they might demand binding and precise norms (to facilitate direct applicability or incorporation into domestic legal systems) but be willing to yield on international delegation, $\{O,P,-\}$.[79]

Activist demandeurs appear to place a high priority on precise normative statements, yielding on other elements when necessary, $\{-,P,-\}$. This compromise often appears to suit the needs of business and other resister groups as well, since it avoids concrete legal enforcement. At the 1992 Rio conference, for example, after business interests blocked legally binding agreements on various issues, environmental groups turned their efforts to obtaining nonbinding but highly elaborated documents like the Rio Declaration, Agenda 21, and the Forest Principles.

Instruments like these are valuable tools for activists. Although they cannot be invoked as law, they support a similar normative discourse. A major technique of activist campaigns is to expose gaps between international commitments and actual government conduct.[80] Legal obligations might be more compelling, but soft undertakings can fuel "accountability politics" if they contain clear normative commitments. Instruments like the Beijing Declaration and the Helsinki Final Act also give legitimacy to issues and initiate political processes that may lead to harder law over time.

Public Choice

In the public choice account, government officials have power to affect political outcomes and act to further their own private redistributive interests. In effect, offi-

---

78. Participation by private actors is also crucial to the political strategies of supranational judges seeking to enhance the strength and scope of their own institutions and the bodies of law they administer. Helfer and Slaughter 1997.

79. The supporters of TRIPs did not have to make this choice: they obtained both domestic implementation and delegation to the strengthened WTO dispute settlement system.

80. Keck and Sikkink 1998, 24–25.

cials become another class of private actor negotiating political bargains. As a result, this perspective is explicitly included in Moravcsik's formulation.

From a public choice perspective, officials pursue forms of legalization that maximize their opportunities for reelection, campaign contributions, bribes, or other personal benefits. Thus, officials might support a highly legalized agreement like TRIPs as a way of making credible commitments to influential private actors in return for electoral support.

Yet soft law will often be appealing in the public choice context, especially to government officials. For one thing, soft legalization allows officials to supply present benefits to private demandeurs while retaining the possibility of extracting future rents. Legally binding rules are relatively inflexible; strong delegation introduces additional actors who may behave unpredictably. Precise but nonbinding normative commitments, $[-,P,d]$, may be the optimal solution.

Soft legalization also enables rent-seeking officials to minimize political losses in the face of strong private distributional conflicts. In domestic politics, officials facing such conflicts resist taking sides, hoping not to alienate either group of constituents; they use such expedients as calling for further study, supporting vague statements of principle, or passing the buck to administrative agencies. Weak obligation, precision, and delegation are the international counterparts of these actions.

Significant forms of soft law are created in "transgovernmental" institutions, such as the Basle Committee of central bankers or the International Organization of Securities Commissions. Participants do not represent states as such, but rather individual agencies within the "state."[81] Public choice theory suggests that officials concerned with advancing their influence can use these organizations to reinforce their positions or justify new regulations at home.[82] Participating agencies may be forced to rely on soft law because they lack authority to enter binding treaties. Informal arrangements may also avoid executive or legislative approval and public scrutiny. Less cynically, soft law is well suited to the loose coordination these associations normally pursue.

Statism

In a statist account—contrary to the pure public choice view—governments retain (some) autonomy, which they exercise to influence and restrict accommodations among private actors. Government preferences are determined by factors such as national self-preservation and independence, relations with other states, the nature of individual issue-areas, and prevailing ideas and norms, as well as domestic politics.

A simple statist model might assume that governments act as "transmission belts" for private bargains on most issues but intervene when those bargains would impair national autonomy. In these situations, soft legalization allows governments to respond to private demands while limiting sovereignty costs. One would expect governments in these settings to avoid legally binding commitments and to limit delega-

81. See Zaring 1998; and Slaughter 2000.
82. Colombatto and Macey 1996.

tion to competing centers of power. Again, precise but nonbinding norms with weak delegation, {-,P,-}, would be a frequent outcome.

Here, too, the Rio and Beijing conferences are perfect illustrations. Although environmental and women's groups are increasingly influential, at least in many countries, it is extremely unlikely that the United States or virtually any other government would have accepted the innovative and expansive Rio and Beijing declarations as legally binding obligations. Yet in soft law form, with sovereignty costs as well as economic and social costs limited, they were adopted by almost every nation in the world.

A more complex statist model might credit states with a broader range of independent preferences. Soft legalization would then function as an instrument of accommodation between the state and private actors, as well as among private actors. When the United States was considering ratification of NAFTA, for example, labor and other constituencies demanded legally binding rules on labor rights. The Clinton administration wished to respond, but it was also aware—quite apart from countervailing business pressures—of Mexico's sensitivity to interference in its internal affairs. Consequently, the administration addressed labor rights in a side agreement that was legally binding, quite precise in terms of the parties' obligation to enforce national labor laws, and with moderate delegation, {O,P,d}.[83] In addressing the content of national labor laws, though, U.S. negotiators accepted markedly vague rules and weaker delegation, {-,p,d}.

States and private actors might also have divergent discount rates. At the time of the Helsinki conference, activist groups were impatient for progress on human rights, but Western governments were more patient. The United States also hoped to retain flexibility on human rights so that it could pursue trade and security issues. In the end, U.S. negotiators accepted a nonbinding declaration.

Given independent preferences, governments might use different forms of legalization offensively as well as defensively. They could, for example, use binding agreements to forestall demands of moderately powerful domestic groups. Alternatively, they could use nonbinding or imprecise agreements to introduce potentially unpopular new rules to domestic audiences. "Framework" agreements like the Vienna Ozone Convention and the WTO services agreement change political discourse and create incentives for private actors to adjust, but leave costly regulation for the future.

Conclusion

We have analyzed the spectrum of international legalization from soft informal agreements through intermediate blends of obligation, precision, and delegation to hard legal arrangements. Although even hard international law does not approach stereotypical conceptions of law based on advanced domestic legal systems, international

---

83. The parallel agreement on environmental protection included an innovative provision allowing private parties to initiate reviews of compliance.

legalization nevertheless represents a distinctive form of institutionalization. Ultimately, we can only understand the inclination of actors to cast their relations in legal form, and the variety of ways in which they do so, in terms of the value those institutional forms provide for them. Put plainly, international legalization is a diverse phenomenon because it helps a diverse universe of states and other actors resolve diverse problems.

Legalization reflects a series of tradeoffs. States are typically torn between the benefits of hard legalization—for example, mitigating commitment and incomplete contracting problems—and the sovereignty costs it entails. For their part, private actors generally seek hard legal arrangements that reflect their particular interests and values, but these demands often conflict with those of other private actors or of governments. In settings like these, soft legalization helps balance competing considerations, offering techniques for compromise among states, among private actors, and between states and private actors. In addition, soft law helps actors handle the exigencies of uncertainty and accommodate power differentials.

Our analysis necessarily combines the rational incentives associated with "contracts" and the normative considerations associated with "covenants." Legalization is a strategy through which actors pursue their interests and values; it also supplies a body of norms and procedures that shape actors' behavior, interests, and identities. Thus, though we premise our analysis on the notion of actors rationally pursuing goals, we argue that they do so knowing that legalization embeds them in a partially autonomous process and discourse that constrains their behavior and may modify important understandings. The wariness with which states regard the prospect of enmeshment in such normative processes is testimony to the power of legalization—soft and hard.

More generally, the many forms of legalization remind us that international politics and international law are not alternative realms, but are deeply intertwined. Although one goal of law—as of institutions in general—is to settle key issues so that actors can regularize their interactions, the creation and development of legal arrangements is highly political. This is especially true in the international sphere, where most legal regimes are relatively new and undeveloped. Politics permeates international law and limits its autonomy.

Conversely, international politics is rooted in legal considerations. From the principles of sovereignty that define modern nation-states, through the rules of diplomacy, war, and commerce that structure their interactions, to the specific regimes they create, legalized agreements and normative processes guide and constrain the behavior of states. Without this foundation in law, neither states nor analysts could make sense of international interactions.

The deep connection of law and politics is most apparent in the area of delegation. States almost never delegate authority to independent courts of general and mandatory jurisdiction like those of advanced domestic legal systems—although more constrained judicial delegation appears to be increasing and is supplemented in many cases by the participation of national courts. More typically, even in connection with binding legal commitments, they delegate authority only to international organizations or other administrative bodies subject to direct and indirect controls. This choice of venue limits the extent to which interactions can be governed by purely legal procedures and discourse.

In forecasting the future of international legalization, we subscribe to the theories of neither Pollyanna nor Chicken Little. To be sure, the twentieth century and especially the period following World War II witnessed a remarkable expansion of international legalization. But in large part that growth merely allowed international institutions to catch up with the dramatic changes in globalization (née interdependence) that had overtaken the inherited framework. It does not follow that international legalization will continue at the same rate, or that the apparent tendency toward (somewhat) harder legalization will continue. Indeed, a central part of our argument is that states and nonstate actors can achieve many of their goals through soft legalization that is more easily attained or even preferable.

In this light, we argue vigorously against those who discount international legalization because it is so often soft. Soft law is valuable on its own, not just as a stepping-stone to hard law. Soft law provides a basis for efficient international "contracts," and it helps create normative "covenants" and discourses that can reshape international politics. International legalization in all its forms must be considered one of the most significant institutional features of international relations.

Legalized Dispute Resolution: Interstate and Transnational

Robert O. Keohane, Andrew Moravcsik, and Anne-Marie Slaughter

International courts and tribunals are flourishing. Depending on how these bodies are defined, they now number between seventeen and forty.[1] In recent years we have witnessed the proliferation of new bodies and a strengthening of those that already exist. "When future international legal scholars look back at . . . the end of the twentieth century," one analyst has written, "they probably will refer to the enormous expansion of the international judiciary as the single most important development of the post–Cold War age."[2]

These courts and tribunals represent a key dimension of legalization. Instead of resolving disputes through institutionalized bargaining, states choose to delegate the task to third-party tribunals charged with applying general legal principles. Not all of these tribunals are created alike, however. In particular, we distinguish between two ideal types of international dispute resolution: interstate and transnational. Our central argument is that the formal legal differences between interstate and transnational dispute resolution have significant implications for the politics of dispute settlement and therefore for the effects of legalization in world politics.

Interstate dispute resolution is consistent with the view that public international law comprises a set of rules and practices governing *interstate* relationships. Legal resolution of disputes, in this model, takes place between states conceived of as unitary actors. States are the subjects of international law, which means that they control access to dispute resolution tribunals or courts. They typically designate the adjudicators of such tribunals. States also implement, or fail to implement, the decisions of international tribunals or courts. Thus in interstate dispute resolution, states act as gatekeepers both to the international legal process and from that process back to the domestic level.

---

1. Romano 1999, 723–28. By the strictest definition, there are currently seventeen permanent, independent international courts. If we include some bodies that are not courts, but instead quasi-judicial tribunals, panels, and commissions charged with similar functions, the total rises to over forty. If we include historical examples and bodies negotiated but not yet in operation, the total rises again to nearly one hundred.
2. Ibid., 709.

International Organization 54, 3, Summer 2000, pp. 73–104

In transnational dispute resolution, by contrast, access to courts and tribunals and the subsequent enforcement of their decisions are legally insulated from the will of individual national governments. These tribunals are therefore more open to individuals and groups in civil society. In the pure ideal type, states lose their gatekeeping capacities; in practice, these capacities are attenuated. This loss of state control, whether voluntarily or unwittingly surrendered, creates a range of opportunities for courts and their constituencies to set the agenda.

Before proceeding to our argument, it is helpful to locate our analysis in the broader context of this special issue of *IO*. Legalization is a form of institutionalization distinguished by obligation, precision, and delegation. Our analysis applies primarily when obligation is high.[3] Precision, on the other hand, is not a defining characteristic of the situations we examine. We examine the decisions of bodies that interpret and apply rules, regardless of their precision. Indeed, such bodies may have greater latitude when precision is low than when it is high.[4] Our focus is a third dimension of legalization: delegation of authority to courts and tribunals designed to resolve international disputes through the application of general legal principles.[5]

Three dimensions of delegation are crucial to our argument: independence, access, and embeddedness. As we explain in the first section, independence specifies the extent to which formal legal arrangements ensure that adjudication can be rendered impartially with respect to concrete state interests. Access refers to the ease with which parties other than states can influence the tribunal's agenda. Embeddedness denotes the extent to which dispute resolution decisions can be implemented without governments having to take actions to do so. We define low independence, access, and embeddedness as the ideal type of interstate dispute resolution and high independence, access, and embeddedness as the ideal type of transnational dispute resolution. Although admittedly a simplification, this conceptualization helps us to understand why the behavior and impact of different tribunals, such as the International Court of Justice (ICJ) and the European Court of Justice (ECJ), have been so different.

In the second section we seek to connect international politics, international law, and domestic politics. Clearly the power and preferences of states influence the behavior both of governments and of dispute resolution tribunals: international law operates in the shadow of power. Yet within that political context, we contend that institutions for selecting judges, controlling access to dispute resolution, and legally enforcing the judgments of international courts and tribunals have a major impact on state behavior. The formal qualities of legal institutions empower or disempower domestic political actors other than national governments. Compared to interstate dispute resolution, transnational dispute resolution tends to generate more litigation, jurisprudence more autonomous of national interests, and an additional source of pressure for compliance. In the third section we argue that interstate and transna-

---

3. Abbott et al., this issue, tab. 1, types I–III and V.
4. Hence we do not exclude types II and V (Abbott et al., tab. 1, this issue) from our purview.
5. See Abbott et al., this issue.

tional dispute resolution generate divergent longer-term dynamics. Transnational dispute resolution seems to have an inherently more expansionary character; it provides more opportunities to assert and establish new legal norms, often in unintended ways.

This article should be viewed as exploratory rather than an attempt to be definitive. Throughout, we use ideal types to illuminate a complex subject, review suggestive though not conclusive evidence, and highlight opportunities for future research. We offer our own conjectures at various points as to useful starting points for that research but do not purport to test definitive conclusions.

A Typology of Dispute Resolution

Much dispute resolution in world politics is highly institutionalized. Established, enduring rules apply to entire classes of circumstances and cannot easily be ignored or modified when they become inconvenient to one participant or another in a specific case. In this article we focus on institutions in which dispute resolution has been delegated to a third-party tribunal charged with applying designated legal rules and principles. This act of delegation means that disputes must be framed as "cases" between two or more parties, at least one of which, the defendant, will be a state or an individual acting on behalf of a state. (Usually, states are the defendants, so we refer to defendants as "states." However, individuals may also be prosecuted by international tribunals, as in the proposed International Criminal Court and various war crimes tribunals.[6]) The identity of the plaintiff depends on the design of the dispute resolution mechanism. Plaintiffs can be other states or private parties—individuals or nongovernmental organizations (NGOs)—specifically designated to monitor and enforce the obligatory rules of the regime.

We turn now to our three explanatory variables: independence, access, and embeddedness. We do not deny that the patterns of delegation we observe may ultimately have their origins in the power and interests of major states, as certain strands of liberal and realist theory claim. Nevertheless, our analysis here takes these sources of delegation as given and emphasizes how formal legal institutions empower groups and individuals other than national governments.[7]

Independence: Who Controls Adjudication?

The variable *independence* measures the extent to which adjudicators for an international authority charged with dispute resolution are able to deliberate and reach legal

---

6. We do not discuss the interesting case of international criminal law here. See Bass 1998.

7. This central focus on variation in the political representation of social groups, rather than interstate strategic interaction, is the central tenet of theories of international law that rest on liberal international relations theory. Slaughter 1995a. Our approach is thus closely linked in this way to republican liberal studies of the democratic peace, the role of independent executives and central banks in structuring international economic policy coordination, and the credibility of commitments by democratic states more generally. See Keohane and Nye 1977; Moravcsik 1997; Doyle 1983a,b; and Goldstein 1996.

judgments independently of national governments. In other words, it assesses the extent to which adjudication is rendered impartially with respect to concrete state interests in a specific case. The traditional international model of dispute resolution in law and politics places pure control by states at one end of a continuum. Disputes are resolved by the agents of the interested parties themselves. Each side offers its own interpretation of the rules and their applicability to the case at issue; disagreements are resolved through institutionalized interstate bargaining. There are no permanent rules of procedure or legal precedent, although in legalized dispute resolution, decisions must be consistent with international law. Institutional rules may also influence the outcome by determining the conditions—interpretive standards, voting requirements, selection—under which authoritative decisions are made.[8] Even where legal procedures are established, individual governments may have the right to veto judgments, as in the UN Security Council and the old General Agreement on Tariffs and Trade (GATT).

Movement along the continuum away from this traditional interstate mode of dispute resolution measures the nature and tightness of the political constraints imposed on adjudicators. The extent to which members of an international tribunal are independent reflects the extent to which they can free themselves from at least three categories of institutional constraint: selection and tenure, legal discretion, and control over material and human resources.

The most important criterion is independent selection and tenure. The spectrum runs from direct representatives of unconstrained national governments to a more impartial and autonomous process of naming judges. Judges may be selected from the ranks of loyal politicians, leading members of the bar, and justice ministries; or they may be drawn from a cadre of specialized experts in a particular area of international law. Their tenure may be long or short. After serving as adjudicators, they may be dependent on national governments for their subsequent careers or may belong to an independent professional group, such as legal academics. The less partisan their background, the longer their tenure; and the more independent their future, the greater the independence of adjudicators.

Selection and tenure rules vary widely. Many international institutions maintain tight national control on dispute resolution through selection and tenure rules.[9] Some institutions—including the UN, International Monetary Fund, NATO, and the bilateral Soviet–U.S. arrangements established by the Strategic Arms Limitation Treaty (SALT)—establish no authoritative third-party adjudicators whatsoever. The regime creates instead a set of decision-making rules and procedures, a forum for interstate bargaining, within which subsequent disputes are resolved by national representatives serving at the will of their governments. In other institutions, however, such as the EU, governments can name representatives, but those representatives are assured

---

8. Helfer and Slaughter 1997.

9. Even less independent are ad hoc and arbitral tribunals designed by specific countries for specific purposes. The Organization for Security and Cooperation in Europe, for example, provides experts, arbiters, and conciliators for ad hoc dispute resolution. Here we consider only permanent judicial courts. See Romano 1999, 711–13.

TABLE 1. *The independence continuum: Selection and tenure*

Level of independence	Selection method and tenure	International court or tribunal
Low	Direct representatives, perhaps with single-country veto	UN Security Council
Moderate	Disputants control ad hoc selection of third-party judges	PCA
	Groups of states control selection of third-party judges	ICJ, GATT, WTO
High	Individual governments appoint judges with long tenure	ECJ
	Groups of states select judges with long tenure	ECHR, IACHR

long tenure and may enjoy subsequent prestige in the legal world independent of their service to individual states. In first-round dispute resolution in GATT and the World Trade Organization (WTO), groups of states select a stable of experts who are then selected on a case-by-case basis by the parties and the secretariat, whereas in ad hoc international arbitration, the selection is generally controlled by the disputants and the tribunal is constituted for a single case.

In still other situations—particularly in authoritarian countries—judges may be vulnerable to retaliation when they return home after completing their tenure; even in liberal democracies, future professional advancement may be manipulated by the government.[10] The legal basis of some international dispute resolution mechanisms, such as the European Court of Human Rights (ECHR), requires oversight by semi-independent supranational bodies. The spectrum of legal independence as measured by selection and tenure rules is shown in Table 1.

Legal discretion, the second criterion for judicial independence, refers to the breadth of the mandate granted to the dispute resolution body. Some legalized dispute resolution bodies must adhere closely to treaty texts; but the ECJ, as Karen Alter describes in this issue, has asserted the supremacy of European Community (EC) law without explicit grounding in the treaty text or the intent of national governments. More generally, institutions for adjudication arise, as Abbott and Snidal argue in this issue, under conditions of complexity and uncertainty, which render interstate contracts necessarily incomplete. Adjudication is thus more than the act of applying precise standards and norms to a series of concrete cases within a precise mandate; it involves interpreting norms and resolving conflicts between competing norms in the context of particular cases. When seeking to overturn all but the most flagrantly illegal state actions, litigants and courts must inevitably appeal to particular interpretations of such ambiguities. Other things being equal, the wider the range of considerations the body can legitimately consider and the greater the uncertainty concerning the proper interpretation or norm in a given case, the more potential legal independence it possesses. Where regimes have clear norms, single goals, and narrow scope—as in, say, some purely technical tasks—we expect to see limited legal

10. For a domestic case of judicial manipulation, see Ramseyer and Rosenbluth 1997.

discretion. Where legal norms are valid across a wide area—as in the jurisprudence of the ECJ, which is connected to the broad, open-ended EC—there is more scope to promulgate general principles within the context of specific cases.[11] Similarly, greater legal independence exists where cross-cutting interpretations are plausible, such as over the scope of legitimate exceptions to norms like free trade, nonintervention, and individual rights. For instance, GATT and WTO dispute resolution bodies, or human rights courts, are increasingly being called upon to designate the margin of appreciation granted to national governments in pursuing legitimate state purposes other than free trade or human rights protection.

The third criterion for judicial independence, *financial and human resources*, refers to the ability of judges to process their caseloads promptly and effectively.[12] Such resources are necessary for processing large numbers of complaints and rendering consistent, high-quality decisions. They can also permit a court or tribunal to develop a factual record independent of the state litigants before them and to publicize their decisions. This is of particular importance for human rights courts, which seek to disseminate information and mobilize political support on behalf of those who would otherwise lack direct domestic access to effective political representation.[13] Many human rights tribunals are attached to commissions capable of conducting independent inquiries. The commissions of the Inter-American and UN systems, for example, have been active in pursuing this strategy, often conducting independent, on-site investigations.[14] Indeed, inquiries by the Inter-American Commission need not be restricted to the details of a specific case, though a prior petition is required. In general, the greater the financial and human resources available to courts and the stronger the commissions attached to them, the greater their legal independence.

In sum, the greater the freedom of a dispute resolution body from the control of individual member states over selection and tenure, legal discretion, information, and financial and human resources, the greater its legal independence.

Access: Who Has Standing?

Access, like independence, is a variable. From a legal perspective, access measures the range of social and political actors who have legal standing to submit a dispute to be resolved; from a political perspective, access measures the range of those who can set the agenda. Access is particularly important with respect to courts and other dispute-resolution bodies because, in contrast to executives and legislatures, they are "passive" organs of government unable to initiate action by unilaterally seizing a dispute. Access is measured along a continuum between two extremes. At one extreme, if no social or political actors can submit disputes, dispute-resolution institutions are unable to act; at the other, anyone with a legitimate grievance directed at

---

11. Weiler 1994.
12. Helfer and Slaughter 1997.
13. Keck and Sikkink 1998.
14. Farer 1998.

government policy can easily and inexpensively submit a complaint. In-between are situations in which individuals can bring their complaints only by acting through governments, convincing governments to "espouse" their claim as a state claim against another government, or by engaging in a costly procedure. This continuum of access can be viewed as measuring the "political transaction costs" to individuals and groups in society of submitting their complaint to an international dispute-resolution body. The more restrictive the conditions for bringing a claim to the attention of a dispute-resolution body, the more costly it is for actors to do so.

Near the higher-cost, restrictive end, summarized in Table 2, fall purely interstate tribunals, such as the GATT and WTO panels, the Permanent Court of Arbitration, and the ICJ, in which only member states may file suit against one another. Although this limitation constrains access to any dispute-resolution body by granting one or more governments a formal veto, it does not permit governments to act without constraint. Individuals and groups may still wield influence, but they must do so by domestic means. Procedures that are formally similar in this sense may nonetheless generate quite different implications for access, depending on principal-agent relationships in domestic politics. Whereas individuals and groups may have the domestic political power to ensure an ongoing if indirect role in both the decision to initiate proceedings and the resulting argumentation, state-controlled systems are likely to be more restrictive than direct litigation by individuals and groups.

In state-controlled systems, the individual or group must typically lobby a specialized government bureaucracy, secure a majority in some relevant domestic decision-making body, or catch the attention of the head of government. State officials are often cautious about instigating such proceedings against another state, since they must weigh a wide range of cross-cutting concerns, including the diplomatic costs of negotiating an arrangement with the foreign government in question. Such indirect arrangements for bringing a case are costly, prohibiting government action to serve extremely narrow or secondary interest groups.

In other cases, state action under such arrangements can be considered prohibitively expensive because of the government's role as a veto player. The most obvious circumstance is one in which individuals and groups seek to file suit challenging the actions of their home state. (This is generally the type of litigation before most human rights and many regional economic integration bodies—which do not restrict access to states.) Although, in theory, an individual or group could secure access to international adjudication by mustering a large enough domestic bloc to override the outright hostility of the state, this rarely occurs in practice.

Within these constraints, GATT/WTO panels and the ICJ differ in their roles toward domestic individuals and groups. In the GATT and now the WTO, governments nominally control access to the legal process, yet in practice injured industries are closely involved in both the initiation and the conduct of the litigation by their governments, at least in the United States. A firm or industry group, typically represented by an experienced Washington law firm, will lobby the U.S. Trade Representative to bring a claim against another country allegedly engaging in GATT violations. The industry lawyers may then participate quite closely in the preparation of the suit and

TABLE 2. *The access continuum: Who has standing?*

Level of access	Who has standing	International court or tribunal
Low	Both states must agree	PCA
Moderate	Only a single state can file suit	ICJ
	Single state files suit, influenced by social actors	WTO, GATT
High	Access through national courts	ECJ
	Direct individual (and sometimes group) access if domestic remedies have been exhausted	ECHR, IACHR

wait in the halls for debriefing after the actual proceeding. In the ICJ, by contrast, individual access is more costly. The ICJ hears cases in which individuals may have a direct interest (such as the families of soldiers sent to fight in another country in what is allegedly an illegal act of interstate aggression). However, these individuals usually have little influence over a national government decision to initiate interstate litigation or over the resulting conduct of the proceedings. As in the WTO, finally, individuals are unable to file suit against their own government before the ICJ. Because the ICJ tends to handle cases concerning "public goods" provision across national jurisdictions, such as boundary disputes and issues concerning aggression, the groups influenced by ICJ decisions tend to be diffuse and unorganized, except through the intermediation of national governments.

Near the permissive end of the spectrum is the ECJ. Individuals may ultimately be directly represented before the international tribunal, though the decision to bring the case before it remains in the hands of a domestic judicial body. Under Article 177 of the Treaty of Rome, national courts may independently refer a case before them to the ECJ if the case raises questions of European law that the national court does not feel competent to resolve on its own. The ECJ answers the specific question(s) presented and sends the case back to the national court for disposition of the merits of the dispute. Litigants themselves can suggest such a referral to the national court, but the decision to refer lies ultimately within the national court's discretion. Whether the interests involved are narrow and specific—as in the landmark *Cassis de Dijon* case over the importation of French specialty liquors into Germany—or broad, the cost of securing such a referral is the same. As Karen Alter shows in her article in this issue, different national courts have sharply different records of referral, but over time national courts as a body have become increasingly willing to refer cases to the ECJ. These referrals may involve litigation among private parties rather than simply against a public authority.[15]

---

15. It therefore remains unclear, on balance, whether the EC or the ECHR provides more ready access. Whereas the EC system under Article 177 allows only domestic courts, not individuals, to refer cases, the EC does not require, as does the ECHR and all other human rights courts, that domestic remedies be exhausted.

Also near the low-cost end of the access spectrum lie formal human rights enforcement systems, including the ECHR, the IACHR, the African Convention on Human and People's Rights, and the UN's International Covenant on Civil and Political Rights. Since the end of World War II we have witnessed a proliferation of international tribunals to which individuals have direct access, though subject to varying restrictions. Even in the ECHR, a relatively successful system, individual access broadened slowly over time. Under the "old ECHR"—the one that existed prior to very recent reforms—individuals could bring cases themselves only if the government being sued had previously accepted an optional clause in the convention recognizing individual petition; otherwise only states could file petitions. This clause was initially accepted by only a few countries and not by all until the 1980s. NGOs and other third parties were excluded; anonymous petitions were not permitted. Any complaint to the system had, moreover, to be reviewed by the European Human Rights Commission before being passed on to the court—assuming that the government had accepted compulsory jurisdiction. Only if the commission decided in favor of referring the case would it finally be heard before the ECHR.

Although this process only rarely constituted an outright barrier to a suit, it could be time consuming. Recent reforms have abolished this intermediate step. The new ECHR, by contrast, gives individuals direct access to the court without any domestic or international intermediary.[16] Even so, however, it continues to require that any individual or group exhaust all national remedies before appealing to the system, typically meaning that litigants must first sue in a lower national tribunal and appeal the resulting judgment up the chain of administrative tribunals and domestic courts. The path to international dispute resolution is thus long, costly, and uncertain, even in this permissive environment; the process can take six to eight years and requires substantial legal expertise.

The Inter-American, UN, and nascent African systems of formal human rights enforcement are in some ways more permissive. As in the new ECHR, individual petition is mandatory. Under the IACHR, other actors have standing to bring suit on behalf of individuals and groups whose rights may be being violated. Indeed, the individuals and groups need not even consent to the suit, and anonymous petitions are permitted. The IACHR Commission has also adopted a very broad and permissive interpretation of what it means to exhaust domestic remedies.[17] Under the African Charter on Human and People's Rights, individuals and states may submit complaints, which will be heard if a majority on a commission so decide. The commission will soon be able to send cases on to the future African Court of Human and People's Rights only if the state against which a claim is being brought has accepted an op-

---

16. In response to the widespread success of the individual petition mechanism in Europe, the growth of the number of states party to the convention, and an increasing backlog of cases, the Council of Europe had sought to improve upon the existing judicial review machinery. After months of arduous negotiation, a majority of states signed Protocol 11, which, once ratified, will abolish the European Commission on Human Rights and create a permanent European Court of Human Rights. For a discussion of both systems, see Moravcsik 2000.

17. Sands, Mackenzie, and Shany 1999, 233–45.

tional clause. As under the ECHR, domestic remedies must be exhausted. The UN requires individual petitions to trigger a process, though NGOs may be involved in the process. Whereas in the ECHR context, the commission took a relatively permissive attitude toward references to the court, this was not so in the Americas. For many years, the IACHR Commission declined to refer cases to the court—to the point where the court admonished the commission for failing to fulfill its "social duty to consider the advisability of coming to the Court."[18]

Among world courts and tribunals, the Central American Court of Justice, established in 1991 as the principal judicial organ of the Central American Integration System, offers the easiest access. Any state, supranational body, or natural or legal person can bring suit against a state party to assure domestic enforcement of regime norms. In addition, domestic courts can request advisory opinions in a preliminary reference procedure similar to the EC's Article 177.

Legal Embeddedness: Who Controls Formal Implementation?

There is no monopoly on the legitimate use of force in world politics—no world state, police, or army. Therefore, even if authority to render judgments is delegated to an independent international tribunal, implementation of these judgments depends on international or domestic action by the executives, legislatures, and/or judiciaries of states. Implementation and compliance in international disputes are problematic to a far greater degree than they are in well-functioning, domestic rule-of-law systems. The political significance of delegating authority over dispute resolution therefore depends in part on the degree of control exercised by individual governments over the legal promulgation and implementation of judgments. State control is affected by formal legal arrangements along a continuum that we refer to as embeddedness.

The spectrum of domestic embeddedness, summarized in Table 3, runs from strong control over promulgation and implementation of judgments by individual national governments to very weak control. At one extreme, that of strong control, lie systems in which individual litigants can veto the promulgation of a judgment *ex post*. In the old GATT system, the decisions of dispute-resolution panels had to be affirmed by consensus, affording individual litigants an *ex post* veto. Under the less tightly controlled WTO, by contrast, disputes among member governments are resolved through quasi-judicial panels whose judgments are binding unless *reversed* by unanimous vote of the Dispute Settlement Body, which consists of one representative from each WTO member state.

Most international legal systems fall into the same category as the WTO system; namely, states are bound by international law to comply with judgments of international courts or tribunals, but no domestic legal mechanism assures legal implementation. If national executives and legislatures fail to take action because of domestic political opposition or simply inertia, states simply incur a further international legal

---

18. Advisory Opinion OC-5/85, 5 Inter-American Ct. of H.R. (ser. A) (1985), 145, cited in Henkin et al. 1999, 525.

TABLE 3. *The embeddedness continuum: Who enforces the law?*

Level of embeddedness	Who enforces	International court or tribunal
Low	Individual governments can veto implementation of legal judgment	GATT
Moderate	No veto, but no domestic legal enforcement; most human rights systems	WTO, ICJ
High	International norms enforced by domestic courts	EC, incorporated human rights norms under ECHR, national systems in which treaties are self-executing or given direct effect

obligation to repair the damage. In other words, if an international tribunal rules that state *A* has illegally intervened in state *B*'s internal affairs and orders state *A* to pay damages, but the legislature of state *A* refuses to appropriate the funds, state *B* has no recourse at international law except to seek additional damages. Alternatively, if state *A* signs a treaty obligating it to change its domestic law to reduce the level of certain pollutants it is emitting, and the executive branch is unsuccessful in passing legislation to do so, state *A* is liable to its treaty partners at international law but cannot be compelled to take the action it agreed to take in the treaty.

This is not to say that individuals and groups have no impact on compliance. Interstate bargaining takes place in the shadow of normative sanctions stemming from the international legal obligation itself. Even if governments do not ultimately comply, a negative legal judgment may increase the salience of an issue and undermine the legitimacy of the national position in the eyes of domestic constituents. And it is difficult for recalcitrant governments to get the offending international law changed. Multilateral revision is rendered almost impossible by the requirement of unanimous consent in nearly all international organizations.[19]

At the other end of the spectrum, where the control of individual governments is most constrained by the embeddedness of international norms, lie systems in which autonomous national courts can enforce international judgments against their own governments. The most striking example of this mode of enforcement is the EC legal system. Domestic courts in every member state recognize that EC law is superior to national law (supremacy) and that it grants individuals rights on the basis of which they can litigate (direct effect). When the ECJ issues advisory opinions to national courts under the Article 177 procedure described in detail in Karen Alter's article in this issue, national courts tend to respect them, even when they clash with the precedent set by higher national courts. These provisions are nowhere stated explicitly in the Treaty of Rome but have been successfully "constitutionalized" by the ECJ over

---

19. The EC, with qualified majority voting, is an exception. But here the unique power of proposal in the legislative process that generates most EC economic regulations is held by the Commission, which is unlikely to propose such a rollback of EC powers. Tsebelis 1994.

the past four decades.[20] The European Free Trade Association (EFTA) court system established in 1994 permits such referrals as well, though, unlike the Treaty of Rome, it neither legally obliges domestic courts to refer nor legally binds the domestic court to apply the result. Domestic courts do nonetheless appear to enforce EFTA court decisions.[21]

International legal norms may also be embedded in domestic legal systems through legal incorporation or constitutional recognition. Although the direct link between domestic and international courts found in the EC is unique among international organizations, in some situations the national government has incorporated or transposed the international document into domestic law subject to the oversight of an autonomous domestic legal system. Many governments have, for example, incorporated the European Convention into domestic law, permitting individuals to enforce its provisions before domestic courts. Despite the lack of a direct link, there is evidence that domestic courts tend to follow the jurisprudence of the ECHR in interpreting the Convention.[22] Even without explicit statutory recognition, some legal systems—such as that of the Netherlands—generally recognize international treaty obligations as equal to or supreme over constitutional provisions. In the United States, the president and federal courts have sometimes invoked international treaty obligations as "self-executing" or "directly applicable" and therefore both binding on the U.S. government and domestic actors and enforceable in domestic courts—though Congress has increasingly sought to employ its control over ratification to limit this practice explicitly.[23]

Two Ideal Types: Interstate and Transnational Dispute Resolution

The three characteristics of international dispute resolution—independence, access, and embeddedness—are closely linked. This is evident from an examination of the extent to which different international legal systems are independent, embedded, and provide access. The characteristics of the major courts in the world today are summarized in Table 4, which reveals a loose correlation across categories. Systems with higher values on one dimension have a greater probability of having higher values in the other dimensions. This finding suggests that very high values on one dimension cannot fully compensate for low values on another. Strong support for independence, access, or embeddedness without strong support for the others undermines the effectiveness of a system.

Combining these three dimensions creates two ideal-types. In one ideal-type—interstate dispute resolution—adjudicators, agenda, and enforcement are all subject

20. Weiler 1991.
21. Sands, Mackenzie, and Shany 1999, 148.
22. Drzemczewski 1983.
23. Although customary international law is generally viewed as self-executing in the United States, and therefore can be applied by courts as domestic law, most international treaties do not create private rights of action. U.S. courts, moreover, have been hesitant to enforce customary international law against a superseding act of the federal government. See Henkin 1996; and Jackson 1992.

TABLE 4. *Legal characteristics of international courts and tribunals*

International court or tribunals	Legal characteristics		
	Independence	*Access*	*Embeddedness*
ECJ	High	High	High[f]
ECHR, since 1999	High	High	Low to high[c]
ECHR, before 1999	Moderate to high[a]	Low to high[b]	Low to high[c]
IACHR	Moderate to high[a]	High	Moderate
WTO panels	Moderate	Low to moderate[d]	Moderate
ICJ	Moderate	Low to moderate[d]	Moderate
GATT panels	Moderate	Low to moderate[d]	Low
PCA	Low to moderate	Low[e]	Moderate
UN Security Council	Low	Low to moderate[g]	Low

Source: Sands et al. 1999.

[a]Depends on whether government recognizes optional clauses for compulsory jurisdiction of the court.

[b]Depends on whether government accepts optional clause for individual petition.

[c]Depends on whether domestic law incorporates or otherwise recognized the treaty.

[d]Depends on mobilization and domestic access rules for interest groups concerned.

[e]Both parties must consent. Recent rule changes have begun to recognize nonstate actors.

[f]Embeddedness is not a formal attribute of the regime but the result of the successful assertion of legal sovereignty.

[g]Permanent members of the Security Council can veto; nonmembers cannot.

to veto by individual national governments. Individual states decide who judges, what they judge, and how the judgment is enforced. At the other end of the spectrum, adjudicators, agenda, and enforcement are all substantially independent of individual and collective pressure from national governments. We refer to this ideal type as transnational dispute resolution.[24] In this institutional arrangement, of which the EU and ECHR are the most striking examples, judges are insulated from national governments, societal individuals and groups control the agenda, and the results are implemented by an independent national judiciary. In the remainder of this article we discuss the implications of variation along the continuum from interstate to transnational dispute resolution for the nature of, compliance with, and evolution of international jurisprudence.

In discussing this continuum, however, let us not lose sight of the fact that *values on the three dimensions move from high to low at different rates.* Table 4 reveals that high levels of independence and access appear to be more common than high levels

24. We use the term "transnational" to capture the individual to individual or individual to state nature of many of the cases in this type of dispute resolution. However, many of the tribunals in this category, such as the ECJ and the ECHR, can equally be described as "supranational" in the sense that they sit "above" the nation-state and have direct power over individuals and groups within the state. One of the authors has previously used the label "supranational" to describe these tribunals (Helfer and Slaughter 1997); no significance should be attached to the shift in terminology here.

of embeddedness, and, though the relationship is weaker, a high level of independence appears to be slightly more common than a high level of access. In other words, between those tribunals that score high or low on all three dimensions, there is a significant intermediate range comprising tribunals with high scores on independence and/or access but not on the others.[25] Among those international legal institutions that score high on independence and access but are not deeply embedded in domestic legal systems are some international human rights institutions. Among those institutions that score high on independence but not on access or embeddedness are GATT/WTO multilateral trade institutions and the ICJ.

The Politics of Litigation and Compliance: From Interstate to Judicial Politics

Declaring a process "legalized" does not abolish politics. Decisions about the degree of authority of a particular tribunal, and access to it, are themselves sites of political struggle. The sharpest struggles are likely to arise *ex ante* in the bargaining over a tribunal's establishment; but other opportunities for political intervention may emerge during the life of a tribunal, perhaps as a result of its own constitutional provisions. Form matters, however. The characteristic politics of litigation and compliance are very different under transnational dispute resolution than under interstate dispute resolution. In this section we explicate these differences and propose some tentative conjectures linking our three explanatory variables to the politics of dispute resolution.

The Interstate and Transnational Politics of Judicial Independence

What are the politics of judicial independence? As legal systems move from interstate dispute resolution toward the more independent judicial selection processes of transnational dispute resolution, we expect to observe greater judicial autonomy—defined as the willingness and ability to decide disputes against national governments. Other things being equal, the fewer opportunities national governments have to influence the selection of judges, the available information, the support or financing of the court, and the precise legal terms on which the court can decide, the weaker is their likely influence over the decisions of an international tribunal.

Political interference is common in some domestic political systems. The secretary general of the Arab Lawyers Union has described routine "intervention with the judiciary through higher decisions" and by appointment of military and special courts in much of the Arab world.[26] Judges in Central and South America have been subjected to threats and assassinations. Even in domestic systems with strong courts, political selection of judges can affect decisions. And in the United States, where federal judges serve for life, the openly politicized nature of Supreme Court appoint-

---

25. Not surprisingly, domestic legal embeddedness is less common than widespread domestic access, since the former is a prerequisite for the latter.
26. Eissa 1998.

ments is said to induce many aspiring lower federal judges to alter their decisions in anticipation of possible confirmation hearings before the Senate. The Italian and German Constitutional Courts are even more overtly politically balanced.[27] Perhaps the most infamous example of interference with the composition of a sitting court is President Franklin D. Roosevelt's effort in 1937 to "pack" the Supreme Court with additional justices of his choice. Instead, "a switch in time saved nine," as key justices suddenly changed their tune and found delegation to the plethora of new administrative agencies constitutional. In the context of de facto single-party rule in Japan, Mark Ramseyer and Frances Rosenbluth have documented the significant impact of decisions on the career trajectory of domestic judges, permitting the inference that selection processes affected judicial decisions.[28]

Evidence of government efforts to influence an international tribunal's direction through judicial selection is anecdotal. Rarely is the attempt at influence as crude as the case in September 1984, when a Swedish member of the Iran–U.S. Tribunal was assaulted by two younger and stronger Iranian judges.[29] Influence is typically more subtle. It was widely rumored, for instance, that the German government sought to rein in the ECJ by appointing a much less activist judge in the 1980s than previous German candidates, but hard evidence is virtually impossible to find. One leading ECJ judge, a long-time skeptic of the notion that the ECJ could be politicized in this way, nevertheless noted in the mid-1990s that "Things have changed. It is now 8–7 for us [that is, the supranationalists]."[30]

Restrictions on the financial resources available to tribunals may limit their independence. Such limitations have hampered efforts to transform the African Convention on Human and People's Rights into a system as effective as those found in Europe and, recently, the Americas.[31] Similarly, it has been argued that the members of the UN Security Council authorized the creation of the International Criminal Tribunal for the Former Yugoslavia to satisfy public opinion but tried to deny it sufficient resources to do its work.[32] If this strategy failed, it may have been in part because resources were ultimately provided from private sources such as foundations and wealthy individuals.[33] On the other hand, a striking difference between the ECJ and ECHR, as well as bodies such as the UN Human Rights Committee, is the relative distribution of resources, without which even an active court cannot process its caseload and make itself heard to a wider audience. Other drags include excessively cumbersome procedural rules, often designed to frustrate all but the most

27. Weiler 1998. Selection of a judge of an identifiable political stripe does not always guarantee corresponding decisions, however. Once on the bench, judges are subject to a specific set of professional norms and duties and develop their personal conception of the role they have been asked to fill in ways that can yield surprises. A paradigmatic case is President Eisenhower's appointment of Justice William Brennan, who gave little sign of the strong liberal standard-bearer he would become.

28. Ramseyer and Rosenbluth 1997.

29. Feldman 1986, 1004.

30. Lecture by Federico Mancini, Public Representation: A Democratic Deficit? Conference at Harvard University, Center for European Studies, 29–31 January 1993.

31. Welch 1992.

32. Forsythe 1994.

33. See Bass 1998; and Bassiouni 1998.

persistent individual litigants, and limits on judicial capacities, such as a court's autonomous ability to find the facts in a particular case rather than having to depend solely on the representations of litigants. Where one of the litigants is a government, the court is likely to find itself unable to challenge the government's version of events without the independent ability to call witnesses or even conduct inspections.[34]

Such potential restrictions on autonomy—along with the threat of noncompliance or treaty revision—may increase judicial solicitude for state interests. We shall return to this question in our later discussion of long-term dynamism. Broadly, however, this discussion suggests the following conjecture: The more formally independent a court, the more likely are judicial decisions to challenge national policies.

The Interstate and Transnational Politics of Access

What are the political implications of movement from low access (interstate dispute resolution) to high access (transnational dispute resolution)? Our central contention is that we are likely to observe, broadly speaking, a different politics of access as we move toward transnational dispute resolution—where individuals, groups, and courts can appeal or refer cases to international tribunals. As the actors involved become more diverse, the likelihood that cases will be referred increases, as does the likelihood that such cases will challenge national governments—in particular, the national government of the plaintiff. The link between formal access and real political power is not obvious. States might still manipulate access to judicial process regarding both interstate and transnational litigation by establishing stringent procedural rules, bringing political pressure to bear on potential or actual litigants, or simply carving out self-serving exceptions to the agreed jurisdictional scheme. Consider the evidence.

Access to classic arbitral tribunals, such as those constituted under the Permanent Court of Arbitration, requires the consent of both states. With regard to access, the Permanent Court of Arbitration is as close as we come to a pure system of interstate dispute resolution. Slightly more constraining arrangements are found in classic interstate litigation before the Permanent Court of International Justice in the 1920s and 1930s, the ICJ since 1945, and the short-lived Central American Court of Justice. In these systems, a single state decides when and how to sue, even if it is suing on behalf of an injured citizen or group of citizens. The state formally "espouses" the claim of its national(s), at which point the individual's rights terminate (unless entitled to compensation as a domestic legal or constitutional matter), as does any control over or even say in the litigation strategy. The government is thus free to prosecute the claim vigorously or not at all, or to engage in settlement negotiations for a sum far less than the individual litigant(s) might have found acceptable. Such negotiations can resemble institutionalized interstate bargaining more than a classic legal process in which the plaintiff decides whether to continue the legal struggle or to settle the case.

---

34. Helfer and Slaughter 1997.

Under interstate dispute resolution, political calculations inevitably enter into the decision to sue. For instance, in 1996 the United States adopted the Helms-Burton legislation, which punishes firms for doing business with Cuba. Although the EU claimed that this legislation violated WTO rules and threatened to take the case to the WTO, in the end it failed to do so: an agreement was reached essentially on U.S. terms. The forms of legalization do not, therefore, guarantee that authoritative decisions will be honored by third parties. Hence even among formally highly legalized processes, the degree of operational authority of the third-party decision makers may vary considerably. More systematic evidence comes from the EU, where governments tend to be reluctant to sue one another, preferring instead to bring their complaints to the EU Commission. The Commission, in turn, was initially—and to an extent, remains—reluctant to sue member states, due to its fear of retaliation and need to establish its own political legitimacy.[35]

Although in interstate dispute resolution states decide when and whether to sue other states, they cannot necessarily control whether they are sued. If they are sued, whether any resulting judgments can be enforced depends both on their acceptance of compulsory jurisdiction and, where the costs of complying with a judgment are high, on their willingness to obey an adverse ruling. U.S. relations with the ICJ provide an example. After pushing for the creation of the ICJ as part of the UN Charter, the United States promptly accepted the compulsory jurisdiction of the ICJ by Senate resolution.[36] The same resolution, however, included the Connally reservation, providing that U.S. acceptance "shall not apply to . . . disputes with regard to matters which are essentially within the domestic jurisdiction of the United States as determined by the United States."[37] In other words, the Senate insisted that the United States remain judge in its own case as to whether disputes were sufficiently "international" to go to the court.

To be sure, the Connally reservation has always been controversial in the United States, and the State Department has resisted invoking it when the United States has been called before the ICJ. Yet control of access does not stop there. In 1984, when the ICJ appeared to take Nicaragua's complaints against the United States seriously, the United States revoked its agreement to the ICJ's compulsory jurisdiction. The United States deposited with the secretariat of the UN a notification purporting to exclude, with immediate effect, from its acceptance of the court's compulsory jurisdiction "disputes with any Central American state" for two years.[38] It litigated the first round of the case, arguing that its revocation of jurisdiction was effective, but then simply failed to appear in the second round after the court ruled that it did indeed have jurisdiction.[39]

This sort of flagrant defiance is rarely necessary. The de facto system is one in which most states, like the United States, reserve the right to bring specific cases to

35. See Alter 1998b; Stein 1981; and Dashwood and White 1989.
36. S. Res. 196, 79th Cong., 2d sess., 92 *Cong. Rec.* 10706 (1946).
37. Ibid.
38. Briggs 1985, 377.
39. Schwebel 1996.

the ICJ or to be sued in specific cases as the result of an ad hoc agreement with other parties to a dispute of specific provisions in a bilateral or multilateral treaty. This system ensures direct control over access to the ICJ by either requiring all the parties to a dispute to agree both to third-party intervention and to choose the ICJ as the third party, or by allowing two or more states to craft a specific submission to the court's jurisdiction in a limited category of disputes arising from the specific subject matter of a treaty.[40] In the ICJ, procedural provisions govern time limits requiring a state to accept a tribunal's jurisdiction before a particular suit arises, time limits for filing the suit itself, the reciprocal nature of the opposing parties' acceptance of jurisdiction, and rules governing intervention by a third state whose interests may be directly affected by disposition of an ongoing suit.[41] Such procedural provisions are key weapons in the litigator's arsenal, with the result that many interstate cases, like suits between individuals, stalemate for years in procedural maneuvering. Some such provisions are promulgated by tribunals themselves, but the majority are bargained out *ex ante* among states contemplating submission to third-party dispute resolution.

More informally, potential defendants may exert political pressure on plaintiff states not to sue or to drop a suit once it has begun. When confronted by an unfavorable GATT panel judgment (in favor of Mexico) concerning U.S. legislation to protect dolphins from tuna fishing, the United States exercised its extra-institutional power to induce Mexico to drop the case before the judgment could be enforced. Another more subtle example concerns the U.S.–Nicaraguan dispute referred to earlier. Although the United States refused to participate in proceedings on the merits of the case, the ICJ ruled on 27 June 1986 that the United States' mining of Nicaraguan harbors violated provisions of customary international law, which were similar to, and should be interpreted in light of, the UN Charter.[42] The United States refused to comply with the decision, and on 27 October 1986 it vetoed a Security Council resolution, which received eleven affirmative votes, calling for it to comply with the ICJ ruling.[43] Nicaragua asked for more than $2 billion in damages, but with the electoral defeat of the Sandinistas, it requested postponement of further proceedings. In 1990 the United States asked the Nicaraguan government of President Violeta Barrios de Chamorro to abandon its claim; it was reported that the Bush administration told Nicaragua that future U.S. aid would depend on such abandonment.[44]

The preceding discussion of access suggests two conjectures:

1. The broader and less costly the access to an international court or tribunal, the greater the number of cases it will receive.

2. The broader and less expensive the access to an international court or tribunal, the more likely that complaints challenge the domestic practices of national governments—particularly the home government of the complainant.

40. Rosenne 1995.
41. Ibid.
42. ICJ, *Military and Paramilitary Activities in and Against Nicaragua.* (Nicaragua v. United States of America.) Merits, Judgment. ICJ Reports 1986, 97–99.
43. See *New York Times*, 29 October 1986, A3.
44. *See New York Times*, 30 September 1990.

TABLE 5. *Access rules and dockets of international courts and tribunals*

Level of access	International court or tribunal	Average annual number of cases since founding
Low	PCA	0.3
Medium	ICJ	1.7
	GATT	4.4
	WTO	30.5
High	Old ECHR	23.9
	EC	100.1

Source: Sands et al. 1999, 4, 24, 72, 125, 200.

We cannot thoroughly evaluate these conjectures here, but a preliminary analysis suggests their plausibility. Consider, for example, the size of an international tribunal's docket. Broadly speaking, the greater the formal access, the greater the caseload we should expect to observe. Courts cannot work without cases. They are quite literally out of business and without even a toehold to begin building their reputations and developing constituencies that will give them voice and at least a measure of independent power. Thus, for instance, if the access rules of the ECJ only gave states and the Commission the right to sue, the ECJ would—like the ICJ—probably have adjudicated relatively few cases and would play a role on the margins of European politics. The vast majority of significant cases in the history of the EU have been brought under Article 177 by individuals who request (or hope) that national courts will send them to the ECJ for adjudication. Another highly developed example is found in international human rights courts. The optional clause of the ECHR, Article 10, permitting individuals to bring complaints, has been the source of nearly all complaints before the Commission and the ECJ. Interstate complaints have been few in number, less than fifteen (all but a few involving state interest in co-nationals in other countries), compared with thousands of individual complaints.[45] The IACHR functions in a similar manner.

The comparative data summarized in Table 5 further support this conjecture. The average caseload of six prominent international courts varies as predicted, with legal systems granting low access generating the fewest number of average cases, those granting high access generating the highest number of cases, and those granting moderate access in between. The difference between categories is roughly an order of magnitude or more. While we should be cautious about imputing causality before more extensive controlled studies are performed, the data suggest the existence of a strong relationship.

Case study evidence supports the conjecture that transnational dispute-resolution systems with high levels of access tend to result in cases being brought in national

45. Moravcsik 1995.

courts against the *home* government. This is the standard method by which cases reach the ECJ. For example, the *Cassis de Dijon* case—a classic ECJ decision in 1979 establishing the principle of mutual recognition of national regulations— concerned the right to export a French liquor to Germany, yet a German importer, not the French producer, sued the German government, charging that domestic regulations on liquor purity were creating unjustified barriers to interstate trade.[46]

The Interstate and Transnational Politics of Embeddedness

Even if cases are brought before tribunals and these tribunals render judgments against states, the extent to which judgments are legally enforceable may differ. We have seen that most international legal systems create a legal obligation for governments to comply but leave enforcement to interstate bargaining. Only a few legal systems empower individuals and groups to seek enforcement of their provisions in domestic courts. However, in our ideal type of transnational dispute resolution, international commitments are embedded in domestic legal systems, meaning that governments, particularly national executives, no longer need to take positive action to ensure enforcement of international judgments. Instead, enforcement occurs directly through domestic courts and executive agents who are responsive to judicial decisions. The politics of embedded systems of dispute resolution are very different from the politics of systems that are not embedded in domestic politics.

Under interstate dispute resolution, external pressure for compliance stems ultimately from the power and interests of national governments of participating states, which back demands with threats of reciprocal denial or punishment. Reciprocity and retaliation are often effective means of enforcement, at least for powerful states whose interests are engaged. As Judith Goldstein and Lisa Martin point out in their article in this issue, governments have made little use of the escape clause in GATT, arguably because doing so would have required providing compensation at the expense of other industrial sectors. That is, reciprocity on the international level implies that gains from reneging on a given arrangement will have to be balanced by losses to some other sector; and the political protests from that sector are likely to be shrill. Using the concept of "compliance constituencies" articulated by Miles Kahler in his conclusion to this issue, it is important to recognize that even if international law is not embedded in domestic legal processes, past agreements, linked to reciprocity, may create strong political pressures for compliance. If domestic "compliance constituencies" are the key to enforcement, we should expect to see more domestic pressure for compliance in trade regimes, where concentrated, mobilized constituencies like exporters and importers tend to press for compliance with tariff liberalization. Goldstein and Martin find evidence for such pressures for compliance.

Yet despite the real successes, in some circumstances, of interstate dispute resolution, it clearly has political limitations, especially where compliance constituencies

---

46. Case 120/78, *Rewe-Zentrale AG v. Bundesmonopolverwaltung fur Branntwein* (Cassis de Dijon), 1978.

are weak. Under interstate dispute resolution, pressures for compliance have to operate through governments. The limitations of such practices are clear under arbitration, and notably with respect to the ICJ. In the case involving mining of Nicaragua's harbors, the United States did not obey the ICJ's judgment. Admittedly, the Reagan administration did not simply ignore the ICJ judgment with respect to the mining of Nicaragua's harbors, but felt obliged to withdraw its recognition of the ICJ's jurisdiction—a controversial act with significant domestic political costs for a Republican president facing a Democratic Congress. Nevertheless, in the end the United States pursued a policy contrary to the ICJ's decision. Even in trade regimes, political pressure sometimes leads to politically bargained settlements, as in the case of the U.S. Helms-Burton legislation. And a number of countries have imposed unilateral limits on the ICJ's jurisdiction.

More broadly, reciprocity does not work well when interdependence and power are highly asymmetric. Under these circumstances, reciprocal denials of policy concessions may have much more severe consequences for the more dependent party. Furthermore, powerful governments may threaten weaker targets not only with reciprocal denial of policy concessions but also with further retaliation in linked areas. The United States has, for example, used unilateral threats of sanctions under Section 301 and with respect to antidumping and countervailing duty statutes. It has also threatened numerous governments with economic and military sanctions in an effort to compel compliance with international human rights norms. Overall, interstate dispute resolution presents many opportunities for powerful states to set the agenda for a legal process, to introduce political bargaining into decision making, and to thwart implementation of adverse legal decisions.

The politics of transnational dispute resolution are quite different. By linking direct access for domestic actors to domestic legal enforcement, transnational dispute resolution opens up an additional source of political pressure for compliance, namely favorable judgments in domestic courts. This creates a new set of political imperatives. It gives international tribunals additional means to pressure or influence domestic government institutions in ways that enhance the likelihood of compliance with their judgments. It pits a recalcitrant government not simply against other governments but also against legally legitimate domestic opposition; an executive determined to violate international law must override his or her own legal system. Moreover, it thereby permits international tribunals to develop a constituency of litigants who can later pressure government institutions to comply with the international tribunal's decision.[47] Consider the language of the ECJ in its landmark 1963 decision announcing that selected provisions of the Treaty of Rome would be directly effective as rules governing individuals in national law: "The Community constitutes a new legal order . . . for the benefit of which the states have limited their sovereign rights . . . and the subjects of which comprise not only Member States but also their nationals. Independently of the legislation of the Member States, Community law therefore imposes obligations on individuals but is also intended to confer on them

---

47. Helfer and Slaughter 1997.

rights which become part of their legal heritage."[48] The primary individuals and groups the ECJ had in mind were importers and exporters, many of whom came to understand that they had a direct interest in helping the court hold governments to their word on scheduled tariff reductions. Individuals and groups also have incentives to bring cases in other substantive contexts, including human rights and environmental law.[49]

The politics of compliance under transnational dispute resolution tends to give courts more leverage than they enjoy under interstate dispute resolution. The result is an environment in which judicial politics (the interplay of interests, ideas, and values among judges) and intrajudicial politics (the politics of competition or cooperation among courts) are increasingly important. Judicial politics are subject to a wide range of constraints that may or may not intersect with state interests—for example, the exigencies of legal reasoning, which Thomas Franck has distilled as the legitimacy-based demands of consistency, coherence, and adherence,[50] not to mention simple logic; the texts and case law available to shape a particular decision; and the political preferences and judicial ideology of individual judges.[51] More broadly, however, the relationships between international and national courts are central to the politics of transnational dispute resolution. In the words of Joseph Weiler, "The relationship between the European Court and national courts is the most crucial element for a successful functioning of the European legal order."[52]

Transnational dispute resolution does not sweep aside traditional interstate politics, but the power of national governments has to be filtered through norms of judicial professionalism, public opinion supporting particular conceptions of the rule of law, and an enduring tension between calculations of short- and long-term interests. Individuals and groups can zero in on international court decisions as focal points around which to mobilize, creating a further intersection between transnational litigation and democratic politics.

This discussion of the politics of interstate and transnational dispute resolution suggests that the following two conjectures deserve more intensive study.

1. Other things being equal, the more firmly embedded an international commitment is in domestic law, the more likely is compliance with judgments to enforce it.

2. Liberal democracies are particularly respectful of the rule of law and most open to individual access to judicial systems; hence attempts to embed international law in domestic legal systems should be most effective among such

---

48. Case 26/62, *N. V. Algemene Transp. and Expeditie Onderneming Van Gend and Loos v. Nederlandse administratie der belastingen*, 1963 E.C.R. 1, 12.

49. This dynamic is not limited to Europe. David Wirth explains it succinctly in his analysis of compulsory third-party dispute resolution as a mechanism for enforcing international environmental law. Wirth 1994.

50. Franck 1990.

51. Mattli and Slaughter 1995.

52. Weiler 1998, 22. The ECHR has experienced considerable variation in its effectiveness, which does not seem on its face to be well explained by embeddedness. With respect to the ECHR, we believe that more research is needed to evaluate explanations that rely on embeddedness.

regimes. In relations involving nondemocracies, we should observe near total reliance on interstate dispute resolution. Even among liberal democracies, the trust placed in transnational dispute resolution may vary with the political independence of the domestic judiciary.

Although embedding international commitments does not guarantee increased compliance, we find good reason to conclude that embeddedness probably tends to make compliance more likely in the absence of a strong political counteraction. However, as Goldstein and Martin argue in this issue, by removing loopholes, legalization also takes away "safety valves" that can reduce political pressure for drastic changes in rules. As they argue with respect to the WTO, "moving too far in the direction of legalization could backfire, undermining the momentum toward liberalization that the weakly legalized procedures of GATT so effectively established." To be genuinely successful, international law needs to rest on a strong basis of collective political purpose and shared standards of legitimacy: where these conditions exist (as in the EU), embedding international law in domestic legal processes is more promising than when they are absent.

The Interstate and Transnational Dynamics of Legalization

We have considered the static politics of legalization. Yet institutions also change over time and develop distinctive dynamics. Rules are elaborated. The costs of veto, withdrawal, or exclusion from the "inner club" of an institution may increase if the benefits provided by institutionalized cooperation increase. Sunk costs create incentives to maintain existing practices rather than to begin new ones. Politicians' short time horizons can induce them to agree to institutional practices that they might not prefer in the long term, in order to gain advantages at the moment.[53]

What distinguishes legalized regimes is their potential for setting in motion a distinctive dynamic built on precedent, in which decisions on a small number of specific disputes create law that may govern by analogy a vast array of future practices. This may be true even when the first litigants in a given area do not gain satisfaction. Judges may adopt modes of reasoning that assure individual litigants that their arguments have been heard and responded to, even if they have not won the day in a particular case. Some legal scholars argue that this "casuistic" style helps urge litigants, whether states or individuals, to fight another day.[54]

Although both interstate and transnational dispute resolution have the potential to generate such a legal evolution, we maintain that transnational dispute resolution increases the potential for such dynamics of precedent. The greater independence of judges, wider access of litigants, and greater potential for legal compliance insulates judges, thereby allowing them to develop legal precedent over time without trigger-

---

53. See Keohane and Hoffmann 1991; Alter 1998a; and Pollack 1997.
54. See White 1990; Glendon 1991; and Sunstein 1996.

ing noncompliance, withdrawal, or reform by national governments. We next consider in more detail the specific reasons why.

The Dynamics of Interstate Third-party Dispute Resolution

In interstate legal systems, the potential for self-generating spillover depends on how states perform their gatekeeping roles. As we will show, where states open the gates, the results of interstate dispute resolution may to some degree resemble the results of transnational dispute resolution. However, in the two major international judicial or quasi-judicial tribunals—the Permanent Court of Arbitration and the ICJ—states have been relatively reluctant to bring cases. The great majority of arbitration cases brought before the Permanent Court of Arbitration were heard in the court's early years, shortly after the first case in 1902. The court has seen little use recently—the Iran Claims Tribunal being an isolated if notable exception.

States have been reluctant to submit to the ICJ's jurisdiction when the stakes are large.[55] Hence the ICJ has been constrained in developing a large and binding jurisprudence. Even so, it has triggered overt and effective national opposition. Before the United States revoked compulsory jurisdiction in advance of the Nicaragua case, France had previously revoked its acceptance of the ICJ's compulsory jurisdiction in response to suits brought against it by Australia and New Zealand concerning its nuclear testing in the South Pacific in the 1960s.[56] Since the USSR and China had never accepted compulsory jurisdiction, Great Britain stood alone by late 1985 as the only permanent member of the UN Security Council willing to expose itself to the risk of being brought before the ICJ on an open-ended basis. What has emerged in the ICJ is essentially a system of discretionary submission to its jurisdiction, allowing states to control access case by case. In 1945 75 percent of all states that had ratified the Statute of the Permanent Court of International Justice also accepted the ICJ's compulsory jurisdiction; as of 1995 only 31 percent of states party to statute accept compulsory jurisdiction.[57] As measured by the level of legal obligation, legalization in the ICJ has moved *backwards* over the last half-century.

Still, it is fair to note that use of the ICJ did increase substantially between the 1960s and 1990s, reaching an all-time high of nineteen cases on the docket in 1999.[58] Although this increase does not equal the exponential growth of economic and human rights jurisprudence in this period, it marks a significant shift. In part this reflects pockets of success that have resulted in expansion of both the law in a particular area and the resort to it. The ICJ has consistently had a fairly steady stream of cases concerning international boundary disputes. In these cases the litigants have typically already resorted to military conflict that has resulted in stalemate or determined that such conflict would be too costly. They thus agree to go to court. The ICJ,

---

55. Chayes 1965.
56. Rosenne 1995, 270 n. 17. See also *Nuclear Tests (Australia v. France)*, 1974 I.C.J. 253 (20 December); and *Nuclear Tests (New Zealand v. France)*, 1974 I.C.J. 457 (20 December).
57. Schwebel 1996.
58. Ibid.

in turn, has profited from this willingness by developing an extensive body of case law that countries and their lawyers can use to assess the strength of the case on both sides and be assured of a resolution based on generally accepted legal principles.[59]

Another factor in the expansion of the ICJ's caseload over the past two decades may have been the court's willingness to find against the United States in the Nicaragua case, thereby enhancing its legitimacy with developing countries.[60] At the same time, it has received a number of very high profile cases that seem likely to have been filed in the hope of publicizing a particular political dispute as much as securing an actual resolution. Examples include the suit brought by the United States against Iran over the 1979 taking of diplomatic hostages, Iran's suit against the United States for the destruction of oil platforms in the Persian Gulf, two suits brought by Libya against the United States and Great Britain arising out of the Lockerbie air disaster, and Bosnia's suit against Yugoslavia for the promotion of genocide. Although such cases are vigorously litigated by teams of distinguished international lawyers on both sides, the likelihood of compliance by the losing state seems dubious.

The ambiguous, even paradoxical consequences of the Nicaragua case suggest that the interaction between dispute resolution mechanisms and substantive agreement over time is complex. Not only does the nature of substantive agreement influence the probable development of legal systems over time, as we have seen, but the nature of legalization may influence the nature of substantive cooperation. In some cases legalization may even lead to more contention and conflict over the nature of the rules. This is an area where more research would be welcome.

The Dynamics of Transnational Dispute Resolution

The key to the dynamics of transnational dispute resolution is access. Transnational dispute resolution removes the ability of states to perform gatekeeping functions, both in limiting access to tribunals and in blocking implementation of their decisions. Its incentives for domestic actors to mobilize, and to increase the legitimacy of their claims, gives it a capacity for endogenous expansion. As we will see with respect to GATT and the WTO, even a formally interstate process may display similar expansionary tendencies, but continued expansion under interstate dispute resolution depends on continuing decisions by states to keep access to the dispute settlement process open. Switching to a set of formal rules nearer the ideal type of transnational dispute resolution makes it much harder for states to constrain tribunals and can give such tribunals both incentives and instruments to expand their authority by expanding their caseload. Indeed, tribunals can sometimes continue to strengthen their authority even when opposed by powerful states—particularly when the institutional status quo is favorable to tribunals and no coalition of dissatisfied states is capable of overturning the status quo.[61]

---

59. See, for example, Charney 1994.
60. Schwebel 1996.
61. See Alter 1998a; and Alter, this issue.

The pool of potential individual litigants is several orders of magnitude larger than that of state litigants. Independent courts have every incentive to recruit from that pool. Cases breed cases. A steady flow of cases, in turn, allows a court to become an actor on the legal and political stage, raising its profile in the elementary sense that other potential litigants become aware of its existence and in the deeper sense that its interpretation and application of a particular legal rule must be reckoned with as a part of what the law means in practice. Litigants who are likely to benefit from that interpretation will have an incentive to bring additional cases to clarify and enforce it. Further, the interpretation or application is itself likely to raise additional questions that can only be answered through subsequent cases. Finally, a court gains political capital from a growing caseload by demonstrably performing a needed function.

Transnational tribunals have the means at their disposal to target individual litigants in various ways. The most important advantage they have is the nature of the body of law they administer. Transnational litigation, whether deliberately established by states (as in the case of the ECHR) or adapted and expanded by a supranational tribunal itself (as in the case of the ECJ), only makes sense when interstate rules have dimensions that make them directly applicable to individual activity. Thus, in announcing the direct effect doctrine in *Van Gend and Loos*, the ECJ was careful to specify that only those portions of the Treaty of Rome that were formulated as clear and specific prohibitions on or mandates of member states' conduct could be regarded as directly applicable.[62] Human rights law is by definition applicable to individuals in relations with state authorities, although actual applicability will also depend on the clarity and specificity of individual human rights prohibitions and guarantees.

In this way, a transnational tribunal can present itself in its decisions as a protector of individual rights and benefits against the state, where the state itself has consented to these rights and benefits and the tribunal is simply holding it to its word. This is the clear thrust of the passage from *Van Gend and Loos* quoted earlier, in which the ECJ announced that "Community law . . . imposes obligations on individuals but is also intended to confer on them rights that become part of their legal heritage." The ECHR, for its part, has developed the "doctrine of effectiveness," which requires that the provisions of the European Human Rights Convention be interpreted and applied so as to make its safeguards "practical and effective" rather than "theoretical or illusory"[63] Indeed, one of its judges has described the ECHR in a dissenting opinion as the "last resort protector of oppressed individuals."[64] Such rhetoric is backed up by a willingness to find for the individual against the state.[65]

Ready access to a tribunal can create a virtuous circle: a steady stream of cases results in a stream of decisions that serve to raise the profile of the court and hence to

---

62. Case 26/62, *N. V. Algemene Transp. and Expeditie Onderneming Van Gend and Loos v. Nederslandse administratie der belastingen.* 1963 E.C.R. 1, 12.

63. Bernhardt 1994.

64. *Cossey v. United Kingdom,* 184 E.C.H.R., ser. A (1990).

65. Helfer and Slaughter 1997.

attract more cases. When the ECJ rules, the decision is implemented not by national governments—the recalcitrant defendants—but by national courts. Any subsequent domestic opposition is rendered far more difficult. In sum, transnational third-party dispute resolution has led to a de facto alliance between certain national courts, certain types of individual litigants, and the ECJ. This alliance has been the mechanism by which the supremacy and direct effect of EC law, as well as thousands of specific substantive questions, have been established as cornerstones of the European legal order.[66]

The significance of the alliance between domestic and supranational courts lies in part in the fact that it was an unintended consequence of European integration. There is no doubt it was unforeseen by the member states; Article 177 was an incidental provision suggested by a low-level German customs official in the Treaty of Rome negotiations. However welcome the functional benefits of ECJ jurisprudence may subsequently have been—and the fact that in recent years member states have deliberately strengthened the enforcement power of the ECJ while limiting its jurisdiction suggests that they were—the founding members of the EC intended to create something much closer to a classical interstate dispute-resolution system. Individual member states often opposed the efforts of the ECJ to transform the institutions set forth in the treaty into a functioning transnational dispute-resolution system. Nothing similar exists in the annals of interstate dispute-resolution bodies.

The assertion of the importance of the ECJ in this process—in particular, the assertion of the supremacy of European law and its direct effect in domestic legal systems—was not automatic. International tribunals with transnational jurisdiction deliberately exploit this link to deepen domestic enforcement. The role of the ECJ in encouraging the cooperation of national courts has been amply documented.[67] A new generation of scholarship has focused much more on the motives driving the national courts to ally themselves with the ECJ, noting substantial variation in the willingness both of different courts within the same country and of courts in different countries to send references to the ECJ and to abide by the resulting judgments. What is most striking about these findings is the extent to which specific national courts acted independently not only of other national courts but also of the executive and legislative branches of their respective governments.[68] A German lower financial court, for example, insisted on following an ECJ judgment in the face of strong opposition from a higher financial court as well as from the German government.[69] The French

---

66. See Burley and Mattli 1993; and Weiler 1991 and 1999.
67. See Stein 1981; Weiler 1991; and Burley and Mattli 1993.
68. This conclusion is not uncontroversial. Some political scientists argue that these national courts were in fact following the wishes of their respective governments, notwithstanding their governments' expressed opposition before the ECJ. The claim is that all EC member states agreed to economic integration as being in their best interests in 1959. They understood, however, that they needed a mechanism to bind one another to the obligations undertaken in the original treaty. They thus established a court to hold each state to its respective word. See Garrett 1992; Garrett and Weingast 1993; and Garrett, Kelemen, and Schulz 1998. On this view, intrajudicial politics within the EU were either anticipated by the founding states or were epiphenomenal. For a debate on precisely this point, see Garrett 1995; and Mattli and Slaughter 1995.
69. Alter 1996b.

Court of Cassation accepted the supremacy of EC law, following the dictate of the ECJ, even in the face of threats from the French legislature to strip its jurisdiction amid age-old charges of *"gouvernment par juges."*[70] British courts overturned the sacrosanct doctrine of parliamentary sovereignty and issued an injunction blocking the effect of a British law pending judicial review at the European level.[71]

The motives of these national courts are multiple. They include a desire for "empowerment,"[72] competition with other courts for relative prestige and power,[73] a particular view of the law that could be achieved by following EC precedents over national precedents,[74] recognition of the greater expertise of the ECJ in European law,[75] and the desire to advantage or at least not to disadvantage a particular constituency of litigants.[76] Similar dynamics of intracourt competition may be observed in relations between national courts and the ECHR.[77] National courts appear to have been more willing to challenge the perceived interests of other domestic authorities once the first steps had been taken by other national courts. Weiler has documented the cross-citation of foreign supreme court decisions by national supreme courts accepting the supremacy of EC law for the first time. He notes that though they may have been reluctant to restrict national autonomy in a way that would disadvantage their states relative to other states, they are more willing to impose such restrictions when they are "satisfied that they are part of a trend." An alternative explanation of this trend might be ideational; courts feel such a step is more legitimate.[78]

The incentives for expansion of a transnational docket also assume a certain familiarity and comfort with litigation as a means of dispute resolution among the potential pool of litigants. Litigants in countries with a tradition of "public interest litigation," for instance, whereby NGOs use the courts to vindicate the rights of particular minorities or otherwise disadvantaged social groups, may readily see a transnational tribunal as another weapon in their arsenal.[79] More fundamentally, litigants in any country must perceive some use in resorting to the courts at all, suggesting a correlation between the most successful transnational tribunals and those presiding over countries with at least a minimum tradition of the rule of law. Alternatively, litigants in countries with a once-functioning legal system that has been corrupted or otherwise damaged may be quicker to resort to an international tribunal as a substitute or corrective for ineffective or blatantly politicized domestic adjudication.[80]

Yet even within the EU legal system, the most studied of all transnational litigation processes, we still know "surprisingly little about the behavior and organization of

70. See Alter 1996b; and Plötner 1998.
71. Craig 1998.
72. See Weiler 1991; and Burley and Mattli 1993.
73. Alter 1996b, and 1998a,b.
74. Mattli and Slaughter 1998b.
75. Craig 1998.
76. Plötner 1998.
77. Jarmul 1996.
78. See Weiler 1994; and Finnemore and Sikkink 1998.
79. See Harlow and Rawlings 1992; and Alter and Vargas 2000.
80. See Helfer and Slaughter 1997; and Stone Sweet 1999.

litigators of EC law, and nothing from a comparative perspective [across EU countries]."[81] Even within apparently dynamic and expansive jurisdictions, the process is not unidirectional, varying considerably across different national courts, different issue-areas in the same court, and across countries.[82] Direct institutional links between individual litigants and an international tribunal create an internal logic of legalization that can become a powerful catalyst for growth, yet more research is required to explain precisely how this decisively important evolution unfolds.

The evolution of the ECHR has been less purely legal. In the ECHR system, as we have seen, litigants have been encouraged over time by the publicity accorded ECHR judgments and the growing willingness of national legislatures and administrative entities, as well as courts, to comply, rather than by a direct legal link on the model of Article 177 of the Treaty of Rome. The clauses in the European Human Rights Convention allowing individuals to bring cases before the Commission (Article 10) and recognizing the compulsory jurisdiction of the ECHR (Article 25) were initially optional among the members of the Council of Europe. It was three decades until individual access and recognition of the court's jurisdiction became universal. These practices were then codified in Protocol 11 to the convention, signed in 1994, whereby all parties recognized the compulsory jurisdiction of the permanent ECHR and permit individuals direct access to it in all cases. Signature of the new protocol was made a condition of admission for any new members, a simultaneous recognition of the greatly enhanced effectiveness of transnational over interstate litigation. In many cases new democracies strongly committed to a successful political transition enthusiastically embraced the clauses.[83] In other cases such willingness may have reflected the relative weakness of the candidate states relative to the members of the largely West European club they were seeking to join.

Beyond Formalism: The Dynamics of GATT and the WTO

The contrast between the two ideal types of dispute resolution we have constructed—interstate and transnational—illuminates the impact of judicial independence, differential rules of access, and variations in the domestic embeddedness of an international dispute-resolution process. The ICJ fits the interstate dispute-resolution pattern quite well; the ECJ approximates the ideal type of transnational dispute resolution. The form that legalization takes seems to matter.

Form, however, is not everything. Politics is affected by form but not determined by it. This is most evident when we seek to explain more fine-grained variations in the middle of the spectrum between the two ideal types. The evolution of the GATT, and recently the WTO, illustrates how politics can alter the effects of form. Formally, as we pointed out earlier, GATT is closer to the ideal type of interstate dispute resolution than to transnational dispute resolution. The independence of tribunals is coded

---

81. Stone Sweet 1998, 330. See also Harlow 1992.
82. Golub 1996.
83. Moravcsik 2000.

as moderate for both GATT and WTO. On the embeddedness criterion, GATT was low and WTO, with its mandatory procedures, is moderate (see Table 4). Most important, however, are access rules: in both the old GATT and the ITO (since 1 January 1995), states have the exclusive right to bring cases before tribunals. In formal terms, therefore, states are the gatekeepers to the GATT/WTO process.

We noted in the first section, however, that the relationships between actors in civil society and representatives of the state are very different in GATT/WTO than in the ICJ. In the GATT/WTO proceedings the principal actors from civil society are firms or industry groups, which are typically wealthy enough to afford extensive litigation and often have substantial political constituencies. Industry groups and firms have been quick to complain about allegedly unfair and discriminatory actions by their competitors abroad, and governments have often been willing to take up their complaints. Indeed, it has often been convenient for governments to do so, since the best defense against others' complaints in a system governed by reciprocity is often the threat or reality of bringing one's own case against their discriminatory measures. In a "tit-for-tat" game, it is useful to have an army of well-documented complaints "up one's sleeve" to deter others from filing complaints or as retaliatory responses to such complaints. Consequently, although states retain formal gatekeeping authority in the GATT/WTO system, they often have incentives to open the gates, letting actors in civil society set much of the agenda.

The result of this political situation is that the evolution of the GATT dispute-settlement procedure looks quite different from that of the ICJ: indeed, it seems intermediate between the ideal types of interstate and transnational dispute resolution. Dispute-resolution activity levels have increased substantially over time, as the process has become more legalized. Adjudication in the GATT of the 1950s produced vague decisions, which were nevertheless relatively effective, arguably because GATT was a "club" of like-minded trade officials.[84] Membership changes and the emergence of the EC in the 1960s led to decay in the dispute resolution mechanism, which only began to reverse in the 1970s. Diplomatic, nonlegalized attempts to resolve disputes, however, were severely criticized, leading to the appointment of a professional legal staff and the gradual legalization of the process. With legalization came better-argued decisions and the creation of a body of precedent.

Throughout this period, the formal procedures remained entirely voluntary: defendants could veto any step in the process. This "procedural flimsiness," as Robert E. Hudec refers to it, is often taken as a major weakness of GATT; but Hudec has shown that it did not prevent GATT from being quite effective. By the late 1980s, 80 percent of GATT cases were disposed of effectively—not as a result of legal embeddedness but of political decisions by states. This is a reasonably high level of compliance, though not as high as attained by the EC and ECHR. The WTO was built on the success of GATT, particularly in recent years, rather than being a response to failure.[85]

---

84. This paragraph and the subsequent one rely on Hudec 1999, especially 6–17.
85. The annual number of cases before the WTO has risen to almost twice the number during the last years of GATT; but Hudec argues that this change is accounted for by the new or intensified obligations of

We infer from the GATT/WTO experience that although the formal arrangements we have emphasized are important, their dynamic effects depend on the broader political context. Our ideal-type argument should not be reified into a legalistic, single-factor explanation of the dynamics of dispute resolution. Even if states control gates, they can under some conditions be induced to open them, or even to encourage actors from civil society to enter the dispute resolution arena. The real dynamics of dispute resolution typically lie in some interaction between law and politics, rather than in the operation of either law or politics alone.

The foregoing discussion of dynamics suggests that the following three conjectures deserve detailed empirical evaluation:

1. Compared with interstate dispute resolution, transnational dispute resolution offers greater potential for the widening and deepening of dispute resolution over time, for unintended consequences, and for progressive restrictions on the behavior of national governments.

2. Judges in transnational dispute-resolution systems are more likely than those in interstate dispute-resolution systems to exploit the potential for independence, access, and embeddedness to centralize political authority in international institutions, particularly dispute-resolution bodies themselves.

3. Whereas very large political differences between ideal-typical systems are well explained by formal institutional characteristics of international legal regimes, more fine-grained differences reflect differences in the ability of domestic political groups to exploit those institutional characteristics.

Conclusion

We have constructed two ideal types of legalized dispute resolution, interstate and transnational, which vary along the dimensions of independence, access, and embeddedness. When we examine international courts, we find that the distinction between the two ideal types appears to be associated with variation in the size of dockets and levels of compliance with decisions. The differences between the ICJ and the ECJ are dramatic along both dimensions. The causal connections between outcomes and correspondence with one ideal type or the other will require more research and analysis to sort out; but the differences between the ICJ and ECJ patterns cannot be denied. Their dynamics also vary greatly: the ECJ has expanded its caseload and its authority in a way that is unparalleled in the ICJ.

The GATT/WTO mechanisms do not reflect our ideal types so faithfully. States remain formal legal gatekeepers in these systems but have often refrained from tightly limiting access to dispute resolution procedures. As a result, the caseload of the GATT processes, and the effectiveness of their decisions, increased even without high formal levels of access or embeddedness. Hence, GATT and the WTO remind

---

the Uruguay Round, rather than being attributable to changes in the embeddedness of the dispute resolution mechanism. Hudec 1999, 21. Hudec acknowledges, however, that he is arguing against the conventional wisdom.

us that legal form does not necessarily determine political process. It is the interaction of law and politics, not the action of either alone, that generates decisions and determines their effectiveness.

What transnational dispute resolution does is to insulate dispute resolution to some extent from the day-to-day political demands of states. The more we move toward transnational dispute resolution, the harder it is to trace individual judicial decisions and states' responses to them back to any simple, short-term matrix of state or social preferences, power capabilities, and cross-issues. Political constraints, of course, continue to exist, but they are less closely binding than under interstate dispute resolution. Legalization imposes real constraints on state behavior; the closer we are to transnational third-party dispute resolution, the greater those constraints are likely to be. Transnational dispute-resolution systems help to mobilize and represent particular groups that benefit from regime norms. This increases the costs of reversal to national governments and domestic constituents, which can in turn make an important contribution to the enforcement and extension of international norms. For this reason, transnational dispute resolution systems have become an important source of increased legalization and a factor in both interstate and intrastate politics.

The European Union's Legal System and Domestic Policy: Spillover or Backlash?

Karen J. Alter

The legal system of the European Union (EU) offers domestic actors a powerful tool to influence national policy. European law can be drawn on by private litigants in national courts to challenge national policies. These challenges can be sent by national judges to the European Court of Justice (ECJ), which instructs national courts to apply European law instead of national law, or to interpret national law in a way compatible with European law. Combining victories in front of the ECJ with political mobilization and pressure, litigants and groups have used the European legal system to force their governments to change national policies.

Using Europe's legal tool involves overcoming four successive thresholds: First, there must be a point of European law on which domestic actors can draw and favorable ECJ interpretations of this law. Second, litigants must embrace EU law to advance their policy objectives, using EU legal arguments in national court cases. Third, national courts must support the efforts of the litigants by referring cases to the ECJ and/or applying the ECJ's legal interpretations instead of conflicting national policy. Fourth, litigants must follow through on their legal victory, using it as part of a larger strategy to pressure the government to change public policy.[1] A litigation strategy can fail at any of the four steps. When private litigants can surmount these four thresholds, the EU legal system can be a potent tool for forcing a change in national policy. Stated as such, these four steps may sound onerous. But litigants have used this tool successfully many times. In one of the most well-known examples, equal opportunity groups used the EU legal system to force a Conservative British government to make considerable reforms to British equality policy at the height of British antagonism toward the EU and EU social policy.[2]

I thank Benjamin Cohen, Lisa Conant, Peter Gourevitch, Brian Hanson, Robert Keohane, David Lake, Harm Schepel, Anne-Marie Slaughter, Martin Shapiro, Steve Weatherhill, the anonymous reviewers, the editors of *IO*, and participants of the Domestic Politics and International Law project for their helpful comments on earlier versions of this article. Special thanks to Jeannette Vargas, who helped develop the framework used in this article, and to Smith College, which provided funds and time to write this article.
    1. Alter and Vargas 2000.
    2. See Alter and Vargas 2000; Barnard 1995; Harlow and Rawlings 1992; and Mazey 1998. The reforms included extending work benefits to part-time workers, eliminating the cap on the size of discrimination awards, and stopping their policy of dismissing women from the military because of pregnancy.

Because the EU's legal tool can be so effective, some analysts have hypothesized that litigants will use EU litigation strategies whenever a potential benefit exists. Resurrecting Ernst Haas' neofunctionalist framework, Anne-Marie Burley and Walter Mattli have asserted that the self-interests of private litigants, national judges, and the ECJ align such that the mutual pursuit of "instrumental self-interest" leads to the expansion and penetration of European law into the domestic realm. They expected pursuit of self-interest to lead in a unidirectional way, toward ever further integration, positing that the ECJ was careful to create a system in which pursuing one's self-interest served as a "one-way ratchet" advancing legal integration.[3] Alec Stone Sweet and Thomas Brunell adopt similar assumptions, with similar predictions. They posit that transnational trade, when combined with third-party dispute resolution, leads to the expansion of legal rules and the construction of supranational governance.[4]

In this article I investigate the factors shaping each step of the litigation process. The analysis reveals many factors that keep private litigants and national courts from facilitating the expansion of European law. Furthermore, the pursuit of self-interest may also lead litigants and national courts to challenge advances in European integration. Indeed, there is much to suggest that the very factors that have led to the success of the EU legal process in expanding and penetrating the national order have provoked national courts and European governments to create limits on the legal process and to repatriate powers back to the national level. Thus the dynamic expansion created by the ECJ may well have provoked a backlash that contributed to disintegration.

I first explain how the ECJ has transformed the preliminary ruling mechanism, furthering the legalization of the EU and creating a means for private litigants to use the EU legal system to influence domestic policy. Second, I examine the different factors influencing each of the four steps, identifying sources of cross-issue and cross-national variation in the influence of EU law on national policy and summarizing a number of hypotheses about when we can expect private litigants and national judges to use the EU legal system to influence national policy. Third, I discuss the interactive effect of the four steps and suggest implications for neofunctionalist theory. Fourth, I show how the framework developed here may be generalizable outside of the EU. Many of the specifics discussed apply only to the European case, but the four-step framework and some of the factors influencing the steps are applicable in other domestic and international legal contexts.

Legalization in the EU and the Role of Private Litigants and National Courts

The EU is perhaps the most "legalized" international institution in existence. It is at the far end of all three continuums for the dimensions of legalization defined in this issue of *IO*:

Obligation: All member states are legally bound to uphold the *acquis communautaire*, the body of European law including treaties, secondary legislation, and

---

3. Burley and Mattli 1993, 60.
4. Stone Sweet and Brunell 1998b, 64.

the jurisprudence of the ECJ. A failure to fulfill a legal obligation can lead to an infringement suit in front of the ECJ, and as of 1993 the failure to obey an ECJ decision can lead to a fine.[5]

Precision: Many European rules are extremely specific, unambiguously defining how states must comply with their European obligations. When there is doubt, the ECJ is there to give a precise meaning to the rules.

Delegation: The ECJ is perhaps the most active and influential international legal body in existence, operating as a constitutional court of Europe.

The advanced level of legalization in Europe is in part a consequence of the institutional design of the EU. Member states set out to create a supranational political entity, giving the EU Council the power to pass legislation that is directly applicable in the national realm and creating a supranational Commission to oversee implementation of the EU treaties, monitor compliance with EU law, and raise infringement suits against states. They also created the ECJ, authorizing it to hear disputes between states and the EU's governing institutions; to hear infringement suits against member states raised by the Commission; to review challenges to EU laws and Commission decisions; and to review and, if necessary, invalidate EU rules. States gave the ECJ these powers believing that the court would help them keep the other supranational bodies of the EU in check. They even created a preliminary ruling mechanism (Article 234 EEC) that allows private litigants and national courts to refer cases to the ECJ, so that they too could challenge the validity of EU law and thus hold EU legislative and executive bodies in check.[6]

Although member states created an unusual supranational court, the advanced state of legalization in Europe is in no small part a result of the court's own efforts. The ECJ was not designed as a tool for domestic actors to challenge national policies; these powers the ECJ created for itself, despite the intention of member states. In the 1963 *Van Gend and Loos* decision, the ECJ declared that European law can create direct effects in national law (individual rights that European citizens can draw upon in national courts).[7] Shortly thereafter in the *Costa v. Enel* decision, the ECJ declared that European law was supreme to national law and created an obligation for national courts to enforce EU law over conflicting national law.[8] Together these two doctrines turned the EU's preliminary ruling mechanism from a conduit for national court questions and challenges to *EU law* into a mechanism that also allows individuals to invoke European law in national courts to challenge *national law.*[9]

The transformation of the preliminary ruling system increased the extent of member state obligations under EU law, the precision of EU law, and the use of third

---

5. A system of sanctions was adopted as part of the Maastricht Treaty on a European Union. For a discussion of the origin and use of this sanction, see Tallberg 1999.

6. The overall model of the ECJ was the French Conseil d'État, which holds the French government accountable to correctly implementing laws as passed by Parliament. Robertson 1966, 150. The preliminary ruling mechanism was an adaptation of a feature from the Italian and German legal systems adopted to facilitate national court reviews of EU decisions and laws. Pescatore 1981.

7. *Van Gend en Loos v. Nederlandse Administratie Belastingen,* ECJ decision of 26/62 (1963) ECR 1.

8. *Costa v. Ente Nazionale per L'Energia Elettrica (ENEL)* ECJ decision of 6/64 (1964) ECR 583.

9. See De Witte 1984; Rasmussen 1986; and Weiler 1991.

parties to resolve disputes—significantly advancing legalization in Europe. As the following list shows, the ECJ has played a key role in increasing legalization in Europe.

Obligation: When the ECJ declared the supremacy of European law it turned national courts into enforcers of European law in the national sphere. National courts set aside conflicting national laws, award penalties for the nonimplementation of EU directives, and assess fines for violations of European law, creating an incentive for firms and governments to change national policies that violate European law. In the words of Joseph Weiler, the transformation of the preliminary ruling system "closed exit" from the EU legal system, ending the ability of states to avoid their legal obligations through noncompliance.[10]

Precision: The ECJ has used preliminary ruling cases to specify the meaning of EU legal texts. Furthermore, with individual litigants raising cases and national courts sending these cases to the ECJ, states are less able to exploit legal lacunae and interpret their way out of compliance with European law.[11]

Delegation: By granting private litigants standing to invoke EU law to challenge national law, the ECJ increased the number of opportunities it has to rule on the compatibility of national policy with European law. Most of the court's case load, most of the challenges to national policies that reach the ECJ, and many if not most of the advances in European law have been the result of national courts referring preliminary rulings to the ECJ.[12]

Given the key role private litigants and national judges played in advancing legalization in Europe, Burley and Mattli's neofunctionalist explanation is quite compelling.

Although private litigants and national courts were key actors facilitating legalization of EU law in the past, they do not always play this role now. Scholars are in agreement that the transformation of the EU legal system has advanced legalization in Europe and made the EU legal system a potent tool for private litigants to influence national policy. There is also agreement that cases brought by private litigants continue to play a central role in the EU legal process. The question remains, however, whether the ECJ's success at transforming the system with the help of private litigant cases means that a never-ending process of legal expansion has been set in motion. When do private litigants and national court actions help to advance legal integration? To answer this question, we need to better understand the interests of the ECJ's key intermediaries (private litigants and national judges) and thus the factors shaping where, when, and why they use the EU legal system to promote their objectives.

---

10. Weiler 1991. In 1974 the ECJ extended member state obligations further by granting EU directives direct effects, making them more legally binding. In 1991 it created a financial penalty for states that failed to implement directives in a timely fashion. *Van Duyn v. Home Office Case,* ECJ decision of 41/74 (1974) ECR 1337. *Francovich v. Italy,* C-6, 9/90, ECJ decision of 19 November 1991, ECR 1991.

11. Alter 1996b, chap. 7.

12. Dehousse 1998, 51–52. Member states have raised only four infringement cases against each other. The Commission raised 1,045 infringement cases from 1960 through 1994, 88 percent of which were after 1981 and most of which involved nonimplementation of EU directives in a timely fashion. National courts have referred 2,893 cases to the ECJ from 1960 to 1994, not all of which were challenges to national policy. (Data from the information services of the ECJ and from Commission reports).

How and When Do Private Litigants and National Courts Use the European Legal System to Influence National Policy?

By focusing on private litigants and national judges, I am not implying that private litigant cases are the only factor contributing to increased legalization in Europe or that EU law influences domestic policy only through private litigant suits. Member states advance legalization when they pass new legislation at the EU level and grant EU bodies new powers—of which they do plenty. According to a report by the French Conseil d'État, by 1992 European law included 22,445 EU regulations, 1,675 directives, 1,198 agreements and protocols, 185 recommendations of the Commission or the Council, 291 Council resolutions, and 678 communications. The Community had become the largest source of new law, with 54 percent of all new French laws originating in Brussels.[13] Because national governments fear expansive interpretations of EU rules, and in order to bind each other more fully, they are also now more precise when they draft EU law. The Commission also has a key role in legalization. It offers interpretations of EU rules and raises infringement suits against member states. And even without a legal suit being raised, the EU legal system impacts national policy by creating anticipatory reactions within states. Most national governments automatically review the compatibility of prospective legislation with EU legal obligations.[14] They do this in a good faith effort to comply with EU law.[15]

But private litigant cases can in many instances be the only way to persuade a recalcitrant state to change its policies. Many cases that reach the ECJ through national courts arrive there because other avenues of influencing domestic policy failed. The litigant has tried to negotiate with the national administration about the policy. The litigant might also have worked with the Commission to address the violation, but either the Commission dropped or settled the case, or the ECJ's infringement decision failed to create a change in national policy. If there were no EU legal tool for private litigants, the case would end in noncompliance. But private litigants can use the EU legal system to pressure a government to comply with EU law. Knowing that private litigants will challenge questionable national policies, member states are more likely to avoid violations of EU law in the first place. Thus the existence of the EU's legal tool is crucial to increasing state compliance, even when the tool itself is not invoked. The key is that it must be available for use.

Using the EU legal tool to influence national policy involves overcoming four successive thresholds: First, there must be a point of European law on which domestic actors can draw and favorable ECJ interpretations of this law. Second, litigants must embrace EU law to advance their policy objectives, using EU legal arguments in national court cases. Third, national courts must support the efforts of the litigants by referring cases to the ECJ and/or applying ECJ jurisprudence instead of conflict-

---

13. Conseil d'État 1992, Rapport Public, 16–17.

14. For example, in Germany proposed legislation is reviewed by the Justice Ministry to ensure its compatibility with EU law. In France, the Conseil d'État conducts a similar review.

15. Usually all that is needed is a change in language to avoid a conflict with EU law, with the overall substance and objective of the policy remaining intact.

ing national policy. Fourth, the litigants must follow up their legal victory to pressure the government to change public policy.[16]

Because EU law influences domestic policy in other ways—by being directly applicable in the national realm, by being incorporated into national law by national governments, by creating anticipatory effects in the national government, or by the Commission raising an infringement suit—one cannot say that these four thresholds represent necessary conditions for EU law to influence domestic policy. But at least the first three are necessary if private litigants are to effectively use the EU legal system to influence national policy, with the caveat that if it is clear that these four thresholds are likely surmountable, then a group might be able to get its way simply by threatening to mount a litigation campaign.

In this section I pull together the state of our knowledge about the factors influencing each step of the EU legal process. These factors can potentially help to explain cross-national and cross-issue variation in the impact of EU law on domestic policy.

Step 1: EU Law and Domestic Policy

The first step of the EU litigation process involves identifying a point of EU law on which domestic actors can draw. Not all national policies are affected by European law, and not all aspects of European law can be invoked before national courts.

EU law reaches quite widely. In addition, if a national policy indirectly affects the free movement of goods, people, capital, or services (the four freedoms) there might be an EU legal angle of attack. But EU law contains biases that make it more useful for some issues than for others. EU law creates significant legal rights for its citizens, but these rights are primarily economic citizenship rights directed at obtaining the four freedoms. The EU has created far fewer social rights and civil rights for its citizens.[17] Indeed, women might find EU law helpful in promoting equality in the workplace but not in addressing larger issues of gender discrimination that do not affect their participation in the workplace. Furthermore, the economic rights of EU law are focused on workers and firms engaged in transnational activity. The British worker who stays at home might find EU law far less helpful in challenging national rules than the French worker who moved to the United Kingdom. There are also policy areas that fall under the EU's jurisdiction and tend to be covered by EU law, including customs law, agricultural policy, transport policy, certain taxation issues, and policy areas that have been harmonized. Farmers and shopkeepers might thus find themselves affected by EU law even though they sell all their goods on the domestic market.

In most cases EU law must create direct effects before it can be invoked in national courts to challenge national policy, meaning that the ECJ must determine if the law in

---

16. Alter and Vargas 2000.
17. See Ball 1996; and Shaw 1998. EU law does create some citizen rights regarding consumer protection, environmental protection, and workplace safeguards. Although these rights exist, they are limited. The vast majority of the private litigant cases before the ECJ either directly concern the economic rights created by EU law or are couched in terms of economic rights created under EU law.

question confers legal standing for individuals in national courts.[18] The ECJ decides on a statute-by-statute basis if EU law creates direct effects, taking into account the specificity of the law, whether the statute is clear and unconditional, and whether the statute leaves states significant discretion.[19] Regulations are directly applicable in the national realm, allowing litigants to invoke them directly to challenge national policy. Directives only sometimes create direct effects, mainly when the obligation they impose is very specific and the time period for adoption has expired.

A separate issue is whether the ECJ would be willing to interpret EU law in the litigant's favor once a case is raised. There is relatively little research on the factors shaping ECJ decision making, but it is clear that the ECJ makes strategic calculations in its decision making, avoiding decisions that could create a political backlash. Geoffrey Garrett, Daniel Kelemen, and Heiner Schulz argue that the greater the clarity of EU legal texts, case precedent, and legal norms in support of a judgment, the less likely the ECJ is to bend to political pressure.[20] In addition, the smaller the costs a legal decision creates for a state, the more likely the ECJ is to apply the law even if it means deciding against a powerful member state.[21] But as I argue elsewhere, even when the costs of ECJ decisions are significant, and the decisions are controversial, states usually lack a credible threat to cow the ECJ into quiescence. When a significant consensus exists among key member states against a decision, political threats can become credible and the ECJ is more likely to be influenced.[22] George Tsebelis and Geoffrey Garrett further hypothesize that when the voting rule to overturn an ECJ decision requires a qualified majority, the ECJ will have less leeway to stray from the wishes of member states.[23] Their argument remains rather vague and they do not provide evidence to support their claim—indeed it is far from clear that the ECJ is less bold in cases involving regulations and directives that only require qualified majority votes. Nonetheless, most analysts agree that mobilizing a credible threat will be less difficult, though still difficult, when states only need a qualified majority vote to overturn the ECJ than when unanimity is required (such as when the decision is based on the treaty itself).

These findings offer helpful starts, but they do not lead to many concrete hypotheses of how extralegal factors shape ECJ decision making. What we can say for now is that systematic biases in EU law shape which national policies can be influenced by the EU legal process and which actors will find EU law most helpful to promote their objectives. EU law is mostly concerned with economic issues with a transnational dimension, and thus economic issues involving transnational elements are more likely to be affected by EU litigation. Laws that are more specific are more likely to

---

18. The ECJ's *Francovitch* doctrine implies that plaintiffs can challenge a state's nonimplementation of a directive regardless of whether the directive itself creates direct effects. This is a small exception on the general rule that EU law must create direct effects to be invoked before national courts. I am indebted to Steve Weatherhill for pointing this out.
19. See Chalmers 1997; and Folsom 1995, 86–89.
20. Garrett, Kelemen, and Schulz 1998.
21. See Alter 1996a; and Garrett, Kelemen, and Schulz 1998.
22. Alter 1998b.
23. Tsebelis and Garrett n.d.

create direct effects; and when the ECJ's doctrine is more developed, the ECJ is more likely to rule against a national policy.[24] The ECJ can be influenced by national governments to decide in favor of existent national policy, but in most situations member states lack a credible threat to cow the ECJ into quiescence. Furthermore, even when member states can muster a credible threat, the ECJ may prefer to stick to the letter of the law to maintain support by the legal community[25] or to make a ruling that encourages the Council to enact new legislation or change its legislation at the EU level.

Step 2: Mobilizing Litigants to Use EU Law to Promote Their Policy Objectives

The Commission can raise cases against member states, but for a variety of reasons it often chooses not to.[26] From 1982 to 1995, the number of complaints received by the Commission was more than three times greater than the number of official inquiries undertaken by the Commission and was fourteen times greater than the number of Article 226 cases raised by the Commission.[27] If the Commission will not raise a case, private litigants must pursue the issue on their own. This seems to be the norm; indeed, starting in the 1970s, private litigant cases overtook the Commission in the supply of cases involving conflicts between national law and EU law by a very significant margin.[28]

There are many European legal texts and favorable EU legal precedents that remain unexploited even though they could help litigants promote their objectives and create significant financial gain. When are domestic actors most likely to turn to EU litigation to promote their objectives? Which domestic actors are most likely to find litigation an attractive strategy to influence national policy?

A number of factors specific to national legal systems affect litigants' willingness to use EU law to challenge national policy. Restrictions in legal standing may make litigation harder to pursue in certain countries and certain issue areas. Other factors include procedural rules on how complaints are filed and investigated, variations in the existence of legal aid, requirements that losers in cases compensate winners, time limits for raising cases, rules limiting the size of awards, and rules regarding the burden of proof. In the United Kingdom, for example, a cap on discrimination awards limited the number of claimants willing to raise discrimination suits, but the Equal Opportunities Commission's (EOC) activism led to a number of British cases challenging U.K. equality policy.[29] Groups would be unable to follow the EOC's strategy in France, Belgium, and Luxembourg, where they are excluded from participating in

---

24. But when it is clear from the ECJ's doctrine how it will decide, states are also more likely to settle out of court in the shadow of the law, and thus the case may never go to court. Alter forthcoming.
25. Mattli and Slaughter 1995.
26. On the difficulty of mobilizing the Commission to pursue infringements, see Weatherhill 1997.
27. Conant forthcoming, fig. 1. For a study on the use of the infringement procedure by the Commission, see Tallberg 1999.
28. Dehousse 1998, 52.
29. See Alter and Vargas 2000; and Barnard 1995.

TABLE 1. *Comparison of domestic civil litigation rates (per 100,000 inhabitants)*

	Civil procedures	Cases heard in first instance legal bodies	Cases heard on appeal
West Germany (1989)	9,400	4,911	251
England/Wales (1982)	5,300	1,200	16
France (1982)	3,640	1,950	250

Source: Blankenburg 1996, 295.
Note: In Germany the total volume of litigation initiated by private actors (civil litigation) is unusually high. If the procedures raised in administrative and labor courts were added to the figures for Germany, the rate of civil procedures would increase by another 1,350 per 100,000, and the appeal rate would rise accordingly.

equality cases.[30] In Denmark only union officials can pursue equality issues, since gender-equality clauses are part of collective-bargaining agreements. If the union refuses to pick up the issue, the individual facing discrimination may be out of luck. This type of variation can lead to cross-national and cross-issue variation in the impact of EU law on domestic policy.

The litigiousness of a society also influences whether litigants use the EU legal process. Importers and exporters in Germany regularly challenge decisions of tax authorities in the tax courts, leading to many EU legal cases. Making a veiled reference to numerous German cases involving customs classifications, Adophe Touffait, a former procureur general at the French Court de Cassation, argued that French enterprises would never become preoccupied with the distinction between types of flours, especially given the reluctance of commercial groups to legally challenge acts of tax or customs administrators.[31] Touffait's argument is supported by statistics on domestic litigation rates. As Table 1 shows, German citizens raise far more legal cases than do British or French citizens. Indeed, most commercial disputes in France continue to be resolved by arbitration rather than through the legal system.

A clever lawyer, however, can often find ways to surmount national legal and procedural barriers, if they or their clients are highly motivated. Which litigants are more likely to be motivated and more likely to raise EU law cases? Drawing on U.S. public law scholarship, Lisa Conant argues that law is at the service of the privileged; litigants with financial resources at their disposal and significant legal know-how are more likely and able to use litigation to promote policy objectives. With respect to EU law, Christopher Harding and Conant find that interest groups, large firms, and lawyers who can provide their own services are the privileged actors most able and likely to pursue an EU legal claim.[32] Of the privileged actors, firms and private lawyers are more likely to use litigation than organized interests, although organized

---

30. See Blom et al. 1995; and Fitzpatrick, Gregory, and Szyszczak 1993, 19–20.
31. Touffait 1975.
32. See Conant 1998; and Harding 1992.

interests are often more able to use a test-case strategy, picking cases with favorable fact situations and shopping for a supportive legal forum.

Which firms and groups are most likely to use litigation, and when are they likely to use litigation? Conant argues that when the potential benefits are significant for an individual or group, litigants are more likely to mobilize to use litigation. The more concentrated the benefits, the greater the likelihood of strategic, coordinated litigation campaigns.[33] Karen Alter and Jeannette Vargas argue that independent of the size or concentration of benefits, how interest groups are organized at the national level influences whether or not specific groups employ litigation. They found the more narrow the interest group's mandate and constituency, the more likely it was to turn to a litigation strategy; and the more broad and encompassing the interest group's mandate and constituency, the less likely it was to turn to a litigation strategy to promote gender equality. This is because broad-based groups often have competing objectives. Thus it was unions composed predominately of women and single-issue agencies like the British Equal Opportunities Commission that used litigation to promote gender equality, whereas broad-based unions and women's groups avoided gender-equality litigation and focused instead on broader employment and family issues.[34]

Another important factor was whether an interest group enjoyed influence in and access to policymaking. In political negotiation, groups can usually strike a deal that will leave them at least better off than before. With legal decisions, groups could well end up with a policy that is more objectionable and harder to reverse than the previous policy. For this reason, and because of the risk and relative crudeness of litigation as a means of influencing policy, organized interests generally prefer to work through political channels.[35] The greater the political strength of a group, and the more access the group has to the policymaking process, the less likely a group is to mount a litigation campaign. In Belgium, for example, neither unions nor women's groups use litigation to pursue equality issues, preferring instead to use their access to the policymaking process to influence Belgian policy.[36]

Litigation is more likely in countries where actors commonly use litigation to challenge policy and where the rules on legal standing and procedures make EU law litigation feasible and profitable. One can expect litigation from wealthier individuals and firms or from lawyers who can provide their own legal council, especially when these actors face potential benefits of significant magnitude. Ironically, although interest groups can perhaps most effectively use test-case litigation strategies, they are the least likely actors to adopt such a strategy. But if political channels are closed, groups might find litigation their best option for influencing public policy. Narrowly focused groups and groups that do not enjoy significant influence over policymaking are most likely to find litigation enticing.

33. Conant 1998, chap. 3.
34. Alter and Vargas 2000.
35. Ibid.
36. Fitzpatrick et al. 1993, 89.

TABLE 2. *Reference patterns in EU member states (1961–97)*

Country	1961–69	1970–79	1980–89	1990–98	Total
Germany	30 (40%)	284 (42%)	346 (28%)	463 (26%)	1,123 (30%)
France	7 (9%)	85 (13%)	285 (23%)	216 (12%)	593 (16%)
Netherlands	22 (29%)	108 (16%)	189 (15%)	174 (10%)	493 (13%)
Italy	3 (4%)	84 (12%)	125 (10%)	370 (21%)	582 (15%)
Belgium	10 (13%)	77 (11%)	142 (11%)	124 (7%)	353 (9%)
Luxembourg	3 (4%)	4 (1%)	17 (1%)	18 (1%)	42 (1%)
United Kingdom	—	20 (3%)	85 (7%)	163 (9%)	268 (7%)
Ireland	—	6 (1%)	15 (1%)	16 (1%)	37 (1%)
Denmark	—	6 (1%)	25 (2%)	47 (3%)	78 (2%)
Greece	—	—	21 (2%)	32 (2%)	53 (1%)
Spain	—	—	5 (—)	116 (7%)	121 (3%)
Portugal	—	—	1 (—)	30 (2%)	31 (1%)
Total	75 (100%)	674 (100%)	1,256 (100%)	1,769 (101%)	3,774 (99%)

Source: Based on the statistics in the 1997 annual report of the ECJ.

Step 3: Eliciting National Judicial Support

When there is a point of EU law that creates direct effects, private litigants can draw upon this law in national courts to challenge national policy. Not all potential beneficiaries of EU rules will mobilize to challenge national policy through litigation, and even when they do, formidable barriers to changing national policy lay ahead. One challenge will be to persuade a national court to either refer the case to the ECJ or to interpret EU rules itself and set aside national law.

One can presume that national courts will be more likely to refer a case to the ECJ when asked to do so by one of the parties to the case. But even then, national courts may avoid referring a case for many reasons. Although national courts are supposed to make references to the ECJ any time a question of EU law arises and if they are a court of last instance,[37] in practice national courts cannot be compelled to refer a case.[38] A lower court's refusal can be appealed to a higher court in hopes of a reference or a more friendly interpretation, but often the most reticent courts are the highest courts. If the highest court refuses to refer the case, the litigant is simply out of luck. The varying willingness of national judges to make references and enforce EU law is reflected in part in variation in the total number of references to the ECJ by courts of different countries (see Table 2), a variation that cannot be explained by population size alone (see Figure 1).

37. *SRL CILFIT v. Ministry of* Health (I) ECJ decision of 283/81 (1982) ECR 1119.

38. In Germany it is a constitutional violation for national courts to deny the plaintiff their legal judge by refusing a reference to the ECJ. But appeals of a decision not to refer a case tend to languish on the docket of the German Constitutional Court, and in no other system is there a way to force a judge to make a reference or to apply EU law correctly.

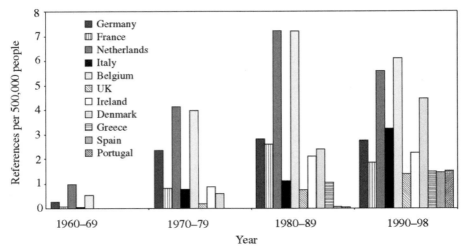

Note: Figure excludes Luxembourg.

FIGURE 1. *Reference per 500,000 population by country*

Early studies explained the relative reluctance of some national judiciaries to refer cases by whether a national legal system was monist or dualist,[39] whether a tradition of judicial review existed in the country,[40] and whether the national legal system had a constitutional court.[41] But none of these explanations holds across countries, nor can they account for significant variation in reference rates within countries.[42]

Stone Sweet and Brunell have done the most complete quantitative analysis of reference rates to the ECJ. They find a correlation between variation in national reference rates and the level of transnational activity; they argue that the more transnational activity, the more conflicts between national and EU law and thus the more references by national courts.[43] There are reasons to question their causal argument and to be suspicious of the data they use to support their claims. Stone and Brunell imply that the numerous referrals to the ECJ involve conflicts between national and EU law and are provoked by transnational activity. But referrals for preliminary rulings also include challenges to the validity of EU rules themselves as well as questions about how national governments are applying these rules. Indeed, when Jürgen Schwartz analyzed the content of German references to the ECJ between 1965 and 1985, he found that only 37 percent of references were about conflicts between EU law and German law; 40 percent were challenges to the validity of EU law and Commission decisions.[44] And of the cases involving national policy, many

39. Bebr 1981.
40. Vedel 1987.
41. Cappelletti and Golay 1986.
42. Alter 1998a, 231–32.
43. See Stone Sweet and Brunell 1998a,b.
44. Schwartz 1988.

are not inspired by transnational activity. Rather, domestic groups may simply be capitalizing on the EU legal system to push their domestic agendas.[45] Conant found that if policy sectors not involving transnational activities were excluded from the reference figures, Stone Sweet and Brunell's correlation would not hold, at least for the United Kingdom.[46] The only way to understand the significance of the reference figures would be to read and analyze the substance of the 3,570 cases that have been referred to the ECJ. Even then, however, one would only capture a fraction of national court cases involving EU law, since the majority of these cases are not referred to the ECJ.[47]

As lawyers will attest, certain courts are more receptive than others to EU legal arguments. National court support cannot be captured by the number of references. Some courts accept ECJ jurisprudence without making a reference, whereas other courts reject key tenets of EU legal doctrine and thus do not make a reference. Some courts refer far-reaching questions of law to the ECJ, whereas other courts only refer narrow technical questions about EU legal texts, resolving the more significant issues about the impact of EU law in the national legal system on their own and only sometimes in accordance with ECJ jurisprudence.[48]

Case study analysis risks being more impressionistic than quantitative. But given the over-aggregated nature of the ECJ's reference data, and the current impossibility of determining the number and content of national court cases that are not referred to the ECJ, it may be the only way to capture the many factors shaping judicial behavior. The following observations come in large part from my own detailed research on the French and German judiciaries. I used variation in reference rates within each judiciary to garner an overall impression of which courts were referring cases to the ECJ; and I interviewed over a hundred judges, lawyers, and government officials to gain insight into the sources of variation in judicial behavior. Research has revealed five factors that contribute to variation in the behavior of national courts vis-à-vis EU law: (1) the substance of EU law and jurisdictional boundaries; (2) rules of access to national courts; (3) the identity of a court; (4) how EU law affects the influence, independence, and autonomy of the national court vis-à-vis other courts; and (5) the policy implication of ECJ jurisprudence. The first four factors create cross-court and

45. See Alter 1996a; Schepel 1998; and Chalmers 2000b.
46. Conant forthcoming.
47. It is hard to know how national judges deal with cases that are not referred. Damian Chalmers has made a heroic effort to find British cases involving EU law. He found 1,088 cases where British judges addressed questions of EU law. This number is nearly five times the number of British references to the ECJ (269). And Chalmers' data include only "reported cases" that were passed on to the Registry of the ECJ or published in one of twenty-seven publications. Lower court cases involving EU law are significantly underrepresented. Chalmers analyzes these cases for the most comprehensive study to date on how national courts are applying EU law. Chalmers 2000b.
48. For example, the German Federal Tax Court has sent over 140 references to the ECJ, probably more references than any other national court in the EU. But the tax court is well known for referring picky technical questions about the meaning of EU laws, wanting to know, for example, how to classify turkey tails and jeans with button flaps. Zuleeg 1993. The tax court is also well known for openly flouting the ECJ's doctrine on the direct effect of directives, reversing a lower court reference to the ECJ, and deciding important questions of legal principle on its own, without reference to the ECJ. Behr 1983.

cross-branch variation and can cumulatively lead to cross-national variation. The last factor contributes to both cross-court and cross-national variation. I will briefly address each factor.

The influence on judicial behavior of variations in the substance of the law and in jurisdictional boundaries.   Variation in reference rates is caused in part by variation in legal substance and in the jurisdictional divisions of courts. The more harmonized EU legislation is, the more courts having to deal with this legislation will consult with the ECJ. In Germany, for example, because customs regulations of the EU were the first to be harmonized (in the 1960s) and because tax law is one of the most harmonized areas of EU law, tax courts have been more involved in legal integration from an early period than penal courts, which deal almost exclusively with national law.[49] Because the Federal Office of Nutrition and Forestry and the Federal Office for the Regulation of the Agricultural Market are located in Frankfurt, the Frankfurt administrative court hears nearly all challenges to the validity of EU agricultural policies. This helps to explain why the administrative court in Frankfurt accounted for 9 percent of all German references from 1960 to 1994.[50]

The influence of access rules on judicial behavior.   We have seen that access rules shape litigant incentives and their ability to pursue an EU law litigation strategy. They also influence judicial behavior vis-à-vis EU law because they affect the ability of national courts to influence the development of European and national law and the incentives of judges to refer cases to the ECJ. France provides a good example of how access rules shape judicial behavior vis-à-vis EU law.

Compared with the active role played by the German and Italian Constitutional Courts in EU legal issues, the French Conseil Constitutionnel's position is bizarre: in all but a few narrow issues the Conseil Constitutionnel refuses to be involved in controlling the compatibility of French law with international law.[51] Access rules explain this position. Laws only make it to the Conseil Constitutionnel for review before they have actually been promulgated and only if political disagreement exists within the government or between the government and the legislature. Many laws of questionable constitutionality are never referred to the Conseil Constitutionnel, and when laws are referred, the Conseil Constitutionnel has only two months to make a decision. According to Bruno Genevois, the secretary general of the Conseil Constitutionnel, the Conseil Constitutionnel is concerned that a national law it finds to be compatible with EU law could be implemented in a way that violates EU law or could be found to be incompatible with EU law by the ECJ or—even more embarrassing for a court charged with upholding the rights of its citizens—by the European Court of Human Rights (ECHR). Because of its inability to systematically ensure that national law complies with international law, and because of the embarrassing

---

49. Indeed, in Germany tax courts, the smallest branch of the judiciary, with less than 3 percent of all judges, account for 49 percent of German references.

50. Seidel 1987.

51. Luchaire 1991.

possibility that it could later be contradicted by the ECJ or the ECHR, the Conseil Constitutionnel prefers not to be involved in enforcing the supremacy of international law.[52]

Access rules also make it hard for French litigants to seek out the most friendly national courts for EU legal challenges. The "ordinary courts" are clearly the most willing to make references to the ECJ (indeed they account for nearly 90 percent of all French references to the ECJ).[53] But constructing a case to challenge EU law is difficult for these courts.[54] The administrative court system deals with direct challenges to administrative acts and national law and, for most of these cases, the Conseil d'État is the court of first and last instance. For reasons that will be discussed, the Conseil d'État is not receptive to EU legal challenges, and in most cases it cannot be circumvented or pressured from courts beneath it.[55] The lack of judicial support from the court best placed to entertain challenges to national policy is a big reason why there are fewer litigant challenges to national policy in France and relatively few significant developments in European law based on references from French courts.

The influence of judicial identity on judicial behavior.   As many scholars have argued, the identity of judges shapes their behavior vis-à-vis EU law.[56] Judicial identity is shaped by the training of judges, the selection process for judges, and the role the court plays in the legal and political process—all factors that can vary by country, by judicial branch, and by court.

Judicial training varies across countries, and even within countries there can be significant variation in how EU legal issues are taught. In most European countries, ordinary court judges participate in specialized training for judges that imparts to them a specific understanding of their role in the political system and how they are to deal with EU legal issues (this education has changed with time, creating generational differences within national judiciaries). Outside ordinary courts are a series of first instance legal bodies (some called courts, others tribunals, and others by other names) which have a different mode of appointment that does not necessarily involve training in judge schools. High court appointees may come from academia or political office, bringing a variety of training experiences and backgrounds. These different life experiences lead judges to act differently when confronted with EU legal issues.

The fairly antagonistic position the French Conseil d'État has taken vis-à-vis EU law, for example, is often explained by the identity of Conseil d'État judges, an

52. Genevois 1989, 827.

53. "Ordinary courts" is a category in France and in other countries. Ordinary courts in France are contrasted to administrative courts and the Constitutional Council.

54. Ordinary courts hear mainly civil and penal law cases. For a civil law case, either the case has to emerge from a dispute between private parties or from a government action against a private actor.

55. In the 1990s the Conseil d'État was more receptive to EU legal arguments, following its change in position on EU law in the *Nicolo* case. Plötner claims that litigants have been more successful in front of the Conseil d'État since then, but it is only a matter of degree. Plötner 1998. Few would say that the Conseil d'État welcomes EU legal arguments, and reference rates from the administrative branch to the ECJ remain abysmally low.

56. See Chalmers 1997; Conant forthcoming; and Mattli and Slaughter 1998b, 200–201.

identity imparted to them in their training at the elite Ecole National d'Administration,[57] which teaches French high administrators to have a strong identification with the French state.[58] Equally important is that members of Conseil d'État float freely in and out of the government and private sector and the Conseil d'État. As Weil has argued,

> the Conseil d'État is too close, by virtue of its recruitment, its composition, and the climate in which it is enmeshed, to the centers of political decision-making to not function on the same wavelength as [the government], to not feel vis-à-vis the authority which it is called upon to control a sympathy in the strongest sense of the word, which explains the self-censorship [the Conseil d'État] imposes on itself and the selectivity in the control it exercises.[59]

The background of a Conseiller d'État affects its jurisprudence on a number of issues, including EU law.[60] A similar argument was made for the German Federal Tax Court by Gert Meier, who claimed that having themselves served many years in the administration before becoming judges, Federal Tax Court judges tended to give the benefit of the doubt to the tax administration.[61]

Variation in how judges understand their legal and political mandates creates cross-national and cross-issue variation in how courts deal with EU legal issues. A number of first instance legal bodies, for example, do not consider themselves to be "courts" and for this reason do not see themselves as qualified under Article 234 EEC to make a reference to the ECJ. In the United Kingdom, for example, first instance industrial tribunals will make references to the ECJ, whereas in the Netherlands and Ireland the legal bodies that deal with equality cases in the first instance do not see themselves as authorized to refer cases to the ECJ.[62] Some countries have legal bodies staffed by lay judges or a mix of lay and professional judges that attempt to be less formal than courts and function more like arbitrating bodies. For example, most commercial disputes in France begin and end in arbitration and thus are not referred to the ECJ.[63] Some countries have mid-level appellate courts that, in essence, are staffed by a few law professors who review the legal basis of lower court decisions and who tend not to make references to the ECJ.

Variations in how EU law affects the influence, independence, and autonomy of national courts in relation to each other. A significant amount of evidence indicates that the more EU law and the ECJ are seen as undermining the influence, independence, and autonomy of a national court, the more reluctant the national court will be to refer far-reaching and legally innovative cases to the ECJ. As I have argued elsewhere, lower courts are often more willing to make references because a

57. Plötner 1998, 55–56.
58. See Bodiguel 1981; and Kessler 1986.
59. Weil 1972, ix.
60. Loschak 1972.
61. Meier 1994.
62. Fitzpatrick et al. 1993.
63. Touffait 1975.

reference bolsters their authority in the national legal system and allows the court a way to escape national legal hierarchies and challenge higher court jurisprudence.[64] Lawyers attest to the greater openness of lower courts when it comes to making a reference to the ECJ, and statistics support this claim, showing that even though lower courts are not legally obliged to make a reference to the ECJ, lower and midlevel courts refer the vast majority of all references to the ECJ (73 percent). Judges and scholars have also argued that lower courts have in many instances been the driving force in expanding ECJ doctrine and in promoting change in national doctrine.[65] Indeed, of the ECJ's preliminary ruling decisions discussed in two legal textbooks (and thus by implication the most significant of the ECJ's jurisprudence) 62 percent of the references had been made by lower courts.[66]

Last instance courts are often more reluctant to make a referral to the ECJ, especially when they are threatened by the existence of the ECJ as the highest court on questions of European law or are upset at how EU law undermines their own influence and the smooth operation of the national legal process. Indeed, courts with constitutional powers have made virtually no references to the ECJ, and doctrinal analyses reveal clear efforts by national high courts to position themselves vis-à-vis the ECJ to protect their independence, authority, and influence.[67]

Variation in the impact of EU law on national law.   Judges do take into account the political implications of their decisions. Some ECJ decisions have created a divergence in the levels of legal protection and in legal remedies available under national law and under EU law, advantaging citizens who can draw on EU law over those who must rely on national law alone. ECJ jurisprudence has also resulted in great complexities for national legal systems and problematic outcomes. The seeming perversities created by the ECJ and EU law, as well as interpretations with which national courts simply disagree, can sap the willingness of national judiciaries to support the ECJ.

Many scholars (including early neofunctionalist theorists) believed that the largest barrier to national judicial support was ignorance about the EU legal system. With knowledge, they assumed, should come support. Although hearing more cases does seem to lead to more references to the ECJ, it does not necessarily lead to greater acceptance of ECJ jurisprudence. As Renaud Dehousse explains,

> From the standpoint of a national lawyer, European law is often a source of disruption. It injects into the national legal system rules which are alien to its traditions and which may affect its deeper structure, thereby threatening its coherence. It may also be a source of arbitrary distinctions between similar situa-

64. Alter 1996a.
65. See Alter forthcoming; Alter and Vargas 2000; Mancini and Keeling 1992; Burley and Mattli 1993; and Weiler 1991.
66. Alter forthcoming, chap. 2.
67. My study of national court acceptance of EU law supremacy shows how the highest national courts are demarcating the borders of the national constitutional order so as to limit future encroachments of European law and ECJ authority into the national domain. Alter forthcoming.

tions. . . . What appears as integration at the European level is often perceived as disintegration from the perspective of national legal systems. . . . Moreover, preliminary references are one of the central elements in the interface between Community law and national law. The ECJ is therefore perceived as the central agent in a process of perforation of national sovereignty.[68]

Controversial ECJ decisions have led to rebukes by judges as well as attempts to avoid references to the ECJ and the application of EU law. For example, the ECJ's jurisprudence regarding labor law and especially its decision that employers must accept medical certificates from other member states, even when an Italian family of four working in Germany had for four years in a row all "fallen ill" during their vacations in Italy, have led the German Federal Labor Court to openly criticize the ECJ and assert that EU law creates a danger for the consistency of codified law in Germany.[69] According to Jonathan Golub, because British judges believe that the ECJ will interpret environmental directives more broadly than necessary, British judges have withheld references to the court in environmental issues.[70] Chalmers finds a greater resistance to EU law when national judges perceive EU law to undermine the capacity of British institutions to promote social conformity.[71] And Carol Harlow predicts a national judicial backlash against ECJ jurisprudence on state liability, possibly expanding to a larger political backlash.[72]

There is no way to ensure that a national court will refer a case to the ECJ or apply EU law as it should. If the litigant indicates a preference for a reference, presumably the likelihood of a reference will increase. If the ECJ's jurisdictional authority in the area is undisputed, and if the ECJ's jurisprudence is uncontroversial within the national legal community, it is also more likely that national courts will either make a reference or apply the ECJ's case law themselves. Lower courts appear relatively more willing than higher courts to make a reference. Courts where appointees have fewer connections to the government seem more likely to act more favorably to challenges to national policy. Lawyers have a sense of which judges are more "friendly" to EU law arguments. Litigants who can shop for legal venues in which judges are thought to be receptive to EU legal arguments are most likely to succeed in getting their cases referred to the ECJ. Interest groups may be able to select among a variety of potential cases, and firms with numerous offices across regions and countries might have the opportunity to raise a case where judges tend to be more open to EU law arguments. The litigant should look for a court that accepts for itself a role filling in lacunae in legal texts, making references to the ECJ when necessary, and setting aside contradictory national laws. The judges must also be willing to challenge both national legal precedent and political bodies—something required when litigants use the EU legal system to influence national policy.

68. Dehousse 1998, 173.
69. Kokott 1998, 124.
70. Golub 1996.
71. Chalmers 2000a.
72. Harlow 1996, 31.

*Step 4: Following Through on Decisions: Creating Political
and Financial Costs*

Just because the ECJ decides in favor of the plaintiff challenging national policy, one should not assume that the government will change its policy. The government may simply compensate the litigant while leaving the legislation in effect and administrative policy unchanged. Or it can change the language of a national law to technically comply with the decision, without significantly changing domestic policy. Or it can simply ignore an adverse ECJ ruling, knowing that the plaintiff likely will not endeavor to have the decision enforced and that the government will not lose an election because it failed to respond to the ECJ's legal decision.

An ECJ decision is likely to lead directly to a change in national policy in certain cases. Anne-Marie Slaughter has claimed that the more a national political ethos supports the rule of law, the more likely groups are to castigate government actions that violate the rule of law and the more likely a government is to change its policy in light of a legal decision.[73] Also, if a legal decision is made in an area of high political salience, where the government can anticipate copy-cat cases or political pressure, legislators are more likely to respond to the decision automatically. An ECJ decision is also more likely to influence the policy in the country that referred the case, because at least there the national court will be likely to enforce the decision.[74]

In many cases, however, translating a legal victory into a policy victory will take follow-through—a second strategy to show a government that there will be costs (financial, political, or both) to not changing its policy. Follow-through has taken a number of forms. Harlow and Richard Rawlings give examples of interest groups publishing pamphlets advertising the EU legal rights of citizens and including a complaint form and of groups distributing videos explaining how to use the EU legal process. In some cases groups have solicited complaints through mass mailings, simultaneously submitting them to the government and the Commission with demands for legislative change.[75] Michael McCann highlighted another strategy where litigation was used to dramatize issues to strengthen political movements, and favorable decisions were invoked in bargaining with employers and public bodies.[76] Combining a legal victory with a political strategy shows the government that the legal case will not be isolated and that faced with a legal challenge, the government would likely lose.

When are we most likely to find follow-through from an EU law legal victory and thus have a legal decision that leads to policy change? Little research has been done

---

73. Slaughter 1995a. Technically, all EU member states are rule-of-law liberal democracies, thus there should be little variation in compliance across them. Yet it is clear that certain EU countries have worse compliance rates than others with ECJ decisions. Furthermore, even the clearly more law-abiding countries have been willing at times to ignore an ECJ decision.

74. Studies have found that national courts nearly always enforce ECJ rulings they receive as a result of their preliminary ruling reference. See Dashwood and Arnull 1984; Kellermann, Levelt-Overmars, and Posser 1990; and Wils 1993.

75. See Harlow and Rawlings 1992, 276; and Meier 1994.

76. McCann 1994.

on this question; thus most of what follows should be taken as hypotheses rather than findings.[77] Private litigants might be satisfied with winning their cases and have less incentive to make sure that the government changes its policy. However, when organized interests or repeat players use litigation with the intent of influencing public policy, the resulting decision is more likely to be invoked in bargaining with the government. From this one can hypothesize that interest group or repeat-player litigation (when successful) is more likely to create policy change than a decision in a one-shot case raised by a private litigant.[78]

It is also possible that legal victories can be picked up by groups to create broader policy change. Drawing on Mancur Olson, Conant argues that distribution of the costs and benefits will influence whether groups mobilize in the aftermath of a legal decision. If there are significant benefits to be won by securing a change in policy, and these benefits fall narrowly on a group of people, it is more likely that individuals and groups will mobilize around a legal decision. When the benefits are distributed widely, an ECJ decision will garner less mobilization. Conant also points out that if the costs of policy change are narrowly focused, there can be a countermobilization against a legal decision. In this case the outcome will be a "compromised acceptance" of an ECJ decision, with the government working out a compromise with the groups involved, and perhaps also with the EU institutions. ECJ decisions where the costs are distributed widely, and the benefits distributed narrowly, may lead to policy change without countermobilization and thus a full acceptance of the decision.[79]

Certainly groups are more likely to mobilize when benefits are narrowly focused than when they are widely distributed, but there are numerous examples of groups mobilizing even when the benefits are unevenly distributed.[80] In each case, however, the groups mobilizing around the legal victory were preexisting. One could add to Conant's hypothesis that legal decisions in areas where there are preexisting mobilized interests are more likely to provoke follow-through. The earlier hypotheses on group mobilization may be less important at the follow-through stage: groups with narrow mandates and single issue concerns that start a litigation strategy are likely to follow through on it; however, even encompassing groups may draw on a favorable legal decision in bargaining.

Interaction Effects of the Four Steps in the Litigation Process

I summarize in Table 3 the factors that can influence each step of the litigation process. I have categorized the factors according to whether they create cross-national and/or cross-issue variation, and, where possible, I have developed hypoth-

---

77. Most work on the political impact of ECJ decisions has focused on the influence of ECJ jurisprudence on EU policy.

78. Dehousse 1998, 111.

79. Conant 1998, chap. 3. Conant supports these arguments with case study analyses of national responses to EU liberalization and ECJ jurisprudence involving two industries (electricity and telecommunications) in three countries (the United Kingdom, France, and Germany).

80. Alter and Vargas find groups mobilizing around issues of equal pay, and Harlow and Rawlings significant mobilization of consumer groups and environmental groups. See Alter and Vargas 2000; and Harlow and Rawlings 1992.

TABLE 3. *Factors influencing the four steps in the EU legal process*

Step of legal process	Sources of cross-national variation	Sources of cross-issue variation	Where and when the EU legal system will most likely be used to influence domestic policy
Step 1: When will EU law provide a legal basis to challenge national policy?	For most EU legal texts, all states have the same legal obligations; thus these texts do not give rise to cross-national variation. Opt-out clauses in a few EU agreements could create some cross-national variation in the effect of EU law on domestic policy, but this will be the exception.	Variation based on substance of EU law. Variation based on whether EU law creates direct effects. Variation based on jurisprudence of the ECJ. Variation based on political consensus of member states.	EU law is mostly concerned with economic issues with a transnational dimension, but the EU has jurisdiction in some national policy areas (such as agriculture, value-added tax, and external trade); these are the areas of national policy most likely to be affected by EU litigation. Direct effects are likely to be created by laws that take the form of regulations and by directives and treaty articles that are specific. The ECJ is more likely to rule against a national policy in areas where ECJ doctrine is well developed than where it is not.[a] The ECJ is more likely to rule against a national policy when the material and political costs of the legal decision are relatively low than when they are relatively high.[b] The ECJ is more likely to rule against a national policy when there is no political consensus against the ECJ's decision among member states.[c] When only qualified majority voting is required, the ECJ may be more susceptible to influence.[d]
Step 2: When will litigants mobilize to use EU law to promote their policy objectives?	Variation based on national procedural and legal standing rules. Variation based on litigiousness of population. Variation based on how interests are organized at domestic level (narrow groups vs. encompassing groups). Variation based on access of domestic groups to policy-making process.	Variation based on wealth and legal know-how of litigants. Variation based on magnitude of potential benefits of litigation. Variation based on how interests are organized at domestic level (narrow groups vs. encompassing groups). Variation based on access of domestic groups to policy-making process.	Private litigant challenges to national policy are more likely to arise in countries where citizens and businesses commonly use litigation to pursue interests and where the legal system generally works. Wealthy individuals and large firms are more likely than others to raise cases and be able to use the legal system to their advantage. Private litigants are more likely to raise cases when the benefits of doing so are significant.[e] Narrowly focused groups are more likely to turn to litigation than groups with broader mandates and more encompassing constituencies.[f] Groups with limited or no access to the political process are more likely to turn to litigation to promote their objectives than groups with greater access.[f]

TABLE 3. continued

Step of legal process	Sources of cross-national variation	Sources of cross-issue variation	Where and when the EU legal system will most likely be used to influence domestic policy
Step 3: When will national judges refer cases and apply ECJ jurisprudence?	Variation in rules of access to legal bodies (influences judicial behavior toward EU law). Variation in national legal training (may influence judicial identity and judicial behavior toward EU law).	Variation in rules of access to legal bodies (influences judicial behavior toward EU law). Variation in legal substance (leads some national courts to deal with EU legal issues more than other courts, influencing number of references but not necessarily judicial openness to EU law and ECJ jurisprudence). Variation in judicial identity (influences judicial behavior toward EU law). Variation in how EU law affects the independence, influence, and authority of judges (influences judicial willingness to send references and accept ECJ jurisprudence). Variation in the policy and legal impact of EU law on national law (influences judicial willingness to refer cases and accept ECJ jurisprudence).	If litigants indicate a willingness to pay and wait for a preliminary ruling decision, the likelihood of a referral increases. Legally uncontroversial ECJ decisions are more likely than controversial decisions to be accepted by national courts. A legal issue is more likely to be heard by the ECJ when litigants can forum-shop for sympathetic judges than when they cannot. Lower courts are often more willing than higher courts to make a reference.[g] Courts with judges who have not previously served for long periods in the national administration are more likely than others to be sympathetic to challenges to national policy.

TABLE 3. continued

Step of legal process	Sources of cross-national variation	Sources of cross-issue variation	Where and when the EU legal system will most likely be used to influence domestic policy
Step 4: When will a legal victory lead to policy change? When are litigants likely to follow through on a legal victory?	Variation based on effectiveness of national legal system and political elite's belief in and general adherence to a rule of law.	Variation based on the political salience of the ECJ decision and the likelihood that the decision will mobilize domestic actors. Variation based on whether the ECJ decision was made in a case referred by a national court in the country targeted to change its policy. Variation based on whether the case was brought by a "repeat player" and/or has interest group support. Variation based on the size and distribution of potential benefits of policy change in light of a legal decision. Variation based on the organization of domestic interests.	The more a country tends to abide by its own court's decisions, the more it is likely to abide by a decision in an EU legal case.[h] National legal decisions of high political salience are more likely than other decisions to provoke mobilization and thus be respected (or legislatively overturned). Follow through on challenges to national policy is more likely to occur in cases constructed by groups or repeat players than in isolated cases raised by private litigants.[i] Follow through is more likely to occur when the benefits of policy change are narrowly focused and the costs of policy change are widely distributed.[e] Follow through is more likely to occur in policy areas where groups are mobilized and vigilant toward government behavior. Preexisting groups are more likely than others to mobilize around favorable legal decisions.

[a]Garrett et al. 1998.
[b]See Garrett et al. 1998; and Alter 1996.
[c]Alter 1998b.
[d]Tsebelis and Garrett n.d.
[e]Conant 1998.
[f]Alter and Vargas 2000.
[g]Alter forthcoming.
[h]Slaughter 1995.
[i]Dehousse 1998.

eses about where and when private litigants are most likely to successfully use the EU legal system to influence national policy.

A Challenge to Neofunctionalist Theory: Negative Interactive Effects and the Process of Disintegration

While different factors influence each step of the EU litigation process, there will clearly be interaction effects across steps. Neofunctionalist theory assumes positive interaction effects. Burley and Mattli envisioned a general harmony of interest among private litigants, national judges, legal scholars, and the ECJ propelling the process forward while they pursued their instrumental self-interests in a mutually reinforcing way.[81] Stone Sweet and Brunell expect the legal process to have its own dynamic, with litigants raising ever more cases and judges inevitably building law as they attempt to resolve disputes where the law is not clear.[82] It is true that the body of EU rules is expanding, driven by national governments who want to build a common market and now a monetary union. Levels of trade are expanding, driven by the completion of the common market and globalization more broadly. As a result, litigants have more opportunities and incentives to draw on European law. Furthermore, evidence indicates that one litigant's success in utilizing EU law can trigger other actors to mimic the strategy. Thus plenty of suggestive material exists to support any theory that predicts legal expansion. The key question is whether neofunctionalist theory can predict or account for the limits to the process of integration that appear along the way. The failure of neofunctionalist theory to account for these limits is what originally led Ernst Haas to abandon the theory.[83]

A virtuous circle, where successful litigation encourages more cases to be raised, and more references to the ECJ may certainly emerge, but it is not the only possibility. Negative feedback loops may also emerge. Factors that undermine each step of the litigation process can reverberate through all four steps, leading to fewer cases involving EU law and a diminishing impact of EU law on national policy. Once litigants are stung by an undesirable ECJ ruling, they may hesitate to raise ambiguous cases in the future. And though reference rates continue to increase, the ambivalence of national courts toward EU law and their opposition to key tenets of ECJ jurisprudence are also increasing. If national courts are not receptive to EU legal arguments, lawyers may well advise their clients not to pursue an EU legal case. The less domestic actors are mobilized to capture the benefits of EU law, the less pressure states will be under to comply with EU law.

In addition to negative interactive effects, the success of EU legal integration may have instigated a larger backlash. Faced with unacceptable ECJ decisions, member

---

81. Burley and Mattli 1993.
82. Stone Sweet and Brunell 1998b.
83. Haas 1975. It has historically been the case that neofunctionalist theory works as long as (and only when) integration is moving forward. For a review of the rise and fall of neofunctionalist theory in the study of the EU, see Caporaso and Keeler 1995.

states have passed protocols and laws at the EU level that reverse or qualify the effects of ECJ rulings, such as the famous Barber Protocol of the Maastricht Treaty that limits the retrospective effects of the ECJ's *Barber* ruling. Although there are relatively few examples where member states have reversed the effects of ECJ rulings, states have sought to constrain the ECJ's activism. Having seen how the ECJ used legal lacunae to seize new powers and delve into areas that member states considered to be their own exclusive realm, national governments have constructed legislative barriers to ECJ legal expansion. Member states have also taken to writing clauses into EU treaties and legislation protecting national policies, sometimes in ways that violate the spirit of the EU and contradict ECJ doctrine. For example, the Danish government insisted on a provision in the Maastricht Treaty that allows it to ban Germans from buying vacation homes, and the Irish government demanded a protocol making it clear that nothing in EU law will interfere with Ireland's constitutional ban on abortion. According to the *Economist*, EU legislation is filled with secret footnotes designed to protect national policies. For example,

[The 1994] directive on data protection attracted 31 such [exception] statements. Britain secured an exemption for manual filing systems if—work this one out—the costs involved in complying with the directive outweigh the benefits. Germany secured the right to keep data about religious beliefs under wraps. Since these and other statements are not published, Joe Bloggs will know about these maneuverings only by chance or if his government chooses to tell him.[84]

These protections are designed to limit the reach of EU law, so that states do not have to change a valued national policy. States have also excluded the ECJ entirely from some of the new areas of EU powers (such as common foreign and security policy, and issues of justice and home affairs that affect domestic security and a country's internal order). And states are writing provisions into EU law that limit the ECJ from expanding the legal effects of EU law into the domestic realm. The new Treaty of Amsterdam, for example, states that policies adopted under the EU framework with respect to Article K.6 will not create direct effects—making private litigants unable to draw on them to challenge national provisions.

Having figured out that lower courts are much more willing to send references to the ECJ, and that their references are allowing the ECJ to expand its own authority and compromise national sovereignty, member states are much more reluctant to open new access to the ECJ for lower courts. Since 1968, the extension of preliminary ruling rights to lower courts has been contested and often limited when the ECJ's legal authority has been expanded to new areas of EU law.[85] Most recently, member states allowed national governments to limit the reference rights of lower courts with respect to new areas of ECJ competence gained in the Treaty of Amsterdam.[86] These efforts are aimed at limiting the future expansion of EU law into the national realm.

---

84. Seeing Through It, *The Economist*, 16 September 1995, 59.
85. Alter 1998b.
86. Article K.7 of the Treaty of Amsterdam.

Member states have also sought to regain national control over certain policy issues. The Maastricht Treaty articulates a "subsidiarity principle" authorizing the Community to undertake actions only "if and so far as the objectives of the proposed action cannot be sufficiently achieved by the member state."[87] This principle has provided a political/legal basis to repatriate powers back to the national level. Politicians, citizen groups, and journalists invoke the subsidiarity principle to argue against EU legislation. And member states have used this principle to reclaim power that the ECJ had claimed for the EU.[88] The ECJ has also invoked the concept of subsidiarity to revise its earlier jurisprudence in favor of national prerogatives.[89]

National high courts are also concerned that the EU and the ECJ have gained too much power, and they are creating their own limits on the expansive reach of EU law. Indeed, though early neofunctionalist theory predicted that greater experience would induce greater support for the process of integration, the opposite seems to have occurred. The more national courts have seen how the process of European integration is influencing the domestic administrative, political, and legal order, the more they seem willing to question the validity of EU law, of ECJ and Commission decisions, and even of their own governments' decisions taken at the EU level. For example, having seen the ECJ give expansive interpretations to the EU treaties in the past, in 1993 the German Constitutional Court ruled that ECJ interpretations that extend the treaty will not be valid in Germany.[90] The court warned the ECJ to protect Germany's subsidiarity rights, and it set limits on the German government's authority to transfer decision-making authority to the EU level.[91] In France the Conseil Constitutionnel has asserted its authority to evaluate the constitutionality of EU rules and declared that the French parliament may not ratify, validate, or authorize an international (that is, EU) engagement contrary to the constitution.[92]

87. Article 3b TEU. This clause pertains to areas that do not fall under the Community's exclusive competence. For more on this clause, see Bernard 1996.

88. For example, member states included Article 126 TEU, which instructs the EU to respect "the responsibility of the member states for the content of teaching and organization of the educational system." This clause asserts state power in an area that the ECJ had previously denied states power. Dehousse 1998, 166.

89. *French Penal Authorities v. Keck and Mithouard,* ECJ decision of 24 November 1993, C-267 and 268/91 ECR I-6097.

90. They stated: "Whereas a dynamic extension of the existing Treaties has so far been supported . . . in future it will have to be noted as regards interpretation of enabling provisions by Community institutions and agencies that the Union Treaty . . . interpretation may not have effects that are equivalent to an extension of the Treaty. Such an interpretation of enabling rules would not produce any binding effects for Germany." Interestingly, the German citizens who raised the challenge to the Maastricht Treaty were members of the European Parliament and a high-level civil servant of the European Commission. *Brunner and Others v. The European Union Treaty,* BVerfG decision of 12 October 1993, 2 BvR 2134/92 and 2 BvR 2159/92: published in *Common Market Law Reports* (hereinafter CMLR), January 1994, 57–108. Quoted from p. 105 of the decision.

91. *Brunner and Others v. The European Union Treaty,* BVerfG decision of 11 January 1994, 2 BvR 2134/92 and 2 BvR 2159/92, 57–108. For an analysis of this decision, see Weiler 1995; and Alter forthcoming, chap. 3.

92. See Maastricht I *Conseil Constitutionnel,* decision of 9 April 1992, 92–308 DC; and Case 91-294 *Conseil Constitutionnel,* decision of 25 July 1991, Schengen Decision, 1991, 173. For an analysis of these decisions, see Pellet 1998; and Zoller 1992, 280–82. Both the French and German rulings are designed to position these courts to serve as a second review, a national-level review, of the validity of EU law in the

By opening up the possibility of national constitutional constraints to EU law, supreme courts have also created a national means for individuals, groups, and minority factions to challenge deals made at the EU level.[93] German Länder governments have drawn on the German constitution to challenge an EU directive regarding television programming that the ECJ had upheld,[94] and German importers of restricted bananas have used German courts and the German constitution to challenge the EU's banana regime.[95] These examples show that national and EU legal systems can also be used by private litigants to challenge advances in European integration agreed to by their governments.

Certainly, as long as European governments seek to facilitate more trade through drafting common rules, the present trajectory toward more integration and more EU law will continue. But negative feedback between the four steps of the litigation process can undermine the influence of EU law on domestic policy. Clearly, even in the legal realm the forces that led to increased legalization in the past are not now nearly so unidirectional. Indeed, even Burley and Mattli have backed away from their neofunctionalist argument, noting that neofunctionalism has "no tools to determine when self-interest will align with further integration . . . and when it will not."[96]

Burley and Mattli suggest returning to midrange theories about private litigant and national court behavior, like the hypotheses explored here. But there is certainly also room to theorize more broadly on the systematic factors that contribute to moves toward disintegration. There is much to suggest that the forces for disintegration are created by the process of European integration itself.[97] As European integration expands, it upsets more national policies. As more power is transferred to EU institutions, national actors (national courts, national administrators, national parliaments, and national interest groups) find their own influence, independence, and autonomy undermined. These actors may in the past have used the EU legal and political system to promote their objectives, and they may continue to do so when convenient. But they are also quite willing to use both EU and national political and legal systems to challenge EU authority in order to protect their influence, independence, and authority, and when doing so promotes specific objectives. The ECJ's intermediaries are often fair-weather friends. Much to the surprise of the ECJ and pro-integration actors, they are increasingly vocal critics, too.

---

national realm. Their goal is to pressure the ECJ to scrutinize the validity of EU law more carefully, to take national judicial concerns into account in its decision making, and to be more sensitive to national sovereignty considerations. Supreme courts also hope to influence their governments to be more careful in what they agree to at the EU level. Alter forthcoming.

93. Because French citizens cannot bring cases to the Conseil Constitutionnel, they are less able to use the French legal system to challenge the constitutionality of EU law. Some observers speculate that the Conseil d'État may eventually create a means for private litigants in France to invoke the French constitution to challenge EU law.

94. *Bayerische Staatsregierung v. Bundesregierung,* BVerfG decision of 11 April 1989, 2 BvG 1/89, *CMLR* 1990 1 649–655; and BVerfG decision of 22 March 1995, 2 BvG 1/89, EuGRZ 1995, 125–37.

95. See Cassia and Saulnier 1997; Everling 1996; and Reich 1996.

96. Mattli and Slaughter 1998b, 185.

97. For an argument to this effect, see Dehousse 1998, 173; and Suleiman 1995.

Generalizing from the European Case to Elsewhere

The European legal system has some unique attributes that have allowed it to contribute to legalization in Europe and that give it leverage to influence domestic policy. Access to the ECJ is far wider than for most international legal bodies, with states, the European Commission, and private litigants empowered to use the EU legal system to challenge national policy. The wide access gives the ECJ more opportunities to influence national policy, and the numerous cases have allowed the ECJ to develop EU law incrementally, a strategy that has been important in building support for its jurisprudence and enhancing the effectiveness of the EU legal system.[98] The EU's preliminary ruling system is also unique. It is hard to underestimate how much the preliminary ruling mechanism has mattered in creating a national source of pressure to comply with EU law and in coordinating national legal interpretation across countries.

Because of the unique nature of the EU legal system, the EU experience is not necessarily the model of what will happen in other international legal systems. The framework developed in this article, however, can help one think about how international legal mechanisms can be used to influence national policy in other contexts.[99] The four steps of the litigation process identified in this article still need to be fulfilled for international legal mechanisms to be a tool for domestic actors to pressure for change in domestic policy. But the factors influencing each step will vary because both the source of international law and the intermediaries in the legal process will be different.

The first step in the EU litigation process involves having a body of EU law that can be invoked in a legal system to challenge national policy. There are many international legal texts that can be invoked by legal bodies (national and international) to challenge national policies. But the ability of litigants to invoke this law will vary depending on the binding nature of the legal text, on whether the national system recognizes the legal text as creating direct effects, and on access and legal standing rules that will influence whether or not litigants can effectively use the legal system to challenge a country's policy. As in the EU case, limitations created by the law and the allocation of legal standing will engender biases by which actors can benefit from the law. Because of biases, international rules may significantly advantage some domestic groups (such as economic actors favoring liberalization) over other domestic groups. This bias helps explain why some actors oppose increased international legalization.

The second step of the litigation process involves mobilizing the potential beneficiaries to draw on international law and use the international legal mechanisms. Where private litigants have access to international legal mechanisms, the factors identified in this article—such as the magnitude of potential benefits and how interests are organized—could matter. Indeed, Christina Sevilla's study on the use of the

---

98. See Burley and Mattli 1993; Hartley 1994; Helfer and Slaughter 1997; and Weiler 1991.
99. The framework could apply to domestic situations as well.

GATT legal mechanisms confirms Conant's hypothesis that most cases are brought by and targeted at the largest trading countries where the potential benefits are the highest.[100]

Where only states have access to legal systems, the dynamics will be different. States tend to be more reluctant than private litigants or national courts to use international legal mechanisms. Governments often fear that the outcome of a legal case could be worse than a negotiated outcome, that a legal ruling could create domestic backlash, or that a legal ruling will be less flexible, tying the hands of governments in the future.[101] This is in large part why Robert Keohane, Andrew Moravcsik, and Anne-Marie Slaughter expect legalization to progress further in transnational compared with interstate legal systems.[102] National governments still might have an incentive to please a domestic group by raising a case. In this situation, domestic political factors, such as the extent to which interest groups can penetrate the political system,[103] the political strength of the domestic group desiring the legal case, and where the party in charge of the government finds its largest domestic political support, will likely be important. International-level factors, such as the relations between the state raising the case and the target state and the number of other interstate issues of potentially higher priority, will also likely influence a state's calculations.[104]

The third step in the EU case—finding national judicial support—is not a factor in legal systems where states or litigants raise their cases directly in front of an international legal body. But in some international systems an international commission or a public prosecutor acts as a gatekeeper deciding whether or not to bring a case to court (such as the original system of the European Convention on Human Rights, the present system for the Inter-American Court of Human Rights, and the proposed system for the International Criminal Court). Where it is up to the discretion of a commission or prosecutor to pursue a legal violation, the factors shaping these actors' decisions will matter. Some of the factors identified here will surely matter, such as the legal rules defining the mandate of the commission or prosecutor, how the commission or prosecutor understands its mandate, and how a case influences the political process. In addition, the ability or inability of the commission or prosecutor to find relevant facts or gather evidence will likely shape what types of cases are pursued.[105]

Follow-through, the fourth step, will also be important in other international legal contexts. Few international legal bodies are able to issue sanctions against states. In most cases a political body must authorize or take a separate action to create a penalty for a violation of international law. It cannot be assumed that states will follow through on their legal victories. Following through on a legal victory might be more

---

100. Sevilla 1997.
101. See Alter 2000; and Levi 1976.
102. See Keohane, Moravcsik, and Slaughter, this issue.
103. For example, Super 301 in the United States virtually forces the executive branch to investigate and act on complaints raised by U.S. firms.
104. Alter 2000.
105. Helfer and Slaughter 1997.

costly than initiating legal proceedings. And time will certainly have elapsed between the original decision to raise a legal case and the potential decision to pressure for sanctions against the offending state, allowing other political factors to be put on the agenda and other political actors to assume control of the government. Because states—not groups, as in the European context—are the actors that must follow through, the factors influencing whether follow-through will occur will be different. But in contexts outside of Europe, this step will be no less important, and possibly even more important, than in the EU.

The European legal system is unique in its ability to be used by domestic actors to pressure for change in national policy. There is great variation in the ways private litigants actually do use the EU legal system to influence national policy, and private litigants can also use the EU legal system to challenge EU policies and rules. For political scientists who prize parsimony, the answer to the questions of where and when domestic actors will use the EU legal system to influence national policy is, unfortunately, complex. Even assuming rational behavior, no human error, and full information—unsustainable assumptions to be sure—where EU law influences national policy depends on the wording of the EU law, on ECJ legal doctrine and ECJ decision making, on private litigant mobilization, on national court support, and on follow-through. Some of these factors will matter in other international contexts. And there are likely additional factors that are important because the main intermediaries in other international legal systems differ. I have been able to suggest only a few factors that might matter in other contexts. There is fertile ground for future research.

NAFTA and the Legalization of World Politics: A Case Study

Frederick M. Abbott

In this article I analyze the North American Free Trade Agreement (NAFTA) in the context of a broader project examining the causes and consequences of the legalization of world politics.[1] Governments are continuously engaged in the process of negotiating international trade agreements, and in each case negotiators are confronted with choices regarding the best mode of legalization to accomplish their agreed upon objectives. By closely analyzing the choices made by governments over time and correlating those choices with the results achieved (in the context of stated objectives), political scientists and lawyers may aid in directing government negotiators to preferred legalization options.

The form of legalization represented in NAFTA is characteristic of a trend toward higher levels of precision, obligation, and delegation in international trade regulation that has been ongoing since the adoption of the General Agreement on Tariffs and Trade (GATT) in 1947.[2] The specific institutional and juridical framework of NAFTA reflects particularized objectives of Canadian, Mexican, and U.S. trade negotiators, pursued under constraints imposed by their political negotiating environment. NAFTA embodies a high degree of precision and obligation and a moderate degree of delegation of decision-making authority. The legalization formula of the World Trade Organization (WTO) agreement is substantially similar.[3] The charter of the European Union (EU), in contrast, embodies a high degree of obligation and delegation and a moderate level of precision. Though the negotiators of the NAFTA, WTO, and EU

I thank Robert Keohane and Anne-Marie Slaughter as well as the editors of *International Organization* for their helpful comments and suggestions.

1. Canada–Mexico–United States: North American Free Trade Agreement, done 8–17 December 1992, entered into force on 1 January 1994, 32 I.L.M. 289 and 605.

2. General Agreement on Tariffs and Trade, opened for signature on 30 October 1947, 61 Stat. A3, T.I.A.S. No. 1700, 55 U.N.T.S. 187.

3. Agreement Establishing the World Trade Organization, done 15 April 1994, entered into force 1 January 1995. World Trade Organization 1995. The WTO agreement incorporates by reference a number of multilateral trade agreements, including GATT 1994, as well as agreements and understandings ancillary to GATT 1994. I use the term *WTO agreement* to refer to the Agreement Establishing the WTO plus the multilateral trade agreements and ancillary texts, unless otherwise indicated expressly or by context.

International Organization 54, 3, Summer 2000, pp. 135–163

agreements adopted somewhat different institutional and juridical models, they each preferred "hard" law to "soft" law. In this article I analyze NAFTA and explain the preference for using hard law in international economic arrangements. I suggest that hard law (1) reduces intergovernmental transaction costs associated with trade and investment, (2) reduces private risk premiums associated with trade and investment, (3) promotes transparency and provides corollary participation benefits, (4) tends to restrain strategic political behaviors, and (5) may increase the range of integration effects by encouraging private actions to enforce intergovernmental obligations.

The trend toward hard law in international economic relations is rooted in governmental experience with the legal charter of the institution formed in the wake of World War II to promote trade and development—GATT 1947. GATT 1947 was drafted in relatively imprecise terms and incorporated a relatively low level of obligation and delegation of dispute settlement authority.[4] As governments implemented that "soft" agreement, it became apparent that its legalization formula was not adequate to address complex second- and third-generation trade barriers.[5] Beginning with the Tokyo Round negotiations in 1974–79,[6] and through the Uruguay Round negotiations that formally commenced in 1986, governments sought to enhance the levels of specificity, delegation of dispute settlement authority, and obligation in GATT, culminating with the conclusion of the WTO agreement in 1994.[7] The Canada–U.S. Free Trade Agreement,[8] on which the NAFTA was modeled, and NAFTA were negotiated during the Uruguay Round by trade negotiators participating directly and indirectly in the GATT negotiations.

NAFTA was designed to promote market liberalization and to encourage capital flows, not to create a political union. Precise rules were adopted along with regional institutions that lack the power to adopt supplementary legislation. The agreement manifests a high level of obligation by way of terms that import binding commitment; these terms are not offset by exceptional opt-out provisions. However, a moderate level of authority is delegated to dispute-settlement mechanisms. There was no political support for a strong regional judicial body that would significantly restrict the autonomy of the parties. The creation of such a judicial body would have raised serious constitutional issues within the parties and may have precluded the conclusion of an agreement.

4. For a definitive description of GATT as a soft-law system, see Long 1985. I traced the evolution from soft to hard legalization in the GATT/WTO context and undertook a detailed analysis of that trend in Abbott 1997a.

5. Second-generation trade barriers refer to nontariff governmental measures directed toward trade, such as quotas, export subsidies, antidumping measures, and voluntary restraints. Third-generation trade barriers refer to internal government regulatory measures not specifically directed toward trade, but which may distort international competition, such as services regulatory measures, intellectual property norms (over- or under-protection), and competition policies (over- or under-regulatory). See, for example, Cottier 1992; and Hillman 1997.

6. On the Tokyo Round negotiations, see Glick 1984.

7. For background regarding the objectives of the Uruguay Round negotiations, see Jackson 1989; Petersmann and Hilf 1988; and Hudec 1993. For details concerning the negotiating history, see Stewart 1993–99.

8. Free Trade Agreement Between Canada and the United States of America, signed on 2 January 1988, entered into force on 1 January 1989, 1989 Can. T.S. No. 3.

The European Community (EC) treaty—the charter of the EU—employs a different legalization formula than employed by NAFTA or the WTO agreement. Hard legalization in the EU trade context is achieved by a relatively imprecise charter coupled with a high degree of delegation to institutions that may promulgate secondary legislation with more precise content. The objective of providing rules that more adequately address second- and third-generation trade barriers is achieved, but only through a continuing legislative and judicial process. The EU contemplates achieving substantially broader social objectives than NAFTA or the WTO.[9] Neither the parties to NAFTA nor the members of the WTO had the political option of establishing the high level of delegation represented in the EU institutions, and neither arrangement sought to broadly address social issues. Determining whether the legalization formula in NAFTA or in the EU is better suited to achieving its objectives is not feasible at this stage. The objectives of the arrangements are not the same, which argues against directly comparing the formulas.[10]

A counter-example to the NAFTA/WTO formula is represented by the Asia-Pacific Economic Cooperation (APEC) forum. APEC is characterized by low levels of precision, delegation, and obligation.[11] The APEC formula was adopted in the context of historically nonlegalized cultures and by governments that had not agreed on particular objectives.[12] APEC is not a successful model of regional economic integration. It may be viewed as a failed experiment in alternative legalization or as a transitional model serving as a predicate to harder legalization.[13]

NAFTA has so far been implemented largely in accordance with its terms, despite the period of economic turbulence generated by the Mexican peso crisis of 1994–95. The period of NAFTA implementation has witnessed substantial increases in cross-border trade among its parties and significantly heightened transborder capital flows. On their face, these developments might suggest that NAFTA has aided in achieving the economic objectives of its parties; however, the parties have maintained political policies supportive of NAFTA's objectives throughout this period. The period of NAFTA implementation has coincided with sustained economic expansion in the United States, the dominant economic actor in the arrangement. It may plausibly be argued that the parties would have achieved the same objectives, with comparable results, without NAFTA. NAFTA has yet to face sustained circumstances in which

---

9. For detailed comparison of underlying social and economic policies, see, for example, Abbott 1992a,b and 1997b. For general background regarding the EU legal and social framework, see Weiler 1991. For a review of EC governance preceding the Single European Act and subsequent reforms, see Riesenfeld 1974.

10. Moreover, an empirical comparison of the two arrangements would require a large-scale investment of resources well beyond the scope of the present project.

11. See Fried 1998; and Schoenbaum 1998.

12. Kahler, this issue.

13. Other counter-examples to the NAFTA model of legalization are the NAFTA supplemental agreements on the environment and labor. In preliminary drafts of this article I suggested that these soft agreements have had a very modest effect on the conduct of the parties and that their major impact has been in promoting transnational cooperation among NGOs. To keep this article to a manageable length, I have excluded discussion of these supplemental agreements.

legal norms and political policies diverge, and the durability of its legalization effects are thus relatively indeterminate.

The implementation of NAFTA has yielded certain unanticipated results. The transnational (investor-to-state) investment-related dispute settlement mechanism has been invoked by private investors in circumstances that were not contemplated by NAFTA negotiators. This lends support to the postulate that transnational dispute settlement may broaden the scope of subject matter affected by an international trade agreement.[14] The record of NAFTA implementation to date supports the use of hard law instruments in international economic relations.

Factors Generally Influencing the Choice of the NAFTA Legalization Formula

The negotiation of NAFTA was initiated following the conclusion and entry into force (in 1989) of the Canada–U.S. Free Trade Area (CUSFTA). Mexico proposed a bilateral free trade agreement to the United States; this proposal was accepted by the United States, and the negotiations were thereafter trilateralized to include Canada. Mexico sought to accelerate a domestic transition from a protectionist/statist economy to an open/market economy, and to ameliorate the internal social disruption accompanying this transition.[15] The United States sought to improve conditions of market access in Mexico for U.S. investors and traders, which had been a long-term U.S. economic objective. A corollary economic objective was to provide a counterweight to the growing economic influence of the EU.[16] The United States also sought to improve economic conditions in Mexico so as to relieve pressures that resulted in emigration to the United States.[17] Canada joined the NAFTA negotiations largely for defensive economic purposes.[18] Canada had little economic interest in Mexico prior to the NAFTA negotiations but understood the U.S. design for a phased opening of the Latin American market and wanted to be an active participant in this longer-term process.

Neither Canada, Mexico, or the United States entered into NAFTA negotiations with the objective of creating a political or social union on the North American continent. An enduring theme of Canadian politics is the maintenance of independence from the United States. The CUSFTA negotiations were perceived by a significant portion of Canadians as a threat to Canadian independence, and this factor nearly resulted in Parliament refusing to approve the agreement.[19] Mexican politics has likewise been dominated by a theme of independence from the United States, and the government of Mexico did not approach the NAFTA negotiations with an intention for political integration with its northern neighbor.[20] The United States has his-

---

14. Keohane, Moravcsik, and Slaughter, this issue.
15. See Nadal 1997; and Ramos Uriarte 1995.
16. Abbott 1993a.
17. Johnson 1994.
18. Kennish 1995.
19. Hurtig 1992.
20. Ramos Uriarte 1995, 90–91.

torically resisted participation in international institutional arrangements perceived as jeopardizing its political autonomy.[21] There was nothing about the proposed NAFTA that suggested a change in this long-running U.S. perspective.

For the United States, NAFTA negotiations were initiated and largely concluded under the Republican administration of President George Bush and under the direction of U.S. Trade Representative Carla Hills.[22] The U.S. Republican party and its industry-producer base of support espouse the minimization of government intrusion into activities of the business sector; from the standpoint of the Republican party and the Bush administration there was no perceived incentive for creating a regional institutional/bureaucratic structure with the power to regulate business activities.[23] Canada generally pursues more interventionist social welfare policies than the United States, and a significant part of the Canadian electorate would perceive the possible integration of Canadian regulatory institutions with those of the United States and Mexico as a threat to its social policies.[24] Mexican trade negotiators would logically fear, in light of the trade-weighted imbalance in the power of the two governments, that joint regulatory institutions with the United States would be dominated by the United States.[25] There was no political motivation on any side of the NAFTA negotiations for establishing a strong regional bureaucracy comparable to the EU.

The European Economic Community (preceded by the European Coal and Steel Community) was created in the early 1950s under a much different political dynamic than that confronted by the NAFTA parties.[26] Continental Europe had been devastated by war, and there was a very strong economic incentive to rationalize the continental economy so as to accelerate rebuilding and growth. The political institutions within the continental European nations were relatively weak, and a group of political leaders encouraged the creation of regional institutions as a means to promote long-term European security. Furthermore, industry and labor leaders believed that regional European institutions might work to their advantage. This confluence of political and economic interests allowed the formation of relatively strong regional political institutions—that is, political institutions embodying a high degree of authority delegated from member states. No comparable confluence was present in respect to NAFTA.

NAFTA and Precision

NAFTA is drafted in precise terms in order to: (1) reduce potential transaction costs of *ex post facto* intergovernmental bargaining, (2) clarify the environment in which business will be conducted and thereby reduce risk premiums paid by private enter-

21. Keohane, Moravcsik, and Slaughter, this issue.
22. Abbott 1992a.
23. Abbott 1997b, 910–12.
24. Barlow and Campbell 1993.
25. Although both Canada and Mexico might see advantages to having regional regulatory institutions in which each country was a co-equal with the United States, this prospect was most unlikely, and thus there was little incentive for establishing a regional regulatory/bureaucratic framework.
26. Haas 1958.

prises, (3) constrain government strategic behaviors, (4) guide government bureaucrats in its administration, and (5) provide transparency. The high level of precision in NAFTA is coupled with a moderate level of delegation to regional institutions for *ex post facto* decision making. The NAFTA model was chosen as a consequence of the particular political constellation in which its trade negotiators were operating.

NAFTA is among the most highly detailed international trade agreements ever negotiated between governments. It comprises twenty-two chapters setting forth specific obligations on trade in goods, services, financial services, investment, intellectual property rights, technical barriers to trade, sanitary and phytosanitary measures, safeguards measures, and dispute settlement.[27] It incorporates a panoply of annexes that elaborate the extent (and limits) of obligations by reference, among other things, to the internal legislation of its parties. NAFTA is broader in scope of coverage (for example, addressing general investment measures) than the WTO agreement, and it is comparable in level of detail to the WTO agreement. NAFTA was drafted at a level of detail substantially higher than the EC treaty, bearing in mind that NAFTA does not envision the adoption of secondary legislation in the sense of the EC treaty.

As a general proposition, increasing the level of detail in a written agreement should result in reducing ambiguity or uncertainty concerning its meaning, unless the drafters deliberately set out to create uncertainty. The precise terms of NAFTA appear designed to clarify rather than obscure its meaning. This can be objectively demonstrated by generally accepted sentence structure, use of terms common to the field of international trade, and the incorporation of definitions in cases in which ambiguity might otherwise be substantial. Although certain highly technical provisions of NAFTA (such as the rules of origin for automobiles and parts) have been criticized for their complexity,[28] this complexity may reflect the complexity of the underlying subject matter.[29] Although no legal text is without ambiguity, it appears reasonable to conclude that the meticulous drafting of NAFTA accomplishes the objective of clarifying the obligations of its parties.

The criterion of precision does not address the substantive content of legal norms. Precise rules may be used to accomplish disparate goals. In the trade regulation context, a precise rule may enhance or inhibit trade and economic welfare.[30] That NAFTA is characterized by a high level of precision does not imply any value judgment about the content of NAFTA rules.

The level of precision in NAFTA is similar to the level of precision in CUSFTA, which preceded it.[31] For this reason, we may assume that the high level of precision in NAFTA is not the result of factors specific to Mexico. The contemporaneous evolution of precise international and regional trade agreements may be explained by

---

27. Abbott 1995a.

28. See interview observations of the Japanese business sector reported in Abbott 1995a, chap. 8.

29. As noted *infra* tan 49, the very high level of precision regarding rules of origin for automobiles and parts addressed a major Canadian government concern over alleged prior misuse of CUSFTA rules of origin by the United States.

30. Abbott 1997a, 45–46.

31. The annexes to NAFTA include a somewhat higher level of detail in relation to party legislative measures than set forth in CUSFTA.

the prior experience of governments in implementing less precise rules, particularly in the absence of a high level of delegated authority.[32] For Canada, Mexico, and the United States, the same groups of individuals who negotiated in the GATT also negotiated CUSFTA and NAFTA.[33] Each of the agreements was drafted to interface with the others.[34] The lessons of GATT 1947 and the Tokyo Round agreements were appreciated in relation to NAFTA.[35] Among these lessons was that imprecise trade rules would lead to higher intergovernmental transaction costs and create a drag on private-sector economic activity.

Intergovernmental Transaction Costs

More precise rules should provide clearer signals to governments about the nature of their obligations. Such rules should reduce intergovernmental bargaining subsequent to the conclusion of an agreement.[36] They should reduce the need to bargain over the mechanics of implementation.[37] Dispute settlement is an *ex post* bargaining mecha-

---

32. As is well known, GATT 1947 entered into force as a provisional agreement in contemplation of a more extensive set of trade rules that would have been established by the Havana Charter for the International Trade Organization. GATT 1947 was framed largely as a broad set of negative rules, prohibiting governments from engaging in certain types of discriminatory and trade restrictive conduct. The history of GATT 1947 through to the Uruguay Round was a process of refining broad rules into more precise obligations. This process took place most particularly in the Tokyo Round, which culminated in 1979 and resulted in a series of codes (or supplemental agreements) covering a number of subject matter areas already addressed in general terms by GATT 1947. The GATT contracting parties negotiated more precise rules because the existing general provisions of GATT 1947 did not provide an adequate basis on which governments could demand compliance and were not capable of sufficiently precise application by dispute-settlement panels. For example, the GATT contracting parties were considerably dissatisfied with the application of antidumping and countervailing duty measures by the United States (and the EU); there was considerable concern with the EC's flexible interpretation of GATT export subsidy provisions; and GATT panels had considerable difficulty interpreting the safeguards provisions of GATT 1947 insofar as they related to health and safety measures. See texts cited in note 7.

33. Regarding the structure of the U.S. trade policy apparatus that, because of the small number of USTR negotiators, virtually assures that the same individuals will participate in important negotiations, see Abbott 1997b, 941–42. It was accepted that NAFTA negotiations diverted attention from the Uruguay Round negotiations because the same individuals at USTR could not be negotiating in two fora at the same time. Ibid. The Canadian trade policy apparatus operates along much the same lines.

34. Abbott forthcoming.

35. The Tokyo Round Antidumping Code, the Subsidies and Countervailing Duties Code, and the Technical Standards Code each represented the efforts of the GATT contracting parties to clarify obligations that were generally embodied in provisions of GATT 1947. The Uruguay Round negotiations were in substantial measure devoted to further clarifying the general rules in the aforementioned areas, as well in the areas of import licensing, rules of origin, sanitary and phytosanitary measures, agricultural subsidies, and trade-related investment preferences. The Uruguay Round also added precise new rules regarding third-generation trade barriers in the areas of services and trade-related aspects of intellectual property rights.

36. Coase suggested that transaction costs associated with the bargaining process may have a significant impact on economic efficiency. Coase 1960. Robert Hudec observes that, "A rule-based system is the most resource-efficient way to resolve conflicts with other countries." Hudec 1999, 10.

37. If the NAFTA parties agree that tariffs will be phased out between them, but do not indicate which tariffs will be phased out over what period of time, the chances are great that they will need to bargain *ex post* over the specific mechanics of tariff reduction. If the parties agree that imports from third countries will not enjoy tariff-free transit between the parties, but do not agree on the conditions under which third-party goods will be deemed to have been transformed into regionally originating goods, then the

nism. It would seem likely that, other things being equal, the chances of disputes being referred to arbitration would decrease as rules become more precise; that is, as the apparent scope for deviations from norms are reduced, governments should be less likely to differ over what measures are within and outside their prescriptions.[38]

The two major adverse consequences of *ex post* bargaining among governments are slower implementation of intergovernmental commitments and the uncertainty generated in respect to private operators seeking to transact business in an unsettled environment.[39] That the slower implementation of commitments will have adverse economic consequences assumes that governments have agreed on measures that promote economic efficiency and economic welfare (for example, that governments have agreed to implement commitments enhancing market access). If governments have agreed on commitments whose implementation would have adverse economic consequences, then increased *ex post* bargaining and delay might be beneficial.

There are transaction costs involved in *ex ante* bargaining (that is, in the process of negotiating an international trade agreement); and in order to determine a preference for more precise rules *ex ante* it is necessary to establish that the *ex ante* transaction costs of reaching a precise agreement will be lower than the *ex post* transaction costs of elaborating the terms of an imprecise agreement.[40]

For several reasons, *ex ante* bargaining costs over the terms of a precise agreement are likely to be lower than *ex post* bargaining costs over the terms of an imprecise agreement, particularly in the absence of delegation of decision-making authority regarding implementation of the agreement to standing institutions.[41] Governments

---

chances are great that the parties will need to bargain *ex post* over rules of origin and criteria for transformation.

38. If an increase should occur in the frequency of disputes because governments are in a better position to assert claims concerning their entitlements, then the precise terms on which such claims are based should reduce the duration of these disputes. Precise terms should provide better guidance to parties as to the extent of their obligations, and this should decrease the frequency of disputes over the nature of implementation obligations. Paradoxically, however, precise terms may also encourage a greater frequency of *ex post* dispute-settlement actions as parties become more certain about their capacity to vindicate perceived rights. Yet, if the nature of obligations is precisely defined, it would also be expected that parties would more frequently settle disputes in the course of consultations. While more precise rules might at least initially increase the frequency of dispute-settlement actions, it is also foreseeable that such actions would be of shorter duration (and thus result in relatively low transaction costs). As governments became more certain that the outcome of disputes would be strongly correlated to precise legal rules, the necessity for pursuing claims to a litigious end would likely diminish. Abbott 1997a, 43–44. Empirical support for the proposition that more precise rules may lead to an increased frequency of disputes, but that these disputes may be substantially more prone to settlement, can be found in Hudec 1999, 25–27. Hudec found that in the first three years of operation of the WTO, the frequency with which consultations had been initiated was greater than in respect to the GATT 1947 dispute-settlement system, but that a significantly lower percentage of disputes resulted in the issuance of panel reports.

39. The effect of uncertainty on private operators is considered in the next section.

40. We might assume that the *ex ante* costs of negotiating an imprecise trade agreement would be lower than the *ex ante* costs of negotiating a precise agreement. The government negotiators involved would have fewer tasks to accomplish. Agreement would be easier as each government considered itself to retain flexibility in implementation. There are, however, caveats to this premise.

41. Recall that bargaining costs not only relate to costs imposed on governments to conduct negotiations but also include delays in the implementation of commitments assumed to have beneficial economic welfare effects.

are able *ex ante* to focus their attention on a particular trade agreement and to intensively consult across a broad range of subjects.[42] The start-up costs associated with conducting fresh negotiations on each aspect of implementation of an imprecise general framework are thereby reduced.[43] If approval or implementation require legislative action, the difficulties of persuading the legislature as to each successive element of an agreement would almost certainly be greater than seeking approval for a single set of commitments. During a single set of *ex ante* negotiations, governments are able to exchange concessions across various subject matters in a bargaining context.[44] This possibility is diminished *ex post* because adding subject matter areas to a bargaining agenda necessarily implicates additional constituencies and interests that will make demands on the process, increasing its complexity and adding transaction costs. *Ex post* dispute settlement of an ad hoc character is costly, and for each government involved opens the possibility that the result will be different than that which it would have bargained for *ex ante*. Though in an isolated case it might be demonstrated that *ex post* bargaining on the means of implementing commitments would be less costly to the governments involved than *ex ante* bargaining, it seems highly unlikely that case-by-case *ex post* bargaining over the terms of an imprecise trade agreement would be cheaper than *ex ante* across-the-board bargaining over the terms of a precise agreement.

The disadvantage of *ex ante* bargaining is that it requires the parties to anticipate the future. Since information about the future is by nature imperfect, *ex ante* solutions are bound to be imperfect. Precise terms that imperfectly anticipate future requirements under a trade agreement will generate *ex post* costs as the parties renegotiate the terms. Mechanisms for reducing the transaction costs associated with imperfect predictions of the future include the creation of standing institutions with the power to adopt supplementary rules.

The *ex post* costs of bargaining over the terms of implementing an imprecise agreement may be reduced by establishing standing institutions with the authority to adopt more precise rules as interpretative issues arise. There will be a cost of establishing and maintaining such institutions. Standing institutions that may respond to the requirements of the parties to a trade agreement "in real time" will be more likely to prescribe terms that are suitable to existing circumstances. Terms that are prescribed to fit specific circumstances are less likely to require additional bargaining, or to generate additional transaction costs, and so should result in savings to the parties.

Unlike NAFTA, the EU has established a set of standing institutions with the authority to prescribe rules as developments warrant. Such institutions were costly to establish and are costly to maintain. However, when developments in the EU point to

42. Hudec 1999, 11 ("A rule-based system is . . . the most effective way to negotiate and capture desired policy changes in achievable incremental steps").

43. This would include briefings and study on the issues, arranging negotiating schedules and venues, and so forth.

44. In the context of the WTO negotiating round, this is generally referred to as the possibility of providing cross-concessions. There is a recognized risk that a single set of trade negotiations may become overburdened by the incorporation of disparate subject matter, and trade negotiators must take this risk into account when establishing a negotiating agenda.

the need for new legislation, the member states do not need to engage in ad hoc efforts to establish the arrangements under which new terms will be agreed.

Determining whether the *ex ante* formulation of precise rules, as in the case of NAFTA, or the *ex post* formulation of secondary legislation, as in the case of the EU, is more beneficial in terms of reducing transaction costs would require an enormously complex empirical analysis even if NAFTA and the EU had identical objectives. Since the NAFTA and EU arrangements maintain different overall objectives, an empirical comparison of the effects of each legal model on transaction costs appears impracticable.

Private Risk Premiums

The principal objectives of NAFTA were to increase trading opportunities and encourage foreign direct investment among its parties. Trade and investment are mainly undertaken by private actors.

Business planners generally prefer to operate under stable economic conditions in which the rules applicable to transactions are known in advance.[45] Precise rules reduce the need for business planners to insure against risks, reduce the costs of doing business, and increase the prospects that transactions will be undertaken. Precise agreements provide business planners with a greater level of certainty than imprecise agreements and thereby reduce risk premiums more effectively than imprecise agreements.[46] Precise rules are inherently more capable of application by courts and other decision makers, and enforceable legal rules encourage trade and investment.[47] This same principle may be restated in the context of transaction costs.[48] Imprecise rules increase the chance that states will differ over the content of their implementation obligations. The results of intergovernmental disputes are unpredictable to varying degrees. Private enterprises that attempt to transact business when the outcome of a dispute is pending must take additional steps to protect against outcomes that may adversely affect their interests.[49] These additional steps involve increased transaction costs.

In regard to NAFTA, Canada insisted on adding precision to rules of origin and transformation with respect to automobiles and parts, because imprecise rules of CUSFTA had been interpreted by the United States to the detriment of Japanese investors in Canada.[50] This U.S. interpretation created substantial uncertainty among

---

45. There are, of course, exceptions to this general rule. A small proportion of business operators prefer to operate in high-risk environments that may present higher profit opportunities. Such operators may forgo purchasing risk insurance that would reduce the potential for profit. Abbott 1997b, 912–15.

46. Hudec 1999, 10 ("A rule-based system creates the most predictable conditions for business decisions").

47. The availability of enforceable legal rules is a point repeatedly made by Alan Greenspan in distinguishing successful and unsuccessful economies.

48. Coase postulated that uncertainty over the meaning of legal rules would increase private transaction costs as enterprises were forced to bargain under conditions of uncertainty. Coase 1960.

49. Economists generally refer to these additional steps under the rubric of increasing risk premiums.

50. The United States interpreted the parts roll-up rules in a way that increased the local content requirement for transformation to duty-free status, making it less attractive for Japanese automobile com-

prospective Japanese investors and increased the effective cost to Japanese investors of further investment in the Canadian automobile sector.

Strategic Behaviors

More precise legal rules may aid in constraining strategic behaviors of governments.[51] Precise legal rules—that is, rules that specifically prescribe permitted and unpermitted conduct—would appear in the context of NAFTA to inhibit the parties from seeking to take advantage of the inherent flexibility of imprecise legal rules. The earlier example of rules of origin and transformation with respect to automobiles and parts furnishes a useful illustration. In CUSFTA these rules were substantially less precise than they are in NAFTA. The United States took advantage of this lack of precision in CUSFTA to interpret the rules based on the perceived industrial interest of the United States.[52] Both Canada and Japan alleged that the U.S. interpretation was politically motivated. One of Canada's principal objectives in NAFTA negotiations was to assure that the new rules of origin regarding automobiles were sufficiently precise to prevent a repetition of what it regarded as U.S. strategic behavior.

Transparency

Precise terms of an international agreement such as NAFTA permit persons within and outside the negotiating governments to understand the nature of the bargain that has been reached. The transparency that is achieved through precise terms serves a variety of functions in respect to various constituencies.

NAFTA is implemented by a number of bureaucratic entities in each of its parties, and these entities require information concerning the mechanics of implementation. A precise agreement such as the NAFTA serves an internal governmental information function by providing the bureaucrats responsible for implementing it with operating instructions. Particularly as the identity of government bureaucrats changes over time, a precise written agreement establishes continuity in information concerning the obligations the parties have assumed. NAFTA required congressional or parliamentary approval in each of its parties. Such approval would have been difficult to obtain in the absence of some threshold level of precision. Legislators demand to know the terms of agreement to which they are consenting. More precise terms allow a more complete evaluation by legislators.

Nonparty governments are concerned about the terms of discriminatory trading arrangements that may affect their economies. Precise terms permit these govern-

---

panies to locate in Canada and export to the United States. See Customs Rules that Canadian Honda Civics Failed to Meet Content Standards Under FTA, *BNA International Trade Reporter*, 4 March 1992, 384.

51. Hudec notes in the context of the WTO that a rule-based system helps to cement one's own liberal trade policies against the internal political pressures of protectionism. Hudec 1999, 10. Internal political pressures provide one of the main reasons why governments pursue strategic behaviors, though external political pressures might also underlay such behaviors.

52. Ibid.

ments to evaluate the arrangement and respond to it. A nontransparent arrangement reduces the information flow to nonparties and may increase anxiety about its potential effects.[53] In the context of the WTO, a free-trade-area arrangement such as NAFTA must be evaluated by a working party under the terms of GATT Article XXIV and may be evaluated by a working party under GATS Article V.[54] In order to secure a GATT waiver of most-favored-nation rules under Article XXIV, the terms of NAFTA must be presented to a working party. A threshold level of precision must be achieved by any regional trading arrangement if it is to be compatible with the WTO agreement.

Precise terms allow business interests and nongovernmental organizations (NGOs) to evaluate the potential impact of an arrangement such as NAFTA. The business sector is directly affected by the terms of NAFTA, and specific industries would demand to understand the ways in which they would be affected by the agreement. In the specific context of NAFTA, NGOs made political demands to receive information concerning the prospective terms of the agreement and actively participated in policy discussions. It is doubtful that in today's political environment a democratic government could successfully bring an arrangement such as NAFTA into force in the absence of terms sufficiently precise to provide the business sector and NGOs with adequate information concerning the bargain that had been reached.

As noted earlier, the EU approach of coupling less precise rules with institutions authorized to adopt secondary (more precise) legislation may reduce the transaction costs otherwise associated with imprecise rules. Questions remain, however, as to what extent this alternative addresses concerns with respect to business planning, transparency, and constraining opportunistic behaviors. The answer would seem dependent on the specific form of the standing institutions that are established to act *ex post*.

It would be difficult to determine (or predict) whether business operators find the terms of the EC treaty (and its secondary legislation mechanism) providing a more or less secure environment than NAFTA for business planning purposes. While the EU system provides less advance information to business enterprises about the specific content of rules, it also provides greater leeway for business enterprises to lobby EC legislators regarding the content of evolving rules. Ronald Coase implied that any set of clear rules is preferable to business enterprises over uncertain rules, and his work might suggest a preference for more precise *ex ante* rules. However, it seems likely that such determinations would be context specific to business sectors.[55]

---

53. If the terms of the arrangement are antithetical to third countries, the parties to the arrangement might have a preference for nontransparency. Transparency may be more beneficial when the interests of third countries are adequately addressed by a trade arrangement.

54. Abbott 1995a, chap. 3.

55. Bankers, for example, might prefer a situation in which they could continuously lobby for rules expanding their scope of action, even if this required tolerating uncertainty concerning other rules. Oil refiners might prefer more precise *ex ante* rules that do not leave open the prospects for subsequent legislation (that might, for example, require major additional investments in environmental control equipment).

The EU certainly has faced a transparency problem over the course of its history, and the lack of transparency has affected the business sector, civil society, member governments, and nonmember governments. The EU has taken steps to improve transparency, among other things, to resolve the so-called democracy deficit.[56] The reputation of the European Commission as an opaque authority is an earned one, and the Commission has more recently acted to bring its activities within the realm of public discourse.[57] Nonmember governments have long complained about their inability to obtain information about EU trade policy mechanisms.[58]

It would be difficult to evaluate whether the level of precision in the EC treaty or in NAFTA is more effective at constraining strategic behaviors of party governments. Measurement would present a daunting task, and each regime would doubtless present advantages and disadvantages.

The extreme of imprecision represented by the APEC arrangement would fail to meet the functional requirements sought by NAFTA parties in negotiating a precise agreement. An agreement with nonspecific commitments and without institutions for adopting secondary legislation would result in high transaction costs (including delays in implementation), since all arrangements would require further bargaining. Such an arrangement would not promote business security or reduce risk premiums because it does not provide definite rules to investors and traders. Such an arrangement does not serve substantial transparency functions, since it does not disseminate information until decisions have been made that add specificity to the arrangement.[59] Such an arrangement does not constrain strategic behaviors, since it does not proscribe conduct, though it might have some positive effect on government behavior by fostering a climate of goodwill. The APEC members from the Asian continent have not been politically motivated to negotiate precise legal rules for reasons explored elsewhere in this special issue.[60] This lack of motivation likely stems both from a historical cultural aversion to precise legalization and from the fact that APEC members have not yet defined shared objectives.

Obligation

NAFTA imposes a high level of obligation on its parties that satisfies objectives of each party's trade negotiators. In light of prior ambivalent attitudes toward foreign

56. Weiler 1991, referenced extensively.

57. Much of this enhanced transparency has resulted from the development and use of Internet resources.

58. Abbott 1990. The long-running banana dispute at the GATT/WTO involved a nontransparent decision-making process and regime and is but one reflection of a difficult relationship between the EU and the GATT/WTO that has persisted since the formation of the Community.

59. The APEC Secretariat views the dissemination of information concerning the national laws of APEC members as an important part of its role. This, however, does not constitute providing information about the terms and operation of a regional arrangement; instead it is more in the nature of performing ordinary functions that some APEC members have failed to perform.

60. Kahler, this issue.

investment and trade, Mexico had a particular interest in providing assurance to potential foreign direct investors and traders that its economic policies are secure. Canada and the United States each viewed NAFTA as providing economic advantages greater than anticipated costs and sought to secure their gains from the negotiations. Moreover, they shared the objective of enhancing the security of their investors and traders.

NAFTA was drafted in terms that import binding legal commitment. The parties expressly agree to "give effect" to its provisions.[61] Its rules are generally stated in terms of actions that the parties "shall" take or refrain from taking.[62] When permissive terms (such as "may adopt") are used, they generally appear in the context of provisions pursuant to which the parties are permitted to adopt internal measures that are otherwise consistent with restrictive rules of the agreement.[63] NAFTA incorporates "safeguards," that is, measures that permit the parties to escape from legal obligation under defined circumstances, such as to temporarily protect against import surges[64] or to take action during balance-of-payments crises.[65] These safeguards provisions are generally consistent with those embodied in the WTO agreement.[66] The express terms of NAFTA generally reflect a high level of obligation.

As discussed later in respect to delegation, the principal NAFTA dispute-settlement provisions refer panel determinations to the parties for potential agreement on implementation. A complained-against party that refuses to agree to implementation of a decision is subject to the withdrawal of trade concessions by the complaining party.[67] The complained-against party is not strictly speaking obligated to remedy a breach. As such, NAFTA incorporates a level of obligation somewhat lower than that of the EC treaty, which requires that member states comply in a strict sense with decisions of the European Court of Justice.[68] There is debate in the academic literature as to whether decisions of the WTO Appellate Body and Dispute Settlement Body require compliance or whether members may opt out of them in exchange for compensation.[69]

NAFTA expressly authorizes its parties to withdraw from the agreement six months following written notice.[70] This is consistent with the WTO agreement, which likewise expressly authorizes withdrawal upon six months' written notice.[71] The express

61. NAFTA, art. 105.
62. See, for example, NAFTA, art. 301, "Each party *shall* accord national treatment."
63. See, for example, NAFTA, art. 712(1), Right to Take Sanitary and Phytosanitary Measures.
64. NAFTA, chap. 8.
65. NAFTA, art. 2104.
66. Some reduce the discretion of the parties, as in the balance-of-payments safeguard. NAFTA, art. 2104.
67. These withdrawn concessions are expected to be equivalent to the level of concessions lost in consequence of the breach. NAFTA, art. 2019(1).
68. See Weiler 1991, 2419 et seq., and Riesenfeld 1974.
69. Compare Jackson 1997 with Bello 1996.
70. Art. 2205.
71. WTO agreement, art. XV. International agreements sometimes include provisions authorizing withdrawal, and a right to withdraw may otherwise be inferred. If not expressly stated, an international agreement is considered not to permit withdrawal, unless this right may be inferred from the context. See Vienna Convention on Law of Treaties, art. 56.

right of withdrawal in NAFTA is mentioned by way of contrast with the EC treaty, which does not expressly confer a right of withdrawal. There is debate among commentators whether the EC treaty permits withdrawal or precludes it because of its constitutional nature.[72] Without seeking to resolve this debate, to the extent that the EC treaty does not permit withdrawal it would evidence a higher level of obligation than NAFTA. This special case should not, however, prevent the conclusion that NAFTA embodies a high level of obligation. It may only suggest a way in which the level of obligation might be higher.

A high level of obligation has both persuasive and compulsive characteristics. By framing legal commitments in terms of binding obligation, governments signal their intention to fulfill their commitments. If a trade agreement such as NAFTA is negotiated under assumptions of reciprocity (that is, one party agrees to provide enhanced market access in exchange for another party's commitment to provide market access, with each believing that it is providing a valuable concession), each side should be more likely to execute the agreement if it believes that the other side will do the same.

NAFTA was negotiated in the context of reciprocal exchange, even if an unequal exchange. Mexico agreed to open its market to trade and investment, and to provide legal security, in exchange for U.S. and Canadian commitments on market access for certain previously restricted categories of Mexican exports. Both the United States and Canada were largely open to investment and trade prior to NAFTA. Mexico provided a relatively higher level of concessions in NAFTA than the other parties.[73] Mexico, however, had specific reasons for preferring a high level of obligation in NAFTA that was distinct from its level of concessions (and made an imbalance in concessions less significant). Mexico sought to persuade potential capital investors that it would provide a secure financial environment.[74] A low level of obligation—that is, one that Mexico might disregard at its discretion—would not be as persuasive to investors. In essence, a low level of obligation would have been inconsistent with Mexico's goals in entering into the agreement.

In light of the imbalance of concessions in favor of the United States and Canada, it would appear to be in their mutual interest to agree to a high level of obligation, since this would increase the prospects that they would receive the benefits of a higher level of concessions from Mexico.

The United States agreed in NAFTA to limitations on its future discretion in trade policy regarding Canada and Mexico. Each of these countries would perceive it to be in their interests to restrain U.S. discretion to deviate from the terms of an agreement that effectively provided them with market access.

The high level of obligation in the NAFTA is enforceable through trade policy mechanisms—that is, a party that has suffered a breach may withdraw trade concessions to offset its loss of benefits. This is the "compulsion" mechanism of NAFTA.

72. See discussion in Weiler 1991, 2412.
73. Nadal 1997.
74. Ramos Uriarte 1995.

The parties might have chosen a stronger compulsion mechanism, such as one obligating them to amend or remove measures inconsistent with NAFTA or to pay direct compensation in the amount of a breach.

The NAFTA compulsion formula was adopted for several reasons. Since dispute settlement is undertaken ad hoc by trade experts, it would be difficult to persuade national legislators that such persons should issue rulings that would compel changes in national legislation. The WTO modified its dispute settlement mechanism to establish a standing Appellate Body to address concerns about the quality and legitimacy of ad hoc arbitration.[75] A dispute-settlement mechanism that issues determinations binding in a strict sense necessarily diminishes party autonomy. This implicates "sovereignty" concerns. The United States in particular has a history of resistance to restraints on its autonomy in foreign affairs and trade policy. It would be a significant undertaking for U.S. trade negotiators to persuade the U.S. Congress to relinquish autonomy in a way that would be contemplated by a more strictly binding NAFTA dispute-settlement mechanism. The lower level of obligation was deliberately chosen to assuage congressional (and executive branch) concerns with reducing autonomy.[76]

NAFTA parties might have chosen a lower level of obligation such as is evidenced by the APEC arrangement[77] or a slightly higher level of obligation as evidenced by the EC treaty. The very low level of obligation evidenced by the APEC arrangement does not raise concerns regarding intrusion on sovereignty and autonomy. This is the main advantage of the nonobligatory form of arrangement from the standpoint of its state participants. However, this autonomy advantage is offset by the disadvantages of providing minimal persuasion and no compulsion.

From a political standpoint, reaching agreement on rules in the context of a high level of obligation may be more difficult than in the context of low obligation. If governments believe they will be required to implement the undertakings specified in an agreement, they are likely to be more cautious in accepting those undertakings.[78] The ease or hesitation with which governments approach proposals is partly a function of the relative level of obligation of the proposals. In theory a level of obligation that is perceived as too stringent might reduce the willingness of governments to pursue beneficial trade policies.

The EU member states have arguably entered into an arrangement from which they are not entitled to withdraw. This level of obligation may be consistent with an intention to form a federal or constitutional polity since it signals permanence and commitment. The parties in NAFTA, however, did not intend to create such a polity, and their decision to permit withdrawal was consistent with their intention to form an economic arrangement. Although a higher level of commitment may have increased

---

75. Abbott 1997a. If NAFTA were to incorporate a higher level of compulsion, a similar appellate mechanism or other arrangement might be required.

76. Whether Canadian or Mexican negotiators would have agreed to a more strictly binding dispute-settlement arrangement is superfluous under these conditions.

77. See Kahler, this issue; and Fried 1998.

78. Abbott 1997a, 46–47.

the perceived security of investors and traders with regard to Canada and Mexico, it seems likely that private business operators would discount such a commitment on the part of the United States in light of its historical record regarding international commitment.[79]

Delegation

As defined in the introduction to this special issue, delegation "means that authority has been granted to third parties for the implementation of rules, including their interpretation and application, dispute settlement, and (possibly) further rule making."[80]

The main difference between NAFTA and the EU in their approaches to hard legalization involves the degree to which decision-making authority is delegated to regional institutions. The NAFTA parties have not delegated authority for promulgating secondary rules to supplement or clarify the precise rules set out in its charter document, whereas the EC treaty establishes regional institutions with substantial authority to promulgate secondary legislation. The NAFTA parties maintain effective control over the selection of arbitrators and the implementation of dispute-settlement decisions, and NAFTA rules are not directly applicable in the law of Canada or the United States. Decisions of the European Court of Justice, a standing judicial institution, require implementation by the EU member states, and EU law may be directly applied in all member states (under appropriate circumstances). NAFTA's moderate approach to delegation reflects political and juridical/constitutional constraints within its parties. An approach to delegation modeled on the EU was not politically feasible. The NAFTA model may be the more politically viable option for establishing hard law international economic arrangements in parts of the world where "sovereignty" concerns continue to weigh on national political decision makers.

NAFTA's main political decision-making institution, the Free Trade Commission, acts to oversee the implementation of the agreement, to make recommendations to the parties, to appoint arbitrators in the context of dispute settlement, and to negotiate accession agreements. The commission acts by consensus, and it has no power to adopt legislative measures with binding effect on the parties in the sense of secondary legislation promulgated by the Council of the European Communities.

NAFTA does not establish any form of legislative or parliamentary body elected directly or indirectly by individual citizens of the parties. The EC treaty established the European Parliament, which has evolved over the course of EU history to play a substantial role in the EU governance process. The European Parliament forms part

79. See, for example, U.S. withdrawal from the compulsory jurisdiction of the International Court of Justice during the pendency of the Nicaragua proceedings, and the text of Section 301 of the Trade Act of 1974, as amended, which specifically authorizes the USTR to take actions inconsistent with U.S. obligations under international trade agreements.
80. See the introduction to this issue. A second article by these authors refers to delegation in more limited terms, that is, to the delegation of authority for the settlement of disputes. Keohane, Moravcsik, and Slaughter, this issue.

of the member states' delegation function in respect to EU secondary legislation and is generally understood to enhance the democratic character of delegated EU decision making.[81]

Arbitrators appointed pursuant to NAFTA's dispute-settlement provisions are third parties to whom the task of interpreting the agreement and resolving issues concerning compliance may be referred. NAFTA incorporates several distinct dispute-settlement procedures. The generally applicable procedure is set forth in Chapter 20. This is an interstate procedure that may be initiated only by the parties.[82] It involves the appointment of arbitrators on a case-by-case basis from a roster of panelists that has been jointly approved by the parties.[83] The panel ultimately prepares a final report with determinations and recommendations concerning the dispute. This report is transmitted to the parties, which shall agree on the resolution of the dispute and normally shall conform with the determinations and recommendations of the panel.[84] If a complained-against party fails to agree to a settlement based on the panel's report, the complaining party may suspend the application of benefits under NAFTA.[85] The decisions of NAFTA panelists are not binding in the sense of requiring party compliance. Though NAFTA states a preference for compliance,[86] it does not demand it. Instead, NAFTA refers third-party dispute-settlement decisions back to the political arena for further consideration by party decision makers. In contrast, decisions of the European Court of Justice are directly binding on those they are addressed to and require compliance.

Chapter 19 of NAFTA establishes a separate dispute-settlement mechanism in respect to antidumping and countervailing duty (AD/CVD)-related complaints. NAFTA contains no rules regarding the substance of the AD/CVD laws of the parties[87] but requires that each party act in domestic AD/CVD actions in compliance with its own laws. Under the AD/CVD dispute-settlement procedure, arbitral panels are appointed on a case-by-case basis, generally from a roster established by the parties. A person in a NAFTA party that has been the subject of a final administrative AD/CVD determination may require its government to initiate a Chapter 19 proceeding.[88] In addition, that person is entitled to participate in the proceeding. Thus, although the AD/CVD procedure is nominally interstate, the fact that private actors may initiate and participate in the procedure effectively transforms it into a quasi-transnational procedure. Panels decide whether a complained-against party has complied with its own AD/CVD laws in a particular action, and the decisions are directly

---

81. See Weiler 1991, 2466.
82. NAFTA, art. 2008.
83. Ibid., art. 2009 and 2011. A panelist who is not on the roster may be proposed but is subject to peremptory challenge. Art. 2011(3).
84. Ibid., art. 2018(1).
85. Ibid., art. 2019.
86. Ibid., art. 2018(2). "Whenever possible, the resolution shall be non-implementation or removal of a measure not conforming with this Agreement or causing nullification or impairment . . . or, failing such a resolution, compensation."
87. Chapter 19 contains a weak "stabilization" clause, largely directed at transparency.
88. NAFTA, art. 1904(5).

binding on the country parties.[89] An extraordinary challenge procedure exists that entitles a party to appeal to a committee of judges on limited grounds that a panel exceeded its authority or engaged in abusive practices.

NAFTA also permits private investors of parties to pursue third-party arbitration against a host government in the International Centre for the Settlement of Investment Disputes (ICSID) or under UN Conference on International Trade Law (UNCITRAL) rules.[90] NAFTA obligates the parties to make adequate provision for the enforcement of resulting arbitral awards.[91] Private persons may seek enforcement of awards by national courts under international agreements to which the parties may belong.[92] Note, however, that these agreements allow some scope to national courts to refuse to recognize and enforce awards based on considerations of overriding public policy, so that the enforcement of an arbitral award rendered by ICSID or under UNCITRAL rules is not automatic.[93] An arbitral award may provide for the payment of monetary damages or restitution of property (which may be avoided by a party by payment of compensation), but it may not direct a government to amend its legislation.[94] If a party fails to comply with an award, it is subject to NAFTA Chapter 20 dispute-settlement proceedings.[95] On the whole, this mixed investor-to-state procedure is more in the nature of a transnational dispute-settlement procedure than an interstate procedure.

The question of whether NAFTA may be directly effective in the law of the parties is related to the question of the extent to which NAFTA delegates decision-making authority to third parties or neutral decision makers. In this context the issue is whether decision making might be delegated to national courts and judges and away from political branches (that is, executive and legislative decision makers).[96] As an international legal instrument, NAFTA would appear capable of being given direct effect in national law, at least in substantial part, except where direct effect has been expressly precluded. The terms of NAFTA are sufficiently precise to be applied by

89. Ibid., art. 1904(9).

90. Ibid., arts. 1115, et seq. See Abbott 1995a, 102.

91. Ibid., art. 1136(4).

92. Ibid., art. 1136(6), referring to the ICSID Convention, the New York Convention on the Recognition and Enforcement of Foreign Arbitral Awards, and the Inter-American Convention on International Commercial Arbitration.

93. See, for example, New York Convention on the Recognition and Enforcement of Foreign Arbitral Awards, art. V.

94. Ibid., art. 1135.

95. Ibid., art. 1136(5). This may result in a recommendation that a party comply with the award.

96. A treaty may have direct effect in the law of a state that is party to it. See Riesenfeld and Abbott 1994a. If a treaty (or part of a treaty) is directly effective, it may be relied on in the courts of a state as a source of rights. The question whether a treaty has direct effect has both an international law and national law component. A treaty may be intended by its parties to be capable of direct effect, as determined by an examination of its terms and context under international law. However, whether a treaty that is capable of direct effect under international law will be given that effect in national law is determined by the constitution of the state in which the treaty is invoked. Some national constitutions permit treaties to be directly effective and others do not. Both the U.S. and Mexican constitutional systems permit treaties to have direct effect, whereas the Canadian constitution (modeled on the British constitutional system) does not. See notes 102–103. In some states in which a treaty may be given direct effect, the national parliament or legislature may deny direct effect to it in its approving or implementing legislation.

courts in concrete cases or controversies.[97] Insofar as NAFTA might be directly invoked in the courts of one party against the measures or conduct of another party, this potential avenue for direct effect is expressly barred by the terms of the agreement. NAFTA provides that no country party may be sued in the courts of another party "on the ground that a measure of another Party is inconsistent with the Agreement."[98] Private actors are thus precluded from using the domestic courts of one party to challenge the legislative measures or conduct of another party under NAFTA, and cross-border disputes are channeled into the intergovernmental dispute-settlement mechanism (that is, Chapter 20).[99]

NAFTA might also be directly invoked by a person in the national courts of a party to challenge the measures or conduct of that party. An importer in the United States, for example, might attempt to challenge a decision by the U.S. Customs Service regarding the application of NAFTA rules of origin directly on the basis of the NAFTA text. The U.S. Congress expressly denied the possibility of domestic direct effect for NAFTA in the legislation approving and implementing the agreement, and it may not be relied on as a source of rights in U.S. law.[100] This rule extends to the Supplemental Agreements on Environment and Labor. Litigation may be brought only on the basis of the implementing legislation and other domestic legislation.[101] A private litigant in the United States may not directly challenge the consistency of federal, state, or local measures with provisions of NAFTA.

The Mexican Constitution allows for the direct effect of international agreements, and the Mexican legislature has not acted to deny potential direct effect to NAFTA.[102]

---

97. It may have been understood by U.S. trade negotiators that NAFTA implementing legislation would deny the agreement direct effect in U.S. courts, and this may argue that neither Canada nor the United States intended the agreement to be directly effective (since Canadian law bars direct effect). The U.S. Supreme Court has held (as has the European Court of Justice) that whether another state permits an agreement to be directly effective does not determine whether it will be directly effective under the U.S. Constitution (i.e. there is no test of reciprocity). *Ware v. Hylton,* 3 U.S. (3 Dall.) 199 (1796). The failure of the Parties to proscribe direct effect under national law in the body of the NAFTA, the possibility of direct effect in Mexico, and the U.S. decision to expressly legislate against direct effect each suggest that the agreement might be directly effective absent specific national legislative action.

98. NAFTA, art. 2021.

99. The North American Agreement for Environmental Cooperation (NAAEC) Secretariat factual report procedure provides an alternative outlet for private actors but does not result in enforceable decisions.

100. Ibid. 102(a) provides that "no provision of the Agreement, nor the application of any such provision to any person or circumstance, which is inconsistent with the law of the United States shall have effect." Though this appears to leave room for the direct application of provisions of NAFTA that would not amend existing federal legislation, the Implementation Act at 102(c) provides that "no person other than the United States (1) shall have any cause of action or defense under (A) the Agreement or by virtue of Congressional approval thereof, or (B) the North American Agreement on Environmental Cooperation or the North American Agreement on Labor Cooperation; or (2) may challenge, in any action brought under any provision of law, any action or inaction by any department, agency, or other instrumentality of the United States, any State, or any political subdivision of a State on the ground that such action or inaction is inconsistent with the Agreement, the North American Agreement on Environmental Cooperation, or the North American Agreement on Labor Cooperation." See Abbott 1993b (written prior to publication of the NAFTA Implementation Act).

101. In addition to its general statement on direct effect, the NAFTA Implementation Act states that "nothing in this Act shall be construed—(A) to amend or modify any law of the United States, including any law regarding—(i) the protection of human, animal, or plant life or health, (ii) the protection of the environment." Ibid., 102(a)(2).

102. Gal-Or 1998.

Since the Canadian constitutional system generally bars the direct effect of international agreements in national law, NAFTA may not be relied on directly as a source of rights in Canada.[103]

The EC treaty and EU secondary legislation may be directly effective in the law of the EU member states.[104] In other words, EU citizens may directly invoke the EC treaty and secondary legislation in the courts of the member states (and the European Court of Justice) under appropriate circumstances. Whether or not the EC treaty or secondary legislation may be directly relied upon depends on factors such as the precision of terms and the form of the secondary legislation. As previously noted, NAFTA does not establish a permanent regional judicial body comparable to the European Court of Justice. Nationals of NAFTA parties may therefore not seek to invoke the agreement directly before a regional judicial authority that might render decisions binding upon the parties.

The preceding description indicates that NAFTA provides for a moderate level of delegation to nonparty decision makers. Virtually no authority has been conferred upon regional institutions to autonomously formulate policy or to adopt legislative measures binding upon the parties. A significant level of decision-making authority has been delegated to neutral arbitrators for dispute resolution, but this delegation does not generally obligate the parties to amend or withdraw measures inconsistent with NAFTA. In the limited case of AD/CVD measures, there is a high level of delegation. In the case of investment disputes, there is also a fairly high level of delegation of decision-making authority; although investment arbitral awards may not order a party to modify its legislative measures, they are subject to enforcement by national courts and may ultimately result in referral to Chapter 20 dispute settlement. The combination of low delegation in respect to legislative measures, moderate delegation in respect to general dispute settlement, and higher delegation in respect to AD/CVD and investment dispute settlement suggests that NAFTA on the whole incorporates a "moderate" level of delegation.

Political factors in the parties militated against the creation of regional institutions with the power to make decisions on behalf of the parties. The political bias against creating such institutions was accompanied by constitutional constraints within the parties that would have raised serious legal obstacles to their creation.[105] In the following discussion I focus on constitutional constraints within the United States, recognizing that similar constraints also affected Canada and Mexico.[106]

103. Ibid. In approving and implementing NAFTA Parliament indicated that Canadian courts should interpret domestic implementing legislation consistently with NAFTA. Fried 1994, n.78.

104. See Weiler 1991, 2413 et seq.; and Riesenfeld 1974. In relation to secondary legislation, for example, a directive that obligates the member states to bring national law into conformity with EU rules generally may only be directly relied upon if the national legislature has failed to implement the directive within the prescribed time period.

105. The potential constraints that the U.S. constitution imposes upon the formation of regional political institutions and a regional judicial institution are analyzed in Abbott 1995b.

106. Regarding Canada, see Gesser 1998. Regarding Mexico, see, for example, Ramos Uriarte 1995, 90–92.

The U.S. Constitution authorizes the president, with the consent of Congress, to enter into international agreements such as NAFTA.[107] The Constitution provides that treaties are the supreme law of the land,[108] and it does not impose any explicit limitations on the subject matter that might be addressed by an international agreement.[109] However, based on Supreme Court precedent, it is generally accepted that a treaty may not be used to deprive U.S. citizens of their constitutional rights.[110]

The Constitution very specifically sets out the ways in which federal legislation will be made by Congress and the president. The Supreme Court has refused to approve deviations from this process adopted in the name of legislative efficiency.[111] If the president and Congress were to approve an international agreement that delegated legislative decision-making authority to a regional institution, a conflict might arise between constitutional provisions authorizing the making of treaties that are the supreme law of the land and those prescribing the means by which federal legislation should be made.[112] Although the Supreme Court has never struck down a treaty on grounds that it preempted the legislative prerogatives of Congress, it has never addressed a general delegation of legislative authority to an international institution. How the Supreme Court would react in such a situation is uncertain.

The question whether the parties to NAFTA would create a North American court of justice along the lines of the European Court of Justice was never seriously entertained during the negotiations. However, if such a NAFTA court were agreed upon, it would certainly face constitutional challenge in the United States. This would arise from a tension between Article III of the Constitution, which vests the judicial power of the United States in its federal courts, on one side, and the treaty power on the other.[113] The creation of the Chapter 19 AD/CVD dispute-settlement procedure generated substantial constitutional opposition despite its very limited nature. A more general vesting of the judicial power in a regional institution would be certain to generate an intensive constitutional debate.

---

107. U.S. Constitution, art. II, sec. 2.

108. Ibid., art. VI, cl. 2.

109. Riesenfeld and Abbott 1994b. Perhaps the widest delegation of decision-making power by the United States to an international institution is the delegation of power to the UN Security Council to make decisions regarding threats to the peace, including the power to authorize the use of force to address such threats. The United States maintains a veto at the Security Council, and it does not face the possibility of decisions being made and carried out without its consent. U.S. participation in the Security Council was approved by the Senate in ratifying the UN Charter and by the Congress in the UN Participation Act (UNPA). There is a potential conflict between the power of the president to vote in favor of the use of force in the Security Council and the residual constitutional power of the U.S. Congress to declare war. This conflict surfaced during the Gulf War when President Bush asserted the right to use U.S. military force based on Security Council action, which right was challenged by members of Congress. Without conceding the point, the president sought and received consent from Congress to the use of force against Iraq. For details, see Abbott 1995b, 148–49.

110. *Reid v. Covert*, 354 U.S. 1223 (1957).

111. *INS v. Chadha*, 462 U.S. 817 (1983).

112. The question of whether the procedure used by the president and Congress in approving NAFTA comported with the requirements of the Constitution was discussed at length by a federal district court that rejected a constitutional challenge in *Made in the USA v. United States*, 56 F. Supp. 2d 1226 (N.D. Ala. 1999).

113. Bermann 1998.

By pointing out the potential constitutional obstacles inherent in delegating legislative and judicial functions to regional institutions I am not suggesting the unconstitutionality of such delegation, but rather showing that more extensive delegation would have substantially hindered the NAFTA approval process. The political resistance to delegation—that is, to losing autonomy—was overcome in two specific contexts.

The Chapter 19 procedure in NAFTA is closely modeled on the AD/CVD procedure incorporated in CUSFTA, and its policy roots must be sought in those earlier negotiations. The reasons for the special status of AD/CVD panel determination are well documented.[114] The Canadian government considered that its exporters were subject to unfair treatment under U.S. AD/CVD law, particularly since U.S. trade law judges hearing appeals from Commerce Department/International Trade Commission AD/CVD determinations showed a high degree of deference to initial agency determinations.[115] The normalization of AD/CVD rules was one of Canada's principal objectives in entering into CUSFTA, since it perceived that advantages it gained in trade with the United States were often attacked and offset by AD/CVD rulings. The Canadians proposed to negotiate a uniform set of AD/CVD actions in CUSFTA, potentially modeled on a competition law approach. U.S. trade negotiators rejected this approach because of internal congressional resistance and under pressure from domestic industries that expressed particular concern with Canadian subsidy practices. The CUSFTA procedure was adopted as a compromise, allowing the United States to retain its domestic AD/CVD laws intact, while satisfying Canada's demands that its exporters not be subject to what it perceived as arbitrary and discriminatory treatment.

A high level of delegation was agreed on in CUSFTA following the failure of Canada and the United States to agree on common rules. The objective was to make each side abide by its domestic rules by eliminating some of the local advantage of domestic administration. That the parties agreed on binding delegation in this context, though not in others, may to some extent be attributed to Canada's particular insistence that AD/CVD measures be adequately addressed as a condition to entering into CUSFTA. Mexico had also been concerned with U.S. AD/CVD practices. However, the constellation of interests in the United States during the NAFTA negotiations was similar to that during the CUSFTA negotiations, and there was little prospect of moving beyond the solution achieved in CUSFTA. The NAFTA Chapter 19 rules and procedures are substantially similar to the CUSFTA AD/CVD procedures.[116]

CUSFTA incorporated rules regarding foreign direct investment similar to those in NAFTA, but it did not establish a separate dispute-settlement mechanism.[117] In CUSFTA, a dispute between Canada and the United States regarding the treatment of

---

114. See, for example, Carman 1997; and Gesser 1998.
115. Carman 1997, 7.
116. NAFTA modestly expanded the scope of the extraordinary challenge procedure that permits a party to challenge a panel determination when an abuse of process is alleged to have occurred. Fried 1994, 48.
117. CUSFTA, arts. 1608, 1806–1807.

a private investor was to be resolved by reference to the general dispute-settlement procedure, similar to the NAFTA Chapter 20 procedure. During the CUSFTA negotiations, Canada agreed to amend its foreign investment review legislation to provide additional flexibility for U.S. investors. Canadian decisions under this review procedure were exempted from CUSFTA dispute resolution.[118]

One of Mexico's principal objectives for entering into NAFTA was to encourage additional foreign direct investment.[119] Mexico's historical treatment of foreign direct investment was inconsistent, and it might be characterized as hostile during the 1970s and 1980s.[120] The Mexican legal system did not have a reputation for transparency, nor would it encourage investor security.[121] From Mexico's perspective, adopting a neutral dispute-settlement procedure that would enhance the security of U.S. and Canadian investors was an aid to achieving an important goal.[122]

The investor-to-state dispute-settlement mechanism incorporated in NAFTA is common to both Canadian foreign investment protection agreements and to U.S. bilateral investment treaties.[123] These agreements have been fairly widely used in relations with developing countries and countries-in-transition.[124] From the perspective of the United States, the motivation for including third-party investor-to-state arbitration in an agreement with Mexico is plain. U.S. investments would be more secure if investors could avoid litigation in the Mexican courts and Mexico assured the enforcement of arbitration awards.[125] Canada did not contemplate a major investment presence in Mexico and so did not have the same incentive as the United States for concluding a third-party arbitration provision. However, so long as it was able to maintain its reservation regarding investment review (which it did), and since the provision was consistent with its general policies regarding relations with developing countries, this was not a major issue to Canada.[126]

From the standpoint of investors, the Chapter 11 investor-to-state third-party dispute-resolution procedure would be far preferable to the Chapter 20 state-to-state arbitration procedure. The state-to-state procedure requires reliance on the government to initiate a claim, which it might refuse to do for political reasons. It requires the government to evaluate the legal merits of the claim, and its evaluation may differ from the investor's. Government lawyers would undertake the representation (albeit with assistance from the investor's counsel), and there is no assurance that such

---

118. See CUSFTA, art. 1608; and Kennish 1995, 16–17.

119. Ramos Uriarte 1995, 88–92.

120. Ibid., 88–90.

121. Ibid., 98.

122. Ibid., 98–99, 107–109. Note that the Mexican government faced constitutional obstacles to concluding the investor-to-state arbitration provisions of NAFTA and may yet face constitutional challenges to this aspect of the agreement. Ibid., 90–91.

123. Fried 1994, 48–49.

124. See, for example, Treaty Between the United States of America and the Republic of Senegal Concerning the Reciprocal Encouragement and Protection of Investment, done December 1983, entered into force 25 October 1990, at art. VII, <http://www.mac.doc.gov:80/tcc/data/commerce-html/tcc-2/Senegal.html>.

125. Kennish 1995, 7–8.

126. Ibid., 1–3.

representation would be satisfactory. Finally, any award by a panel would be subject to political implementation, at which stage political considerations might again interfere with the investor's perceived entitlement. In short, from the standpoint of a private investor, the capability to directly force a government into arbitration, and to enforce the resulting award, are significant benefits. The U.S. government had the strong support of its investor community in negotiating the investor-to-state dispute resolution procedure.

The incorporation of a high level of delegation in respect to investor-to-state relations was consistent with important objectives of both the Mexican and the U.S. governments. From the standpoint of Mexico, the security of investment would be promoted, and this would encourage inward investment. From the United States' perspective, its investors would be made more secure, and this would enhance the value of its outward foreign direct investment stock. As discussed later, the consequences-in-fact of the third-party investment-dispute procedures may not have been foreseen by the negotiating governments.

The NAFTA provisions precluding private actors of one party from suing another party (in the first party's domestic courts) were adopted to protect the autonomy of the NAFTA party governments. The NAFTA parties would have substantially limited their political control over the way in which NAFTA was implemented if they allowed direct access to private actors to sue governments (other than their own). When direct effect is precluded, the parties may choose not to seek enforcement of their rights, or they may negotiate compromise outcomes of potential disputes among themselves. If private actors may sue to enforce the agreement, judges become the enforcers of the agreement, and judges generally are not empowered to exercise political discretion in the administration of legal norms.[127]

The United States legislatively denied direct effect to NAFTA because of congressional concerns that private-party enforcement might lead to unanticipated legal consequences.[128] By specifically legislating the domestic impact of NAFTA, Congress sought to retain a higher level of control over domestic affairs. The history of the direct application of the EC treaty supports the thesis that private-party access may lead to unanticipated consequences.[129] These consequences may be positive ones. In the U.S. constitutional framework, if Congress becomes dissatisfied with the domestic consequences of a treaty, it may legislate a binding alternative. There is therefore no compelling justification for denying the direct effect of agreements such as NAFTA.

Preliminary Observations Regarding Effects of Legalization Choices

NAFTA has so far been implemented largely in accordance with its terms.[130] Tariffs and quotas have been eliminated and market access commitments have been met.

127. Judges may invoke "political question" doctrines to avoid deciding cases.
128. Abbott 1993b.
129. Keohane, Moravcsik, and Slaughter, this issue.
130. See, generally, U.S. Executive Branch 1997.

The 1994–95 peso crisis did not significantly affect Mexico's level of compliance with the agreement, even though the government was under domestic political pressure to take some form of action to address it. In response to earlier monetary crises, the reaction of the Mexican government had been to restrict access to the internal market.[131] The United States provided large-scale financial aid to Mexico during the peso crisis, and this relieved pressure on the Mexican government to take measures that might have been inconsistent with NAFTA.

There have been a few notable instances of apparent noncompliance with the terms of the NAFTA. The United States has failed to open its borders to cross-border trucking (and bus service) despite terms of NAFTA that obligate it to do so.[132] Mexico has initiated a Chapter 20 proceeding in respect to the alleged U.S. cross-border trucking (and bus service) breaches, but the parties have moved exceedingly slowly in constituting panels to hear the cases. The United States enacted Helms-Burton legislation that appears to be inconsistent with NAFTA's investment rules.[133] Each of these instances of U.S. noncompliance is based on demands of powerful domestic political constituencies. Mexico has, on its side, delayed providing market access for U.S. express courier services,[134] and Canada has imposed restrictions on split-run periodicals.[135] In the context of a far-reaching set of trilateral commitments, however, the level of noncompliance is very modest.

To date, two Chapter 20 panel determinations have been concluded. In the Canadian Agricultural Tariffs case (initiated by the United States) the panel found that Canada had not violated the terms of NAFTA and made no recommenda-

131. For example, following the collapse of the peso on international currency markets in 1982, Mexico nationalized the Mexican banking system and imposed a two-tier system of exchange controls designed to curtail capital flight and restrict imports. See Buira 1983; Hobbs 1990; Philip 1985; and Skiles 1991. The 1982 peso crisis resulted in a substantial enhancement of government intervention in the domestic marketplace, at least for the short term. See, for example, Buira 1983, 54–60. State control over private-sector activity was intensified as the means to bring the domestic economic situation into equilibrium. In 1982 the Mexican government was not without international legal constraints responding to the peso crisis. Specifically, in order to satisfy the International Monetary Fund in respect to emergency borrowing, the Mexican government undertook to meet criteria regarding budget deficit control and agreed to other fiscal and monetary constraints. See Hobbs 1990, 187–89. In 1982 the Reagan administration made a $600 million loan to Mexico from the Exchange Stabilization Fund, the same fund that was used to extend loans to Mexico in 1994. Covey 1996.

132. Mexico announced its request for the formation of a panel regarding its cross-border trucking dispute with the United States on 23 September 1998. Mexico Seeks NAFTA Arbitration Panel on U.S. Resistance to Mexican Truckers, *BNA International Trade Reporter,* 30 September 1998, 1645. As of this date, the panel has not yet been constituted.

133. Lowenfeld 1996. This legislation was challenged by the EU in the WTO, and a temporary negotiated settlement was reached between the EU and the United States.

134. Clinton Mexico Trip to Include Little Discussion of Trade Issues, *Americas Trade*, 11 February 1999, 1.

135. A split-run periodical is one that is produced with different content in two markets. Canada sought to effectively prohibit U.S. magazine publishers from selling U.S.-generated works with Canadian advertisement in Canada. Canada's theory was that U.S. publishers were able to sell advertising space in Canada at unfairly low cost because U.S. advertisers had in essence already paid for the production of magazine content. The WTO Appellate Body found these Canadian restrictions to violate GATT 1994. WTO Appellate Body, *Canada—Certain Measures Concerning Periodicals,* 1994. WT/DS31/AB, 30 June 1997 <http:///www.wto.org>.

tion.[136] In the Broom Corn Brooms case (initiated by Mexico) the panel found that the United States had failed to comply with NAFTA procedural requirements for adopting safeguard measures.[137] It recommended that the United States remedy this procedural failure. More than fifty Chapter 19 cases have been initiated, and more than fifteen panels decisions have been rendered.[138] To date, the decisions have not resulted in significant controversy.

Investor claims have been threatened and initiated under Chapter 11 against Canada, Mexico, and the United States. One of these claims has been resolved by an arbitral determination.[139] These claims have been based on a variety of circumstances alleged to constitute breach of NAFTA's investment rules. Of particular note are a claim brought by a Canadian investor against the United States, alleging that a judgment rendered by a state court in Mississippi violates international standards of nondiscrimination and due process;[140] and claims threatened against both the Canadian and U.S. (California) governments, alleging that environment-related business restrictions represent arbitrary takings under international law.[141] These claims have led the Canadian government to request the negotiation of a clarification of Chapter 11 rules.[142] Public interest groups in the United States and Canada have demanded the reopening of Chapter 11 negotiations,[143] expressing dissatisfaction with the lack of transparency inherent in an ICSID arbitration proceeding and with the idea that NAFTA rules might undermine traditional avenues of court adjudication of claims.

It is doubtful that NAFTA negotiators anticipated that allegations of discrimination by U.S. state courts and arbitrary U.S. and Canadian environmental regulations would be the subject of Chapter 11 arbitration.[144] This lends support to the postulate that opening dispute-settlement procedures to private actors increases the scope of subject matter involved in dispute-settlement proceedings. Expanding the subject matter scope is consistent with experience in the EU, which maintains a doctrine of direct effect and access to private actors and has witnessed a wide range of subject matter claims based on the EC treaty. Many of these claims may have been unanticipated by the drafters of the Treaty of Rome.[145]

Continued use of Chapter 11 proceedings as a business tool to challenge environmental regulations is likely to exacerbate NGO dissatisfaction with NAFTA and

---

136. Final Report of the Panel in the Matter of Tariffs Applied by Canada to Certain U.S.-Origin Agricultural Products, 1997 BDIEL AD LEXIS 24 (2 December 1996).

137. Final Panel Report, in the Matter of the U.S. Safeguard Action Taken on Broom Corn Brooms from Mexico (USA-97–2008–01), 30 January 1998.

138. See index of proceedings and reports available at <http://www.nafta-sec.org>.

139. ICSID Additional Facility, Robert Azinian et al. v. United Mexican States, Case No. ARB (AF)/97/2, 1 November 1999 <http://www.worldbank.org/icsid/cases>.

140. Lutz and Trice 1998.

141. Peter Menyasz, NAFTA Chapter 11 Provisions Said to Threaten Environmental Protection Rights, *BNA International Trade Reporter*, 7 July 1999, 1146.

142. NAFTA Ministers Lock Horns on Investor, Environment/Labor Issues, *Americas Trade,* 6 May 1999, 1.

143. Menyasz, Chapter 11 Provisions.

144. See Lutz and Trice 1998; and NAFTA Ministers Lock Horns.

145. Keohane, Moravcsik, and Slaughter, this issue.

other trade agreements. The practice might ultimately be cited in support of U.S. congressional efforts to limit the direct effect of NAFTA because of unanticipated consequences. Yet if Chapter 11 can be used to challenge environmental regulations in a way that does not adequately account for environmental interests (and a conclusion to this effect would seem premature), this may be a consequence of specific rules embodied in Chapter 11. The provisions of NAFTA were drafted with limited environmental goals. Before concluding that Chapter 11 transnational dispute settlement fails to protect environmental interests, it might be well to examine the content of the substantive rules of Chapter 11.

During the implementation period to date, trade between Canada, Mexico, and the United States has increased significantly.[146] Mexico has experienced a surge in foreign investment inflow.[147] These economic developments might be attributed to the market-access opening and stabilizing effects of a highly legalized trilateral trade and investment agreement. They might also stem from a very strong U.S. economy combined with, among other things, the peso crisis, which reduced the effective price of Mexican exports and investment stock.[148] The U.S. government's analysis of the first three years of NAFTA implementation concedes that the effects of peso crisis and a strong U.S. economy make disaggregation of NAFTA's economic effects highly problematic.

The durability of the NAFTA legalization formula has yet to undergo a major test involving policy divergence.[149] During the six-year period from January 1994 to January 2000 in which NAFTA has been in force, the economy of the United States has been very strong, and the political leaders of the United States, Canada, and Mexico have supported implementation of the agreement. Policy divergence might be precipitated by a significant slowdown in U.S. economic growth, by the election of protectionist/isolationist political leaders in one of the parties, or by other developments. Whether NAFTA's legalization formula will effectively withstand policy divergence will be determined as events unfold.

---

146. In the period from 1994 through 1996 covered by the U.S. Executive Branch Study, there was a substantial increase in two-way trade between the United States and Mexico. The share of U.S. imports in the Mexican market also substantially increased as did the share of Mexican imports in the U.S. market. Economic movements in NAFTA services markets were not significant during the same three-year measurement period. U.S. Executive Branch 1997, 8–11, 29–44.

147. The U.S. Executive Branch Study reported only a modest increase in the level of U.S. foreign direct investment in Mexico in the 1994–96 period. U.S. Executive Branch 1997, 22–24. A later Mexican government report indicates a significant acceleration of foreign direct investment inflows. Mexico Economic Update, *NAFTA Works*, March 1999, 1.

148. The U.S. Executive Branch Study confirms that it is difficult to isolate the effects of NAFTA on regional trade or investment flows during the first three years of its operation because the peso crisis overwhelms NAFTA-specified changes. The U.S. economy was exceptionally strong during the measurement period, and this alone might account for changes in import-export trends. U.S. Executive Branch 1997, 12–14.

149. Ernst Haas observed that the progress of regional integration is rendered unpredictable by turbulence and by the close linkage between regional integration mechanisms and external global economic and political factors. Haas 1975. The peso crisis was a turbulent event that NAFTA survived intact. This demonstrates some measure of durability, even if factors other than legalization (for example, U.S. interest in preserving Mexican political stability) affected developments.

Concluding Observations

In this article I have sought to analyze and explain why trade negotiators have increasingly relied on hard law instruments to pursue international economic objectives and why a particular hard law model was used to create NAFTA. International economic agreements that incorporate high levels of precision, obligation, and delegation reduce intergovernmental transaction costs, reduce risk premiums for investors and traders, constrain strategic governmental behaviors, provide guidance to bureaucrats, and promote a variety of transparency functions. These hard law objectives may be achieved using different legalization formulas. NAFTA evidences a high level of precision and obligation and a moderate level of delegation. The formula evidenced by the WTO agreement is substantially similar to that of NAFTA. The EU evidences a high level of obligation and delegation and a moderate level of precision. NAFTA and the EU were negotiated in rather different historical contexts and in pursuit of different objectives. For a variety of reasons, it is not practicable to measure whether the NAFTA hard legalization formula is better or more effective than the EU formula. To date, each of these regional integration arrangements appears to have been effective in pursuit of its objectives.

The NAFTA transnational dispute-settlement mechanism for direct investments has yielded certain unanticipated results that may broaden the scope of subject matter regulated by the investment chapter of the agreement. This lends some support to the postulate that granting rights of dispute-settlement access to private actors will broaden the legalization effects of an international agreement. This broadening may in some instances be contrary to positive social policies. This may lead some parties to conclude that international agreements such as NAFTA should be constrained within tight limits (that is, not be allowed direct effect) because of their potential unintended consequences. In the case of NAFTA, a more deliberate conclusion might be that the rules of the investment chapter require reevaluation.

The legalization effects of NAFTA remain to be tested against a significant change in political and economic policy in one of its parties. The extent to which NAFTA is able to survive a policy change will provide insight into the durability of hard law agreements. For the time being, the success of NAFTA, the WTO, and the EU suggest that hard legalization is preferable to soft legalization for accomplishing international economic objectives.

Legalization as Strategy: The Asia-Pacific Case

Miles Kahler

Legalization of international institutions is often cast as a global phenomenon driven, through a functionalist logic, by increasing economic integration or the simple density of international relations in the late twentieth century. An alternative view portrays legalization as spatially circumscribed. Institutions that display rules with high levels of obligation and precision and that delegate rule interpretation and enforcement to third parties are heavily concentrated in West Europe and North America, a zone of long-standing liberal democracies and high levels of economic integration. This concentration, and the regional variation in legalized institutions it implies, offers leverage in explaining legalization in world politics. Closer examination of regional variation also permits a better estimate of the benefits and costs of legalized institutions in sustaining cooperative and predictable outcomes for both governments and private agents.

If Europe and North America provide an implicit benchmark for high legalization, the Asia-Pacific region offers an important example of low legalization and possibly an explicit aversion to legalization. Before the end of the Cold War, the Asia-Pacific region had produced few formal multilateral institutions, given the region's growing economic and security interdependence.[1] A modest wave of institution building in the 1990s narrowed the institutional difference with other regions, although the density of institutions spanning the region remains lower than that in Europe or the Americas. More important, those regional institutions constructed with significant Asian participation remained highly informal and explicitly rejected legalization in their design. Formal rules and obligations were limited in number; codes of conduct or principles have been favored over precisely defined agreements; and disputes have been managed, if not resolved, without delegation to third-party adjudication.

I wish to thank Robert O. Keohane, Andrew MacIntyre, Richard Steinberg, the editors of *International Organization*, the participants in the June 1997 conference "Domestic Politics and International Law" and an anonymous reviewer for their comments on previous drafts of this article. Hilary Hicks, Cory Firestone, and Pablo Pinto provided valuable research assistance.
    1. Kahler 1988.

International Organization 54, 3, Summer 2000, pp. 165–187

Documenting this institutional record in the Pacific is less difficult than in other regions, since institution building has often explicitly excluded legalization. Three institutions, their formation, and their evolution are examined in the first section: the Association of Southeast Asian Nations (ASEAN), Asia-Pacific Economic Cooperation (APEC), and the ASEAN Regional Forum (ARF). These institutions span economic and security issue-areas.

Explaining this pattern of regional variation in legalization is more challenging. In the second section of this article I advance competing explanations for the apparent failure of legalization to take hold in Pacific regional institutions. Each explanation offers different predictions of future institutional evolution. Demand-driven, functionalist arguments associate legalization with economic integration. As levels of integration grow, the binding character of liberalizing agreements becomes more important, and, as levels of obligation and precision increase, delegation of rule interpretation and adjudication of disputes is often observed. A second explanation, widely espoused within the region, portrays regional institutions as reflective of domestic legal culture and institutions. Culturally grounded institutions are predicted to change very slowly, if at all, on the dimensions of legalization. A third cluster of explanations rests on domestic politics. Some features, such as a high assessment of the sovereignty costs of legalization, are shared by the developing countries in the region. Other domestic political variables, such as authoritarianism versus democracy, are likely to divide regimes in the region and influence their attitudes toward institutional forms. Political heterogeneity itself may influence institutional development when institutional change requires consensus on the part of members. Finally, the choice of informal institutions may be an instrumental and strategic choice on the part of governments: instrumental in that institutional choices are not in themselves fundamental but rather are a means to accomplishing other national ends; strategic in that the choice of legalization is highly dependent on other actors and their capabilities in a prospective institutional setting. No generalized preference for or against legalized institutions would be observed, as a cultural explanation might predict; instead, national choices for or against legalization would vary according to the context of bargaining.

Recent developments in the region, the subject of the third section, permit some discrimination among these explanations. One key regional institution, ASEAN, has embraced increased legalization. Asian governments have also made clear their willingness to employ legalized global institutions to resolve both economic and territorial disputes. Two other regional institutions, the ARF and APEC, however, continue to resist clear-cut legal obligations and third-party dispute settlement. This pattern, if sustained, undermines cultural and political explanations that predict a uniform and persistent resistance to legalization and lend support to both demand-driven and strategic accounts of legalized institution building.

The final section is devoted to understanding the implications of these findings for the Asia-Pacific region after the Asian economic crisis of 1997–98. The sharp economic downturn produced a crisis of confidence in regional institutions, which were widely seen as weak and ineffectual. Whether the future of the Pacific will be more legalized than its past has become part of the region's debate on its institutional course.

ASEAN, ARF, and APEC: Institutions Without Legalization

Three regional institutions and their histories are central in an assessment of legalization in the Asia-Pacific region. The long history (by regional standards) of ASEAN and its self-proclaimed status as an alternative Asian model for international institutions make its evolution particularly important.[2] Its members, all developing countries, and its institutional model of incremental institutionalization and low legalization directly influenced APEC, founded in 1989, and the ARF, a multilateral security group that first met in 1994. Combining both proponents of greater legalization and critics of this "Western" style of international collaboration, the internal debate within APEC also sheds light on the reasons for endorsing or resisting a legalized model of institution building.

The "ASEAN Way": Collaboration Without Legalization

ASEAN was one of many regional institutions constructed in the developing world during the 1960s. In contrast to many of those now-fossilized organizations, ASEAN has played a significant role in Southeast Asia for three decades, while developing in directions unforeseen by its founders. Despite an emphasis on economic cooperation at the time of its formation in 1967, ASEAN remained primarily a mechanism for diplomatic cooperation for much of its history. Its success in the first decades was measured in managing, if not resolving, disputes among the ASEAN states that might have disrupted their economic development and provided an opening for hostile external powers. From this initial security collaboration, ASEAN evolved, after the Vietnamese invasion of Cambodia, into a diplomatic community that worked in collaboration with powers outside the region to thwart the Vietnamese occupation.[3] Economic collaboration was limited until ASEAN governments took steps to liberalize their economies, boosting low levels of economic interdependence among the member economies. Even the security agenda in the first decades was dominated by internal threats from Communist insurgents, a threat largely outside the design of the fledgling regional organization.

As Michael Leifer describes, ASEAN was the "institutional product of regional conflict resolution" (or, more precisely, conflict management). The institutional form chosen by ASEAN's members was strictly intergovernmental and informal. Its founding document was a "multilateral declaration and not a treaty" nor was it a "legal

---

2. The original members of ASEAN, founded in 1967, were Indonesia, Malaysia, the Philippines, Thailand, and Singapore. Brunei became a member in 1984; Vietnam, Cambodia, Laos, and Myanmar were admitted to membership in the 1990s.
3. Leifer 1989.

regime embodying a commitment to some form of political integration."[4] Legalization was low, and institutions were rudimentary at the start. An annual meeting of foreign ministers, chaired on a rotating basis by one of their number, provided its governing structure, together with a Standing Committee for consultation between these meetings. Informally, the central arena for consultation and bargaining during ASEAN's first decade was the Senior Officials Meeting (the top senior officials of the foreign ministries), a group awarded no formal role in ASEAN.

ASEAN's institutions developed slowly; a modest increase in obligation and precision was not accompanied by any increase in delegation from member states to the organization, however. The Declaration of ASEAN Concord and the Treaty of Amity and Cooperation in Southeast Asia signed in 1976 established core principles of behavior and a code of conduct for regulating relations among the states of the region. Although the Treaty of Amity and Cooperation (TAC) legally bound its signatories to this code of conduct, which included respect for sovereignty, non-interference in domestic affairs, peaceful settlement of disputes, and renunciation of the use of force, no sanctions were included to enforce the norms of conduct.[5] These ground rules formed the basis for ASEAN's method of dispute management, the much-studied (and touted) ASEAN way. ASEAN's treaty structure did not produce an elaboration of military cooperation, however; nor did it sustain any delegation from member states to the small secretariat established in 1976.

The institutional design and procedures of ASEAN—the ASEAN way—are normally described as starkly different from the formal legalism of most Western international institutions. Relations among ASEAN's members emphasize "informality rather than a legalistic framework, adopting the principles of accommodation and consensus in decision making and non-interference in the domestic affairs of its members, and accommodating the needs of members at different levels of economic development."[6] Two principles lie at the core of ASEAN's official ideology and standard operating procedures: *musyawarah* (consultation) and *mufakat* (consensus). These two terms are taken to characterize decision making in village society in Southeast Asian societies (or at least Malay societies). The first defines a process of decision making that involves painstaking and lengthy discussion and consultation in which decisions emerge from the bottom up. That process aims to achieve eventual consensus—unanimity or near-unanimity—as a much-valued result.[7] This alleged transfer of a domestic decision-making style (clearly informal and antilegal) to international negotiation implies a strong cultural component in the choice of international institutions, at least in the rhetoric of ASEAN's members.

ASEAN did not remain a skeletal institution, despite its resistance to legalization. As its mandate grew to include cooperation in a larger number of domains, the density and frequency of intergovernmental meetings (eventually over two hundred each year) served to cement its consultative and consensual institutional model. A deepen-

---

4. Ibid., 25.
5. Hoang 1996, 63–71.
6. Chia 1996, 59.
7. Thambipillai and Saravanamuttu 1985, 11–13.

ing of intergovernmental cooperation followed the Manila Summit in 1987: ASEAN formally incorporated the Senior Officials Meeting (already at the core of its permanent operation) and created a Senior Economic Officials Meeting to handle all aspects of ASEAN economic cooperation. Consultation widened to include Senior Officials Meetings on the environment, drug trafficking, social development, science and technology, and other policy domains. The creation of national secretariats in each foreign ministry that were responsible for ASEAN-related activities at the national level strengthened this move from intergovernmental to transgovernmental collaboration.

The product of this increasingly elaborate ASEAN cooperation umbrella was difficult to measure. Ironically, for all of the *gemeinschaft* aura of the ASEAN way, few if any major disputes were settled by means of consultation and consensus building: dispute management (preventing the outbreak of militarized disputes or military conflict) best characterizes the achievements of ASEAN in security collaboration. Even the means of dispute settlement specified in the 1976 treaty—a High Council that would recommend ways of settling disputes—has never been activated. Nevertheless, ASEAN's success as a mechanism of diplomatic collaboration was unique in the developing world. It has also been labeled a security community in formation in which the use or threat of force among members has become increasingly rare.[8]

Economic cooperation among ASEAN members produced mediocre results until the formation of the ASEAN Free Trade Area (AFTA) in 1992. ASEAN's pattern of economic cooperation and the reasons for its limited achievements are familiar: inward-looking economic policies and economies at different levels of income and industrialization. The absence of formal regional institutions and the failure to negotiate precise and binding obligations reflected those shortcomings rather than creating them. Although the ASEAN economies were among the most successful in the developing world by the 1990s, very little of that success could be attributed to intraregional trade liberalization.[9]

A long list of economic initiatives—Preferential Trading Arrangements, Industrial Projects, Industrial Complementation Projects, and Industrial Joint Ventures—was succeeded by AFTA, agreed to at the Singapore Summit in 1992. AFTA was designed in part to deflect competitive pressures within the region, particularly China and India. Widespread economic liberalization in Asia had removed both the distinctive policy and cost advantages of ASEAN. Substantial unilateral liberalization in ASEAN member economies and the prospects of greater intraregional trade argued for accepting more binding obligations to liberalize trade.[10] AFTA also reflected the emerging economic agenda for developing economies in the 1990s: to attract foreign investment by creating wider markets, a dynamic that would influence NAFTA as well as other regional arrangements.

---

8. See Acharya 1998; and Khong 1998.
9. Excluding Singapore, a crucial entrepot, intra-ASEAN trade was less than 5 percent of total trade. Chia 1996, 63.
10. See Chia 1996; and Ravenhill 1995.

Despite the fanfare that accompanied AFTA's introduction and a new strategy of creating a common effective preferential tariff that made national exceptions more difficult, ASEAN faced a serious credibility problem. Its half-hearted attempts at regional trade liberalization in the past and the informal institutional preferences of ASEAN members produced skepticism on the part of many observers. Institutional innovations did not seem to match the new commitments.[11] Apparently, AFTA would continue to rely on unilateral measures with a minimum of peer pressure. Even as the agenda of AFTA widened beyond merchandise trade to include services and other contentious issue-areas, a mechanism for mobilizing member governments to speed the process of liberalization and to bring pressure on those who defected from liberalization commitments remained unclear.[12]

ASEAN's institutional design was modified by two innovations that were designed to add political weight to the AFTA liberalization project and to increase the organization's ability to monitor compliance with commitments. At the same time, these changes did not represent an increase in legalization. The 1992 Singapore Summit that approved AFTA added political oversight to the new liberalization program by establishing a calendar for regular summits of ASEAN heads of government. In addition, the ASEAN secretariat was delegated increased responsibilities for initiation, advice, coordination, and implementation of ASEAN activities. Expanded delegation was related to the requirements of AFTA as was acceptance that the Senior Economic Officials would recommend decisions to the economic ministers by "flexible consensus," a break with ASEAN traditional insistence on effective unanimity.[13] The secretariat's staff doubled—but only to thirty-one, an indication of the limits of delegation and the persistence of ASEAN's intergovernmental model.

In evaluating the original design of AFTA, John Ravenhill notes two prominent shortcomings that were linked to the ASEAN way of institution building and its aversion to legalization: inadequate precision and limited delegation. In contrast to other regional free-trade agreements, AFTA was a sparse document of about fifteen pages (compared to NAFTA's more than one thousand). The lack of concrete and specific provisions in the original version of AFTA produced the derisory nickname "Agree First, Talk After." In the absence of more precise obligations, nontariff barriers (more important in many sectors than tariffs) and rules of origin threatened to undermine the new strategy for trade liberalization.[14] Given the ambiguities and contested interpretations that were likely to arise with such a sketchy blueprint, ASEAN also seemed to require new institutional capabilities for interpreting rules or adjudicating disputes. Despite modest increases in delegation to the permanent apparatus of ASEAN and a widening of intergovernmental collaboration, those capabilities did not exist.

---

11. Ravenhill 1995.
12. Kieran Cooke and Peter Montagnon, A Liberal Pinch of Eastern Spice, *Financial Times*, 18 October 1995, 12.
13. ASEAN Secretariat 1997, 15–36.
14. See Ravenhill 1995; and Chia 1996.

ASEAN in the early 1990s was a model of institutional development without legalization. ASEAN institutions were far more elaborate than they had been at the founding of the group twenty-five years earlier, moving from an intergovernmental model to a transgovernmental one. The scope of cooperation had widened to encompass a broad swathe of government policies. Binding and precise legal obligations among the member states remained relatively few, however, and delegation of interpretation or enforcement to judicial or quasi-judicial institutions did not exist.

The ARF: Security Initiatives the ASEAN Way

Although security arrangements have generally been less legalized than institutions and agreements in other issue-areas, arms control regimes during the Cold War often included precise and binding obligations. (The third dimension of legalization—delegation—has been less characteristic of security regimes.) As in other spheres, legalization in security arrangements was particularly characteristic of Europe. In the Pacific the European model of confidence building and arms control was rejected in favor of a weakly institutionalized multilateral arrangement that reflected the influence of ASEAN and the high sovereignty costs attached to constraints on security policies.

The ARF, which met for the first time in 1994, was the first intergovernmental multilateral security initiative that covered the entire Asia-Pacific region. Its heterogeneous membership includes the ten members of ASEAN and twelve other governments.[15] Wide membership has been matched by a thin institutional framework, deeply influenced by the ASEAN model. As one observer remarked, the ARF was "so underinstitutionalized the members don't even call themselves members."[16] The ARF began (and continues) without a secretariat (ASEAN provided the services of a secretariat) and with no clear obligation to convene between the forum's annual meetings.[17] Its operational conventions resemble those of ASEAN: consensus (and nonvoting); progress at a pace comfortable to all participants.

In self-conscious contrast to "Western-style legalism," the modest agenda of the ARF was not based on binding commitments of any kind.[18] Although ASEAN's TAC was adopted early on as a code of conduct for the ARF, its import was "more symbolic than practical."[19] The more legalized alternative of having participants accede to the TAC would have been opposed by China and treated warily by Indonesia and other members of ASEAN. Instead, the ARF based its initial program on a set of modest seminars on noncontroversial topics.

---

15. In addition to ASEAN members, the membership of the ARF includes Australia, Canada, China, the European Union (presidency), India, Japan, Mongolia, New Zealand, Papua New Guinea, Republic of Korea, Russia, and the United States.

16. Johnston 1999, 287.

17. Ibid.

18. Garofano 1999, 76–77.

19. Leifer 1996, 35.

The model of a weakly institutionalized and continuing dialogue on security in the Pacific is regarded by some as the principal achievement of the ARF.[20] Although China's deep suspicion of precise and binding multilateral commitments threatened the ARF, its supporters claim that China's "comfort level" has shifted over time with participation in the forum and that China's incorporation in such a framework, however loose and imprecise, is valuable for regional cooperation and conflict management.[21] Rather than movement forward by a pattern of negotiation and commitment, the ARF relies heavily on its nonofficial track two for forward momentum and new ideas.[22] Whatever the shortcomings or strengths of the ARF, however, few of its members seem eager to have the organization move in a more legalized direction: sovereignty costs in the sphere of security relations may simply be too high. However, in the case of the third regional institution, APEC, conflict between an Asian (or ASEAN) model of nonlegalized institution building and a more legalized approach backed by the United States and others has been more apparent and persistent.

APEC and the Rejection of Legalization

ASEAN and its institutional design were awarded a central role in the development of the ARF; ASEAN preferences were also crucial in the initiation of APEC. As Yoichi Funabashi describes, Japan and ASEAN were the central Asian players in the formation of APEC.[23] Since ASEAN's opposition had blocked the development of a Pacific economic organization in the past, the institutional preferences of the Southeast Asian governments had to be accommodated. ASEAN was promised a prominent role from the beginning by Australia, which had proposed the formation of APEC.[24] One way of insuring that APEC would not be dominated by Japan and the United States was to shape the organization in the ASEAN image. ASEAN preferences were close to those of Japanese policymakers, who viewed even the Organization for Economic Cooperation and Development (OECD) as too formal a model for the planned Pacific economic organization.

As the name of APEC itself indicates, its precise character as an institution has been a matter of debate since its foundation. Lawrence Krause defends APEC as a process that constrains and informs governments through ongoing dialogue, a process that also explicitly engages the private sector, which has been the source of Pacific economic integration.[25] Ippei Yamazawa labeled APEC an "open economic association" that represents economic integration without formal institutions.[26] Unlike ASEAN, whose members were all Asian developing countries, or the ARF, in which sovereignty costs produced a broader consensus against legalization, APEC contained what Ravenhill calls two "competing logics" that coalesced around the

---

20. Khong 1997.
21. See Johnston 1999; and Foot 1998.
22. Garofano 1999, 87.
23. Funabashi 1995, 52–53.
24. Ibid., 64.
25. Krause 1994.
26. Yamazawa 1992.

dimensions of legalization: Asian preferences for "lack of specificity in agreements" and "an informal, incremental bottom-up approach to regional cooperation" were juxtaposed with Western models based on "formal institutions established by contractual agreements."[27]

In its first years APEC emphasized consultation and dialogue, rather than binding commitments, a trajectory that clearly placed it in a nonlegalized mold that resembled other regional institutions. This pattern matched the preferences of ASEAN and of China (the two key constraints on the ARF's construction as well). ASEAN's wariness of "dilution" within the larger APEC framework found voice in its Kuching Consensus, which laid out the ground rules for ASEAN participation in APEC. The consensus specified opposition to legalization within the new regional organization, stipulating that APEC "should not lead to the adoption of mandatory directives for any participant to undertake or implement" and that it should proceed "gradually and pragmatically."[28] The ASEAN position did not foreclose further institutionalization of APEC through one of two avenues: either agreeing on nonbinding principles that would evolve into a more binding code or permitting some members to opt out if they were unwilling to participate in more binding agreements. China, an early participant in APEC, expressed even less willingness to enter into binding commitments, opposing "a strong organization with mandatory powers that can force it to change beyond its ability and desire."[29]

By 1993, as a new U.S. administration took greater interest in APEC, APEC's future as a purely consultative institution was challenged by a more ambitious alternative. The gradualist view of APEC's future was soon pitted against an "American" approach that was viewed by Asians as "too legalistic and too institutional."[30] The first APEC summit in November 1993 was preceded by an ambitious report from the Eminent Persons Group that had been formed to advise the APEC member governments on the organization's future course. The report urged a timetable and a target date for achieving free trade in the Pacific as well as a "GATT-plus" agenda of trade and investment facilitation measures. For the U.S. member of the Eminent Persons Group, the 1993 summit demonstrated that APEC had "become a negotiating forum rather than a purely consultative body."[31] This turn in APEC's agenda and instrumentalities appeared to be confirmed at the Bogor Summit in 1994, which endorsed a region-wide program for liberalizing trade and investment. The timetable was multispeed, offering more time to developing countries. Nevertheless, a high-level political commitment was made to an agenda that appeared to move beyond the global GATT/WTO agenda, including investment as well as behind-the-border policies. Skeptics noted that the Bogor Declaration was "very much in the Asian tradition of lack of specificity about institutional design and agreement implementation."[32] Asian

27. Ravenhill 1998, 159.
28. See Soesastro 1994, 47; and Plummer 1998.
29. Zhang 1998, 222.
30. Soesastro 1994, 50.
31. Bergsten 1994.
32. Ravenhill 1998, 159.

observers saw the United States transforming the APEC mandate "at its root," by replacing its model of "consultation and consensus" with "more formal and binding commitments to scheduled liberalization programs."[33]

The record of APEC following the Bogor Summit, however, demonstrated the familiar regional pattern of limited institutionalization with little or no legalization. APEC's institutional design has included a prominent role for informal advisory groups, such as the Pacific Economic Cooperation Council, the Eminent Persons Group, and the APEC Business Advisory Council, but it remains an intergovernmental group. Its small secretariat relies heavily on working groups to arrive at consensus. After Bogor, debate centered on two issues: on the one hand, the priority to be awarded to the liberalization agenda, as compared to APEC's other goals of trade and investment facilitation and technical cooperation and, on the other, the means by which the Bogor commitments would be reached. Developing-country members of APEC emphasized building on the success already achieved in the region through unilateral means: the addition of peer pressure within APEC councils would produce Concerted Unilateral Action (CUA) without moving toward binding commitments or deadlines, extensive monitoring, or the application of sanctions. The United States and others from the industrialized world were skeptical of the CUA model and stressed the need for clearly measured reciprocity to overcome the temptation of free-riding within APEC and between APEC and the rest of the world.[34]

In subsequent development of individual action plans and the Manila Action Plan for APEC (MAPA) to implement the Bogor commitments, it became clear that any movement toward more binding and precise APEC commitments had been a false start. APEC remained resolutely nonlegal; its members "have shown little willingness to formalize APEC by means of binding agreements on a defined set of substantive economic or trade issues, nor have its members sought to create a regional institution with rule-making, interpretative, enforcement, or adjudicative powers."[35] On the legalization dimensions of precision and obligation, the MAPA clearly fell short: even a sympathetic observer labeled it "complex" but "vague on overall goals and short on specifics."[36] Even more revealing was APEC's foray into liberalizing investment regimes, a set of principles that were explicitly labeled "nonbinding." As Merit Janow points out, these principles were, on several key points, imprecise and weaker than commitments already made under the WTO's Trade-Related Investment Measures negotiations. Although the principles included a dispute-settlement provision, they did not incorporate a mechanism or procedure beyond suggesting settlement through acceptable arbitration procedures.[37]

Delegation, the third dimension of legalization, was necessarily linked to obligation and precision. If there were no binding rules to be interpreted or adjudicated, then little need existed for a formal dispute-settlement mechanism. Perhaps the clear-

---

33. Yamakage 1997, 293.
34. Ostry 1998.
35. Janow 1996/97, 948.
36. Petri 1997, 41.
37. Urata 1998, 108.

est indication of the skepticism that APEC's Asian members—particularly Japan, China, and ASEAN—have toward legalized models was found in proposals for an APEC dispute-mediation service rather than a dispute-settlement mechanism. The Eminent Persons Group, which moved the APEC agenda forward in the 1990s, had recommended the creation of a dispute-settlement mechanism, "based on either the 'Dunkel text' [of the proposed WTO dispute-settlement mechanism] or the Canada-United States/NAFTA model, as soon as possible."[38] The second and third Eminent Persons Group reports, however, transformed this recommendation into a dispute-mediation service that would not compete with the WTO's new Dispute Settlement Understanding and would only "provide assistance in resolving (and thus, over time, perhaps avoiding) economic disputes among its members."[39] The Eminent Persons Group justified this endorsement of a less-legalized formula with a reference to APEC's own evolving institutions: a binding dispute-settlement mechanism required "the existence of agreed rules against which to judge compliance" or (on the NAFTA model of judging compliance by implementation of domestic laws) "a significant degree of comparability of those laws among the participating economies."[40] As soon became clear, even this less-legalized version of a dispute-settlement mechanism would prove unacceptable or unnecessary for Asian members of APEC.

Why Legalization Is Low in the Asia-Pacific Region

By the mid-1990s three key regional institutions in the Pacific had taken an institutional form that appeared to reject legalization. The obligations undertaken were seldom binding and were often imprecise. In part because of the character of members' commitments, little delegation to interpret or adjudicate those commitments was evident. The emergence of legalized models outside the region—particularly the WTO, the European Union, and NAFTA—seemed to have inspired little imitation.

The characteristics of these three Asia-Pacific institutions seem to undermine simple *demand-driven, functionalist* models of legalization: economic integration and security interdependence have grown in East and Southeast Asia as well as across the Pacific, yet the demand for legalized institutions seems to remain low.[41] Growing regional economic integration might produce legalized institutions through the domestic political demands of increasingly internationalized economic interests. Their interests in a stable, rule-governed environment for international economic transactions should be reflected in more legalized institutions to govern market access and constrain government policies. A somewhat different model relies on the growth of specific assets related to intraregional trade and investment.[42] Specific assets—investments tightly linked to intraregional economic exchange and having few alter-

---

38. APEC Eminent Persons Group 1993, 40.
39. APEC Eminent Persons Group 1994, 23–24.
40. Ibid., 23.
41. Models of this kind are elaborated by Kenneth W. Abbott and Duncan Snidal in this issue.
42. Yarbrough and Yarbrough 1992.

native uses—will increase concerns over government opportunism in regional economic partners. Legalized institutions may deal more effectively with the threat of opportunism and backsliding from commitments through easier identification of violations and mechanisms for sanctioning those violations. Although the rejection of legalized institutions in the Pacific appears to undermine these arguments, a final demand-driven approach may help to explain the pattern of institutional design in the region. If alternative institutions are available outside the region to supply the legalized characteristics required by the new economic circumstances, then demand for such institutions within the region may be lower.

A second explanation for the region's rejection of legalization is widely accepted in regional rhetoric: ASEAN and APEC are set apart from "Western-style" institutions on the basis of radically different Asian *legal culture and institutions.* International expression of those domestic institutions and cultures produces the ASEAN (or APEC) way and a distrust of Western-style legalization. This argument is often connected to wider assertions of "Asian values"—less adversarial and litigious, less intent on demonstrating right and wrong, more concerned with avoiding conflict. One commentator on APEC dispute management argues that an "Asian way" of approaching disputes—"an emphasis on group harmony, consensus, and informality and avoidance of legalism"—is at the core of disagreements between Asian and Western members: "These differences of 'legal culture' reflect deeply held values and are unlikely to change in the near future."[43] According to this model, institutional preferences are expressive of deep-seated cultural norms that are reflected in domestic legal practices and international institutional choices.

Arguments from dominant legal culture to international institutional design fail for several reasons, however. Most Asian societies, particularly in Southeast Asia, display legal pluralism rather than monolithic legal cultures and homogenous legal institutions.[44] Domestic legal institutions were produced by successive layers of legal influence—some imposed by colonial powers, some borrowed by successor regimes. This process of melding legal traditions preceded Western influence in some cases. In Indonesia, for example, "Islamic law was never taken over fully anywhere. . . . Indonesian societies picked and chose among rules that were then adapted to suit their own organizational values and needs."[45] Complexity increased in many societies when modernizing nationalists, whether those of Meiji Japan or postcolonial Indonesia, embraced the centralizing and unifying tendencies of Western law against local and religious traditions. Local legal and political traditions, such as the *musyawarah* and *mufakat* of ASEAN, were typically rejected by nationalists or reserved for a poorly educated rural population: "How could a unified and independent country survive without a unified regime of law? How could 'primitive' adat law be a suitable vehicle of modernization?"[46] Not only is Asia characterized by legal pluralism within individual societies; its heterogeneity across societies, given different religious and

43. Green 1995, 730–31.
44. Hooker 1978.
45. Lev 1972, 5–6.
46. Fasseur 1992, 256.

colonial histories, is also manifest. Legal cooperation within ASEAN has made little progress because of the diversity of legal systems within Southeast Asia.

What appear to be cultural differences may in fact represent strategies pursued by political actors. Legal "traditions" are sometimes rooted in a cost-benefit calculus that is skewed by governments. Frank Upham describes the sources of persistent national ideologies—such as the belief that Japan is a deeply harmonious society averse to litigation—in a political or bureaucratic elite's desire to deflect social pressure in particular directions (that is, away from the judicial system).[47] The ASEAN or Asian way of managing disputes or favoring informal institutions may result from not only the construction of social myths about harmony and a national past untouched by Western influence but also conscious political programs to dampen adversarial conflict internally and internationally.

Domestic political explanations for regional institutional design represent a third category of explanation independent of culture and reflective of national histories. Domestic politics includes variables that are shared by most of the Asian societies that are members of these institutions as well as other variables that discriminate among them. Both political homogeneity (a shared history of responding to colonialism) and heterogeneity (divisions over political regime and the status of domestic legal institutions) may undermine a move to legalized institutions. A common assessment of the sovereignty costs associated with legalization (and their political consequences) may lead states to reject legalized institutions; resistance by authoritarian regimes skeptical of the rule of law will also hold back institutional evolution in a legalized direction, so long as decision making occurs by consensus.

All of the states in Southeast Asia, with the exception of Thailand, share a history as colonial territories. Other regional powers, such as China, have also been marked by the experience of unequal treaties imposed by Western imperial powers and by invasion and occupation by Japan. These histories are embedded in the domestic politics of Asian societies, creating a strong attachment to norms of state sovereignty and a bias against legalized institutions. Consensus decision making protects national prerogatives, and external, binding constraints that might challenge internal legitimacy and political order are viewed with deep suspicion. This postcolonial syndrome, which increases what Kenneth W. Abbott and Duncan Snidal call sovereignty costs, should erode over time as new political cohorts take power, although certain domestic interests, such as the military and state security bureaucracies, may have an organizational interest in sustaining nationalist programs.[48]

The Asia-Pacific region, apart from its relatively uniform response to colonialism, is marked by political heterogeneity. To the degree that legalization is based on the interaction of liberal democratic states, the region may not meet a crucial threshold condition. Authoritarian regimes are likely to reject constraints on their behavior (the rule of law) internally and internationally. Authoritarian regimes and states that im-

---

47. Upham 1987.
48. Abbott and Snidal, this issue.

pute high sovereignty costs to legalized institutions are unlikely to entertain transnational dispute resolution, which offers direct access to nonstate actors. As Robert Keohane, Andrew Moravcsik, and Anne-Marie Slaughter argue, transnational dispute resolution may deepen and reinforce legalization over time.[49]

Domestic legal institutions and practices in the region are also diverse. Peter Katzenstein has argued that Asian states inherited "rule by law" institutions rather than the West European tradition of "rule of law."[50] However, Asian societies display considerable variation in the strength of their legal institutions and the power of their legal professions and judiciary. Whatever the current level of political intervention in the administration of justice, some states (Singapore, Malaysia, the Philippines) have histories of judicial autonomy and legal redress, whereas others (Vietnam, China) possess only the rudiments of independent legal institutions.

Each of the preceding explanations predicts a uniform response on the part of regional states toward legalized institutions. Functionalist and demand-driven explanations predict an increase in legalization with growing economic integration; explanations based on legal culture or domestic politics predict persistent resistance to legalization. (Democratic and rule-of-law states might be predicted to deviate from authoritarian states in their acceptance of legalized institutions, but those preferences may not find expression within institutions that are embedded in politically heterogeneous settings.)

The most significant flaw in explanations for the persistent rejection of legalization in the Asia-Pacific region, however, is that a uniform rejection of legalization has *not* persisted. Outside regional institutions, Asia-Pacific governments have embraced legalization in particular issue-areas when it serves national purposes. Within the region, ASEAN's members have accepted legalization as a concomitant of their free trade area. APEC and the ARF, on the other hand, remain institutions that are not legalized on any of the three dimensions of obligation, precision, or delegation.

These recent developments lend support to a fourth explanation for legalization: the choice of legalization is both *instrumental* and *strategic*. The choice of legalized institutions is instrumental in that it does not express deeper cultural preferences (or aversions). Instead, legalized institutions are primarily a means to other ends. The governments of the region share common goals of economic integration and opening (without such a minimal consensus, AFTA and APEC would not exist). The national choice of legalization in a particular context, then, results from a calculus that legalized institutions serve those goals, even when costs (particularly sovereignty costs) are taken into account. The choice for or against legalized institutions is also strategic, since it will be influenced by the competing strategies and capabilities of other actors in particular institutional settings. Governments may reject binding and precise obligations in a setting that requires bargaining with a government (the United States) that not only has greater economic and legal capabilities but also has demonstrated an attachment to unilateral enforcement. As described in the next section, this

49. Keohane, Moravcsik, and Slaughter, this issue.
50. Katzenstein 1997, 28.

type of discriminating calculus goes some distance in explaining both institutional innovations and stasis in the Pacific region.

A Legalized Future? Recent Institutional Evidence in the Asia-Pacific Region

Discriminating among alternative explanations for the pattern of legalization in the Pacific would be difficult were it not for two recent developments: acceptance by Asian governments of legalized arenas outside the region and divergence between the institutional evolution of ASEAN on the one hand and APEC and the ARF on the other. These developments lend support to the strategic explanation for legalized institutions and undermine those explanations, particularly cultural and political explanations, that rely on homogeneous or unchanging preferences toward legalization within the region.

Asian Governments and the WTO

The WTO's Dispute Settlement Understanding is widely regarded as a victory for those who wished to move the global trade organization in a more legalized direction. Although Japan, the largest Asian economy, had endorsed a diplomatic rather than a legal view of GATT dispute resolution at the start of the Uruguay Round, there is little evidence that Japan actively opposed the legalized direction that the negotiations eventually took.[51] On the contrary, Funabashi claims that Japan, and particularly the Ministry of International Trade and Industry, had long been interested in strengthening dispute-settlement mechanisms in world trade as a way of constraining American unilateralism.[52]

The record of Asian governments under the new WTO dispute-settlement procedures undermines arguments that they are reluctant to engage in legalized institutional settings. Certainly Asian countries, and particularly developing countries, underutilized the GATT dispute-settlement mechanism, relative to their importance in world trade.[53] The short history of the WTO Dispute Settlement Understanding suggests that this pattern may be changing, even though few concessions were made to developing countries in the negotiations that produced the procedure. Although Asian governments continue to underutilize the new procedure when compared with their importance in world trade, the proportion of complaints brought by Asian governments has doubled as a share of total complaints when compared to the historical average under GATT.[54] The first complaint lodged under the new procedure was

---

51. Croome 1995, 149.
52. Funabashi 1995, 196–97.
53. McGivern 1996, 101.
54. Under GATT only nine complaints were brought by Asian governments (4.35 percent of the total). Three of these were brought by Hong Kong. In the short time that the WTO procedure has been operational, 10.63 percent of the complaints have been brought by Asian states. The proportion of complaints made against Asian countries has remained roughly the same.

brought by Singapore against Malaysia. (It was withdrawn before a panel was established.) Japan has used the WTO procedures vigorously to challenge U. S. sanctions directed to opening the Japanese automobile market and European Union restrictions on "screwdriver" assembly plants. An even more sensitive case was the complaint lodged by Japan against Indonesia, challenging Indonesia's National Car Program. Thailand and Malaysia were party, with other developing countries, to a successful and high-profile complaint against U.S. restrictions on imported shrimp for which the United States claimed environmental justification. Apart from the European Court of Justice, the WTO Dispute Settlement Understanding is the most legalized dispute-settlement mechanism in world trade. Nevertheless, Asian governments appear comfortable using it to challenge the major trading powers and each other.

Territorial and Other Interstate Disputes

Acceptance of third-party adjudication by Asian states has been even more striking in other issue-areas. The execution of Flor Contemplacion, a citizen of the Philippines convicted of murder in Singapore, produced a crisis between Singapore and the Philippines. The conflict was resolved in part by referral to a panel of three U. S. forensic experts who conducted a joint autopsy on the remains of the murder victim and reached the same conclusion as the Singaporean coroners.[55]

The Asia-Pacific region is dotted with long-standing territorial disputes. Few disputes have been resolved through judicial or quasi-judicial means. Recently, however, economic development has driven ASEAN states toward resolving territorial disputes that have lingered since decolonization. Singapore and Malaysia agreed in 1994 to submit their dispute over the island of Pulau Batu Putih/Pedra Branca to the International Court of Justice. The choice of venue was determined strategically by Malaysia: rather than using ASEAN's dispute-settlement mechanism, which could have been activated, it viewed the World Court as more appealing. As one senior ASEAN official pointed out, "Malaysia has territorial disputes with practically every country in ASEAN. They felt that if they go the [sic] High Council it may be difficult to get an objective decision from the other members."[56] By June 1998 the two governments had negotiated a special agreement to refer Malaysia's claim to the International Court of Justice; formal signing and ratification remain.

Malaysia and Indonesia followed suit in their dispute over Sipadan and Ligitan Islands. The need to settle the territorial claims was heightened once again by economic development: Malaysian development of Sipadan—touted as one of the ten most beautiful islands in the world—as a tourist destination brought protests from Indonesia over this breach of a 1969 status quo agreement. Malaysia once again preferred the disinterested International Court of Justice to its ASEAN partners who held territorial claims against it; Indonesia held out for bilateral avenues of settlement or the ASEAN High Council. The two disputants agreed to take their claims to

---

55. Hoang 1996, 69–70.
56. Frank Ching, Resolving ASEAN's Problems, *Far Eastern Economic Review*, 23 January 1997, 28.

the International Court of Justice in October 1996; a memorandum of understanding on the procedures for submitting their respective claims was agreed in May 1997, and in May 1998 the two countries formally agreed to accept any ruling made by the court. The two countries jointly seised the court of their dispute in November 1998, and it now appears on the court's docket.

These territorial disputes are not the most important in the region. Recent and limited judicial proceedings hardly confirm a larger movement to legalization in this issue-area. So far, legalized resolution of more important territorial conflicts, such as those in the South China Sea, has not occurred. Nevertheless, these longstanding disputes were taken to a global judicial body for settlement rather than to an available, nonlegalized forum in the region (the ASEAN High Council). These cases demonstrate that resistance to legalization is not uniform and, in the case of Malaysia, that governments make careful strategic calculations of when and where legalized dispute resolution will serve national purposes.

Legalization and ASEAN

In addition to their willingness to resolve disputes in legalized forums outside the region, the ASEAN governments have also endorsed legalization in ASEAN itself. The adoption of a dispute-settlement mechanism by ASEAN in 1996 was clearly related to AFTA and the growth of economic exchange among ASEAN economies. First proposed by Thailand in April 1995, the idea of a dispute-settlement mechanism for ASEAN grew from the dispute between Singapore and Malaysia over the Malaysian government's decision to increase tariffs on petrochemical products (a major Singaporean export). Singapore believed that this action was a breach of the agreement within AFTA to lower tariffs by 2003. A means for determining which member's interpretation was correct did not exist within ASEAN, however. As a result, Singapore took Malaysia's action to the new WTO dispute-settlement mechanism. Bringing an intra-ASEAN trade dispute to the WTO was an embarrassment to the organization and its members; it also sparked a realization that disputes of this kind were likely to increase as economic integration deepened among the ASEAN economies.

It was fitting that the ASEAN decision to adopt a dispute-settlement mechanism was taken at the same meeting that crafted a compromise on the knotty issue of liberalizing trade in rice and sugar. AFTA's liberalization demands were beginning to bite; consensus and consultation might not sustain the momentum of liberalization without additional institutional supports. The dispute-settlement mechanism was designed to apply to all ASEAN economic agreements, past, present, and future. A senior ASEAN official also noted that requests for a formal mechanism had come mainly from the private sector, even though the private sector would not have direct access to the mechanism.

Much of the commentary on the ASEAN dispute-settlement mechanism referred to a change from ASEAN's consensus decision making to a more legalized approach. The model of dispute resolution chosen bore little resemblance to an ASEAN way of settling disputes. Closer to the WTO design, its time limits from conciliation or mediation to final appeal were tighter than those of the global trade organization (a total of 290 days). Decision on the panel report by the Senior Economic Officials Meeting and any final appeal to the ASEAN Economic Ministers is to be by simple majority, and that decision will be final and binding. The use of majority vote was a dramatic first use of nonconsensual decision making within ASEAN. If the offending party does not comply, the complainant can request compensation; if compensation cannot be agreed, the ASEAN Economic Ministers may grant authorization to suspend trade concessions.

Although no ASEAN government has yet utilized the new dispute-settlement mechanism, ASEAN governments have undertaken to create "a more predictable and rules-based free trade area" in the wake of the Asian economic crisis. In particular, governments agreed in 1998 to a protocol that required sixty days' notification of any changes in AFTA commitments or obligations. The possibility of permitting private parties direct access to the ASEAN dispute-settlement mechanism has also been discussed, a sharp turn toward transnational dispute resolution if it should occur.[57] Outside the realm of trade relations, the Philippine president Joseph Estrada has called for establishing a "formal mechanism for the resolution of disputes within ASEAN and of situations inimical to regional peace." Once again, ASEAN's strategic use of legalization was apparent. China and its South China Sea territorial claims were the target of Estrada's initiative; since China was even more averse to legalized settings than ASEAN, such a mechanism could only advantage the Southeast Asian states. Moving to have the TAC endorsed as a "binding code of conduct" (recommended in the ASEAN Vision 2020) would serve the same purpose.

APEC Resists Legalization

ASEAN governments have accepted third-party dispute settlement—the dimension of legalization least favored in the past—in both ASEAN and other venues. ASEAN's acceptance of legalization has not been paralleled in APEC's recent evolution, however. The final report of the APEC Eminent Persons' Group in 1995 once again advocated an APEC dispute-mediation service, but it concluded that such a service "should avoid duplicating or competing with the arrangements already in place at the WTO." This conclusion reflected the belief of APEC members that the new WTO Dispute Settlement Understanding, despite its legalized character, should become the principal venue for resolving trade disputes.[58] As described earlier, Asian governments have used the new WTO instrument in resolving trade conflicts.

APEC's Dispute Mediation Experts Group began its work in 1995 on the assumption that "no new institutions should be created within APEC for this purpose."[59] Before the November 1996 Manila Summit, APEC rejected once again the establish-

57. Al Labita, Push for More Transparency in Free Trade, *Business Times* (Singapore), 7 October 1998, 6; and ASEAN to Use Anti-dumping Mechanism Soon, *Businessworld* (Philippines), 6 February 1998.
58. APEC Eminent Persons Group 1995, 12. See also Krause 1997, 245.
59. McGivern 1996, 104.

ment of a formal dispute-settlement body similar to the WTO. Edsel Custodio, joint head of the Philippines negotiating team, stipulated that disputes among members should be resolved using "voluntary mediation"; if such efforts failed, the parties to the dispute should go to the WTO.[60] The Manila Summit's Ministerial Joint Statement made virtually no mention of dispute mediation. The Dispute Mediation Experts Group has directed its attention toward educating APEC's members and publics on WTO dispute-settlement procedures and rendering more transparent the arbitration and dispute-resolution practices available in APEC member economies.[61]

APEC and the ARF, Pacific institutions that incorporate Western legalizers, remain resolutely resistant to legalization in all of its dimensions. The sixth ASEAN Regional Forum in July 1999 confirmed that the ARF would "continue to move at a pace comfortable to all ARF participants on the basis of consensus."[62] ASEAN, on the other hand, whose members were supposed to be culturally predisposed against legalization, had moved some distance toward legalizing its institutions and making use of other legalized venues at the global level. This apparent paradox points toward an explanation of legalization in the region that emphasizes both its strategic utility for national governments and its demand-driven character.

Legalization and Its Regional Limits

The Asia-Pacific region has recently shed its image as the home of informal and nonlegalized institutions in favor of a more differentiated pattern. ASEAN's recent acceptance of more legalized institutional innovations and its members' willingness to make use of third-party adjudication outside the organization lend support to both demand-driven and strategic accounts of legalization. Shifts in the international economic environment and liberalization of the ASEAN economies laid the groundwork for the negotiations that produced AFTA. Regional business leaders, increasingly involved in each other's economies, lobbied for a more stable and rule-governed environment. Governments, facing a higher level of specific assets linked to intraregional trade and hoping to attract foreign investment through a wider market, accepted the need for more binding liberalization commitments. AFTA, which produced commitments with greater precision and obligation, in turn stimulated demands for mechanisms to clarify and interpret its commitments. Reports on the WTO dispute-settlement mechanism negotiations suggest that business had pressed for a more formal mechanism, a pattern that has been seen in other regional economic organizations. Territorial dispute settlement has also been driven in part by desires to exploit the resources in and around contested territory. At the same time, postcolonial sensitivities regarding external legal constraints have diminished.

These regional trends and the demand for institutional innovation that they created affected only one regional institution, however; both APEC and the ARF continued

---

60. Edward Luce, APEC Rejects Rigid Disputes Mechanism, *Financial Times*, 25/26 May 1996, 3.
61. APEC 1998.
62. ASEAN Regional Forum 1999.

to avoid precise and binding commitments or any third-party mechanisms for rule interpretation or adjudication. If demand driven by economic integration moved ASEAN's members toward legalization, one would expect a similar development in APEC. To explain their divergent trajectories, a different aspect of demand-driven models must be deployed: the successful operation of the WTO altered the supply of legalized institutions for the settlement of certain economic disputes. As APEC members (who were members of WTO or aspired to be) became familiar with the WTO Dispute Settlement Understanding, they saw less need for a dispute-settlement or mediation mechanism within APEC. Despite the rhetoric against legalization within APEC, its members appeared willing to utilize the new and highly legalized procedures of the WTO.

An explanation based on alternative institutional supply does not fully account for APEC's failure to follow the logic of adopting more binding and precise liberalization obligations, as ASEAN had through the AFTA. Economic integration in the Pacific was as deep or deeper than integration within Southeast Asia. In order to explain the paradox that has recently emerged—less legalization in regional forums that have more members who strongly endorse legalization—legalization or its absence can best be viewed as a strategic response by governments in particular institutional settings. Governments choose or accept legalized institutions when they represent the best strategy for accomplishing their larger goals, given the strategies and capabilities of other governments.

The ASEAN governments (and China) are able to prevent legalization in APEC. They continue to do so because they do not want the organization's prospective agenda, which goes well beyond that of the WTO, to become binding, and because of the configuration of power within the organization, which could be dominated by the two largest industrialized economies, the United States and Japan. Given the United States' willingness in the past to deploy unilateral enforcement measures in order to force the opening of Asian markets and change "protectionist" Asian policies, Asian members of APEC faced the possibility that the United States (and possibly Japan) would employ legalized institutions in just this fashion. Most of the states in East and Southeast Asia have been targets of U.S. demands in international economic negotiations. They are, therefore, likely to be more wary of legalization in institutions where the United States plays a dominant role (that is, APEC) and less averse to legalization in a setting where the United States is absent or less dominant. For APEC to pursue a more legalized future, the United States would need to credibly commit to ending "aggressive unilateralism."

Since ASEAN is entirely Asian in its membership (and, with the exception of Singapore, restricted to developing countries), these recent changes call into question sweeping claims of opposition to legalization based on legal culture or uniformly high sovereignty costs. Other domestic political variables better supplement demand-driven and strategic explanations for the emerging pattern of legalization. Although sovereignty costs may have declined in economic issue-areas, other domains, such as national security and human rights, have begun to display a divide between democratic and authoritarian regimes over the issue of greater international oversight. One of the region's democracies, Thailand, recently proposed "flexible engagement"—a break with ASEAN's rigid ban against scrutinizing domestic political practices or human rights violations. Not surprisingly, that suggestion was subjected to withering criticism by other, nondemocratic members.[63] The type of political regime is also likely to influence the willingness of governments to accept international legalization that guarantees their citizens' rights against national governments and the influence that legalizing constituencies have on national policy. Both will be reduced in authoritarian regimes. Few members of the ARF, including the United States, seem eager to move that forum in the direction of more binding and precise multilateral security commitments: the sovereignty costs for national militaries and electorates appear too high. So long as decision making is based on consensus, these politically driven cleavages will place these issue-areas off-limits to legalization, in contrast to other regions, such as Europe or Latin America.

The recent pattern of legalization in the Pacific has wider implications for the dilemmas faced by developing countries contemplating the reform of regional and global institutions. On the one hand, weaker states will typically benefit from legalization, since legalization will often impose some constraints on the strong, discouraging unilateral interpretation and enforcement of international obligations. On the other hand, as the Asia-Pacific case suggests, that calculus may hold only in cases of complete legalization (relatively high levels of obligation, precision, *and* delegation). A setting in which levels of obligation and precision increase, and stronger members are able to unilaterally interpret and enforce those obligations, is far less favorable for weaker countries. National legal capabilities will also be critical in determining a government's relative costs and benefits when confronted with a choice for or against legalization. Successful engagement in legalized institutions requires resources and expertise, which are often in short supply in poor countries. The newest (and poorest) members of ASEAN—Vietnam, Laos, Myanmar, and Cambodia—have economies that are not fully market-oriented and demonstrate the greatest concern over sovereignty costs. They are likely to serve as a drag on future legalization within ASEAN. The organization may reach a legalization plateau that remains well below the levels of institutional legalization found in the Western Hemisphere and the European Union.

An explanation for the pattern of legalization in the Pacific that emphasizes demand-driven and strategic elements leaves one puzzle, however. Why do the Asian states decline to trust a legalized APEC and at the same time pursue their economic interests in a legalized WTO? A complete answer to this question awaits a more discriminating and detailed analysis of the policies of individual governments toward particular global and regional institutions. However, several elements of an explanation can be advanced. First, the agenda of APEC was potentially more expansive than the WTO on such sensitive issues as foreign investment and regulatory policies. It was also less subject to control by developing-country members. The addition of influen-

---

63. Nayam Chand with Shada Islam, In the Bunker, *Far Eastern Economic Review,* 6 August 1998, 24–28.

tial and active developing-country governments, such as India and Brazil, in WTO negotiations offered insurance that any new U.S. agenda would be subject to developing-country approval. The question of agenda control, in turn, reflects on the configuration of influence within the two organizations. The relative weight of Japan and the United States within APEC was potentially much greater than it was within the WTO, where their views would be balanced by the European Union and a large number of developing economies.

The strategic explanation for acceptance of or resistance to legalized institutions is supported by historical evidence. Despite the rupture that Western imperialism meant for the traditional Chinese worldview in the nineteenth century, the Chinese imperial government quickly absorbed and deployed Western international law to defend its interests in a dangerous environment. China attended both Hague Peace Conferences (1899 and 1907), joined the Universal Postal Union, and adhered to "many multilateral conventions dealing with the laws of war, the pacific settlement of disputes, and other matters."[64] China's behavior was imitated by other Asian states that were spared absorption into colonial empires: "The strategy generally adopted by China, Japan, and Siam was to learn the 'rules of the game' as quickly as possible. This involved translations of British, French, and American books on international law and the employment of foreign advisers."[65] Whatever their cultural distaste for "Western" legal instruments, Asian states have long demonstrated a willingness to use those instruments when required for their national well-being.

Legalization, Regional Institutions, and the Asian Economic Crisis

The question of legalization and its limits in the Asia-Pacific region has now become entwined with institutional reforms in the wake of the most severe regional economic crisis in decades. Following the Thai devaluation in July 1997, a national currency crisis became, through a process of unexpected contagion, a regional and global economic crisis. Proponents of the existing institutional models emphasize that existing regional institutions did not collapse and that these institutions were not designed for high-profile roles in crisis management.[66] Despite an increase in economic conflict during the crisis, existing commitments to liberalize in AFTA were underscored and accelerated at the ASEAN summit in November 1999. Domestic economic distress has not been externalized into militarized conflicts. Nevertheless, even sympathetic observers do not award key regional institutions a central or constructive role in managing either the economic crisis or the later crisis that surrounded Indonesia's role in East Timor. Others have been harsher in their judgments: "None of the much-touted institutions and forums designed to promote regional stability and economic

---

64. Gong 1984, 181.
65. Brownlie 1984, 365.
66. Harris 1999.

health has had much to contribute, especially not the region's own club: the Association of South-East Asian Nations. . . . The 'ASEAN Way' no longer works."[67]

Defenders of the region's informal model of institution-building had argued before the crisis that these institutions satisfied key goals of national governments without the need for formal and legalized institutions.[68] Debate has now begun on whether that model, already eroding before the crisis, remains adequate to the newly defined international situation and the risks that it presents to governments in the region.

Although the region's governments have demonstrated an instrumental and pragmatic attitude toward the shape of regional institutions, legalized institutions may not immediately address the region's collective needs (for at least two reasons). Legalization is only one dimension on which international institutions can vary, and it is not clear that legalization will provide the institutional improvements required by a new and riskier regional environment. Following Abbott and Snidal, legalization seems particularly suitable for situations in which opportunism on the part of governments is a central concern and legalization can render commitments more credible. Although government opportunism occurred during the Asian crisis (Malaysia's imposition of capital controls, for example), it is far from clear that failure by governments to maintain their existing commitments is a central problem for the region. The region did not demonstrate substantial backsliding from existing liberalization or agreed commitments for the future. Regional financial contagion has produced a consensus on the need for closer surveillance of government policies, but here as well, legalization appears to add relatively little. As Beth Simmons suggests, monetary and financial affairs at the global level have been marked by a decline rather than an increase in legalization since 1976.[69] Although enhanced surveillance may require institutional changes, and particularly a greater commitment to transparency on the part of governments, those institutional changes may not require legalization.

Finally, regional economic institutions in the Pacific have avoided competition with global institutions. The demand for further institutional development in the region may be partially offset if global institutions satisfy the requirements perceived by governments. Global institutional supply has been important in the past and will continue to be important to these globally engaged economies in the future. Although the Asian economic crisis is likely to produce institutional change in the region, more legalized regional institutions may not offer solutions to the new economic and security challenges that the region faces. Choices will not be based on hypothetical cultural affinities to institutions of a particular sort, but rather on hard calculations of institutional performance and regional outcomes.

---

67. The Limits of Politeness, *The Economist*, 28 February 1998, 43–44. For other critical reviews of APEC, the ARF, and ASEAN, see Cheng 1998; Acharya 1999; and Wesley 1999.

68. See Doner 1997, 201; and Petri 1997, 43.

69. Simmons, this issue.

The Legalization of International Monetary Affairs

Beth A. Simmons

Sovereign control over money is one of the most closely guarded national prerogatives.[1] Creating, valuating, and controlling the distribution of national legal tender is viewed as an inherent right of a nation-state in the modern period. Yet over the course of the twentieth century, international rules of good monetary conduct have become "legalized" in the sense developed in this volume. This historic shift took place after World War II in an effort to bolster the confidence that had been shattered by the interwar monetary experience.[2] If the interwar years taught monetary policymakers anything, it was that economic prosperity required credible exchange-rate commitments, open markets, and nondiscriminatory economic arrangements. International legalization of monetary affairs was a way to inspire private actors to once again trade and invest across national borders.

Sensitivity to the sovereignty costs continues to preclude dense hard law in this area. This is especially obvious when compared to other areas of economic relations, such as trade in goods and services. The Bretton Woods institutions involved only three international legal obligations regarding the conduct of monetary policy. The best known of these was to establish and maintain a par value, an obligation that was formally eliminated by the Second Amendment to the International Monetary Fund's (IMF) Articles of Agreement in 1977. But two other obligations remain: to keep one's current account free from restrictions, and to maintain a unified exchange-rate

Thanks to William Clark and Brian Pollins, the editors of *International Organization* and this special volume, and two anonymous reviewers for very helpful comments. I would like to acknowledge the extremely helpful research assistance of Zachary Elkins and Conor O'Dwyer, who assisted with data management and analysis; Becky Curry, who assisted with the legal research; and Aaron Staines, Maria Vu, and Geoffrey Wong, who assisted with data collection and entry. I would also like to thank the Archives of the International Monetary Fund for access to documents. All errors remain my own.
 1. Cohen 1998.
 2. See Eichengreen 1992; and Simmons 1994.

International Organization 54, 3, Summer 2000, pp. 189–218

system. The first requires that if a bill comes due for imports or an external interest payment, national monetary authorities must make foreign exchange available to pay it. The second proscribes exchange-rate systems that favor certain transactions or trade partners over others. IMF members can voluntarily declare themselves bound by these rules (Article VIII status) or they can choose to maintain, though not augment, the restrictions that were in place when they joined the IMF (a form of grandfathering under Article XIV).

My premise is that legalization of international monetary relations helps governments make credible policy commitments to market actors. As I will argue, the central mechanism encouraging compliance is the desire to avoid reputational costs associated with reneging on a legal obligation. As Kenneth Abbott and Duncan Snidal suggest in this volume, legalization is a tool that enhances credibility by increasing the costs of reneging. The hard commitments encoded at Bretton Woods were thought to be necessary because the soft arrangements of the interwar years had proved useless. Governments have used commitment to the rules contained in the Articles of Agreement as a costly commitment to stable, liberal external monetary policies. This does not mean that compliance is perfect, but it is enhanced when other countries comply and when governments have a strong reputation for respecting the rule of law. When these conditions obtain, rule violation entails disproportionate reputational costs, as I shall argue.

In the first section of the article I examine the international monetary system prior to World War II and show that "hard" international legal obligations played virtually no role in monetary relations during that time. In the second section I demonstrate that the Bretton Woods system ushered in a new "public international law of money" that peaked just prior to the breakdown of the par value obligation in the 1970s. Although governments are no longer legally required to maintain fixed exchange rates, they can still (voluntarily) obligate themselves to maintain a unified exchange-rate system and to keep their current accounts free from restrictions. Thus the trajectory of legalization in this issue area is far from linear. In the third section I investigate why, given a choice, governments commit to and comply with the IMF's monetary rules. Since commitment to these rules is voluntary, why do governments obligate themselves to abide by them? I argue that governments are much more likely to choose to commit under conditions in which such a commitment would be credible, but that commitment is also conditioned on other countries' willingness to commit. In the fourth section I examine the conditions under which commitment affects behavior. Since the IMF is unlikely to enforce these rules in a direct way, what explains compliance? The findings suggest that the desire to avoid reputational costs is crucial. Costs are higher if comparable countries are complying, and if a state has heavily invested in maintaining a strong reputation for respecting the rule of law. In short, legalization strengthens commitment. It is this quality that makes formal treaty arrangements desirable in the first place.

The International Monetary System Before 1945:
National Laws and International "Understandings"

The Nineteenth-Century Gold Standard

The stability of the international monetary system in the nineteenth century owed nothing to international legal agreements. Not a single international treaty addressed obligations of countries under the gold standard. Rather, the international system was anchored in national rules, often in the form of statutes, that specified the rights of private parties to import and export gold. In Britain, at the center of the system, the Peel Act of 1819[3] gave individuals the right to convert bank notes to gold by presenting them to the Bank of England. The Bank Charter Act (1844) extended to individuals the right to acquire notes for gold, and created a legal obligation on the part of the Bank of England to maintain gold backing pound for pound, for all outstanding Bank of England notes beyond the "fiduciary issue" of 14 million pounds.[4]

Although the gold standard certainly had a clear legal basis, there was nothing international about the legal structure on which it rested. It was, at most, a decentralized system of regulatory harmonization.[5] To access international capital and trade, other countries had an incentive to follow Britain onto gold. So in 1871 the German Empire made gold its standard (even though this required Germany to hold much more gold in reserve than did Britain). Switzerland and Belgium followed in 1878. France adopted the gold standard but restricted convertibility when the franc was weak. The Austro-Hungarian gulden floated until the passage of (what was purported to be) gold standard legislation in 1891. In 1900 the United States declared gold as the "standard unit of value," which put the country officially on the gold standard (though silver coins still circulated). None of these national decisions involved the international community in their making. Indeed, when international conferences did take place, they tended to favor bi-metalism.[6]

Nor was this system managed through international legal arrangements. Even if one does not accept the traditional description of balance-of-payments adjustment under the classical gold standard as fully "automatic," its cooperative aspects knew no international legal guidelines. W. M. Scammell described the adjustment mechanism as "quasi-organizational, being operated by a team of central bankers under the leadership of the Bank of England on behalf of the world community."[7] But at no point in the pre–World War I period could one point to an international legal framework within which such cooperation was to take place. It is not difficult to see why this should be so. This decentralized system of harmonized national rules seemed to provide a good degree of stability—at least for international traders and investors at

---

3. Amended in 1921.
4. Dam 1982, 23–25.
5. See, for example, the description by the MacMillan Committee on Finance and Industry, Cmd. 3897, HMSO 1931, as reprinted in Eichengreen 1985, 185–99.
6. Dam 1982, 23.
7. Scammell 1985, 105.

the industrialized core of the system.[8] As long as investors were confident that the system would be maintained,[9] there was little reason to design an elaborate international legal structure for its maintenance.

The Interwar Years

World War I disrupted not only the economic relationships but also the domestic political and social stability that underlay the confidence in the gold standard.[10] As a result, the interwar years were a "largely unsuccessful groping toward some form of organizational regulation of monetary affairs."[11] Increasingly, the major governments turned to negotiated agreements that had the feel of "soft law" as described by Abbott and Snidal. For example, the Brussels Conference of 1920 met to consider creating a new addition to the League of Nations, the Economic and Financial Commission, to which some responsibilities for economic stabilization might be delegated. In 1922 the governments of the major European countries met in Genoa to agree informally to the principles of a gold exchange standard, which would economize on gold by encouraging smaller financial centers to hold a portion of their reserves in foreign exchange rather than gold. Although this agreement did in fact have an important impact on the composition of reserves, it was at most a soft admonition to economize gold holding. When the Bank for International Settlements was created in 1930, governments were careful to limit their mutual obligations while solidifying the bank as their agent in the collection of reparations from Germany.[12] As the Permanent Court of International Arbitration noted, the international community had quite clearly "accepted [the] principle that a State is entitled to regulate its own currency."[13]

Virtually every important exchange-rate decision made in the interwar years was made unilaterally. On 21 September the British government implemented the Gold Standard (Amendment) Act of 1931, suspending payments of gold against legal tender and officially leaving the gold standard. Even as multilateral negotiations were in progress, the Roosevelt administration unilaterally imposed exchange controls and an export embargo.[14] Even when governments tried to coordinate their actions, diplomatic declarations were chosen over legal commitments. The Gold Bloc, formed in July 1933 among the governments of Belgium, France, Switzerland, and the Netherlands to cooperate to defend existing parities, was a "soft" legal arrangement created

---

8. Ford 1985.
9. Eichengreen writes extensively about the confidence that investors had in the prewar gold standard. Eichengreen 1992.
10. Simmons 1994.
11. Dam 1982, 50.
12. Simmons 1993.
13. *Case of Serbian Loans*, Permanent Court of International Justice, ser. A, nos. 20/21, 44, 1929, cited in Gold 1984b, 1533. Thus, researchers often speak of the "norms" of the gold standard (for example, Simmons 1994), but these were never codified in international agreements.
14. Presidential Proclamations 2039 (6 March 1933) and 2040 (9 March 1933); Executive orders 6111 (20 April 1933) and 6260 (28 August 1933). Cited in Dam 1982, 47, 55.

by declaration and communiqué, rather than a formal treaty. When France left the gold standard, for domestic reasons leaders needed multilateral cover and sought it in the form of the "Tripartite Agreement" of 1936. This agreement was the loosest of arrangements, in which Britain, the United States, and France issued separate declarations rather than sign a single document. Without mentioning devaluation, France announced the "readjustment" of its currency, while promising, as far as possible, to minimize the disturbance of such action on the international exchanges. France, Britain, and the United States agreed to arrange "for such consultations for this purpose as may prove necessary." The declarations also expressed the governments' intentions to take actions to relax the system of trade quotas and exchange controls that were in effect at that time and expressed the "trust that no country will attempt to obtain an unreasonable competitive exchange advantage and thereby hamper the effort to restore more stable economic relations which it is the aim of the three governments to promote."[15] Most historians of the period have concluded that the Tripartite Agreement did little to change international economic relations in the 1930s.[16] For our purposes, it was undoubtedly intended to create only the softest of obligations.

That governments tried at all to coordinate their monetary choices during this period had much to do with the growing incentives governments faced after World War I to externalize their problems of economic adjustment. The international monetary system was still dependent on national law, but the nature of the national rules had changed. Certainly governments could no longer passively accept internal adjustments in the face of mounting political demands to manage the economy. In contrast to the nineteenth century, during the 1930s a number of countries claimed to be on a "gold standard" even though gold had little to do with the money supply and hence held no implications for internal adjustment.[17] Once the national rules no longer commanded respect for internal adjustments, governments were increasingly faced with the need for international rules to put limits on external adjustments. Efforts to formalize international monetary relations arose from the need for credible limits on external adjustment.

The IMF and International Monetary Law: Toward the Formalization of "Rules of Good Conduct"

The legalization of international monetary relations burgeoned after World War II.[18] In rejecting the less formalized arrangements of the past century and establishing for

---

15. All quotations from the Tripartite Monetary Agreements of 25 September 1936 are from the version printed by the Bank for International Settlements, Monetary and Economic Department, Basle, January 1937. The sections quoted can be found nearly verbatim in all three declarations.

16. See Sauvy 1967, 224; Kindleberger 1986, 255, 257, 259; and Clarke 1977.

17. In the United States it was illegal after 1933 (Exec. order 6260) for a resident to hold gold coins or bullion. Sterilization funds in both the United States and Great Britain further severed the relationship between gold flows and international monetary policy.

18. The expression "rules of good conduct" is used by Gold 1965, passim.

the first time a public international law of money,[19] negotiators from the United States and the United Kingdom were consciously choosing an international legal framework to enhance the system's credibility. Moreover, the IMF was to be, among other things, a fund, the purpose of which was to extend loans to members in balance-of-payments trouble. This alone led to a huge increase in legal detail, since these rules are analogous to banking law or at least to banking practice, where terms of loans and their repayment are spelled out in contracts and often limited by statutes and regulations. The IMF was created by a multilateral treaty arrangement, by which signatories agree to pay in subscriptions in exchange for voting and drawing rights. Of course, the decision to create an intergovernmental organization and to codify basic rules required domestic ratification of all signatories. In the United States, this meant that the Articles of Agreement had to be ratified by two-thirds of the Senate and, because of the need for implementing legislation, a simple majority of both houses of Congress. With the entry into force of the IMF's Articles of Agreement, money—like activity on the seas and diplomatic relations among states—was drawn under the system of public international law and became newly subject to its broader norms and principles.[20]

Fixed Exchange Rates: The Rise and Fall of Legalization

The Articles of Agreement set forth two primary regulatory goals that reflected lessons drawn from the interwar years: governments should be obligated to peg exchange rates and to remove exchange controls and discriminatory practices that affected current transactions. Legalization was designed, of course, to fulfill the broader objectives of the IMF's founding members, especially those of the United Kingdom and United States. According to Article IV of the Articles of Agreement, "The essential purpose of the international monetary system is to provide a framework that facilitates the exchange of goods, services, and capital among countries, and . . . a principle objective is the continuing development of the underlying conditions that are necessary for financial and economic stability."[21] To this end, the original White Plan had advocated "the general policy of foreign exchange trading in open, free, and legal markets, and the abandonment as rapidly as conditions permit of restrictions on exchange controls." Controls that were once under the sovereign control of national governments now had to be justified to the international community and were collectively condoned only to the extent necessary "to carry out a purpose contributing to general prosperity."[22] In short, in the postwar monetary system, public international law was to be used as it had been for decades in trade relations: to

---

19. Gold 1984a, 801. A French plan was offered at the beginning of the postwar monetary negotiations. Although it played no direct role, it did indicate the French preference for agreement among the "principal nations" somewhat analogous to the Tripartite Agreement. The French plan saw an international institution as optional. Dam 1982, 76.

20. Gold 1980, 5. Nonetheless, legal treatments of these obligations are surprisingly few. See generally Denters 1996, 16–20.

21. Art. IV, sec. 1.

22. From the White Plan. Horsefield and De Vries 1969, 3:64.

help facilitate the international exchange of goods and services by providing for currency convertibility in open, free, and legal markets.

The international community thus explicitly recognized for the first time that exchange rates were properly a matter of international concern. To become a member of the IMF, a country had to communicate a "par value" for its currency by direct or indirect reference to gold. This might involve minor negotiations with the IMF staff, but it basically established par values very close to those prevailing just prior to membership. Members then had an obligation to maintain that par value within the margins prescribed in the articles.[23] Members were required, without exception, to consult with the IMF before making a change in their initial or subsequent par values; failing to do so constituted a breach of a legal obligation. And although the IMF could not propose a change in a member's par value, by using its resources it could influence a member's decisions to adopt a particular par value. In short, "the authority over exchange rates granted to the Fund by the original articles was unprecedented in international law."[24]

Not all members complied with the obligation to peg. Some were able to do so only by maintaining other undesirable (or illegal) practices, such as multiple currency arrangements or restrictions on current account, which will be analyzed later. Among the industrialized countries, Canada failed to comply and instituted generalized floating for many years,[25] and Germany and the Netherlands briefly were in breach as well.[26] The most spectacular instance of noncompliance—that of the United States in 1971—ultimately reversed the trend begun in the 1940s to harden exchangerate obligations. Outside of the IMF's legal framework, the "Group of 10" (G-10) industrialized countries met in an attempt to stabilize exchange rates by loosening the margins. The ensuing "Smithsonian Agreement" was adopted as a temporary set of rules by the IMF's executive board on the same day that it was announced in the G-10 communiqué.[27] Rules for generalized floating were then negotiated by the "Group of 20"—again, outside of the legal framework of the IMF—and were adopted by the executive board as nonmandatory guidelines.[28] The heyday of multilateral

23. Art. IV, sec. 4. Furthermore, Art. IV, sec. 2 provided that "no member shall buy gold at a price above par value plus the prescribed margin, or sell gold at a price below par value minus the prescribed margin." A central bank could not enter into any gold transaction with another central bank other than at par without one or the other violating the articles.

24. Gold 1988, 48.

25. Canada's decision to float in 1950 was a violation of the Articles of Agreement, but the IMF did not want to force a showdown with Canada; instead it issued an explanation that amounted to pragmatic toleration of floating rates. No major currency followed Canada (at least for the next two decades), so the case was more of an aberration than a precedent.

26. Gold 1988, 31.

27. Executive board decision, Central Rates and Wider Margins: a Temporary Regime, 18 December 1971. See Dam 1982, 191. The board tried to reconcile the Smithsonian Agreement with the articles. The decision stated that the temporary arrangement "would enable members to observe the purposes of the IMF to the maximum extent possible during the temporary period preceding the resumption of effective par values with appropriate margins in accordance with the Articles." Gold 1979, 559.

28. The executive board decision called on members to "use their best endeavors to observe the guidelines." Decision of 13 June 1974 (IMF 1974, 112). The guidelines said that a member "should" intervene "to prevent or moderate sharp and disruptive fluctuations from day to day and from week to week, . . .

legalized exchange-rate relations were effectively over. It was only left for the IMF membership to officially acknowledge the reassertion of national sovereignty in exchange-rate relations by composing the Second Amendment to the Articles of Agreement, which took effect in 1977.

Remaining Monetary Obligations: Article VIII

Despite the softening of legal obligations with respect to the system of par values, governments who are members of the IMF do retain two important obligations in the conduct of their external monetary policy. Both of these are contained in Article VIII of the Articles of Agreement, which spells out the general obligations of members. These rules prohibit restrictions on the making of payments and transfers for current international transactions; they also prohibit multiple currency practices without the approval of the IMF itself.[29] Article VIII section 2(a) provides that governments must make foreign exchange available for goods, services, and invisibles.[30] By agreeing to this standard, governments obligate themselves to make available to their citizens foreign exchange to settle all legal international transactions (it remains up to the government to determine which are legal).[31] They also agree to refrain from delaying, limiting, or imposing charges on currency transfers if these have the effect of inhibiting or increasing the costs of making payments.[32] Interestingly, this provision appears to be the only part of the Bretton Woods Agreements that constitutes an obligation of member states toward their own residents.[33]

Multiple currency practices that establish different rates of exchange have always been prohibited by the Articles of Agreement. Article VIII section 3 creates a hard legal obligation to avoid such practices,[34] which were viewed as a threat to the original parity rule, potentially discriminatory, and always distortionary. As with the restrictions in section 2, the IMF could, however, approve temporarily such practices, which can serve to soften the proscription in the short run. Multiple currency practices were rampant after World War II: about a third of all the countries involved in the Bretton Woods negotiations had multiple currency systems in place. As late as

---

should not normally act aggressively with respect to the exchange value of its currency," should adopt a "target zone of rates," and should consult with the IMF.

29. Art. VIII, sec. 2, para. (a), and sec. 3. Member states are, however, permitted to maintain or impose exchange restrictions under certain conditions: (1) if they are necessary to regulate international capital movements (art. VI, sec. 3); (2) with the approval of the IMF (art. VIII, sec. 2 (a)); (3) if the IMF has declared a currency "scarce" (art. VII, sec. 3 (b)); and (4) if the exchange restrictions were effective at the time the state became a member of the IMF (art. XIV, sec. 2).

30. The restriction applies only to payments and transfers for current international transactions. The IMF articles explicitly permit the regulation of international capital movements (Art. VI, sec. 3).

31. See Executive Board Decision 1034 (60/27), 1 June 1960, para. 1, *Selected Decisions of the International Monetary Fund and Selected Documents*, 11:259 (Washington, D.C.: IMF). See also Horsefield and de Vries 1969, 3:260.

32. Edwards 1985, 391 (see fn. 39 for original documentary sources); and Horn 1985, 295.

33. Boehlhoff and Baumanns 1989, 108.

34. Art. VIII, sec. 3 says: "No member shall engage in, or permit any of its fiscal agencies referred to in Article V, Section 1 to engage in, discriminatory currency arrangements or multiple currency practices . . . except as authorized under this agreement or approved by the Fund."

1971, a major member, France, introduced a multiple exchange-rate system. The United Kingdom also maintained a separate investment rate as late as 1979.

Why were rules forbidding these practices considered necessary? For two general reasons: Governments may want to support developmental objectives that favor certain kinds of imports over others based on established state priorities.[35] More often, however, governments use exchange controls and multiple currency practices as one among a variety of methods to deal with balance-of-payments problems.[36] For either purpose, they may require exporters to surrender foreign currencies received in export sales to government authorities, at governmentally determined rates.[37] In turn, importers are required to obtain foreign currency from the governmental authority or authorized bank. Such systems allow for foreign currency rationing or import discrimination in which foreign currency is made available (or available at favorable rates) for some goods or some transactions but not others.[38]

The IMF has always viewed such systems of control as dangerous substitutes for economic adjustment and inhibitions to the development of free foreign exchange markets. However, because many of the IMF's founding members could not immediately achieve full convertibility at unified rates, Article VIII obligations are made voluntarily. Upon joining the IMF, new members can avail themselves of "transitional" arrangements, under Article XIV, which in effect "grandfather" practices that were in place on their accession to the Articles of Agreement.[39] Even so, Article XIV countries are expected to withdraw restrictions when they are no longer needed for balance-of-payments reasons[40] and are required to consult annually with the IMF about retaining restrictions inconsistent with Article VIII.[41] In the course of these consultations the IMF tries to persuade members gradually to move from "transitional" practices—foreign exchange rationing, multiple exchange rates, foreign exchange licensing systems—to the IMF's traditional approach: reduction of domestic inflation, comprehensive fiscal reform, devaluation if necessary, and simplification of exchange restrictions to remove their tax and subsidy effects. Once these fundamentals are in place the IMF usually urges the Article XIV country to commit itself to Article VIII status.[42]

---

35. See, for example, India and Article VIII, 11 July 1955, S424, Transitional Arrangements, Article VIII Country Studies (Washington, D.C.: IMF Archives).

36. See Edwards 1985, 381–82; and Gold 1988, 255.

37. Edwards 1985, 391. Surrender requirements are not prohibited, because surrender in itself is not considered to be an impediment to the making of payments. Gold 1984a, 813.

38. Edwards 1985, 382. A very comprehensive system of exchange controls might prohibit residents to transfer the state's currency to nonresidents except with the state's permission on a case-by-case basis, or prohibit residents to hold foreign currencies except with the state's permission.

39. Art. XIV, sec. 2. An Art. XIV country can also adapt its restrictions without the need for IMF approval. But an Art. XIV country cannot introduce new restrictions without approval, adapt multiple currency practices without IMF approval, nor maintain restrictions that the member cannot justify as necessary for balance-of-payments reasons. See Horsefield and De Vries 1969, 1:248–59.

40. Art. XIV, sec. 2.

41. Art. XIV, sec. 3.

42. Ideally, the IMF wants the removal of restrictions to coincide with the assumption of Art. VIII obligations, though it has recognized that this might not always be possible and that waiting for the complete removal of every last restriction would only serve to delay the making of such a commitment.

Legal Commitment: Expectations and Evidence

But why should a government voluntarily assume Article VIII obligations? And why should it continue to comply with them? After all, the articles specify neither a time period nor a set of criteria for ending the transitional period.[43] And although the IMF encourages countries they believe are in a position to do so to make an Article VIII commitment, the IMF does not provide direct positive or negative incentives for doing so.[44] Nor does it directly "enforce" these obligations.[45] It does publish data on states' policies from which one can infer compliance (see the data appendix). The executive board can also "approve" restrictions (or not) and has done so as an accompaniment to adjustment programs it is supporting. But the consequences of nonapproval are questionable, since the board does not generally make its decisions public.[46] The executive board can declare a member ineligible to use the IMF's resources if the member "fails to fulfill any of its obligations" under the articles,[47] and noncompliance sometimes does interrupt drawings under standby and extended arrangements.[48] But, in fact, the IMF has used these formal remedies very sparingly. Noncompliers rarely have to worry about retaliation directly from the IMF, since members that vote for some kind of punishment may be concerned about drawing a retaliatory

See Article VIII and Article XIV, memo prepared by Irving S. Friedman, Exchange Restrictions Department, 24 May 1955, S424, Transitional Arrangements, Art. VIII and XIV, September 1954–55, (IMF Archives). In a few cases, developing countries that were not in an especially strong position to accept Art. VIII had no restrictions in place, and the IMF urged them to go ahead and commit, since they had nothing to "grandfather" under Art. XIV. See Haiti, memo from H. Merle Cochran to Irving S. Friedman, 30 October 1953, C/Haiti/424.1, Trans. Arrange., Members' Intent to Use (IMF Archives); and Letter, Ivar Rooth, M.D., to Jose Garcia Ayber, Governor of the Central Bank of the Dominican Republic, 1 August 1953, C/Dominican Republic/424.1, Trans. Arrange., Members' Intent to Use (IMF Archives). These countries often turn out to be long-term noncompliers.

43. Horsefield and De Vries 1969, 2:225. The IMF staff discussed on various occasions the imposition of time limits for the removal of restrictions and the unification of exchange rates, but rejected them as impractical. Article VIII and Article XIV, memo prepared by Irving S. Friedman, 24 May 1955, S 424, Trans. Arrange. (IMF Archives). There were also debates over the IMF's legal authority to declare an end to the transitional period. Furthermore, there were debates in the early period about exactly what "transitional" referred to. Extract, Executive Board Informal Session 54/2, 19 November 1954, S424, Trans. Arrange. (IMF Archives).

44. However, sometimes countries in fairly tenuous balance-of-payments positions who were willing to accept Art. VIII obligations were provided standby arrangements. For example, see Costa Rica (1965), Executive Board Minutes, EBM/65/7, 29 January 1965, C/Costa Rica/424.1, Trans. Arrange., Members' Intent to Use (IMF Archives).

45. In 1948, the executive board explicitly disapproved France's multiple exchange-rate practice and declared France ineligible to use IMF resources, invoking Art. IV, sec. 6 sanctions. The sanction failed to induce France to adopt a unitary rate. The use of sanctions was perceived as a failure and never invoked again. Dam 1982, 132.

46. Although the board is not barred from publishing reports that communicate the board's views, doing so requires a two-thirds majority of the total voting power to make this decision. Gold 1979, 153.

47. Art. XV, sec. 2 (a).

48. According to Gold, "All standby arrangements include a uniform term on measures that directly or indirectly affect exchange rates. Under this term a member is precluded from making purchases under an arrangement if at any time during the period of the arrangement the member: 'i. imposes [or intensifies] restrictions on payments and transfers for current international transactions, or ii. introduces [or modifies] multiple currency practices, or iii. concludes bilateral payments agreements which are inconsistent with Art. VIII, or iv. imposes [or intensifies] import restrictions for balance of payments reasons.' " Gold 1988, 466.

vote in the future. The IMF is much more likely to use persuasion than to apply a remedy for continued noncompliance.[49]

Hypotheses about why countries commit and whether they comply relate to the function that international legal commitments play in international monetary relations. I have argued that the shift to legalization in the postwar regime was an effort to lend credibility to various monetary policy commitments that were shattered after World War I. Governments commit themselves in order to send a costly signal to market actors as well as other governments that they plan to maintain a stable, open, and nondiscriminatory stance. A legal commitment helps make this signal more credible. It does this through many of the mechanisms Abbott and Snidal outline in their paper. An Article VIII commitment is more costly to breach than are other kinds of policies. For one, breaching a commitment has consequences in domestic courts in cases in which contract performance is contested. Exchange contracts that reflect illegal or unapproved restrictions are required by the articles to be unenforceable in the courts of any member state.[50] This should, in theory at any rate, create disincentives to make exchange contracts with private or public entities that operate under national rules that do not comply with international obligations.[51]

More important, however, is the signal that an Article VIII commitment sends to markets. It indicates a serious intention not to interfere in free exchange and thus to protect property rights of those engaged in international transactions.[52] It is a potentially costly signal to send, since noncompliance could be expected to involve domestic political costs. Recall that the proscription of current account restrictions amounts to a right of access to foreign exchange to nationals. Abrogation, then, amounts to the denial of an expected right of a domestic constituency, which is likely to raise criticisms by affected groups. Of course for a signal to be credible, there must be a good possibility that it will be complied with. That is why almost every country considering a move to Article VIII status has tried to assure markets and the IMF staff that they are in a tenable balance-of-payments position.[53]

---

49. Gold 1979, 185

50. Art. VIII, sec. 2, para. (b). This provision was originally designed to support the par value system; in particular to assuage the United Kingdom that New York would not become a significant black market for discounted sterling the value of which the United Kingdom was unable to defend through gold sales. Gold 1989, 73. It was originally placed alongside the exchange-rate provisions (Art. IV). According to Gold, "If a contract is unenforceable as a result of the provision, a court may not decree performance of the contract or give damages for nonperformance. . . . The provision establishes a defense rather than a condition for the institution of proceedings." Gold 1989, 90.

51. In practice, many domestic courts have been reluctant to refuse to enforce such contracts, especially when the interests of national firms or major financial institutions are involved. Gold 1989, 6–7.

52. Archival materials thoroughly support such an interpretation. To cite two examples among many, executive board members, in discussing Argentina's acceptance, "thought that Article VIII status would add substantially to the domestic and external confidence in the intentions of the authorities." Argentina—Acceptance of Article VIII, sections 2, 3, and 4, EMB/68/122, 14 August 1968 (IMF Archives). Executive board members, in discussing Costa Rica's acceptance, noted, "The move to Article VIII status was further proof of its determination to maintain a liberal payments system." Costa Rica (1965), EBM/65/7, 29 January 1965, Trans. Arrange., Members' Intent to Use (IMF Archives).

53. Thus, "it may be assumed that it is countries with relatively strong balance of payments positions that would most likely feel able to assume Article VIII status." Article VIII and Article XIV, memo prepared by Irving S. Friedman, 24 May 1955, p. 5, S424, Trans. Arrange. (IMF Archives).

Thus our first hypothesis is that the decision to commit is tied to expectations regarding the ability to comply in the future.[54] The ability to comply is necessary to making a credible commitment. Accordingly, the commitment is likely to be useful only to those countries with a good chance of complying. Countries with economies that are vulnerable to highly volatile swings in their external position are likely to face future conditions in which current account restrictions provide a handy policy instrument in the short run. Since balance-of-payments problems are the main reason governments interfere with the current account in the first place, it is reasonable to expect that external economic pressure or excessive demands for external payments could discourage governments from making an Article VIII commitment. And why should they? Markets are not likely to respond positively when the commitment is incredible. Hence our first hypothesis: susceptibility to balance-of-payments pressures will make a government less likely to accept Article VIII obligations.

Furthermore, it is likely that one influence on the decision to accept Article VIII status is that others are doing so. If making a legal commitment is a way to credibly commitment in a competitive economic environment, then following the lead of one's major competitors may be necessary. A country's firms may find themselves at a competitive disadvantage in international transactions if competitors make commitments to refrain from foreign exchange restrictions while the home government does not. The risk of government interference could result in a premium charged by foreign firms on transactions with residents. For competitive reasons, a government might want to avoid such a premium and follow the suit of its major economic competitors. In addition, international socialization toward accepted standards of behavior, accelerated by the growing dominance of neoliberal economic ideas touted by the IMF itself, may reinforce expectations of openness.[55]

Governments therefore face something of a dilemma: there are costs to being the first to liberalize (including the possibility of direct balance-of-payments pressures), but there are also costs to lagging too far behind international or regional norms. Governments have keenly felt this dilemma in formulating their policies regarding Article VIII. The major Western European countries, for example, assumed Article VIII obligations in unison, since "None of the six countries wanted to move in advance of the other, and all of them preferred to come under Article VIII at the same time as the United Kingdom."[56] A similar decision was made by the African franc

---

54. Downs and Rocke have used this insight to develop an endogenous explanation of treaty commitments based on uncertainty over future compliance. Downs and Rocke 1995.

55. External normative influences are important in the work of Keck and Sikkink 1998; Legro 1997; Fisher 1981; Kratochwil 1989; and Finnemore 1996. Margaret Levi, in her study of compliance with conscription efforts, combines both rational and normative elements in describing a form of "contingent consent" in which some compliance is "the result of . . . incentives, but at least some compliance expresses a confirmation in the rightness of policies." Levi 1997, 18.

56. Implementation of Article XIV and Article VIII Decision, minutes of staff visit to the United Kingdom, 22 July 1960, S424, Trans. Arrange., Move to Article VIII Mission, minutes of meetings (IMF Archives). The IMF archives contain ample evidence that no European power wanted to pay the potential costs of being the first mover, yet none wanted to lag a decision by other countries in the region. Thus, "The French policy with regards to restrictions depends on the policy followed by other European countries, especially Great Britain. It might even be said in large measure it is conditioned by that policy."

zone countries three and a half decades later. When Argentina committed to Article VIII, executive board members indicated that they were "not surprised to see one more Latin American country assuming the obligation," since most of the other Article VIII countries were from Latin America. Board members predicted that "now that Argentina had assumed the obligations of Article VIII perhaps Brazil would also do the same soon and Chile would follow."[57] In discussions of the timing of Article VIII acceptance with the IMF, Peru's prime minister "agreed Peru should not jump out ahead of the others, but . . . definitely does not want to 'miss the boat.' "[58] These concerns are understandable if legal commitment is viewed as a way to reassure markets in a competitive economic environment. Although there may be few incentives to liberalize first, governments need to be cognizant of the signal they may be sending by refusing to commit, especially when other countries with whom they might compete for capital or trade have done so.

If a legal commitment to Article VIII is a way to improve access to capital and trade by in effect raising the costs of interfering in foreign exchange markets, then we should expect commitment to be influenced by two factors: (1) a basic ability to comply (which is necessary for a credible commitment), and (2) the commitment decisions of other countries (which avoids the costs of being the first to move and reduces the costs of lagging).

We should also consider a set of plausible control variables that could reveal a spurious correlation with these hypothesized relationships. I am not suggesting that a credible commitment is the only reason a government would commit to Article VIII but investigating whether it stands up to a range of plausible alternatives. The first is a straightforward argument based on domestic demands: commitment is likely to be a function of domestic policy demands, just like any other aspect of foreign economic policymaking.[59] Such arguments must consider the source and nature of domestic preferences and the extent to which the political system reflects these preferences. Article VIII provides a right of access to foreign exchange for residents and

---

F. A. G. Keesing, 1 July 1955. S424, Trans. Arrange., Art. VIII Country Studies (IMF Archives). For a similar position by the Netherlands, see Netherlands and Article VIII. 23 June 1955, S424, Trans. Arrange., Art. VIII Country Studies (IMF Archives). On the United Kingdom's unwillingness to move alone, see memo from Rooth to E. M. Bernstein, 20 May 1955, S424, Trans. Arrange., Art. VIII and XIV, Sept. 1954–55 (IMF Archives). On the incentives for a general snowball effect within Europe, see memo from F. A. G. Keesing, 13 May 1955, S424, Trans. Arrange., Art. VIII and XIV, 1954–55 (IMF Archives).

57. Argentina—Acceptance of Article VIII, sections 2, 3, and 4, p. 4, 14 August 1968, EMB/68/122 (IMF Archives).

58. Memo from Jorge del Canto to Per Jacobsson, IMF Managing Director, 23 September 1960, C/Peru/424.1, Trans. Arrange., Members' Intent to Use (IMF Archives). Peru was basically free from all restrictions in 1960, and IMF staff members wondered whether they should be encouraged to assume Art. VIII obligations as soon as possible or wait and go with the Europeans. In a handwritten note in the margins, Per Jacobsson wrote, "No. It would not profit Peru to move first—more advantageous to be 'drawn by movement' with others." Memo from Jorge del Canto to Per Jacobsson, 17 May 1960, C/Peru/424.1 (IMF Archives).

59. The literature linking foreign economic policymaking to domestic political demands is vast. Most of this work concentrates on demands for trade protection. See, for example, Aggarwal, Keohane, and Yoffie 1987; Alt et al. 1996; Destler and Odell 1987; Goodman, Spar, and Yoffie 1996; McKeown 1984; Milner 1988; and Rogowski 1989. For works on financial and monetary policy, see Simmons 1994; and Frieden 1991.

nonresidents, and demands for such a right are likely to be greater in countries where trade is an important part of the national economy. A right of free access to foreign exchange is valuable to importers: it provides a guarantee to foreign firms that the government is not likely to use interference in the foreign exchange market to intervene in international business transactions.[60] It is also likely to be favored by export groups, whom recent research has shown to be concerned with issues of reciprocity and retaliation.[61] For these reasons, economies that depend on trade are likely to be among the most willing to make legal commitments to free and open foreign exchange markets.[62]

The IMF staff, in their discussions of who was ready to commit, clearly recognized the incentives that trade dependence created. Indonesia was deemed unlikely to commit, for example, because "The restrictive system is somewhat peripheral to the broad economic issues in which the public are interested: foreign trade is only 6% of GDP. And non-nationals control the major industries" (jute and tea).[63] On the other hand, when Guyana made the Article VIII commitment, the executive board noted explicitly that "Guyana was one of those very few developing countries in the world whose imports and exports, taken separately, were larger than 50 per cent of GNP, and this necessarily meant that the country was highly vulnerable to swings both in capital and in trading magnitudes." Trade dependence made Guyana a good candidate for Article VIII but also implied a possible need for IMF assistance should liberalization prove destabilizing. A standby arrangement was considered simultaneously.[64]

Furthermore, we might expect that the demand for guaranteed foreign exchange access is most likely to be addressed by a democratic regime. The political organization around this issue area is likely to be that of civil society versus the state: on the one hand, it is difficult to conceive of a private interest that would organize to actively oppose free access to foreign exchange. On the other hand, the concentrated rents go to the government, as the dispenser of limited access to hard currency. If one of the primary characteristics of democracy is the extent to which it empowers civil demands vis-à-vis the state, and if it is also true that these demands are likely to favor those who want free access to foreign exchange, then we should expect democratic governance to be positively associated with the acceptance of Article VIII.

---

60. According to Horsefield and De Vries, for example, "Article VIII status had come to signify over the years either that a country had a sound international balance of payments position, or that if its payments position was threatened, it would avoid the use of exchange restrictions." Horsefield and De Vries 1969, 2:285–86.

61. Gilligan 1997.

62. Relatedly, the IMF staff thought that Art. VIII obligation created the most advantages for countries whose currencies tended to be traded internationally. See the staff discussion contained in Peru—Aspects of Article VIII, C/Peru/424.1, Trans. Arrange., Members' Intent to Use (IMF Archives).

63. Indonesia and Article VIII, 14 July 1955, S424, Trans. Arrange., Art. VIII Country Studies (IMF Archives).

64. Guyana—Acceptance of Obligations of Article VIII, Sections 2, 3, and 4, Initial Par Value, and Stand-by Arrangement, 13 February 1967, EMB/67/10, C/Guyana/424.1, Trans. Arrange., Members' Intent to Use (IMF Archives).

It is also important to control for the institutional incentives provided by the IMF for those who commit. An early inducement for countries to choose Article VIII status was the fact that multilateral surveillance applied only to Article XIV countries until the Second Amendment (revisions to Article IV) extended mandatory surveillance to the entire IMF membership.[65] Prior to 1977, governments willing to announce acceptance of Article VIII obligations could actually avoid multilateral surveillance.[66] Article XIV countries, on the other hand, were subject to wide-ranging, even invasive "consultations," during which the staff broadly reviewed the member's balance-of-payments position. The executive board would then follow up with an official "view" of the member's situation. Thus until 1977, members faced a perverse incentive to accept Article VIII obligations: the commitment gave them the ability to avoid discriminatory and potentially humiliating surveillance and formal board review. We can hypothesize that the acceptance rate was therefore higher, all else being equal, before 1977 than after.

Finally, controlling for time is appropriate in this analysis. One important reason is that countries may have been reluctant to commit to Article VIII in the early years of the IMF because it was unclear just how the executive board would interpret the obligation. Countries clearly did not want to commit and then be surprised that the executive board considered them in breach of their obligation.[67] As time went on, this kind of uncertainty could be expected to wane through approval decisions and executive board clarification.

Our control variables suggest that four other factors might influence commitment: (1) the degree of trade dependence of the economy, (2) whether the country is democratic, (3) whether those who commit are exempt from surveillance, and (4) the passage of time.

Before proceeding to more complicated analyses, it is useful to make a visual inspection of the data. The data set used is a panel of 138 countries. The only criterion for their inclusion was membership in the IMF by 1980. Of these countries, we have time varying and case varying data for 110 countries that have chosen Article VIII status since 1966. Using yearly observations for these countries, it is useful to construct a Kaplan-Meier "survival function" that describes the period of transition prior to making an Article VIII commitment (see Figure 1).[68]

---

65. James 1995, 773, 775.

66. Gold 1983, 474–75. Consultations with Art. VIII countries were established in 1960 but were completely voluntary. Horsefield and De Vries 1969, 2:246–47.

67. For example, the United Kingdom did not want the stigma of a board decision that they maintained an illegal multiple currency practice as a result of what the United Kingdom considered a legitimate way to control capital movements. Implementation of Article XIV and Article VIII Decision, minutes of staff visit to the United Kingdom, 27 July 1960, S424, Trans. Arrange., Move to Art. VIII Mission (IMF Archives). Uncertainty over board interpretation inhibited early commitment. Generally, see Policy Aspects of the Article VIII and Article XIV Problem, 21 October 1954, S424, Trans. Arrange., Art. VIII and XIV, 1954–55 (IMF Archives).

68. The literature usually terms the event of interest a "failure" and the time elapsed until its occurrence as "survival" regardless of the substantive problem modeled. Proponents of international openness and free markets would in this case view "survival" analysis as "transition" analysis, and an Art. VIII commitment as a "success"; those who favor closer government management of markets might agree that the customary appellations are in fact more apt.

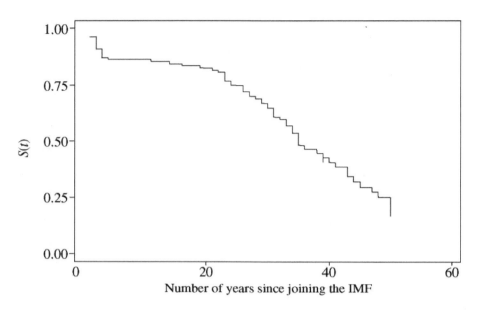

Number of years since joining the IMF

Note: The Kaplan-Meier estimator for maintaining Article XIV status beyond time *t* is the product of the probability of maintaining this status in time *t* and the preceding periods:

$$S(t) = \prod_{j=t0}^{t} \{(nj - dj)/nj\}$$

where *n* represents those cases that neither accepted Article VIII status nor were censored, and *d* represents the number of acceptances during the time period.

	Country-years at risk	Incidence rate	Number of countries	Survival time		
				25%	50%	75%
Total	3,125	.01999	110	24	35	50

FIGURE 1. *The Kaplan-Meier survival function: Duration of Article XIV status over time*

One fact becomes obvious from this visual representation of the data: the "transitional" regime could in fact last a long period of time for a number of countries. The Kaplan-Meier function estimates about a 25 percent chance of accepting Article VIII status in the first twenty-four years of IMF membership, a 50 percent chance within thirty-five years, and about a 75 percent chance after fifty years. Clearly, many countries have been in no rush to commit legally to keeping their current account free from restrictions.

What affects the rate at which governments make the commitment? Table 1 presents the findings of the Cox proportional hazard estimation for a combination of variables discussed earlier. (Note that ratios of more than 1 indicate an increase in the rate of Article VIII acceptance, and ratios of less than 1 indicate a reduction in the rate of acceptance. Thus the null hypothesis is that the hazard ratio is not significantly different from 1.) Consider first the ability to comply, which I argue is essential for a credible commitment. My expectation is that countries are more unlikely to make Article VIII obligations when their payments are volatile and they tend toward deficit. In the models developed here, balance-of-payments levels (the average balance of payments for the period as a whole) are interacted with balance-of-payments volatility.[69] This specification is meant to distinguish volatility effects conditional on whether the balance-of-payments position is relatively strong or weak. The results displayed in Table 1 show that, as anticipated, balance-of-payments volatility reduces the proportional hazard rate substantially. In model 3, it reduces the rate by (1 −.390), or .610, when mean deficits are equal to zero. Substantively, volatility is very likely to reduce the rate at which countries accept Article VIII obligations. Also as expected, countries that have better balance-of-payments positions are more likely to accept Article VIII obligations (36.4 percent more likely for every percentage point of balance of payments as a proportion of gross domestic product, GDP, according to model 3). Interestingly, the negative effects of volatility may be slightly greater in countries with better payments positions on average, as indicated by the statistically significant but substantively small impact of the interaction term. These findings about the balance of payments support the hypothesis that countries that are more capable of compliance are more likely to commit. The commitment is, in turn, more likely to be credible.

The next two variables, "universality" and "regional norm," are meant to test the proposition that taking on an obligation is likely to be contingent on similar actions by others. "Universality" is the proportion of all IMF members who have accepted Article VIII status, and "regional norm" is the proportion of countries within each subregion (as defined by the World Bank) that have done so. (All variable measures and sources are discussed in the data appendix.) Both of these variables have a large and positive influence on the acceptance rate. According to model 3, for example, every 1 percent increase in the proportion of IMF members accepting Article VIII increases the likelihood of acceptance by 38.5 percent. Similarly, a 1 percent increase in the regional proportion of Article VIII adherents increases a country's likelihood of acceptance by 4.1 percent. This translates into a 49 percent increase for every 10 percent increase in regional accession.[70] Clearly, as the number of countries who accept Article VIII increases, there is a greatly increased chance that an uncommitted government will do so. Note that this impact is significant even if we control for time ("year" in model 4). We can be fairly confident, then, that the universality and regional norms variables evaluated here do not simply reflect the fact that adherents

69. Reserve levels and volatility, as well as terms of trade volatility, were also analyzed, but because the results were insignificant they are not reported here.

70. Which is calculated by raising the estimated hazard ratio to the tenth power.

TABLE 1. *Influences on the rate of Article VIII acceptance*

	Rate of Article VIII acceptance (hazard ratios)			
	Model 1	*Model 2*	*Model 3*	*Model 4*
Average balance of payments	—	—	1.364**	1.352**
			(.145)	(.180)
Balance-of-payments volatility	—	—	.390**	.400*
			(.170)	(.205)
Balance-of-payments (volatility*mean)	—	—	.887**	.891**
			(.035)	(.046)
Universality	1.073***	1.330***	1.385***	1.553***
	(.015)	(.092)	(.111)	(.386)
Regional norm	1.030***	1.043***	1.045***	1.040***
	(.005)	(.009)	(.010)	(.010)
Surveillance	.608	.047***	.041***	.061**
	(.289)	(.042)	(.047)	(.087)
Openness	1.009***	1.015***	1.018***	1.018***
	(.003)	(.003)	(.004)	(.005)
Democracy	—	1.078*	1.081*	1.079*
		(.050)	(.044)	(.044)
Year	—	—	—	.904
				(.199)
N	1,988	1,757	1,754	1,754
Time "at risk"	2,517.97	2,296.98	2,294.98	2,294.98
Log likelihood	−182.45	−93.39	−90.15	−89.96
χ^2	132.12	75.63	66.09	74.76
Prob. $> \chi^2$	0.00	0.00	0.00	0.00

Note: Table shows estimated hazard rates using a Cox proportionate hazard model with time varying covariates. Robust standard errors are in parentheses.
***$p > |Z| = .01$.
**$p > |Z| = .05$.
*$p > |Z| = .10$.

increase over time. What most influences the acceptance rate is not time, but the proportion of adherents. This finding is consistent with the incentives of the competitive economic environment in which governments declare their legal adherence to Article VIII.

Domestic political demands that flow from trade openness also have an important impact on the acceptance rate. Openness to the international trade system raises the proportional hazard rate significantly. According to model 3, every one point increase in imports plus exports as a proportion of GDP increases the likelihood of Article VIII acceptance by 1.8 percent. This could account for a 67 percent difference in acceptance probability for countries with trade profiles as different as, say, Malaysia (imports plus exports totaling approximately 80 percent of GDP for the period under consideration) and the Philippines (where the corresponding figure is about 50 percent).[71] Certainly, the demands of importers and exporters have much to do with the government's willingness to commit. Interestingly, whether or not a country was democratic only marginally affected the decision, if at all. In the improbable event that a country transformed itself from a complete nondemocracy to a highly democratic society, the possible impact on the probability of accepting Article VIII would only be about 19 percent. Our confidence in this effect barely reaches standard levels of significance, however.[72]

There is also evidence that institutional incentives have made a big difference in Article VIII acceptance. "Surveillance" here is a dummy variable that takes on a value of zero prior to 1977 and 1 thereafter. Once surveillance has been extended to all countries—not just those availing themselves of the Article XIV transitional regime—the impact has been to reduce drastically the probability of accepting Article VIII, as we expected, though our confidence in this result is reduced somewhat by the exclusion of democracy as an independent explanation. The hazard ratio indicates that once the surveillance advantage of Article VIII states was removed, countries were anywhere from 40 percent to as much as 96 percent less likely to accept Article VIII status, other conditions held constant. The end of discriminatory surveillance seems to have mattered greatly to governments' willingness to commit. On the other hand, the simple passage of time had little effect. This could be because the uncertainty regarding obligations that motivated the inclusion of this variable was highly concentrated in the very earliest years of the IMF. There is little reason to believe that time itself accounts for changes in the rate of commitment.

The evidence suggests that governments are more likely to commit to Article VIII status when the commitment is credible and when other countries, especially countries in their own region, have done so as well. Although other factors influence the decision to commit, these results are consistent with the use of legal commitments as a signal to markets of a serious intent to maintain open and nondiscriminatory foreign exchange markets.

Who Complies? Explaining the Compliance Decision

Members of the IMF are legally required to comply with their commitments to keep the current account free from restrictions and to maintain unified exchange rates, and twenty-six members in our sample have perfect compliance records on both counts.[73] However, a number of Article VIII countries have far from a perfect record (see Tables 2 and 3). Most of the long-term noncompliers are concentrated in Latin

---

71. Calculated in this case by raising the estimated hazard ratio to the twenty-ninth power.

72. Subtracting the polity scores on autocracy from those on democracy, yielding a scale from −10 to 10, does not significantly alter this general conclusion.

73. Among the countries who were members of the IMF in 1980, as of 1997, Bahrain, Canada, Denmark, Djibouti, Finland, Gambia, Germany, Indonesia, Lebanon, Malaysia, Mauritius, New Zealand, Norway, Panama, Portugal, Qatar, Saudi Arabia, Seychelles, Spain, Sweden, Switzerland, Thailand, Trinidad and Tobago, United Arab Emirates, United States, and Yemen Arab Republic all had perfect records of compliance with their Art. VIII status.

TABLE 2. *Article VIII noncompliers, restrictions on current account (rates and years of noncompliance, 1967–95)*

Country	Rate of noncompliance (1967–95)	Years committed (1967–95)[a]	Dates of restrictions
Dominican Republic	1.000	29	1967–95
El Salvador	.931	29	1967–93
Jamaica	.862	29	1968–69, 1973–95
Guyana	.828	29	1967, 1971–93
Iceland	.750	12	1984–92
Chile	.722	18	1983–95
South Africa	.682	22	1979–93
Argentina	.630	27	1972–77, 1983–93
Fiji	.600	5	1989–92
Costa Rica	.586	29	1972–73, 1975, 1982–95
Guatemala	.552	29	1967–73, 1981–86
Peru	.552	29	1971–78, 1985–92
Nicaragua	.517	29	1979–93
Ecuador	.440	25	1983–93
Honduras	.414	29	1982–93
St. Lucia	.400	15	1981–86
St. Vincent	.357	14	1982–86
Morocco	.333	3	1993
Italy	.276	29	1975–82
Austria	.241	29	1967–73
Bolivia	.179	28	1982–86
Mexico	.172	29	1983–87
France	.138	29	1969–71, 1983
Haiti	.138	29	1968–71
Japan	.107	28	1968–70

Source: IMF, various years, *Exchange Arrangements and Restrictions.*
Note: Noncompliers are defined as countries that have declared themselves obligated by Article VIII but have implemented restrictions on current account. These are in apparent contravention of Article VIII, section 2(a), but no effort is made here to distinguish between "approved" and "unapproved" restrictions.
[a]Countries with fewer than two years of observations have been omitted.

America, though liberalization increased markedly in this region in the mid-to-late 1990s. Although data limitations prevent the inclusion of very recent years, almost all of the noncompliance associated with the global financial crisis of 1996–97 elicited foreign exchange restrictions rather than the implementation of multiple exchange rates. A few Article VIII countries have implemented one measure inconsistent with their obligations but not the other. Belgium, Hong Kong, and the Netherlands, for example, have in the past implemented multiple exchange rate systems but not restrictions on current account, whereas Austria, Korea, Singapore, and Japan have made the opposite choice.

What explains this variance among countries that chose to obligate themselves to openness? The strategy in this section is to examine only cases in which governments

TABLE 3. *Article VIII noncompliers, multiple exchange-rate systems (rates and years of noncompliance, 1967–95)*

Country	Rate of noncompliance (1967–95)	Years committed (1967–95)[a]	Dates of multiple exchange rates
Bahamas	1.000	24	1974–97
Costa Rica	.81	31	1967–91
Belgium/Luxembourg	.77	31	1967–90
Peru	.77	31	1968–91
Chile	.75	20	1983–97
Dominican Republic	.68	31	1973–91, 1996–97
Nicaragua	.68	31	1967–74, 1979–90
Venezuela	.67	21	1977–90
Argentina	.59	29	1972–77, 1982–92
South Africa	.54	24	1977–82, 1986–92
Bolivia	.43	30	1967, 1983, 1985–95
United Kingdom	.42	31	1967–79
Guyana	.39	31	1967–68, 1984–85, 1987–91, 1993–95
Ireland	.39	31	1967–78
El Salvador	.32	31	1982–91
Guatemala	.32	31	1985–94
Honduras	.32	31	1986–93, 1996–97
Jamaica	.29	31	1967–68, 1978–79, 1987–91
Mexico	.29	31	1983–91
Italy	.26	31	1973–74, 1976–78, 1980–82
France	.10	31	1972–74
Netherlands	.10	31	1972–74
Ecuador	.07	27	1972–73
Haiti	.06	31	1991–92
Hong Kong	.06	31	1970–71
Kuwait	.06	31	1970–71
Australia	.03	31	1968
Suriname	.03	31	1994

Source: IMF, various years, *Exchange Arrangements and Restrictions.*

Note: Noncompliers are defined as countries that have declared themselves obligated by Article VIII but have some form of multiple exchange-rate system. These are in apparent contravention of Article VIII, section 2(a), but no effort is made here to distinguish between "approved" and "unapproved" systems.

[a]Countries with fewer than two years of observations have been omitted.

have committed to Article VIII and then to explain the decision nevertheless to implement restrictions on current account or multiple exchange rate regimes.[74] The first and most obvious explanation for noncompliance is unexpected economic pressures that make the maintenance of an open current account and unified exchange rates

74. This is presented as a priori evidence of noncompliance, even though at this point I do not examine the technical question as to whether or not the executive board of the IMF has approved of the restrictions in place, thus rendering them "legal" temporarily.

very difficult. Certainly economic conditions are likely to have influenced Latin American noncompliance in the 1980s. Thus in the tests that follow I control for the changes in economic growth, current account balance, and current account volatility, all standardized over GDP.

If legalization is an attempt to make a commitment more credible, then governments should resist violating international law because they want to preserve their reputations as law abiding. The incentive for such a reputation in the monetary area is clear: governments want to convince markets that they provide a desirable venue for international trade and investment. Investors and suppliers seeking opportunities for international commerce should prefer to do business with firms in countries that provide a more certain legal framework with respect to the nondiscriminatory fulfillment of international contracts. Although there is no central enforcement of this obligation, the desire to avoid reputational costs should motivate compliance.

The question is, when will reputational costs have their greatest impact? My first hypothesis is that costs are greatest when a violator is an outlier among comparable countries. That is, rule violation is most costly when comparable countries manage to continue to comply. On the one hand, the more competitors are willing to comply, the greater the pressure for any one country to comply, even in the face of economic pressure to protect the national economy through restrictions or multiple exchange rates. On the other hand, if it is common for Article VIII countries in the region to disregard their commitment, this should increase the probability that any given country in that region will decide against compliance. Rampant violation makes it difficult for markets to single out any one violator for "punishment." Thus, we should expect compliance to be positively influenced by what other countries choose to do.

Consider next characteristics of the domestic polity itself. Several analysts have implied that compliance with international legal commitments is much more prevalent among liberal democracies, pointing to the constraining influence exercised by domestic groups who may have interests in or a preference for compliant behavior.[75] In this view participatory politics might put pressure on the government to comply, especially in the case where noncompliance involves curtailing the rights of residents to foreign exchange (it is less clear how this argument relates to the choice to implement or maintain a unified exchange-rate system). Others have argued that the most important characteristic of liberal democracy when it comes to international compliance is its strong domestic commitment to the rule of law. There are many variants of the argument—from Anne-Marie Slaughter's view that independent judiciaries in liberal democracies seem to share some of the same substantive approaches to law to a more general argument that domestic systems that value rule-based decision making and dispute resolution are also likely to respect rules internationally.[76] In essence, these are affinity arguments: they seem to suggest that domestic norms regarding limited government, respect for judicial processes, and regard for constitutional con-

---

75. See Young 1979; and Schachter 1991. See also Moravcsik 1997.
76. Slaughter 1995a. This captures the flavor of some of the democratic peace literature, for example, Doyle 1986; Dixon 1993; and Raymond 1994.

straints[77] "carry over" into the realm of international politics. They rest on an intuitively appealing assumption that policymakers and lawmakers are not able to park their normative perspectives at the water's edge.[78]

There are other reasons, however, to expect the rule of law to be associated with Article VIII compliance. Countries respecting the rule of law have a strong positive reputation for maintaining a stable framework for property rights. Markets expect them to maintain their commitments, and to undermine this expectation would prove costly. Countries that score low with respect to the rule of law do not have much to lose by noncompliance; erratic behavior is hardly surprising to investors and traders. I use an indicator for the rule of law that is especially appropriate to test the market's assessment of the reputation for rule of law: a six-point scale published by a political risk analysis firm expressly to assess the security of investments.[79] The scale represents the willingness of citizens peacefully to implement law and adjudicate disputes using established institutions. Higher scores on this six-point measure indicate the presence of such institutional characteristics as a strong court system, sound political institutions, and provisions for orderly succession. Low scores reflect an increased use of extra-legal activities in response to conflict and to settle disputes.

Since I have argued that the purpose of legalization is to make more credible monetary commits, that compliance is market enforced, and that markets prefer certainty in the legal framework, the comparison between the participatory characteristics of democracy and rule of law regimes should be especially telling. We have little reason to expect that democracy alone provides the stability that economic agents desire; on the contrary, popular participation along with weak guarantees for fair enforcement of property rights can endanger these rights. Clearly, these two variables are positively correlated (Pearson correlation $=.265$), but they are certainly conceptually distinct and may have very different effects on the decision to comply with Article VIII obligations. Thus we are able directly to compare two regime characteristics that are often conflated: democracy with its participatory dimensions on the one hand and the rule of law with its emphasis on procedural certainty on the other. Monetary compliance should therefore be conditioned by (1) compliance by other countries in the region, and (2) a country's reputation for respecting the rule of law. Participatory democracy is expected to have no effect.

The central explanation for compliance should revolve around these reputational factors. Still, it is important to control for other factors that could influence the compliance decision. Consistent with the reputational argument, it may be more costly for a country that is highly dependent on world trade to violate Article VIII. Certainly, retaliation would be more costly to nationals of such a country. Second, it is plausible that countries defending a fixed exchange rate might find it more difficult to maintain Article VIII obligations; countries that had shifted to more flexible regimes

---

77. "International law is not unlike constitutional law in that it imposes legal obligations on a government that in theory the government is not free to ignore or change." Fisher 1981, 30. Constitutional constraints most often rest on their shared normative acceptance, rather than on the certainty of their physical enforcement, providing another possible parallel to the international setting.

78. See Risse-Kappen 1995b; and Lumsdaine 1993.

79. See Knack and Keefer 1995, 225.

would not be under the same pressure to conserve foreign exchange for purposes of defending the currency's peg.[80] Third, use of the IMF's resources could provide an incentive to comply. Pressure from the IMF should be especially strong when countries are in need of a loan. Fourth, it may be the case that compliance is enhanced by the nesting of the Article VIII regime within a broader regime of free trade. Membership in the General Agreement on Tariffs and Trade (GATT) might encourage a country to maintain free and nondiscriminatory foreign exchange markets.[81] Finally, compliance may simply become easier with the passage of time. Thus the following control variables provide a small sample of other factors that could encourage compliance: (1) positive economic conditions, (2) a high degree of trade dependence, (3) flexible exchange rates, (4) use of IMF resources, (5) membership in the GATT, and (6) the passage of time.

In this case the compliance decision is modeled using logistical regression (logit), with the dependent variable taking on a value of 1 for the presence of restrictions or multiple exchange rates and zero for the absence of both. (Since we are analyzing only Article VIII countries, each instance of restrictions or multiple-rate systems is also a case of apparent noncompliance.) Because the data consist of observations across countries and over time, with a strong probability of temporal dependence among observations, a logit specification is used that takes explicit account of the nonindependence of observations.[82] The results are reported in Table 4.

One of the most important findings of this analysis is, again, the clustering of compliance behavior within regions. Article VIII countries are much more likely to put illegal restrictions on current account or use illegal multiple exchange-rate regimes if other countries in the region are doing so. The impact of regional behavior is substantial: the difference between a region with no violators compared to one with nearly all violators increased the probability of noncompliance by 79 percent. Could this be the result of common economic pressures sweeping the region? This explanation cannot be completely ruled out, but it is rendered less likely by the range of economic variables included in the specification. The inclusion of various measures of current account difficulty and GDP growth failed to wash out apparent regional convergence. Compliance decisions are apparently not being made on the basis of

---

80. The board clearly recognized this was the case: "It was quite evident that flexible rates made it easier for a country to eliminate payment and trade restrictions. This made the fact that several European countries were now accepting the obligations of Art. VIII on the basis of a fixed parity all the more significant." Peru's currency was still fluctuating. Executive board minutes, 8 February 1961, EBM/61/4., p. 15, C/Peru/424.1, Trans. Arrange., Members' Intent to Use (IMF Archives).

81. Indeed, the date of GATT's entry into force was conditioned on the acceptance of Art. VIII, sec. 2, 3, and 4 obligations by the contracting parties to the GATT. According to a memo circulated among the staff of the IMF, "The date of entry into force of the revised [GATT] rules concerning discrimination and quantitative restrictions is linked specifically to the date at which the obligations of Article VIII, Sections 2, 3, and 4 of the Fund Agreement become applicable to such contracting parties as are members of the Fund, the combined foreign trade of which constitutes at least 50 per cent of the aggregate foreign trade of all contracting parties." Article VIII and Article XIV, memo prepared by Irving S. Friedman, 24 May 1955 (IMF Archives).

82. Beck, Katz, and Tucker 1998. A counter vector was employed using the STATA routine made available on Richard Tucker's Web site at <http://www.fas.harvard.edu/~rtucker/papers/grouped/grouped3.html>. Three cubic splines were included in the analysis but are not reported here.

TABLE 4. *Influences on the decision to violate Article VIII obligations*

Explanatory variables	Model 1	Model 2	Model 3	Model 4
Constant	−17.8***	−17.13***	−17.3***	−17.9***
	(4.75)	(4.88)	(4.89)	(4.77)
Rule of law	−.340***	−.346***	−.272**	−.333***
	(.020)	(.119)	(.133)	(.120)
Democracy	.017*	.016	.018*	.018*
	(.010)	(.010)	(.010)	(.010)
Regional noncompliance	5.57***	5.47***	5.21***	5.45***
	(.554)	(.540)	(.567)	(.553)
Balance of payments/GDP ($t − 1$)	−.030**	−.031**	−.029**	−.030**
	(.013)	(.013)	(.013)	(.012)
Balance-of-payments volatility	.753***	.794***	.793***	.716***
	(.257)	(.262)	(.276)	(.266)
Change in GDP	−.055*	−.057*	−.056*	−.055*
	(.032)	(.032)	(.033)	(.031)
Openness	−.014***	−.014***	−.014***	−.014***
	(.003)	(.003)	(.003)	(.003)
Year	.198***	.188***	.186***	.203***
	(.051)	(.053)	(.052)	(.052)
Flexible exchange rates	—	.270	—	—
		(.404)		
Use of fund resources	—	—	.601	—
			(.404)	
GATT member	—	—	—	−.377
				(.334)
N	593	593	593	593
Wald χ^2	(11)	(12)	(12)	(12)
	207.63	207.04	215.52	220.2
Prob. $> \chi^2$	0.000	0.000	0.000	0.000
Log likelihood	−137.7	−137.4	−136.6	−137.3

Note: The dependent variable is an apparent Article VIII violation, either a restriction on current account or multiple exchange-rate system. This analysis covers Article VIII countries only. Logit coefficients are reported with correction for nonindependence of observations. Robust standard errors are in parentheses. Estimation includes three cubic splines, which are not reported here.
***$p > |Z| = .01$.
**$p > |Z| = .05$.
*$p > |Z| = .10$.

economic conditions alone, but with an eye to standards of regional behavior. The most obvious reason for this concern would be reputational consequences in a competitive international economic environment.

The domestic political variables tell an interesting story about regime characteristics. In contrast to theories of international behavior that concentrate on the law consciousness of democracies, the evidence presented here suggests that, in this set of countries, democracy may be associated with a greater tendency to violate the country's international monetary obligations.[83] Substantive interpretation of the coef-

83. This conclusion is not significantly altered by the use of the combined democracy-autocracy variable.

ficients reveals a highly asymmetrical impact; however, a move from zero to 5 on the democracy scale increases the chances of violating a commitment by only 2.89 percent, whereas a move from 5 to 10 on that scale increases the probability of violating by 10.8 percent. Why this might be so is not difficult to understand. A rich literature in political economy suggests that a potential cost of democracy is that the public does not always fully anticipate the consequences of its aggregate demands. For example, if democracies allow for macroeconomic policies that exhibit an inflationary bias,[84] participatory politics may complicate the international compliance problem. However, a strong domestic commitment to the rule of law contributed positively to Article VIII compliance. Again, the impact is somewhat asymmetrical for values on the explanatory variable. A move from 1 to 3 on the six-point rule-of-law scale reduced the probability of violating Article VIII by 17.7 percent, whereas a move from 4 to 6 reduced the probability of violating by about 4 percent. The effect of the rule of law is understandable in light of the argument about uncertainty and reputation: governments that have invested heavily in a reputation for respecting the rule of law—one aspect of which is protecting property rights—have a lot to lose by reneging on their international obligations.

None of the control variables affects these findings. As anticipated, a weakening balance of payments, as well as higher volatility, contributes to violation, as does a worsening business cycle. Governments of more open economies work hard to abide by their obligation of policy openness, consistent with our expectation. Surprisingly, compliance with these obligations does not improve over time; if anything, violations worsen over the years when other variables in the model are held constant. Flexible exchange rates, GATT membership, and the use of IMF resources may be important institutional contexts for international economic relations, but they do not systematically affect the compliance decision.

Conclusions

The legalization of some central aspects of the international monetary regime after World War II allows us to examine the conditions under which law can influence the behavior of governments in the choice of their international monetary policies. Historically, this policy area has been devoid of international legal rules. The classical gold standard did not depend on international legal commitments for its reputed stability. "Soft" international legal commitments began to develop only in the interwar years, largely in response to markets' shattered confidence in the ability of governments to maintain the commitments they had made unilaterally in the previous period. Driven by the need to limit the externalization of macroeconomic adjustment costs, some governments sought international commitments as a way to enhance certainty and reassure markets. However, these commitments were in the softest

---

84. See the review of this literature in Keech 1995.

possible form and did little to constrain behavior or encourage the confidence of economic agents.

The Bretton Woods agreement brought to an end the unbridled national legal sovereignty over monetary affairs. They hardly represent the triumph of legalization over market forces, however, as attested to by the breakdown of the original legal obligation to defend a par value system. Legal obligations cannot stifle market forces: capital mobility has made fixed rates very nearly unmanageable, treaty arrangements to the contrary notwithstanding. The end of the legal obligation to defend pegged rates is a clear reminder that legalization cannot be viewed in teleological terms. Obligations that increasingly frustrate major players as market conditions change are not likely to remain obligations for long.

Members of the IMF still have legal obligations regarding the conduct of their monetary policy. In fact, a growing number of members voluntarily assume these obligations every year. Article VIII Section 2(a) obligates members to keep their current accounts free from restrictions and proscribes the use of multiple exchange-rate systems. Conveniently, the IMF then publishes information on whether countries have imposed what the staff believes constitute restrictions or multiple rate systems. Thus it has been possible in this case to establish a precise account of, first, the rate of commitment and, second, the rate of compliance with international monetary law by looking at states' decisions to accept the obligations of nondiscriminatory current account convertibility and their subsequent behavior. My strategy in this article has been to model the factors contributing to the rate of Article VIII acceptance and to test a set of hypotheses regarding compliance with this commitment.

Legalization is one way governments attempt to make credible their international monetary commitments. The evidence shows that governments are hesitant to make international legal commitments if there is a significant risk that they will not be able to honor them in the future. The hazard models of the rate of acceptance of Article VIII indicate that commitment is associated with conditions that one can reasonably anticipate will make compliance possible. Balance-of-payments weakness and volatility could and did delay the acceptance of obligations for openness significantly. Furthermore, economic downturns and unanticipated balance-of-payments difficulties were associated with noncompliance among Article VIII countries. However, both the archival evidence and the quantitative analysis presented here suggest that governments wanted to be relatively sure they could comply before they committed legally to the open foreign exchange regime. Legal commitment was part of a strategy to make a credible commitment to maintain a liberal foreign exchange regime.

Among Article VIII countries, two regime effects had clear consequences for compliance. Surprisingly for those who view the international behavior of democracies as somehow distinctive with respect to law and obligation, the more democratic the Article VIII country, the more likely it may have been ($p = .10$) to place restrictions on current account. On the other hand, regimes that were based on clear principles of the rule of law were far more likely to comply with their commitments. This finding indicates that rules and popular pressures can and apparently sometimes do pull in opposite directions when it comes to international law compliance. There is no reason to think, based on these findings, that democracy itself is a positive influence on the rule of law in international relations. On the contrary, there is more reason to associate compliance with the extent to which the polity in question respects institutional channels for mediating domestic conflict and protecting property rights than with a participatory or competitive political system. Some analysts have argued that this finding can be understood as a normative constraint on foreign policy choice. But it is also consistent with rational market incentives, since rule-of-law regimes have more to lose reputationally than do capricious regimes in the event of a legal violation.

One of the most interesting findings of this research has been the evidence that commitment and compliance are related to the commitment and compliance patterns beyond one's own borders. The hazard model clearly indicates that the breadth of acceptance influenced acceptance by uncommitted governments. Both worldwide and regional acceptance of Article VIII status had this effect, even when controlling for time. Furthermore, the pervasiveness of restrictions within a region has a negative effect on the compliance decision among Article VIII countries. It is impossible to know from these associational effects, of course, exactly what kinds of mechanisms might be at play in such a relationship. I have argued that these kinds of regional and universal effects likely reflect the strategic nature of implementing restrictions: punishment by economic agents and retaliation or other pressures by trading partners, for example, may be minimal where restrictions are common (since it is prohibitively costly to punish everyone). Those who offer more normative explanations of state behavior might interpret this pattern as an example of the importance of regional norms of appropriate behavior. Or perhaps it is simply the case that although governments feel some moral obligation to obey the law, their willingness to comply breaks down as others abandon the rules at will. Although these tests cannot distinguish these distinct explanations, the ability to document a degree of contingent compliance provides a basis for disentangling the possible mechanisms in future research. What we can say is that compliance and commitment are likely influenced, for whatever reason, by the actions taken by other members of the international system.

This research has broader implications for the study of legalization and compliance with international legal obligations. It shows that legalization as a tool for commitment is limited by economic conditions and market forces. International monetary legalization can be characterized by an inverted "J" pattern: legalization was nonexistent under the classical gold standard and soft during the interwar years. It peaked between 1946 and 1971, when treaty obligations regulated the central relationship among currencies, and now involves definite obligations over a more limited range of policies. Much of the behavior that constitutes international monetary relations remains completely outside of legalized relationships, especially rules and practices with respect to the provision of liquidity.[85]

---

85. Art. VII, sec. 2 empowered the IMF to borrow from a member but also provided that no member should be obliged to lend to the IMF. Thus the General Agreement to Borrow was negotiated by the

Rather than debating whether compliance is pervasive or minimal,[86] my purpose here has been to examine the conditions under which compliance is likely. The study of international law compliance is rife with problems of conceptualization and measurement,[87] but in this case it has been possible to match a treaty obligation with authoritative assessments of behavior over time for a large number of countries and to match the suggested mechanisms with contextual archival materials. The evidence taken together points to law as a hook for making a credible commitment, with compliance largely "enforced" by the anticipation of reputational consequences.

Data Appendix

Dependent Variables

Article VIII Acceptance: Coded 1 if the country has accepted Article VIII status and zero if it remains subject to Article XIV transitional arrangements. Acceptance indicates the end of a "spell" for purposes of the Cox proportional hazard model.[88]

Violate: Coded 1 if restrictions exist and/or if a multiple exchange rate system is in place, zero otherwise. Since this dependent variable is used only to analyze policies of Article VIII countries, it is interpreted as noncompliance.[89]

Explanatory Variables

Universality: Proportion of current IMF members who have accepted Article VIII status.[90]

Regional norms: Proportion of current IMF members within each region who have accepted Article VIII status. Classification of economies by region (East and Southern Africa, West Africa, East Asia and Pacific, Eastern Europe and Central Asia, Rest of Europe, Middle East, North Africa, Americas) is based on World Bank categories.[91]

---

managing director and representatives of the signatory countries outside normal IMF channels. Reminiscent of the Tripartite Agreement, it was enshrined as a series of identical letters among participating countries. Swaps are also soft arrangements created by central banks and operating through the Bank of International Settlements. These were developed completely outside of the IMF framework. Dam 1982, 150. Nor are IMF standby arrangements a contract in the legal sense. Failure to carry out the performance criteria in the letter of intent is not a breach of any agreement and certainly not a breach of international law. All the "seal of approval" effects come despite the nonlegal nature of this commitment. The Executive board's decision of 20 September 1968 explicitly concerns the nonlegal status of standby arrangements. Gold 1979, 464–66.

86. On this point, compare Chayes and Chayes 1993 and 1995 and Henkin 1979 with Downs, Rocke, and Barsoom 1996.

87. These issues are discussed in Simmons 1998.

88. IMF various years, analytical appendix.

89. Ibid.

90. Ibid.

91. Ibid.

Surveillance: A dummy variable indicating whether the time period is before (coded zero) or after (coded 1) 1978, indicating a comprehensive regime of IMF surveillance for all members, whether Article XVI or Article VIII status.

Openness: Imports (total value of goods and services: sum of merchandise f.o.b., imports of nonfactor services, and factor payments at market prices in current U.S. dollars) plus exports (total value of goods and services; sum of merchandise f.o.b, exports of nonfactor services, and factor receipts at market prices in current U.S. dollars), as a proportion of GDP, multiplied by 100.[92]

Democracy: Democracy score (ranging from a low of zero to a high of 10) denoting the degree to which democratic institutions exist within each country.[93]

Mean balance of payments: The mean current account balance (the sum of net exports of goods and nonfactor services, net factor income, and net private transfers as a percentage of GDP, before official transfers) as a proportion of GDP for each country for the period under observation.[94]

Balance-of-payments volatility: The log of the standard deviation of current account balance as a proportion of GDP (defined earlier).[95]

Change in GDP: GDP average annual growth rate, for sum of GDP at factor cost and indirect taxes, less subsidies.[96]

Regional noncompliance: Proportion of current IMF members within each region who place restrictions on their current account and/or used multiple exchange-rate systems. Classification of economies by region (East and Southern Africa, West Africa, East Asia and Pacific, Eastern Europe and Central Asia, Rest of Europe, Middle East, North Africa, Americas) is based on World Bank categories. Since this explanatory variable is used only to analyze policies of Article VIII countries, it is interpreted as noncompliance.[97]

Rule of law: A six-point scale measuring the extent to which a country's domestic polity is based on practices and institutions that respect the rule of law.[98]

Use of IMF credit: Coded 1 if a country has made use of IMF credits during a given year and zero if it has not.[99]

Exchange-rate flexibility: Coded 1 if exchange rates are relatively flexible and zero if they are relatively inflexible; coded individually for each country-year.

GATT member: Coded 1 if a country had acceded to GATT and zero if had not.

---

92. World Bank 1995 and 1998, indicators (210 + 119)/38.
93. POLITY III data set. For a complete discussion of the conceptualization and coverage of this data set and comparisons with other measures of democracy, see Jaggers and Gurr 1995.
94. World Bank 1995 and 1998, indicator 181.
95. World Bank 1995 and 1998.
96. World Bank 1995 and 1998, indicator 181.
97. IMF, various years, analytical appendix.
98. International Country Risk Guide. For a full discussion of the conceptualization of this variable, see Knack and Keefer 1995.
99. World Bank 1995.

Legalization, Trade Liberalization, and Domestic Politics: A Cautionary Note
Judith Goldstein and Lisa L. Martin

Political scientists attempt to explain why governments adopt the policies they do. In political models, policy is the result of calculated choices made by political and economic actors. Actors' resources, and their incentives to mobilize and demand that governments attend to their interests, are the key forces explaining the policy choices we observe. When considering the impact of international legalization on political outcomes, the way in which legalization changes the interests and demands of actors provides the mechanism by which policy changes. In this article we consider how increases in the legalization of the international trade regime interact with the trade-related interests of domestic actors. Although legalization may reduce incentives for cheating by individual nations, we identify ways in which the unintended effects of legalization on the activities of domestic economic actors could interfere with the pursuit of progressive liberalization of international trade. Domestic politics cannot be treated as extraneous or as an irrational source of error that obstructs the purposes of legalization. Instead, politics operates in systematic ways and is the mechanism through which legalization exerts its effects. These effects range far beyond reducing opportunism by unitary states.

Through incremental change in the postwar years, the international trade regime has evolved away from its origins as a decentralized and relatively powerless institution and become a legal entity. The number of countries and the amount of trade covered by the rules agreed to in 1947 have expanded greatly. After 1995 and the creation of the World Trade Organization (WTO), the regime further increased its demands on members by elaborating and expanding commercial rules and procedures, including those that relate to the system of settling disputes. In practice the expansion of the regime in the post–World War II period has made trade rules more precise and binding. The result is that the implications or behavioral demands of rules have become increasingly transparent to all participants.[1]

We thank Bob Keohane, Marc Busch, Eric Anderson, James Fearon, Erica Gould, Barry Weingast, Simon Jackman, Brian Hanson, Richard Steinberg, an anonymous reviewer, and the editors of *IO* for comments on a previous version of this article.

1. Legalization refers to three aspects of international law: obligation, precision, and level of delegation to a centralized authority. Abbott et al., this issue.

International Organization 54, 3, Summer 2000, pp. 219–248

We argue that this increased legalization does not necessarily augur higher levels of trade liberalization, as suggested by supporters. The weakly legalized General Agreement on Tariffs and Trade (GATT) regime was remarkably successful at liberalizing trade; it is not apparent that the benefits of further legalization will outweigh its costs. This finding derives from an analysis of domestic politics and, in particular, from the incentives facing leaders to join and then adhere to the dictates of a liberal international trade regime. We support our position through an analysis of two aspects of trade politics.

First, we examine the effect of legalization on the incentives of domestic groups to mobilize and pressure their governments to adopt policies that favor them.[2] In that legalization entails a process of increasing rule precision, a more legalized trade regime will provide more and better information about the distributional implications of commercial agreements. Information on who will gain and lose from some international action will affect the incentives of groups to mobilize for and against trade agreements. This effect on both the mobilization of groups and the balance among them will vary depending on numerous factors. In general, however, we believe that better information will empower protectionists relative to free traders on issues relating to the conclusion of new agreements and free traders relative to protectionists on issues of compliance to existing agreements.

Second, we examine the implications of a more "binding" GATT/WTO on member governments. Although GATT rules were always obligatory in a legal sense, the provisions for using escape clauses and other loopholes interacted with domestic political realities in a way that made their use increasingly rare. This fact, combined with a strengthened dispute-resolution mechanism under the WTO, has increased the extent to which governments are "obliged," in a political sense, to maintain their liberal commitments. Reducing the ability of governments to opt out of commitments has the positive effect of reducing the chances that governments will behave opportunistically by invoking phony criteria for protecting their industries. On the other hand, tightly binding, unforgiving rules can have negative effects in the uncertain environment of international trade. When considering the realities of incomplete information about future economic shocks, we suggest that legalization may not result in the "correct" balance between these two effects of binding.

In this article we develop both the theoretical reasoning and the empirical support for our cautionary note on the domestic effects of legalization. We begin by examining information and group mobilization and suggest that the predictability that comes with legalization has both positive and negative effects on the trade liberalization goal of the regime. We then investigate the "bindingness" of trade rules. Through examination of the use of safeguards and the new dispute-resolution procedure, we

---

2. The number and variety of groups participating in the politics of trade has grown in the last decades. Where the classic models assumed three groups with trade-related interests—consumers, import-competing groups, and exporters—other groups, whose interests span from human rights to a clean environment, have come to believe that their interests are influenced by trade negotiations. The logic of this article, explaining the interaction among international regimes, social mobilization, and domestic politics, applies to any interest that groups perceive to be influenced by international trade agreements.

argue that trade rules have become more binding, even if *pacta sunt servanda* has always applied to such rules, and that enforcement of rules is now more certain.

Given the relatively short history of the WTO, it is not possible to collect the empirical evidence that can conclusively demonstrate whether legalization has gone "too far." Instead, the theoretical reasoning about the impact of legalization on domestic politics points to trends that demand close attention. Our purpose in this article is to raise questions about the potential downside of legalization that have not received sufficient attention. Appropriately legalizing international agreements is a tricky business, as the theoretical articles in this issue attest. Governments must perform a balancing act between binding themselves tightly enough to avoid cheating and allowing the flexibility to deal with the vagaries of changing information and domestic politics. Performing this balancing act well requires a clear-headed analysis of the impact of legalization on domestic politics.

Legalization, Information, and the Mobilization of Domestic Groups

The logic of precision, delegation, obligation, and increased transparency played a large role in negotiations over transforming the GATT into the WTO. The intended effect of these modifications in the WTO was to expand the breadth of the trade regime and enhance compliance so as to increase the benefits of membership. The problem with this logic is that it neglected domestic politics. Maintenance of free trade is politically difficult and is a function of the differential mobilization of those who favor liberalization and those who oppose a further opening of the economy to foreign products. Mobilization itself is a function of a number of factors, including the cost of mobilizing and the potential gains from collective action. One consequence of legalizing the trade regime has been greater transparency and predictability about the effects of trade agreements. Increased information of this sort has mixed effects on the mobilization of domestic interests and therefore on the ability of governments to maintain support for liberal trade policies.

The Logic of Mobilization

Consider first the impact of increased precision of trade rules during the process of trade negotiations. The ability of leaders to sign an accord will depend on the groups mobilized for or against the accord. The pattern of mobilization is not always predictable; mobilizing interest groups requires overcoming collective-action problems that can be quite intense. Actors within these groups must realize first that they have a common interest in government policies. They must then come to believe that it is worthwhile to bear the costs of collective action. A number of factors can undermine mobilization. The factors most relevant to international trade include the large and diffuse nature of some economic interests, lack of information that the interests of actors are at stake in particular international negotiations, and possible calculations that the costs of influencing government policy outweigh anticipated benefits.[3]

From the perspective of encouraging the liberalization of international trade, the fact that groups who prefer economic closure might suffer from collective-action problems is a blessing. If all antitrade forces were well organized and able to exert substantial pressure on their political representatives, the prospects for liberalization would be dim. The interaction with legalization enters the analysis at this point. In that legalization entails a process of increased precision of rules and transparency of agreements, it affects the behavior of domestic groups by increasing the information available to actors about the distributional implications of trade agreements. To the extent that such knowledge enhances the mobilization of antitrade forces relative to already well-organized protrade groups, legalization could undermine liberalization. Information matters for both protectionist and proliberalization interests. However, if these groups are differentially mobilized prior to the process of legalization, information will have the larger marginal effect on the groups that are not as well organized. The structure of the multilateral trade regime, based on the principle of reciprocity, has provided strong incentives for exporters to organize throughout the post-1950 period.[4] Growing dependence on exports and the multinational character of economic interests has also led to strong and effective lobbying efforts by free-trade advocates.[5] We therefore concentrate on the likely impact of greater information on the incentives facing protectionist groups.

Oran Young, writing on this relationship between international arrangements and the collective action of groups in the context of environmental negotiations, also argues that one important aspect of international negotiations is the distributional information available about the effects of agreements.[6] He argues that if actors know precisely the distributional effects of negotiations, they will concentrate on distributive issues rather than on "integrative" bargaining that searches for arrangements that benefit all. Negotiating behind a "veil of ignorance" can have the benefit of focusing minds on the mutual advantages of international cooperation, rather than arguing about how the costs will be distributed.

Young does not bring differential patterns of domestic mobilization into his analysis. Doing so increases the force of his central argument. If antitrade groups know for certain that their interests will suffer as a result of an agreement, their expected utility of collective action increases and they should be more willing to bear the costs of political participation. Thus legalization that involves highly precise and transparent rules can have the unintended effect of encouraging the mobilization of protectionist forces that see themselves as probable losers from an agreement. To the extent that these forces can now better balance already well-organized free-trade forces, negotiations about liberalization are made more difficult.

---

3. Collective-action problems have been central to the literature on endogenous tariff formation. See, for example, Magee, Brock, and Young 1989; and Mayer 1984.
4. Gilligan 1997.
5. Milner 1988.
6. Young 1989.

Transparency of winners and losers also has an effect on export groups. According to Michael J. Gilligan, one explanation for the liberalization that has occurred since World War II is that the process of setting tariffs encouraged the participation of export groups.[7] Reciprocal agreements made the gains from trade more transparent to exporters, resulting in greater support for trade liberalization than had existed fifty years earlier. Just as the potential losers from a trade agreement will attempt to undercut agreements, the potential winners will have an interest in pushing their states to sign treaties. In the absence of import-competing groups, or where the relative power between the two favors exporters, we assume policy will reflect exporters' interests. To the extent that information activates protectionists, other things being equal, nations will find it harder to build a consensus around a new liberalizing agreement.

A simple model clarifies the posited relationship between information and mobilization. Define p to be the probability with which a group believes that its interests will be at stake in negotiations. This subjective probability, p, is a random variable that takes on different values as information conditions change. We begin by assuming a poor information environment, where groups know only the total number of groups affected, not which of them will be affected.

Assume that there are N groups with an interest in trade. These groups are not mobilized initially. Assume they know that n groups will be affected by negotiations but have no information about which n groups this will be. This is an extreme assumption of poor information but a useful starting point. Each group therefore estimates that it will have a stake in negotiations with probability n/N, the ratio of affected groups to all groups. Given a lack of information, this is their best guess of the probability of being affected by negotiations. Thus, in the prelegalization environment, the variable p takes on the value n/N; $p = n/N$. The value of p will change as information improves.

Given this value of p prior to legalization, does it make sense for a group to mobilize? The calculation depends on the relationship between the expected benefits and costs of mobilization. The benefits of mobilization, B, are realized only if the group is in n. If the group is not in n, it gains no benefits, but will have to bear the costs of mobilization if it chooses to mobilize. Given the pre-legalization value of p, the expected benefits from negotiations are $p*B$, or nB/N. Groups will mobilize if the expected benefits outweigh mobilization costs C; $p*B > C$. Thus each group will mobilize if $nB/N > C$ in the poor information environment. N is a large number, and the ratio n/N is typically small. Thus, unless B is extremely large or the costs of mobilization negligible, groups will not have an incentive to mobilize. Our expectation is that few groups will meet this stringent pre-legalization mobilization condition. As information improves, p increases above the n/N minimum. However, with uncertainty about the distributional implications of negotiations, p remains small and the ratio of B to C must be large to allow mobilization.

After legalization, we assume that groups know with certainty whether they will be included in negotiations; that is, their estimate of the probability p now becomes

7. Gilligan 1997.

either zero or 1, as groups know whether their interests are at stake or not. The value of the random variable p changes as information conditions change. Groups that do not have their interests at stake will not mobilize. However, the condition for groups that are affected by negotiations to mobilize is now $p*B > C$ with $p = 1$, which is simply $B > C$. This is a much easier condition to meet, as long as collective-action costs are not prohibitive (as they may be for large, diffuse groups such as consumers). Therefore, we expect that many more groups will find it worthwhile to mobilize in the richer information environment postlegalization. Even if p does not improve to the extreme values of zero or 1, it approaches these limits, with the expected effects.

As suggested earlier, information has effects on groups that may be harmed as well as helped by negotiations. Our intention here is not to make precise predictions about the policy outcomes of relative mobilization of exporters and protectionists, but simply to draw attention to the political problems created by enhanced mobilization of antitrade groups. Clearly, information will lead both groups to mobilize, given increased certainty on how interests will fare in an agreement. However, a number of factors suggest that increased information is likely to favor proprotectionist mobilization. This position goes beyond the classic explanation, for example, Schattschneider's, that protectionist interests are concentrated and free-trade interests diffuse, which still has some force.[8]

The first factor is that the status quo favors protected groups, not potential new exporters. Since changes from the status quo require explicit affirmation—for example, ratification of a treaty—those who benefit from the status quo gain veto power. Thus typical institutional procedures that privilege the status quo will tend to favor protectionist over liberalizing interests. Another factor pointing in the same direction is the uncertain nature of gains for exporters. Exporters only know that some market will open up, not whether they will be able to capitalize on this opportunity in the face of international competition. In contrast, protectionists know precisely what protection they will be losing as a result of liberalization, enhancing their incentives to mobilize relative to exporters. Moving beyond a strictly rationalist model, we could also mention experimental evidence that actors tend to react more strongly to losses than to gains, again favoring protectionist groups in this mobilization dynamic. Finally, if we assume, as does Gilligan, that exporters are either fully or almost fully mobilized and are already participating in the political process, the increase in information should lead to a relatively greater mobilization of the less involved, that is, the antitrade groups.

The logic of precision and mobilization does not necessarily lead one to expect economic closure. When we consider the effects of more information when maintaining as opposed to creating a trade commitment, we get the opposite effect. Although information may mobilize import-competers before the conclusion of an agreement, the effect of a more legalized regime may be to mobilize exporters in cases of certain market losses, *ex post*. In this case, precision about which exporters will bear the costs of retaliation in a trade dispute works to mobilize exporting interests who would

8. Schattschneider 1935.

otherwise have no involvement in the trade dispute. Given the potential of a market loss, they will press governments to uphold trade rules. The higher the probability that the retaliatory action will hurt them, the greater their interests in expending resources to maintain liberal trade at home.

Therefore, logic suggests that increasing rule precision will have two different, and competing, effects on trade liberalization. Increased determinacy can undermine trade deals by activating import-competing groups with veto power. Conversely, precise rules regarding responses to rule breaches will result in more trade liberalization by activating export groups in the offending country. Over time, we should see not only more antitrade groups organizing but also more political activity by export groups if strategies of retaliation are appropriately designed.

Mobilizing Antitrade Groups

Empirical evidence suggests that groups affected by trade policy are often well organized and articulate. Whether the group is farmers in France, auto producers in the United States, or computer companies in Japan, those whose interests will be hurt by either continued or expanded access to foreign goods, services, and markets are articulate spokespersons for specific policies. These groups often act as veto players, and leaders who would like to negotiate the opening of world markets find that fear of competition at home undermines support for their free-trade coalition. The ability of leaders to ignore protectionist pressures rests on the willingness of proliberalization groups, those who benefit from liberalized trade, to organize and be equally active in their support. In the absence of exporters or other interested parties who articulate their free-trade positions, governments find it difficult to maintain a free-trade policy.[9]

Evidence of the effects of this problem of mobilizing and maintaining a free-trade coalition is found in all democracies and partially results from the concentrated benefits of trade barriers and their diffuse costs.[10] Rarely are those who are hurt by higher prices (consumers) present in political debate; more often, trade politics is determined by the balance between groups with specific interests in either openness or closure. In some countries, structural factors affect this balance. For example, groups may be overrepresented because of the electoral process, such as with agricultural producers in Japan, or because they have bureaucratic or corporatist support in government.

Since World War II, protectionist pressures from such groups have been mitigated through changes in the trade policymaking process, both domestic and international.[11] Reciprocal trade agreements, delegation to executive agencies, electoral re-

---

9. Numerous empirical studies document the importance of groups in setting trade policy. For a cross-national, cross-sectional examination of groups' involvement, see, for example, Verdier 1994.

10. On trade and interest groups, see Destler 1995; and Lohmann and O'Halloran 1994.

11. Whether it was a change in the balance of group interests or a shift in trade policymaking that explains the ability of governments to lower barriers to trade is difficult to determine in the early years of the GATT regime. Certainly, in the United States interest-group activity was muted because the costs of

form, and changing legislative voting rules help explain why countries support liberal trade policies that were difficult to defend in the pre–World War II period. The fact of liberalization and the specifics of the process are in equilibrium. The process may change either because underlying interests change or for exogenous reasons. Regardless of the particular reason for change, changes in the process have far-reaching consequences for policy. Process changes have made it more difficult for import-competing groups to find a majority to support their position while encouraging the organization of exporter interests.

The success of groups who support liberalization, however, should not be construed as evidence that policymakers no longer need to worry about veto groups undercutting trade policy. Liberalization may have changed the face of the proprotection lobby, but it has not eliminated its potential power. Even in the United States, long a proponent of the liberal trade regime, elected officials repeatedly face pressures from antitrade groups. Politicians such as Ross Perot and Pat Buchanan have mobilized voters against further trade liberalization, and authorization to join the WTO was garnered only after a significant battle in which continued participation was made contingent upon a reauthorization by Congress every five years. The potential influence of an antitrade coalition was no better evidenced than during the November 1999 ministerial meeting of the WTO in Seattle as protestors took to the streets. Even though the United States retains open markets, protrade politicians who do not strategize about the creation and maintenance of their coalitions can easily find themselves overwhelmed by protectionist demands.[12]

These social pressures have led strategic trade negotiators to bundle the gains to exporters from access to new markets with the losses to import-competing producers from new competition from abroad. Whatever the specifics of this trade-off at the negotiating table, the result must be an agreement that can garner majority support at home. If information about the distributional implication of agreements affects the propensity of groups to organize during negotiations, it may be easier to get to that "optimal bundle" in situations where some uncertainty exists about who is and who is not affected by the trade deal. Providing this information about the effects of either a potential commercial agreement, the behavior of a trading partner, or the dissolution of a trading pact is a central function of the contemporary trade regime. The WTO collects and disseminates trade data in preparation for rounds of trade talks; it monitors compliance and inventories national practices that undermine the free flow of goods and services.

---

organizing increased when the president obtained increased control of trade policymaking. Still, the shift toward openness would not have occurred without underlying social support. For an analysis of the relationship between institutional and underlying social variables, see Bailey, Goldstein, and Weingast 1997.

12. One simple metric capturing the continued involvement of proprotection groups in the United States is the number of bills entered in Congress pertaining to imports. In the 93rd–97th Congress, 1973–81, over 2,200 bills were entered; in the 98th–101st Congress, 1982–90, almost 2,300 bills were entered; and in the 102nd–105th Congress, 1991–98, over 1,600 bills were considered. Although few of these bills become law, the data suggest that liberal policy exists in the shadow of growing resistance. Numbers were obtained from Thomas Legislative Information on the Internet located at <http://thomas.loc.gov/home/thomas.html>.

Over time, the GATT/WTO regime has dramatically increased its ability to deliver this information to member countries.[13] In initial rounds of negotiations, tariff information was not systematically collected. Nations relied on data supplied by their negotiating partners, and thus the computation of offers and counteroffers for "balance" was done using often-incomplete statistics. Recognizing the need for better data, the secretariat undertook a systematic compilation of tariff and nontariff barriers following the Kennedy Round. By the time negotiators came together for the Tokyo Round, countries could utilize reports, available on computer tape, to measure the degree of reciprocity in trade deals. The information environment became even richer for the Uruguay Round. After 1985, the GATT infrastructure began to provide refined data on tariff and nontariff barriers in member countries. In 1989, the Trade Policy Review Mechanism was authorized at the Montreal midterm review of progress in the Uruguay Round. This began a process of regular country studies, providing sector and product information on practices of GATT members. The four largest trading powers—Canada, the European Union (EU), Japan, and the United States—are reviewed every two years; the sixteen member countries that are next in the value of their trade are reviewed every four years; most other members are reviewed every six years.[14] The result has been a more symmetric information environment.[15]

This increased monitoring activity in itself is not a result of "legalization" according to the definition adopted in this issue. Still, it has been tightly bound up with increased formalization and precision of commitments both at the time of and during the life of an agreement. The result is a far richer information environment than at any previous time. One aspect of WTO operations, for example, that is more public than in the past is the ministerial meeting. The November 1999 meeting was well publicized, including procedures for obtaining observer status. In response, more groups than ever before petitioned for admission to the meeting. Few of these groups were protrade, leading the secretariat to fear that the meeting would be met with pickets and protests, as it was.[16]

Along with changes in WTO policy, a key demand of antitrade groups has been less secrecy in WTO proceedings. Although some Western governments, including the United States, have defended the principle of transparency, most representatives in the WTO strenuously resist this demand.[17] Still, transparency has increased over time. Early rounds were akin to clubs. Deals were struck among a small group of like-minded representatives, behind closed doors. Later rounds eschewed this general negotiating form. Although private negotiations occurred, and were often the most productive, more time was spent in formal settings, with delegates giving pre-

13. Keesing 1998.
14. Ibid.
15. The GATT's move to the Trade Policy Review Mechanism was motivated by the perception that information was key in negotiations but that it was available only to the larger countries. Ibid.
16. More applications were received from groups asking for admission to the talks than at any previous time in the GATT/WTO's history (private correspondence). See also the *New York Times*, 13 October 1999, A12.
17. *New York Times*, 4 December 1999, A6.

pared speeches that offered few, if any, real trade concessions. Thus the demand for more transparency has been met by more open meetings and more press coverage, but the effect of these particular changes has been muted; delegates continue to worry about domestic constituencies and remain wary of saying anything that would get them into trouble at home.

Increased provision of information to delegates is not, we acknowledge, evidence of complete transparency in the trade regime. Although legalization has resulted in a movement toward transparency, we cannot claim to have reached a situation of complete and perfect information. The WTO retains many of the elements of the GATT, including its preservation of member countries' rights to secrecy. The empirical evidence does not adequately allow us to make precise estimates of the level of transparency. We can, however, identify a trend toward greater openness. When the GATT was established in the late 1940s, the confidentiality rule adopted by member countries was the strictest of any adopted by postwar international institutions.[18] The correspondence of any delegate could be claimed as privileged. If a delegate did not formally rescind a confidentiality request within three years, the information became confidential in perpetuity. Why this rule? Simply, delegates did not want information to leak back home. Offers made during negotiations could be highly sensitive, and although the final package would be made public, it came home as a "closed" deal— groups could not easily pick it apart.

The early delegates to the GATT understood that too much information would incur import-competing group pressures and undermine their ability to make trade-offs among groups. Policymakers need to be able to bundle agreements in order to procure majorities in their home countries. For politicians, the logic of membership in a multilateral trade institution is to facilitate the creation of larger bundles than are possible through bilateral bargaining.

Efforts to devise free-trade coalitions in an environment of market liberalization help explain the changing structure of trade rounds. Since the creation of the GATT, negotiators have utilized four different methods of conducting the rounds, each an attempt to finesse potential antitrade interests in member states. In the initial rounds— Geneva 1947, Annecy 1949, Torquay 1951, Geneva 1956, Dillon 1961—talks were conducted on an item-by-item basis. The form of these talks reflected the negotiating discretion of the U.S. representative. Due to the structure of U.S. trade politics, negotiators were relatively unconstrained, since they had in hand, *ex ante,* authorization to reduce tariffs, on average, by a specified amount. They could make cross-sectoral deals without fear of import-competers vetoing a final agreement. The United States abandoned its support for such a form of talks in the 1960s, partially because of efficiency concerns and what Americans perceived as an asymmetric information environment that did not favor the United States.[19] By the mid-1960s, industries were

---

18. Richard Blackhurst interviews.

19. Under 1951 and 1958 laws, U.S. negotiators were forced to consider data on which industries would be hurt by a trade agreement. Under peril point legislation, the U.S. Tariff Commission provided public information on the effect of tariff reductions on particular industries. This list told U.S. trading partners exactly who could and could not be included in a trade deal. This generated more information to

also demanding side payments, in both the United States and Europe, when they felt victimized in the name of other sectors' gains.[20]

Instead of negotiating item by item, participants in the Kennedy Round adopted a linear formula approach. Although advocates of this approach foresaw it as negating the power of specific groups, the formula was never a significant constraint, and the real politics of the round surrounded the balancing of members' exceptions lists. Nations came to Geneva with long lists of producers to be exempted from the linear cuts. Some nations, such as the Nordic countries, had no industries on their exception list. The United Kingdom had about 10 percent of dutiable industrial imports on its list, the United States had 18–19 percent, Japan had 20–25 percent, and the European Community had 40 percent.[21] The United States' exceptions list was compounded by its having made significant concession to textiles and having granted Article XIX relief to carpets and glass.[22] Even so, the agreements did not fare well when sent to Congress for approval.[23] Although initial authorization had elicited minimal resistance, hearings before the U.S. House Ways and Means Committee in 1968, at the close of the round, were more reminiscent of pre-1934 than post-1934 trade politics. Export groups were conspicuously absent, but import-sensitive groups appeared in large numbers and stopped passage of agreements to end the American Selling Price and reform the antidumping law concluded during the round.[24]

With a new interest in nontariff barriers and the role of the developing economies as well as a fear of import pressures, the 1973 Tokyo Round abandoned linear formulas and adopted a formula that harmonized rates. Linear formulas reduced tariffs by the same amount for all industries. Countries with peaked tariff schedules could participate in worldwide tariff reductions and not have to change the relatively high protection granted to certain products. Harmonized formulas force greater cuts on the top, producing more liberalization as well as more resistance, explaining why the formula was adopted amid much controversy. Since the United States was one of the biggest offenders of the skewed tariff schedule, U.S. negotiators had considerable difficulty finding support at home for the cuts. The final U.S. average cut of 31 percent must be considered alongside the far smaller cuts for powerful industries: 4 percent for leather; 15 percent for apparel; 16 percent for autos; and no cuts for a variety of producers, including footwear and TVs. The United States was not alone in offering a "Swiss cheese" set of offers, and agricultural groups kept cuts in their tariffs off the table all together.[25]

Although in the Uruguay Round attention was focused on nontariff barriers and GATT rules, the pattern of interest-group activity helps to explain why the round

---

groups than is even the case under the WTO. One effect, consistent with this analysis, is that access to this information explains the relatively modest tariff changes made in the 1950s. Goldstein 1993.

20. Shonfield 1976, 175.
21. Ibid., 183.
22. Goldstein 1993, 166.
23. Evans 1971, 281.
24. American Selling Price was a valuation system used for chemical imports. Ibid., 300–303.
25. Winham 1986, 17–18. A reviewer suggested the Swiss cheese metaphor, particularly applicable here since the adopted formula was Swiss.

returned to the original item-by-item approach, with deals made within, and less often across, sectors. At its core, the approach was an attempt by participants to garner support by balancing access to the home market with expanded export opportunities within sectors. All of the major nations faced stiff resistance from powerful social actors in the 1980s. The United States had used a variety of instruments, including antidumping, Section 301, and countervailing duty legislation, in response to aid requests from key sectors, such as steel, automobiles, and textiles. Even more important in both the United States and the EU was the agricultural lobby. At one point during the round the power of French farmers nearly led France to veto the Euro-American Blair House Agreement as well as the conclusion of the round itself.[26] Similarly, the textile lobby in both the United States and the EU worked to undermine the attempt to dismantle the Multi-Fiber Arrangement.[27] The power of the textile industry in the United States was no better evidenced than when a coalition of senators from the South held up the final agreement in Congress.

In all these rounds, politics was never removed from the liberalization process, although the regime's structure did affect which domestic groups were able to translate their preferences into policy. Thus, adopted formulas were never intended to be binding on parties, and national offers were rife with exceptions. Preparation for rounds involved difficult negotiations with potentially powerful veto groups, often leading to an assortment of side payments issued in the early phase of negotiations.[28] Drawing on U.S. congressional indexes, we illustrate in Table 1 one way that this phenomenon manifested. The table summarizes the rise in the number of bills that provided side payments, usually in place of a more direct policy to curb imports. During the 1975–94 period, the number of side-payment bills that made their way to the House floor is high, though fairly stable. The data for 1995–98 suggest that under the WTO even more side-payment bills were used, as our analysis predicts.

Our attention to antitrade groups derives from two related observations. First, although liberalization has been extremely successful in the postwar period, it has always occurred in the shadow of organized opposition. Second, groups respond to information about impending trade talks, which motivates them to pursue particularistic policies. The existence of continued openness should not be interpreted as an absence of proprotection group pressures. Although proprotection groups may have been more constrained, had less "voice," and been balanced by well-organized exporter groups, once organized, they have powerful effects on policy.

Has there been a rise in interest-group activity since the creation of the WTO, as suggested by our analysis? Given the WTO's brief existence, assessing the data is difficult. However, as evidenced by the significant rise in the number of groups attending the WTO's November 1999 ministerial meeting, the WTO itself has engendered

---

26. The three major players were all plagued by antitrade pressures during the round. In the EU, differences among member countries developed over the Common Agricultural Policy. In Japan, the issue of rice protection undercut the ruling Liberal party, and in the United States, pressure from groups polarized on fast-track legislation extension. Secchi 1997, 81.

27. Ibid., 79.

28. Goldstein 1993.

TABLE 1. *Trade bills in the U.S. House of Representatives, 1975–98*

	Number of bills	Percentage providing side payments rather than direct protection
1975–78	79	14
1979–82	43	28
1983–86	61	26
1987–90	61	21
1991–94	47	13
1995–98	48	38

Source: Congressional Index, various years.

more attention from a wider range of domestic groups than ever before. For a whole host of reasons, some associated with legalization, the WTO has become a focus of attention not only for labor and producer groups, the traditionally interested parties, but also for environmental, health, and safety groups. Such attention is a result of the expansion of knowledge about what the WTO is doing as well as structural changes in the scope of the regime.

The regime's effect on the mobilization of groups may also explain problems faced in initiating a new round of trade talks. The stated focus for a new WTO Millennium Round of talks is far more targeted than ever before; knowledge of who has been targeted has led to more and earlier activity than in previous rounds. The best exemplar is the agricultural sector, where good information about the locus of talks led to a cross-national campaign of producers to undercut negotiations.[29] These types of increasing pressures, generated by more information about the liberalization process, will make it more difficult to find nations willing to launch trade rounds and, for those who do make it to Geneva, more difficult to make the necessary trade-offs among producers, even if export groups stay mobilized. After the November 1999 ministerial meeting the fate of the Millennium Round remains an open question, with most observers offering pessimistic assessments.

Mobilizing Export Groups

Although the mobilization of groups circumscribes the type of new deals that are possible, it also explains the stability of signed agreements. Leaders rarely renege on a GATT trade deal, even when faced with pressure from powerful rent-seeking industries. This stability was not due to GATT sanctions against such changes. Rather, changing specific tariffs, according to the rules, was relatively easy under a number of safeguard provisions of the GATT regime. Under GATT rules, nations could change

29. Josling 1999.

TABLE 2. *Post-negotiation tariff changes by invoked article for all GATT members, 1961–90*

	Open season[a]	Out of season[b]	Article 28:5[c]
1961–66[d]	9	14	3
1967–72	8	7	15
1973–78	5	3	31[e]
1979–84	1	1	66[f]
1985–90	1	1	19
1991–93/94	4	1	5

Source: GATT Analytical Index 1994.
[a]*Open season* refers to the usage and invocation of GATT Art. XXVIII:1.
[b]*Out of season* refers to the usage and invocation of GATT Art. XXVIII:4.
[c]Before the end of a period of "firm validity," a country may reserve to modify their schedule. The numbers in this column refer not to the election of this right, but to its usage (the actual modification).
[d]The time periods correspond to two periods of "firm validity," except the last time period (1991–93/94) for which we have only three years of data. Art. XIX data are as of 1 December 1993. Art. XXVIII data are as of 30 March 1994.
[e]Of these cases, 22 are either New Zealand's or South Africa's.
[f]Of these cases, 32 are South Africa's.

tariffs every three years during the "open season," in between these times "out of season," and/or under Article 28:5, as long as the general tariff level remained the same. Keeping the overall level of tariffs stable, however, was not easy for politicians at home. The problem with giving compensation was the trade-off it created between the group pressing for aid and some other producer. This type of a trade-off is difficult for politicians.

Table 2 shows the use of these provisions for changing particular tariffs post-negotiation. What is striking is that, although the regime legally provided a substantial amount of flexibility, these provisions have only rarely been invoked. Given the thousands of products affected by cuts, only a few countries rescinded an agreement to bind their tariffs. For GATT members, these provisions were akin to a Pandora's Box. Having to change a schedule, item by item, in the absence of reciprocal benefits meant trading off one domestic sector for another. The political problems this engendered assured that few GATT countries chose to deal with import problems through these means.

Another perspective on mobilization is evident in attempts to mobilize export groups in support of free trade by strategically using threats of retaliation. States making a threat of retaliation that is intended to mobilize exporters in other countries, such as the United States in implementing Section 301, must consider how to maximize the pressure applied by exporters to the other government. Announcing threats of definite retaliation against just a few groups would not have the desired effect. These groups would certainly mobilize, but those left off the short list would not. At the other extreme, announcing a very large or vague list of possible targets of retaliation would also fail to mobilize many exporters. This tactic would create massive collective-action problems, since each exporter would be only part of a potentially universal coalition and therefore face incentives to free ride. In addition, lack of precision in the possible targets of retaliation might encourage exporters to wait and take their chances on being hit, rather than bearing the definite, immediate costs of mobilization.

With these considerations in mind, if our story about mobilization is correct, the strategic use of retaliatory threats should be quite precise. In addition, it should target a group of exporters large enough to put pressure on the government, but not so large as to exacerbate collective-action problems. Section 301 cases provide a good source of evidence on the use of retaliatory threats, since they list the potential targets of retaliation when the other government does not reach a settlement with the United States.

The case of the United States pressuring Honduras to improve its protection of intellectual property provides a clear example of the principles of targeting in action. The U.S. Trade Representative (USTR), after deciding that Honduras was not adequately protecting intellectual property rights, announced on 7 November 1997 that it would impose sanctions on certain exports from Honduras if improvement in its policy were not forthcoming.[30] The annex to this announcement listed approximately thirty groups of products that would be denied preferential tariff treatment if Honduras did not comply. The annex also specified, in case there was any question, the current duty facing these products. Comments on the list were invited from the U.S. business community and due within one month of the announcement. Public hearings were also held on the proposed list.

One noticeable aspect of the target list is its degree of precision in specifying the targets of sanctions. Rather than just citing agricultural products, for example, the list identified specific agricultural exports: "mushroom spawn," "cucumbers, including gherkins, fresh or chilled," and "pineapple juice, not concentrated, or having a degree of concentration of not more than 3.5 degrees." Tobacco exporters of all sorts were singled out, as were exporters of luggage ("trunks, suitcases, vanity cases, attaché cases, briefcases, school satchels, spectacle cases") and wood products. Another target was exporters of "statues, statuettes, and handmade flowers, valued over $2.50 each and produced by professional sculptors or directly from molds made from original models produced by professional sculptors."

By developing this degree of precision in the specification of targets, the USTR left exporters with little doubt about whether they should put pressure on the Honduran government to seek a settlement with the United States. At the same time, the list was extensive without being so comprehensive that exporters could rely on others to carry the lobbying burden for them. It would have been much simpler, for example, to announce a 25 percent across-the-board increase in duties on exports from Honduras, but this procedure would have been so encompassing that it would have exacerbated collective-action problems among exporters. One other interesting aspect of

30. See *Federal Register* 62 (7 November 1997), Docket No. 301–116 (62 FR 60299).

the list of threatened sanctions is that it identified a set of exports from which the USTR would, if sanctions were actually imposed, select a subset. Thus the list of threatened sanctions was longer than the list of actual sanctions would be, again increasing the size of the mobilized exporters' pressure group.

We find similar retaliation strategies in other trade disputes. Lists of products in trade disputes with the EU and China were, as would be expected for larger trading partners, longer than those in the case of Honduras. In 1995 the USTR launched a complaint against the EU for not offering compensation when Austria, Finland, and Sweden entered the EU and adopted the EU's common external tariff.[31] In this instance, the first product on the list of threatened sanctions was "cheese and curd," going on to list various types of cheese in excruciating detail, and clearly aiming to mobilize French farmers to pressure the EU. Perfumes and cosmetics also appeared high on the list, again suggesting a strategy of mobilizing influential French exporters. The United States has been involved in a number of disputes with China over intellectual property.[32] In these cases, textiles made up the bulk of the list, although beer and chemical exporters were also targeted. In the Chinese cases, the USTR threatened to move beyond imposing a duty to imposing quantitative restrictions on imports, limiting them to 15 percent of the previous year's level.

The threat of retaliation, if issued with an appropriate degree of precision, activates export groups. This suggests that the GATT/WTO should allow or even encourage retaliation in the face of deviation from regime rules. The GATT structure, incorporating reciprocal retaliation and/or alternative market access in response to reneging on a concession, even under safeguard clauses, may have been better than the alternative adopted by the WTO. WTO rules waive the right to both compensation and/or retaliation for the first three years of a safeguard action. Those who supported the change argued that this would encourage nations to follow the rules—when nations could defend their reasons for invoking safeguard actions as "just," they should be protected from retaliation.[33] The logic offered here suggests the opposite. Circumstantial evidence in the United States supports the argument that domestic groups organize in response to government threats that affect their market position. For example, in what was supposed to be a simple incidence of using market restrictions in a Section 301 case, the United States found it politically impossible to raise tariffs on a Japanese car, the Lexus, in large part because of resistance from Lexus dealers in the United States. Lexus dealers are not the type of group that generates great sympathy from the American people. However, during a trade dispute with Japan that came to a head in 1995, they found their interests directly at stake. In an attempt to force more opening of the Japanese market, the United States announced a list of 100 percent retaliatory tariffs on Japanese luxury goods that would go into effect on 28 June.[34] Since this list included cars with a retail value over $30,000, Lexus dealers (along

---

31. *Federal Register* 60 (27 October 1995), Docket No. 301–101 (60 FR 55076).

32. *Federal Register* 56 (2 December 1991), Docket No. 301–86 (56 FR 61278); see also 57 FR 38912 and 61 FR 25000.

33. Krueger 1998.

34. *New York Times*, 9 June 1995, D3.

with Infiniti and Acura dealers) found themselves directly threatened. In response they generated a large lobbying and public relations effort. In the end a midnight deal with Japan averted sanctions.

To summarize, we argue that one of the primary political effects of legalizing the trade regime will be an interaction between increased precision about the distributional implications of trade agreements and the mobilization of domestic groups, both protectionist and free trade in orientation. In this section we have surveyed evidence on trade negotiations and the use of retaliatory tariffs during trade disputes to see if mobilization does indeed respond as we expect. From a number of perspectives, we find evidence to support our claims. During negotiations, lobbying activities are conditioned on the information available to particularistic interests. Strategic politicians, who are attempting to design the negotiating process so as to increase their ability to create mutually beneficial bundles of agreements, may find it helpful to have less than complete transparency about the details of negotiations. Antitrade group pressures make negotiations more difficult, and to the extent that transparency encourages mobilization of antitrade groups it will hinder liberalization negotiations.[35] During trade disputes, politicians similarly strategize about how to reveal information so as to mobilize groups appropriately—in this instance to maximize the mobilization of exporters in the target country.

Our findings should not be interpreted as a prediction of trade closure. Rather, we make the more modest claim that attention should be paid to an underexplored effect of international legalization, that is, the mobilization of domestic groups. The analysis of the interaction of legalization, information, and domestic groups is a requisite to understanding the conditions under which legalization of the trade regime will be successful.

Tightly Binding Trade Rules

In the preceding section we argued that legalization enriches the information environment. In this section we examine a second effect of legalization linked to an increase in the obligatory nature of international rules. Legalization at its core refers to *pacta sunt servanda,* or the presumption that, once signed, nations will adhere to treaty obligations. Interpretations of this responsibility are typically rendered by lawyers using a discourse focusing on rules—their exceptions and applicability—and not on interests. Given the expanding breadth of the trade regime, we suggest that the use of legal rule interpretation has made it increasingly difficult for governments to get around obligations by invoking escape clauses and safeguards or by turning to alternative measures, such as nontariff barriers. Partly, this is a result of the increased precision of rules and the inclusion of what were extralegal trade remedies, such as voluntary export restraints, in the regime itself. But the legalization of the trade regime has also moved the nexus of both rule making and adjudicating rule violations into the center of the regime and away from member states.

35. See, for example, the history of agricultural trade in Josling 1999.

The Logic of "Bindingness"

The benefits of increased precision and "bindingness" are identified in the function-alist literature on international institutions.[36] The benefit of international institutions lies primarily in the creation of disincentives for states to behave opportunistically by reneging on trade agreements and acting unilaterally. The problem of incentives to renege on cooperative arrangements, and the role of international institutions in help-ing states to overcome these incentives and so reach Pareto-superior outcomes, has been central to the institutional approach to international relations.[37] The key institu-tional argument is that attaining cooperative outcomes is hindered by the lack of information about the intentions and behavior of others and ambiguity about interna-tional obligations that states can manipulate to their advantage. States are often caught in a "prisoners' dilemma" and find it difficult to sustain the necessary enforcement strategies to assure cooperation in the uncertain environment of international poli-tics. The primary function of international institutions, therefore, is to provide politi-cally relevant information and so allow states to escape from the prisoners' dilemma trap.

This argument about international institutions took shape during an era when re-searchers were anxious to extend their analysis beyond formal international organiza-tions to informal institutions and regimes.[38] By focusing on legalization, the current project returns to the study of formal institutions, but the underlying logic remains the same. Making international commitments precise and explicit makes it more difficult for states to evade them without paying a cost. More precise rules allow for more effective enforcement, and legalization involves a process of increasing preci-sion. Greater precision and transparency about the obligations and behavior of states are also created by other dimensions of legalization. Delegation of monitoring and dispute-resolution functions to centralized organizational agents, away from member states, is intended to increase the quantity and quality of information about state behavior. It therefore leads to more effective enforcement and disincentives to renege on commitments.

As we have argued, legalization has unintended effects on the mobilization of support for and against trade liberalization. Similarly, legal binding has unexpected effects on domestic politics. If agreements are impossible to breach, either because of their level of obligation or because the transparency of rules increases the likelihood of enforcement, elected officials may find that the costs of signing such agreements outweigh the benefits. The downside of increased legalization in this instance lies in the inevitable uncertainties of economic interactions between states and in the need

---

36. We use the term *bindingness* where the term *obligation* would seem appropriate to a political scientist. The reason is that obligation has taken on a particular legal meaning, and that meaning has been adopted in this issue. By *bindingness* we mean the political obligation created by international rules. It is a positive rather than a normative term, meaning the degree to which rules are binding, practically speaking, on governments. Rules with higher probability of enforcement, for example, are more binding (or obliga-tory) in this political sense.

37. Keohane 1984.

38. Krasner 1983.

for flexibility to deal with such uncertainty without undermining the trade regime as a whole. Legalization as increased bindingness could therefore constrain leaders and undermine free-trade majorities at home.

George Downs and David Rocke consider a similar question and conclude that the dynamics of domestic politics create some optimal level of "imperfection" in the application of international rules.[39] They concentrate on the uncertainty that domestic groups, particularly producers, face when they are exposed to the vagaries of the international market. They assume, reasonably, that governments are not able to perfectly anticipate negative economic shocks and the organizational capacities of groups that may be made vulnerable by trade liberalization.

The existence of uncertainty about the costs of trade agreements on the domestic level suggests that fully legalized procedures that apply high, deterministic penalties for noncompliance could backfire, leading to an unraveling of the process of liberalization.[40] Under some conditions it will be inefficient for actors to live up to the letter of the law in their commitments to one another, such as when alternative arrangements exist that increase mutual gains.[41] These alternative arrangements generally involve temporary deviations from the rules with compensation offered to the other party. The problem is to write agreements that recognize the possibility of breach but limit it to the appropriate context, such as when economic shocks occur and all will be better off by temporarily allowing deviation from rules.

At the same time, of course, writing agreements that provide the necessary flexibility creates a moral-hazard problem. If the circumstances that demand temporary deviation are not perfectly observable to other actors, parties will be tempted to cheat. Cheating in this instance would consist of a demand to stretch the rules for a while, which all would benefit from, because of an unanticipated shock, when in fact the actor is simply attempting to get out of inconvenient commitments. Such opportunistic behavior is a constant concern in strategic settings with asymmetric information. In the context of the GATT/WTO, the primary reasons that flexibility is necessary lie in the uncertainties of domestic politics. Flexibility or "imperfection" can lead to stability and success of trade agreements, but incentives also exist for states to evade commitments even when economic conditions do not justify evasion.

The enforcement structures of the GATT/WTO thus face a difficult dilemma: to allow states to deviate from commitments when doing so would be efficient but to deter abuse of this flexibility. If enforcement is too harsh, states will comply with trade rules even in the face of high economic and political costs, and general support for liberalization is likely to decline. On the other hand, if enforcement is too lax, states will cheat, leading to a different dynamic that could similarly undermine the system. Downs and Rocke, drawing on game-theoretic models, suggest that imper-

---

39. Downs and Rocke 1995, chap. 4.

40. Contract law recognizes the same dynamic of uncertainty requiring flexibility in contracts, under the heading of efficient breach. See Roessler, Schwartz, and Sykes 1997, 7.

41. The idea is similar to that behind the Coase theorem: efficient agreements are reached through the mechanism of one party compensating another.

fection in the enforcement mechanism is the appropriate response. Punishment for infractions of GATT commitments should be probabilistic rather than deterministic.

Changes in WTO procedures have made penalties for rule violation more certain and less probabilistic. At this point, it is difficult to say whether negotiators went too far in limiting the availability of safeguards.[42] However, we can point out one unanticipated effect of the tightening of safeguards that both ties this analysis to our earlier discussion of trade negotiations and generates predictions about future attempts to further liberalize trade. There is a direct connection between states' access to safeguard provisions and their stance during trade negotiations. Domestic interests can anticipate the effects of eliminating safeguards and so will bring more pressure to bear on governments during negotiations.[43] Those who fear the possibility of adverse economic shocks without the protection of an escape clause will be highly resistant to inclusion in liberalization. In response they will demand exclusion or, at a minimum, side payments if their sector is included in liberalizing efforts. Thus extensive tightening of safeguard provisions will lead to tougher, more disaggregated negotiations as some groups lobby strenuously for exclusion. The rise in the use of voluntary export restraints and antidumping and countervailing duty cases is almost certainly a result of this difficulty in using safeguards. It is also likely that more bindingness has led to increases in the side payments governments are forced to make to groups in order to buy their support for trade agreements. Not surprisingly, perhaps, the North American Free Trade Agreement, a highly legalized trade agreement, could only gain approval in the United States after extensive use of side payments by the government.[44]

It is also important to ask whether GATT or WTO provisions effectively deter opportunistic evasion. Mechanisms that deter evasion include domestic costs of violations, enforcement provisions, and reputational concerns. These mechanisms are identical to those identified in standard theories of international institutions, suggesting that extensive international cooperation does not always require legalization. Legal theorists studying the GATT have been surprised to find that the level of compliance was high in spite of its reliance on weakly legalized procedures. Friederich Roessler, Warren F. Schwartz, and Alan Sykes see the overall reduction in tariffs under the GATT as evidence that its procedures did in general deter opportunistic evasion.[45] Sykes also finds that reputational mechanisms in the GATT substantially constrained the United States from acting opportunistically, as does Robert Hudec.[46]

Few analysts dispute that the old trade regime was tremendously effective in reducing impediments to trade. Nevertheless, analysts and legal scholars involved in the GATT expressed dissatisfaction about many of its procedures and capacities. One

---

42. As we argue later, the safeguard reforms are counterintuitive for two reasons. First, they may be too difficult to invoke, undercutting their purpose. Second, since retaliation is limited, the stability evoked by activating export groups may have been undermined.
43. See also Sykes 1991, 259.
44. Hufbauer and Schott 1993.
45. Roessler, Schwartz, and Sykes 1997, 13.
46. See Sykes 1992; and Hudec 1999.

concern was that the dispute-resolution procedures seemed to have a fatal flaw, in that member states could undermine the creation of dispute-resolution panels as well as any decision that went against them. Another concern was that powerful states, particularly the United States, evaded GATT regulations when convenient. As the United States increasingly turned to unilateral remedies for perceived trade infractions, such as Section 301, other members grew increasingly concerned that the GATT was powerless in preventing unilateralism and not strong enough to provide effective enforcement.

The remedy to these problems, both in theory and in practice, was greater legalization of the GATT. As the GATT evolved into the more formal WTO, the dispute-resolution procedures were made more legal in nature and the organization gained enhanced oversight and monitoring authority. Multilateral rules of trade extended into new and difficult areas, such as intellectual property, and substituted for unilateral practices. The procedures for retaliation and compensation were made more precise and limiting. The process of negotiating the content of rules—including provisions for addressing rule breaches—led to greater precision.[47] In the next sections we evaluate these changes, asking whether or not the changes portend greater trade liberalization. Our inquiry centers on two questions. First, we ask whether the legal framework allows states to abrogate a contract when doing so would be mutually beneficial. Second, we examine the functioning of the dispute-resolution mechanism.

In sum, theoretical consideration of the problem of complying with commitments in an uncertain economic and political environment provides another angle on the function and process of legalization in the WTO. Moving toward more certain, legalized procedures constitutes a balancing act. Appropriate procedures should deter opportunism while allowing states to deviate from commitments under some circumstances. Focusing only on the problem of opportunism, which would lead us to argue consistently in favor of more legalized procedures, misses the dilemma that the institution actually faces. Given uncertainty on the domestic level, moving too far in the direction of legalizing trade could undermine the momentum toward liberalizing trade that the weakly legalized procedures of the GATT so effectively established.

Exceptions and Escape Clauses

Trade legalization has constrained states by curtailing their ability to utilize safeguards and exceptions. The issue of exceptions, their status and use, has loomed large in many of the rounds of GATT negotiations. Pressure from import-competing groups is strong everywhere, although domestic institutional arrangements vary in how well they can "buy off" or ignore this resistance. The United States, for example, has been notorious for both retaining protection on the upper part of its schedule and for making particular industry side payments before even arriving in Geneva. The United States is also responsible for the inclusion of an escape clause into the GATT's

---

47. On the extent of changes in the WTO, see Krueger 1998.

original design, reflecting a desire by Congress to maintain its prerogative to renege on a trade deal if necessary.[48]

Legalization of the regime has resulted in a tightening in the use of safeguard provisions, including the escape clause. Under Article XIX, a country is allowed to increase protection for a home industry if a past tariff concession does damage to it.[49] If a country backs out of an agreement or imposes some additional trade restriction, it must be applied in a nondiscriminatory way; that is, countries whose exports are not hurting your industry cannot retain a preferential position.[50] When the provision is used, other countries are allowed to retaliate by reducing an equivalent amount of concession; otherwise the country imposing Article XIX must reduce tariffs on other products, equivalent to the amount of the original concession.

Two important domestic groups are potentially affected by these limitations on the use of safeguards. If nations retaliate, exporters suffer; if the government compensates, some import-competing industry will feel increased competition. Unless offered some side payment, industries have a strong incentive to have their political representative veto their inclusion into the compensatory package. Thus both the threat of retaliation and the difficulty of reassigning tariff reductions should constrain countries from raising trade barriers as allowed under Article XIX. The logic here is consistent with that offered in the preceding section.

The data on Article XIX provide support for the argument that using this provision is difficult in practice. Table 3 shows the aggregate use of the escape clause for all GATT members. Since the 1960s, Article XIX has been invoked at a relatively consistent rate. Given increasing levels of trade, stable numbers of Article XIX invocations imply *declining* use of this mechanism. As with the safeguard measures listed in Table 2, the small number of cases, compared with the significant number of industries affected by changing tariffs, should be attributed to the difficult time countries have both with the potential for retaliation and with compensating nations through alternative tariff reductions. This difficulty explains the trend toward alternative methods of protection, such as "administered protection" in the form of subsidies and antidumping and countervailing duty provisions.[51] Nontariff barriers, though not often used in the 1950s, were, by the 1970s, used by most countries to circumvent problems with GATT rules. Licenses, quotas, and voluntary export restraints were all means to finesse the potential problems *at home* with the GATT compensatory system.

48. Goldstein 1993.
49. "Tariff concessions and unforeseen developments must have caused an absolute or relative increase in imports which in turn causes or threatens serious injury to domestic producers . . . of like or directly competitive goods." Although the invoking party is not saddled with the burden of proving that it has met these requirements, the requirements nonetheless have deterred countries from invoking the escape clause.
50. This often leads to a situation where the producers causing the problems in the first place could remain in a competitive position with the higher-cost home producer. The producers who get penalized are the middle-price traders who were not the problem. Shonfield 1976, 224.
51. Baldwin 1998.

TABLE 3. *Use of escape clause by all GATT members, 1950–94*

	Average number of cases per year	Nontariff barrier remedies as percentage of total uses
1950s	1.9	26
1960s	3.5	56
1970s	4.7	70
1980s	3.7	51
1990s[a]	1.2	75

Source: GATT Analytical Index 1994.
[a]Data for the 1990s run only from 1990 to 1 December 1993.

Overall, the figures in Tables 2 and 3 suggest that use of the legally available mechanisms of flexibility in the trade regime is heavily circumscribed by the interaction of the legal provisions for their use and political realities. The increasing extent to which governments are bound by the lack of realistic escape clauses is apparent when we examine the use of compensation. Although the use of safeguards has been relatively constant, compensation or retaliation in response to the invocation of a safeguard provision was more common in the earlier years—ten cases from 1950 to 1959, ten cases from 1960 to 1969, six cases in the 1970s, and three cases in the 1980s.[52]

Use of compensation and retaliation was concentrated. The United States accounted for twelve of the twenty cases between 1950 and 1970 but only one case thereafter. Australia accounted for seven of the sixteen cases between 1960 and 1980. Although American use of Article XIX did not decline until the 1980s, the kind of remedy administrators chose to use did shift over time. Compensation could occur through reducing tariff barriers elsewhere. However, this would hurt other import-competing groups, so the compensation mechanism of Article XIX is unwieldy if these groups are organized. At the same time, rescinding tariff concessions without compensation opens exporters to the threat of retaliation. For these reasons, the United States had moved toward a nontariff barrier remedy by the late 1960s. The change was rather dramatic. In the early years of the regime, between 1950 and 1969, the United States compensated for a tariff hike over 93 percent of the time.[53] Thereafter, both the use of compensation and the number of invocations declined precipitously.

Overall, the evidence on the use of safeguards and compensation suggests that strict legal provisions were not necessary to maintain openness. The pattern of use of safeguard provisions in the GATT suggests that the regime gained in politically relevant bindingness, even when in legal terms the obligatory nature of rules did not change. Still, the WTO reforms attempted to clarify and make more stringent the

52. GATT *Analytical Index,* various issues.
53. The United States invoked Article XIX fourteen times between 1950 and 1969. Of these they used nontariff barriers alone in only one case.

requirements for using safeguards. Drawing on the discussion of economic uncertainty and the need for flexibility in light of the data, we suggest that increased stringency in safeguard use may be misplaced. In fact, even the GATT provisions could be interpreted to have become too tightly binding, not allowing the necessary temporary deviations from rules that contribute to long-term stability. Escape clauses, safeguards, and the like are the legal mechanisms for dealing with a world of economic uncertainty. The provisions for their use must be heavily constrained, so as to reduce the chance that states will invoke them opportunistically. However, it appears that these constraints, interacting with domestic politics, may bind states more tightly than intended.

Our cautionary note may explain why the WTO chose to forestall retaliation for three years in cases where a safeguard provision was sanctioned. Yet the choice of this tool to deal with overbinding may be a problem. Given the logic offered in the preceding section, we suggest that nations abide by their trade agreements because the threat of retaliation mobilizes export groups to counter rent-seeking producer groups. Similarly, our analysis suggests that the mobilization of groups favored those who support openness, which, in turn, deterred states from using even legal exceptions. Given the logic of domestic politics, it is hard to know whether the benefits of this new rule in terms of flexibility will outweigh its effects on the balance between pro- and antitrade groups in WTO members.

Dispute Settlement

One of the major innovations of the WTO was to strengthen the dispute-resolution mechanism. States have lost the ability to wield a veto, which they used under the GATT to protect themselves against GATT-approved retaliation. In effect, residual rights of control have been shifted from states to the WTO, convened as the Dispute Settlement Body. According to proponents of the new system, the existence of veto power encouraged opportunism, whereas not having veto power deters such behavior. If this is the case, we should see predictable effects in the pattern of disputes brought to the WTO.

We suggest that the GATT dispute-settlement structure, by being more attentive to the realities of power and an uncertain economic environment, but also by providing publicity and possible sanctions when states blatantly disregarded regime rules, may have optimized the trade-off between constraint and flexibility that liberalization requires. As a way to examine this hypothesis, we ask whether the pattern of disputes has changed under the WTO in the manner predicted by the logic of reducing opportunism. The strong theoretical argument in favor of legalization claims that legalization is necessary to prevent opportunistic behavior. If we find that the incidence of opportunism has not changed in the face of increasing legalization, the argument in favor of legalization loses much of its force.[54]

---

54. We assume a goal of reducing opportunism on theoretical grounds, without claiming that all negotiators had precisely this goal in mind. Certainly the agendas of negotiators were diverse, and reducing opportunism was only one goal among many.

If the primary effect of further legalization in dispute settlement is reducing opportunism, it should appear in the data as reduced political manipulation of the regime. Eliminating the power to veto should have observable effects on the activities of states and the outcome of disputes. Political scientists are producing a burgeoning literature on GATT/WTO dispute settlement, using sophisticated statistical techniques. However, this literature, regardless of the techniques involved, cannot escape problems of selection bias, since states chose whether to bring disputes and at what stage to resolve them. Here we suggest a few simple hypotheses about how the pattern of disputes should change with legalization if its major effect is a reduction in opportunism. If the data do not support these simple hypotheses, the case for legalization is substantially weakened.

Adopting the unitary state/opportunism model, we derive propositions about how legalization should influence patterns of disputes. Assuming the problem of opportunism suggests that the loss of veto power should have two primary effects: a *deterrent* effect and a *distributive* effect. States will behave strategically both in deciding when to bring disputes and whether to comply preemptively so that others have no cause to bring a dispute. This two-sided strategic behavior could render many predictions indeterminate. To identify refutable hypotheses, we focus on expected changes in the relative behavior of developed and developing states. Since both are subject to the same incentives in deciding whether to comply with changes in GATT/WTO rules, changes in the proportions of disputes brought are likely caused by changed calculations about the chances of success in a dispute and not by changed patterns of compliance. Although developing countries have more trade restrictions than developed countries, the marginal impact of new dispute-resolution procedures on compliance decisions should be the same for both. In addition, we concentrate on just the first few years of experience under the WTO rules. Since states can change their behavior in bringing disputes more quickly than they can change their basic trade regulations, the patterns we observe should be due primarily to calculations about whether bringing disputes is worthwhile, not fundamental changes in compliance.

A deterrent effect refers to the likelihood that the existence of veto power would deter states from bringing disputes. Bringing a formal dispute is costly and time consuming, and states could calculate that doing so is not worth the trouble if the powerful will simply veto any decision that goes against them. Thus we generate a deterrence hypothesis: *the existence of veto power deters some states from bringing disputes, and with the loss of veto power these states are no longer deterred.*

In order to collect data relevant to this general hypothesis, we need to derive some observable implications from it. We do so on the assumption that the intent of legalizing dispute-resolution procedures is to reduce opportunistic behavior by powerful states such as the United States.[55] One implication is that, since powerful states can no longer veto decisions that go against them, *we should expect the proportion of complaints against developed countries to rise under the WTO* (hypothesis 1). If states were deterred from bringing complaints against the powerful because of the

---

55. Jackson 1998.

existence of the veto, then such complaints should have a higher probability of success as a result of the loss of the veto. Therefore, we should see more disputes brought against the powerful. This should be true even if states are, for strategic reasons, complying more fully under the WTO. Better compliance should hold for both developed and developing states; there is no reason to expect the proportion of disputes against the powerful to change as a result of changes in compliance patterns.

Second, since less powerful countries may now have a greater chance of having decisions in their favor implemented, *we should see developing countries increasingly bringing complaints* (hypothesis 2). Simply put, the deterrence hypothesis suggests that under the WTO, weak states should no longer be deterred. Like hypothesis 1, hypothesis 2 should hold even if patterns of compliance have improved, since improved compliance should hold for both developed and developing states. There is no reason to expect strategic compliance behavior to lead to a change in the proportion of disputes brought by developing countries.

Finally, a process marred by opportunism should be most evident in relations between powerful and weak states. Thus a third implication of the deterrence hypothesis is that *we should see an increase in the proportion of cases brought by developing countries against developed countries* (hypothesis 3). As the WTO depoliticizes trade and so encourages the less powerful to demand their legal rights, we should see more of these "asymmetric" disputes.

The evidence on these three hypotheses about deterrent effects is mixed.[56] Regarding hypothesis 1, of the complaints raised under the GATT through 1989, 87 percent were brought against developed states.[57] Under the WTO, this percentage has dropped, contrary to the expectation from the opportunism perspective, to 64 percent. This is likely a result of the expansion of regime rules to cover more developing-country trade. The high percentage of complaints brought under the GATT against developed states is not surprising, considering the value of their market for other states. Yet it indicates that the power to veto did not allow powerful states to deter others from bringing complaints against them. This finding suggests that the GATT, in spite of the decentralized nature of its dispute-resolution process, was able to constrain the behavior of developed countries, as Hudec also concludes.[58] Preventing opportunism does not require high levels of legalization.

Hypothesis 2 posits that developing countries will be more likely to use the WTO procedures than they were to use the GATT mechanism. If this is true, we should see the percentage of complaints brought by developing countries rising under the WTO. This prediction holds up better than the first. Under the GATT (through 1989), only 19 percent of complaints were brought by developing countries.[59] This number has risen to 33 percent in the first few years that the WTO mechanisms have been in effect. However, considering the evidence just discussed on the identity of defen-

---

56. For a more thorough examination of patterns of disputes in the GATT and the WTO, see Hudec 1999; and Sevilla 1998.
57. Hudec 1993, 297.
58. Hudec 1999.
59. Hudec 1993, 296.

dants, it seems likely that this increased reliance on the dispute-resolution mechanism reflects some dynamic other than a decreased ability of the powerful to deter complaints against themselves. In particular, it seems likely that increased legalization has reduced the costs of bringing suits, thus making it more frequently worth the cost of bringing a complaint for poor states, regardless of the identity of the defendant.[60] In other words, legalization has encouraged weaker states to bring more complaints, generally because doing so is easier, not because the powerful will no longer veto them.

Hypothesis 3 predicts an increase in the number of complaints brought by developing countries against developed countries under the WTO. This hypothesis fares badly, because the data show that under the GATT developing countries targeted almost solely the rich world in their disputes. Hudec's data show almost no cases of developing countries bringing complaints against one another. The exceptions are disputes between India and Pakistan. In contrast, the twenty complaints brought by developing countries so far under the WTO have been just about evenly divided between targeting the developed and developing world. Two factors might explain this finding. First, the costs of bringing disputes are now lower, so it is more often worthwhile to bring them against developing countries. Second, the Uruguay Round extended many trade rules to developing countries, so the dispute-resolution procedures can be used against them for the first time. Regardless of the particular mechanism at work, the pattern of complaints shows that the major change under the WTO procedures has been an increased willingness of developing countries to bring complaints against one another. This effect is not consistent with reduced opportunism.

If legalization reduces opportunism as intended, a second effect that should result from eliminating the veto power is enhanced equity in the outcomes of disputes. We can formalize this as a fourth hypothesis: *legalization of dispute resolution has reduced the bias toward the powerful in the settlement of disputes* (hypothesis 4). A distributive effect could be estimated by comparing the outcomes of disputes brought under the GATT versus under the WTO. Unfortunately, since few cases have yet been resolved under the WTO, we can say nothing definitive on this issue. However, we can look at dispute outcomes under the GATT to see if they tended to favor developed countries as expected. If the weakly legalized GATT mechanisms encouraged opportunism, this trend should appear as a bias toward the powerful in the outcomes of disputes under the GATT. Eric Reinhardt has provided a careful statistical study of the factors determining the distributive outcomes of GATT disputes.[61] He tests the hypothesis that powerful states tend to get a larger share of the benefits of resolved disputes. Employing a number of alternative operationalizations, Reinhardt found no evidence that asymmetries of power work in favor of the powerful. Instead, he found a bias in favor of defendants, regardless of power asymmetries.

As with the data on the choice to bring complaints, in looking at the outcomes of disputes we find little evidence that the GATT operated in an overtly politicized

---

60. Sevilla 1998.
61. Reinhardt 1995.

manner, with powerful states using the GATT dispute-resolution procedures to deter weaker states from bringing complaints or to force outcomes of disputes to favor the powerful. The GATT, in spite of its weak level of legalization, provided many of the benefits we expect to see from international institutions. It discouraged opportunism without a resort to highly legalized mechanisms. This finding raises further questions about the benefits that states will be able to derive from further legalization.

Improving the compliance of powerful states with their explicit obligations under the rules of international trade was one of the primary motivations behind the enhanced dispute-resolution mechanisms of the WTO. Thus moving from a politicized process to a more legalized one should have an observable impact on the behavior of powerful states. However, the evidence is weak that the WTO has made the difference intended by proponents of more legalized dispute-resolution procedures. While developing countries appear more willing to lodge formal complaints than they were previously, the complaints do not target the behavior of powerful states any more than they did before. One plausible interpretation of the evidence on the number of complaints being brought is that the GATT was in fact quite influential in constraining powerful states, leading us to ask how much value will be added by increased legalization. Considering the drawbacks of increased legalization discussed earlier, the benefits must be clear in order to justify further moves in this direction. Dispute outcomes do not show evidence of coercion by powerful states, consistent with the idea that the political sensitivity of the GATT was not as much of an impediment to liberalization as legalization proponents presumed.

Conclusion

This article was motivated by questions about the relationship between international legalization and trade. The benefits of legalization lie in the fact that the more efficiently a regime provides information, reduces transaction costs, and monitors member behavior, the harder it is for a unitary state to behave opportunistically and renege on trade agreements. However, an analysis of the domestic requisites of free trade suggests potential negative effects of legalization that must be weighed against its benefits. When we consider cooperation with the trade regime to be a function of the interests of domestic political actors, the assumption that increased legalization leads to more trade openness becomes questionable. Although we cannot demonstrate that legalization has gone so far that it threatens liberalization, we do wish to sound a cautionary note based in the impact of legalization on the mobilization of protectionist groups.

We examined three theoretical issues implicated by the legalization of the trade regime. First, we asked how greater precision at the time of negotiating treaties changes the incentives of antitrade groups to mobilize. In that legalization leads to more and better information about the distributional effects of proposed agreements, we suggested that it could actually deter the conclusion of cooperative deals. Faced with certainty of loss, the expected utility of a group's organizing increases, suggesting that negotiators could find themselves confronted by powerful veto groups, undermining their ability to construct a majority in favor of a treaty. This dynamic of information provided by a legalized regime leading to massive mobilization may help explain the level of social activism at the 1999 WTO meetings in Seattle.

Second, we applied the same logic of information and mobilization to expectations about the maintenance of agreements already in force. The logic of information here predicted a different outcome from that during negotiations. By focusing on the incentives of exporters, we argued that when exporters know that they are likely targets of retaliation, they are more motivated to organize in support of the trade regime than those subject to an imprecise threat of retaliation. Thus the prediction about the effect of changes in the information environment varies, depending upon whether we are considering the expansion of trade liberalization or compliance with enacted treaties.

Finally, we looked at the effects of a system of highly deterministic penalties on domestic actors. Here we suggested that trade regimes need to incorporate some flexibility in their enforcement procedures; too little enforcement may encourage opportunism, but too much may backfire, undermining the ability of domestic actors to find support for an open trade policy. By decreasing the ability to breach agreements, WTO negotiators may have underestimated the inherently uncertain character of the international economy and so the need to allow practical flexibility in enforcement of regime rules.

These theoretical arguments suggest the need to carefully examine the trend toward increasing legalization, weighing both its benefits and its costs. Legalization can increase social resistance to new cooperative agreements by reducing the number and type of instruments available to politicians to deal with a rise in antitrade sentiment. In addition, with less ability to finesse international rules, leaders could find themselves forced to renege on trade agreements.

Given the short history of the WTO, the empirical support for our theoretical arguments is inconclusive. Still, evidence suggests that the effects of legalization may not be as glowing as proponents argue. First, legalization may be one reason for the increased attention and activity of antitrade groups. We cannot say whether this will deter nations from further liberalization, since policy will ultimately depend on the balance of national forces between pro- and antitrade groups. Still, it is clear that those groups who are targeted for liberalization in the new round of discussions have become active proponents of particularistic policies. Second, some evidence suggests that changes in WTO rules undermine the incentive for export groups to mobilize in defense of free trade. In that the WTO makes retaliation more difficult, both because of changes in the rules on safeguard provisions and because of the process of dispute resolution, we expect exporters to mobilize less often to balance the action of rent-seeking import-competing groups.

Consideration of the effect of the more precise and binding safeguard and dispute-settlement provisions also raises questions about the turn toward legalization. Given the difficulty of their use, few countries turned to GATT safeguards, choosing instead alternative methods to deal with difficulties in compliance. Making these safeguards more difficult to use may have been both unnecessary and counterproductive—if countries found it necessary to turn to alternative mechanisms to deal with the political effects of market dislocation before, the change in rules on safeguards does little to solve the underlying problem. Similarly, our investigation of the WTO dispute-settlement mechanism gives us little reason to think that legalization in the realm of settling disputes will have significant effects on trade compliance. The GATT system was relatively effective at deterring opportunism, in spite of its political nature.

The source of stability of trade agreements is found in domestic political mechanisms. The rules of the regime influence countries by making it easier or harder to find majority support for trade openness; if the regime supports rules that are unhelpful to politicians at home, it may well undercut its own purpose. Thus the legalization of international trade could turn on itself if analysis of the benefits of legalization neglects associated political costs. Thomas Franck has argued that the greater the "determinacy" of a rule, the more legitimate it becomes.[62] Determinacy, however, may be of greater value to lawyers than to politicians, whose interests in trade liberalization will be constrained by elections. Elected officials face a dilemma. If there is too little formalism in international trade rules, politicians will be unable to commit for fear of opportunism by others; too much formalism and they lose their ability to opt out of the regime temporarily during especially intense political opposition or tough economic times. Analyses of legalization that focus on maximizing state compliance neglect complex domestic political dynamics. It is well possible that attempts to maximize compliance through legalization will have the unintended effect of mobilizing domestic groups opposed to free trade, thus undermining hard-won patterns of cooperation and the expansion of trade.

---

62. Franck 1995.

International Human Rights Law and Practice in Latin America

Ellen L. Lutz and Kathryn Sikkink

Human rights practices in Latin America provide a lens through which to examine the relationship between international law and domestic politics. International human rights norms are expressed in numerous widely ratified treaties. Many of those norms also are embedded in customary international law. The number of binding human rights norms incorporated into international or regional law as well as the precision and delegation of those norms increased significantly between the mid-1970s and the mid-1990s. In addition, in the 1970s and 1980s an international human rights advocacy network committed to documenting and spotlighting human rights violations, drafting and implementing international human rights standards, and pressuring governments to implement bilateral and multilateral human rights policies emerged.[1]

During the same time period, a transformation occurred in the composition and behavior of political actors in the region. Whereas two decades ago most Latin American states were governed by dictatorial regimes that routinely engaged in torture, disappearance, extrajudicial execution, and prolonged arbitrary detention, today they enjoy electoral regimes that for the most part comply with fundamental international human rights norms.

We explore the extent to which these two parallel processes are linked. We examine state compliance with three primary norms of international human rights law: the prohibition against torture, the prohibition against disappearance, and the right to democratic governance. These three norms vary in their degree of obligation, precision, and delegation. In the context of this legalization framework, the prohibition against torture is the most legalized, the prohibition against disappearance has mid-level legalization, and the right to democratic governance is the least legalized.

Our thanks to the editors of this special issue, the editors of *International Organization,* and two reviewers for helpful comments and suggestions. We also want to thank Martha Finnemore, David Weissbrodt, Richard Price, Timothy Buckalew, Ann Towns, and Maria Florencia Belvedere for comments, advice, and assistance.

1. See Sikkink 1996; and Clark, forthcoming.

International Organization 54, 3, Summer 2000, pp. 249–275

Torture is the most widely outlawed human rights violation. Nearly all Latin American nations have long prohibited torture as a matter of domestic law.[2] It is prohibited by numerous international instruments, and it violates customary international law.[3] Torture is one of a handful of rights in the International Covenant on Civil and Political Rights for which no derogation is permissible. The customary international law prohibition similarly has a *jus cogens,* or nonderogable, character. Thus, under no circumstances may states take measures to annul the prohibition against torture. In 1980 a U.S. federal court judge, considering the customary international law prohibition against torture, declared that "the torturer has become—like the pirate and slave trader before him—*hostis humani generis,* an enemy of all mankind."[4] The British House of Lords recognized the inviolability of the international prohibition against torture when it allowed extradition proceedings against General Augusto Pinochet to go forward. Spain sought Pinochet's extradition from England, where he was visiting to receive medical care, to stand trial for torture that occurred in Chile during the Pinochet regime (1973–90).[5]

In addition to being obligatory, the norm against torture also is precise. Two treaties, the Convention Against Torture and Other Cruel, Inhuman, or Degrading Treatment or Punishment and the Inter-American Convention to Prevent and Punish Torture, contain detailed definitions of torture and the obligations of states to prevent and punish it.[6] Although levels of delegation are not high, third-party authority exists to review state compliance with the international prohibition and to settle disputes involving allegations of torture. Individuals in the Americas may submit complaints of torture to the Inter-American Commission on Human Rights (IACHR), and the commission may refer cases to the Inter-American Court of Human Rights if the country involved has accepted the court's jurisdiction. Individuals in states that have ratified the relevant treaties and protocols may submit petitions to the UN Human Rights Committee or Committee Against Torture. These quasi-judicial bodies issue findings and recommendations.

The prohibition against disappearance is less legalized than that against torture. It emerged almost overnight in response to an epidemic of state-sponsored secret abductions and killings in Chile, Guatemala, and Argentina in the mid-1970s. The legaliza-

---

2. Amnesty International 1975.
3. Restatement of Foreign Relations Law of the United States (Third), Section 702.
4. *Filártiga v. Pena-Irala,* 630 F.2d 876, 890 (2d Cir. 1980).
5. *5 R v Bartle and Commissioner of Police for the Metropolis and others, ex parte Pinochet,* House of Lords, 24 March 1999.
6. The definition in the Convention Against Torture and Other Cruel, Inhuman, or Degrading Treatment or Punishment, the treaty elaborating on the prohibition against torture that is most widely ratified by Latin American states, is:

> any act by which severe pain or suffering, whether physical or mental, is intentionally inflicted on a person for such purposes as obtaining from him or a third person information or a confession, punishing him for an act he or a third person has committed or is suspected of having committed, or intimidating or coercing him or a third person, or for any reason based on discrimination of any kind, when such pain or suffering is inflicted by or at the instigation of or with the consent or acquiescence of a public official or other person acting in an official capacity. It does not include pain or suffering arising only from, inherent in, or incidental to lawful sanctions.

tion process was eased because the violation was seen as analogous to well-institutionalized norms against arbitrary arrest and detention and summary execution. In 1988 a U.S. federal court judge declared that disappearances violate customary international law.[7] However, steps to make the prohibition against disappearance more legalized did not occur until the 1990s. In 1992 the UN General Assembly adopted a Declaration on the Protection of All Persons from Enforced Disappearance, and in 1994 the Organization of American States (OAS) adopted the Inter-American Convention on Forced Disappearance of Persons.[8] The latter contains a precise definition of disappearance,[9] but that treaty only entered into force in 1996 and as of 1999 had been ratified by only seven states.

In principle the norm against disappearance is obligatory, but in fact the norm's obligatoriness is weakened by the nature of the rights violation involved. Disappearances often are difficult to prove because the accuser must show that the victim was deprived of his or her freedom by government agents notwithstanding government claims to the contrary. With respect to delegation of enforcement authority to independent institutions, victims of disappearance in the Americas have the same opportunities as survivors of torture to file complaints with the IACHR of the OAS. In some cases, the IACHR has the discretion to submit disappearance complaints to the Inter-American Court on Human Rights, as it did in the Honduras case discussed later.

The right to democratic governance is the least legalized norm internationally, though its constituent elements, including freedom of expression, freedom of association, freedom of assembly, and the right to participate in free and fair elections, are included in all the major human rights treaties. Until September 1997 the primary norm reference for the right to democracy in the Americas was the Santiago Commitment to Democracy and the Renewal of the Inter-American System (Santiago Declaration), a resolution adopted by the OAS General Assembly in 1991.[10] As a declaration, it lacked the dimension of formal legal obligation. It also lacked precision, since its definition of democracy is vague. Finally, there is no legal delegation to a third party for dispute resolution, though in a resolution adopted the following day the OAS General Assembly established a process for convening an ad hoc meeting of the region's ministers of foreign affairs in the event of any occurrence giving rise to the sudden or irregular interruption of democratic governance in a member state.[11]

7. *Forti v. Suarez Mason*, 697 F. Supp. 707 (N.D. Cal. 1988).

8. Inter-American Convention on Forced Disappearance of Persons, done at Belém, Brazil, 9 June 1994, 33 I. L. M. 1529.

9. That treaty provides

forced disappearance is considered to be the act of depriving a person or persons of his or their freedom, in whatever way, perpetrated by agents of the state or by persons or groups of persons acting with the authorization, support, or acquiescence of the state, followed by the absence of information or a refusal to acknowledge that deprivation of freedom or to give information on the whereabouts of that person, thereby impeding his or her recourse to the applicable legal remedies and procedural guarantees.

10. Reproduced in Vaky and Munoz 1993.

11. AG/RES. 1080-(XXI-0/91), Representative Democracy, Resolution Adopted at the Fifth Plenary Session, 5 June 1991, reproduced in Vaky and Munoz 1993.

TABLE 1. *Issue-area legalization in Latin America (mid-1990s)*

Issue-area	Level of obligation	Level of precision	Level of delegation
Torture	High	High	Medium
Disappearance	Medium	Medium	Medium
Democracy	Low	Low	Low

Note: The table reflects the level of legalization of democracy before the Protocol of Washington entered into force in 1997. After 1997, we could say that democracy was characterized by a medium level of obligation but still had low levels of precision and delegation.

After September 1997 the level of obligation of the democracy norm in Latin America increased substantially when the Protocol of Washington, an amendment to the OAS Charter, entered into force. The protocol provides that two-thirds of the OAS General Assembly may vote to suspend a member state whose democratically elected government has been overthrown by force.[12] The levels of precision and delegation are still low, however, since the protocol does not include a definition of democracy or an explanation of what constitutes being "overthrown by force." Nor are decisions delegated to a neutral third party, since the decision on suspension is made by two-thirds of the OAS General Assembly in a process that would clearly involve more political bargaining than legal argument. Table 1 summarizes the extent of legalization of the three issue-areas—torture, disappearance, and democracy—in Latin America in the mid-1990s.

We explore in this article the consequences of legalization on human rights practices in countries in the region. The impact of legalization varies considerably in relation to each of the three issue-areas. If legalization is significant, we would expect it to have the most impact on the prohibition on torture and the least impact on the right to democratic governance. However, the degree of legalization within any issue-area also varies across countries, since some countries ratified treaties and thus accepted more obligation and delegation. We devote our exploration primarily to the effect of legalization within the context of comparative country case studies. Before we turn to those cases, it is useful to explore the hypotheses in the context of the region as a whole to see how legalization has affected human rights practices.

Despite the unambiguous prohibition against torture both in international law and in domestic law, torture has been widely practiced in Latin America and was particularly prevalent in the 1970s and early 1980s when the majority of states in the region were governed by military dictatorships.[13] In the early 1980s Amnesty International

12. 1-E Rev. OEA Documentos Officiales OEA/Ser.A/2 Add 3 (SEPF). Signed 14 December 1992; entered into force 25 September 1997.

13. Amnesty International says that Costa Rica is the only country in Latin America from which they had received no torture allegations of any kind in the year preceding the preparation of the report. Amnesty International 1975, 191.

reported that it had credible evidence of torture in fifteen Latin American countries: Argentina, Bolivia, Brazil, Chile, Colombia, El Salvador, Guatemala, Guyana, Haiti, Honduras, Mexico, Paraguay, Peru, Suriname, and Uruguay.[14] By the mid-1990s, most analysts agree that torture was less widespread throughout the region than it was in the 1970s. Nevertheless, in 1999 Amnesty International reported that torture was frequent or widespread in four countries in Latin America (Brazil, Colombia, Mexico, and Venezuela) and that "some" or "several cases" of torture had been reported in nine additional countries.[15] The UN Special Rapporteur on Torture in his 1999 report discussed numerous cases of torture in Brazil, Colombia, Mexico, and Venezuela, and added Peru as a country where torture was frequently used. The Special Rapporteur discussed six additional Latin American countries from which he had received cases alleging torture.[16] Despite the high legalization of the prohibition against torture, the practice has far from disappeared from the hemisphere.

Unlike torture, which has occurred for centuries, the widespread and systematic practice of disappearance is a more recent phenomenon in the region. The IACHR first expressed concern for the practice in its 1976 annual report to the OAS General Assembly, arguing that "disappearances seem to be a comfortable expedient to avoid application of the legal provisions established for the defense of personal freedom, physical security, dignity, and human rights itself." In 1978 the UN General Assembly adopted a resolution calling on governments to investigate and punish those responsible for disappearances and calling on the UN Commission on Human Rights to take up the matter.[17] The commission subsequently created the UN Working Group on Disappearances.

In its first report in 1981 the UN Working Group reported that it had received information about 11,000 to 13,000 cases of disappearances from fifteen countries, ten of which were Latin American: Argentina, Bolivia, Brazil, Chile, El Salvador, Guatemala, Mexico, Nicaragua, Peru, and Uruguay.[18] By 1996, however, the UN Working Group concluded that political disappearances had almost ended in the Western Hemisphere. "Argentina, Bolivia, Brazil, Chile, Ecuador, El Salvador, Guatemala, Haiti, and Nicaragua were among the nations where no disappearances were reported in 1996, although several countries still have backlogs of unexplained cases."[19] By 1998 the UN Working Group and Amnesty International reported disappearances in only two countries in Latin America: Colombia and Mexico.[20] It appears that despite being less legalized than the prohibition against torture, the prohi-

14. Amnesty International 1984, 143–79.

15. Amnesty International 1999.

16. United Nations 1992–1999. 1999 Report of the Special Rapporteur on Torture.

17. UNGA Res.33/173, 20 December 1978.

18. United Nations 1991. The list of countries in Latin America that practiced disappearance almost completely overlaps with the list of countries that practiced torture during the same period, so it should be clear that although we examine these rights separately, they are linked in practice.

19. *New York Times,* 25 May 1997, 4.

20. See Amnesty International 1999; and United Nations 1998. The UN Working Group also reported it had received one newly transmitted case from Ecuador.

TABLE 2. *Changes in human rights practices in Latin America*

Practices	Late 1970s	Mid 1990s
Torture	Very high	Medium
Disappearance	Very high	Low
Nondemocracy	Very high	Low

bition against disappearances has coincided with a more dramatic decline in disappearances in the region.

The region has witnessed a similarly dramatic change with respect to democracy. Preceded by a century of swings between democratic and authoritarian regimes, every Latin American country except Cuba either retained or returned to electoral democracy between 1978 and 1991.[21] These electoral regimes are far from perfect democracies, but as a result of these changes, Latin America today faces a new set of issues—not the problem of military coups, but the problems involved in expanding existing electoral regimes into fuller democracies.

Table 2 summarizes these very broad regional trends. It suggests that each of these issue-areas followed a similar trend during the period from the late 1970s to the mid-1990s, moving from a very poor situation to an improved situation. In part that is because the three issues are related to each other. Although some democratically elected governments still use or tolerate torture, the transition to democracy contributed to a reduction in the use of torture and disappearance. A comparison of Table 1 and Table 2 suggests that legalization alone cannot explain the trend described here.

We conclude that to understand the improvement in human rights practices illustrated by Table 2 we need to consider two additional factors. The first is a broad regional norm shift that led to an increased regional and international consensus concerning an interconnected bundle of human rights norms, including the three discussed in this article. The popular, political, and legal support and legitimacy these norms now possess is reinforced by diverse legal and nonlegal practices designed to implement and ensure compliance with them. This factor is consistent with the conclusions of a prominent group of legal scholars at the University of Chicago who argue that, even within a domestic setting, understanding compliance requires attention to the pervasive influence of social norms on behavior.[22] In the 1980s Latin America experienced a regional human rights "norm cascade"—a rapid shift toward recognizing the legitimacy of human rights norms and international and regional action on behalf of those norms.[23]

21. Palmer 1996, 257–58.
22. See Sunstein 1997; and Lessig 1995. For an interesting overview by a journalist, see Jeffry Rosen, The Social Police: Following the Law Because You'd Be Too Embarrassed Not To, *The New Yorker* (20–27 October 1997), 170–81.
23. On "norms cascades," see Sunstein 1997; and Finnemore and Sikkink 1998.

The second factor influencing improved human rights practices is the extent to which decision making is centralized with respect to norm compliance. Decisions about military coups or whether to hold free and fair elections are made by a country's top political or military authorities and are therefore highly centralized. Decisions about disappearances also tend to be centralized, since the ability to use security forces to kidnap and clandestinely detain large numbers of prisoners requires a high level of coordination. Decisions about torture, however, can be either centralized, like decisions about disappearances, or decentralized. If torture decisions are decentralized, even where state policy categorically outlaws the practice, police and security officers at local or regional levels may continue to use it to extract confessions in criminal cases, intimidate local political actors (such as campesino leaders, trade unionists, and political opponents), or strike fear in the local populace. In countries whose legal systems are penetrated with corruption or unresponsive prosecutorial or judicial procedures, or that lack the political will to investigate and prosecute police or security officers who engage in such conduct, decentralized torture is likely to continue despite declared or legalized national policy to the contrary. Thus international norms and the pressures exercised to enforce them will be more effective in securing compliance when decisions are made by a handful of powerful, central political actors than when decision making is decentralized.

Background

Human rights principles have long resonated in Latin America, and Latin American policymakers, legal scholars, and activists have historically been vocal supporters of the development of international human rights law. Long before the founding of the UN and the OAS, they perceived such law as a means of protecting weaker states and their people from unlawful interventions of more powerful states, particularly the United States. Many early Pan American leaders also stressed the importance of international law in promoting the doctrines of sovereignty and nonintervention, but they argued that the doctrine of nonintervention needed to be harmonized with other principles of international law, including human rights.[24] This legal tradition led Latin Americans to support human rights language in the UN Charter, to adopt in 1948 the American Declaration of the Rights and Duties of Man, and to unanimously support, later that same year, the UN General Assembly's adoption of the Universal Declaration of Human Rights.

Actual practice in adhering to international law in the region often fell far short of this commitment, especially in the 1970s and 1980s, when many Latin American governments carried out unprecedented levels of human rights violations. Latin American military leaders often argued that international human rights pressures were a violation of sovereignty and a form of moral imperialism. But this argument was less persuasive in Latin America because of the region's long discursive tradition of sup-

---

24. See, for example, Alvarez 1943. For a survey of this historical tradition, see Sikkink 1997.

port for international law and human rights. Domestic human rights organizations demanded that their governments respect human rights and allied with international human rights networks to publicize human rights violations and demand change.

The primary international human rights norms are found in the Universal Declaration of Human Rights and the American Declaration of Human Rights. In addition, international human rights norms relevant to Latin American states are articulated in the International Covenant on Civil and Political Rights, the International Covenant on Economic, Social, and Cultural Rights, and the American Convention on Human Rights. These treaties were adopted by the UN and the OAS in the late 1960s and entered into force between 1976 and 1978. More highly elaborated norms were subsequently expressed in such treaties as the Convention Against Torture and Other Cruel, Inhuman, or Degrading Treatment or Punishment, the Inter-American Convention to Prevent and Punish Torture, and the Inter-American Convention on Forced Disappearance of Persons—treaties that were drafted and entered into force in the late 1980s and early 1990s.

Because many of these norms are expressed in treaties, they impose legal obligations. They are not highly legalized, however, since formal international mechanisms for delegation in the area of human rights are limited and weak. Individual petition procedures are available to victims complaining of human rights violations by states that have ratified the First Optional Protocol to the International Covenant on Civil and Political Rights or have consented to the authority of the Committee Against Torture to consider individual petitions submitted under Article 22 of the Convention Against Torture, but neither of these bodies has the power to enforce its findings or recommendations. Individual victims in the Americas alternatively can elect to petition the IACHR. Those complaining of violations by states that have not ratified the American Convention may do so under the IACHR's authority to examine violations of certain human rights included in the American Declaration.[25] Those complaining of violations by states that have ratified the American Convention may apply to the IACHR in its quasi-judicial capacity to consider individual petitions and seek a resolution.[26] None of these bodies, however, has the authority to coerce state compliance. The Inter-American Court of Human Rights is the only international adjudicatory body with enforcement capability available to victims of human rights in the Americas. But access is limited. Victims must complain of rights violations by a state that has both ratified the American Convention and accepted the jurisdiction of the Inter-American Court of Human Rights.[27] They must then exhaust domestic remedies and

---

25. The human rights include those in Art. 1 (right to life, liberty, and personal security); Art. 2 (right to equality before the law), Art. 3 (right to religious freedom and worship), Art. 4 (right to freedom of investigation, opinion, expression, and dissemination of information), Art. 18 (right to a fair trial), Art. 25 (right of protection from arbitrary arrest), and Art. 26 (right to due process of law). See OAS Resolution XXII of the 2nd Special Inter-American Conference OEA/Ser. E/XIII.I Doc. 150 Rev. (1965); and Medina Quiroga 1990, 439–41.

26. Articles 44–51 of the American Convention on Human Rights.

27. In 1999, twenty-five of the thirty-five members of the OAS had ratified the American Convention, and twenty-one had accepted the contentious jurisdiction of the court, including most of the key members of the organization, but significantly excluding the United States. This number is a significant increase from the ten members accepting the contentious jurisdiction of the court in 1990.

file a petition with the IACHR. Should the IACHR be unable to resolve the matter, it may, at its discretion, refer the case to the court. Individuals do not have independent standing to invoke the court's jurisdiction.

The paucity of formal international delegation to third-party judicial authority does not mean international human rights law is never enforced. Active enforcement occurs in a variety of ways. Transnational human rights advocacy networks promote adverse international publicity about a state's violations of human rights so that non-compliance leads to embarrassment or a blow to reputation. Moreover, once a state's human rights misconduct has been exposed, more damaging bilateral or multilateral enforcement measures may follow. Bilateral foreign policy sanctions may be imposed on states that violate human rights. Courts in other countries, relying on their own domestic civil and criminal law, may hold individuals who fall within their jurisdiction responsible for violations of international human rights that occurred in other countries. In recent years there has been increased multilateral willingness by regional or international organizations to apply sanctions to rights-violating states. Although bilateral and multilateral enforcement continues to be selective, such measures frequently impose high costs on recalcitrant states.

Not only do the issues differ in their degree of legalization, but countries differ as well with respect to their acceptance of obligation and delegation in each of these areas. While the degree of obligation is implicit in the nature of the agreement, it also depends on whether a state has ratified a treaty. Thus countries that have ratified a treaty have more binding obligations than countries that have not. In turn, treaty ratification often implies delegation, or the acceptance of some third-party authority. Thus in the following section, for each of the issue-areas we consider—torture, disappearances, and democracy—we compare two countries with different levels of obligation and delegation with respect to that issue.

We look at the degree to which international law reflects preexisting domestic norms and the extent to which international law has penetrated and influenced domestic law and its enforcement. We also look at whether external enforcement measures have been applied to pressure states to comply with international human rights norms, the types of enforcement measures used, and the extent to which states have responded to such pressure. In the case of torture we compare Uruguay and Paraguay; for disappearances, Argentina and Honduras; and for democratic governance, Uruguay and Guatemala.

Case 1: Torture in Uruguay and Paraguay

To explore whether international law contributed to reducing governmental use of torture, we look at Uruguay and Paraguay between 1970 and the present. The two countries differed markedly in their formal acceptance of legal norms against torture. The prohibition against torture was more legalized in Uruguay than it was in Paraguay, so comparing the two countries sheds light on whether domestic acceptance of obligation and delegation of international human rights law leads to compliance with that law.

In the 1970s regimes in both Uruguay and Paraguay made extensive use of torture. Despite their similar size and population, and their physical proximity, the political histories of the two states are dramatically different. Until 1973, when the military was handed unchecked power by an elected civilian president, Uruguay had one of the longest traditions of democratic rule and best records of protecting civil liberties in the region. Paraguay, on the other hand, endured under General Alfredo Stroessner, who held power from 1954 until 1989, one of the region's longest lasting dictatorships. That dictatorship stifled all efforts to develop democratic traditions and hindered the independence and effectiveness of the institutions of civil society. Yet after the military took power in Uruguay, the situations of the two countries shared many characteristics. The independent functioning of Uruguay's courts and other institutions of civil society was suspended, making access to protection from governmental abuse of power more like the situation in Paraguay. Governments in both countries exercised repression, mainly through widespread, arbitrary imprisonment and torture.

The Uruguayan military regime was shorter in duration but more severe in its human rights violations. The Uruguayan military systematically engaged in far-reaching arrests, routine torture of prisoners, and complete surveillance of the population. In 1976 Amnesty International estimated that 60,000—or one out of fifty—people had been arrested and detained in Uruguay for some period of time since the coup. Most were held for a short time and released, though there were between 4,300 and 5,000 political prisoners in 1977, and between 1,000 and 2,500 in 1979.[28] Seventy-eight people died in detention, many as a result of torture.[29] A survey of a sample group of 313 released prisoners conducted after Uruguay returned to democracy found that only 1–2 percent were not tortured during imprisonment.[30]

A comprehensive report on human rights in Paraguay during the Stroessner regime has not been written.[31] Nevertheless, in 1976 Amnesty International estimated that there were about 1,000 political prisoners. That figure dropped to about 300 to 400 in August 1977.[32] Amnesty International further stated that during this period torture was common in Paraguay. It documented ten cases of death under torture in 1976 and another two in early 1977.[33]

Prior to the dictatorship, Uruguay was one of the few countries in the region to ratify the International Covenant on Civil and Political Rights and its First Optional Protocol. The Optional Protocol gave individuals in Uruguay the right to bring their cases to the UN Human Rights Committee if they believed that their government had

28. See *Latin America,* 11 February 1977, XI (6); and Schoultz 1981, 350.
29. Servicio Paz y Justicia Uruguay 1992.
30. Ibid.
31. One preliminary report is Simon 1990, but it does not provide systematic reports of numbers of victims of repression.
32. Amnesty International, "August 1977 Addendum" to Briefing Paper on Paraguay published in July 1976.
33. Amnesty International 1977a, 9–13.

violated rights in the covenant.[34] The decision in 1970 to ratify these treaties was the logical outgrowth of Uruguay's long tradition of support for multilateral human rights efforts and its domestic support for the rule of law. In contrast, Paraguay had not acknowledged the legitimacy of international human rights norms nor ratified any of the major human rights treaties that prohibit torture. For over two decades of authoritarian rule, from 1954 until 1977, Paraguay faced very little international pressure or criticism for its human rights practices.

Although approximately half of all political prisoners in Uruguay were arrested between 1972 and 1974,[35] little international attention to Uruguayan human rights abuses was brought to bear until 1976, the year the International Covenant on Civil and Political Rights and its Optional Protocol entered into force. Once it entered into force, Uruguayan victims, who before the dictatorship had been accustomed to seeking effective remedies from domestic legal institutions, transferred their entreaties to the Human Rights Committee established under the covenant.[36] The committee was responsive to the barrage of petitions it received and in case after case found Uruguay responsible for treaty violations, including torture and arbitrary detention. Its findings, which called on the Uruguayan government to release political prisoners and provide compensation, were publicized and attracted the attention of the then newly burgeoning nongovernmental international human rights movement.[37]

Uruguayan victims similarly appealed to the IACHR to investigate torture in Uruguay. Although Uruguay's military government refused to permit the IACHR to conduct an on-site visit, the IACHR issued several reports outlining abuses of human rights in Uruguay.[38] These reports were later adopted by the OAS General Assembly. In addition, as a result of prodding by Venezuela and the United States, the OAS Permanent Council rejected on human rights grounds Uruguay's offer to host the 1978 meeting of the OAS General Assembly.[39]

Between 1976 and 1980, several nongovernmental human rights organizations, including the International League for Human Rights, the International Commission of Jurists, the Secretariat International des Juristes Pour l'Amnistie en Uruguay, and particularly Amnesty International, took up the cause of human rights in Uruguay. These organizations held symposia, issued reports, sent missions and trial observers to Uruguay, and lobbied governments.[40] They also used evidence from the UN and OAS human rights bodies to pressure governments, particularly the United States, which around the same time began to adopt bilateral human rights foreign policies, to

34. See the article in this issue by Robert Keohane, Andrew Moravcsik, and Anne-Marie Slaughter, which also discusses the different dynamics that result when individuals have direct access to legalized international regimes.

35. Servicio Paz y Justicia Uruguay 1992.

36. After taking power, the military could have rescinded Uruguay's ratification of the covenant but chose not to do so, perhaps because it saw no harm from continued embrace of an international human rights treaty that was not yet in force.

37. Macdermot 1981. During its early years, the UN Human Rights Committee decided more cases against Uruguay than against any other country.

38. See, for example, Inter-American Commission on Human Rights 1978.

39. *Latin American Political Report,* 10 February 1978, XII (6).

40. Macdermot 1981, 88.

suspend bilateral aid to Uruguay on human rights grounds. Thus the work of both nongovernmental and intergovernmental human rights bodies contributed to the legitimacy of bilateral political pressure against Uruguay.

With its 1976 report detailing extensive human rights abuses, Amnesty International brought the human rights situation in Uruguay to the attention of U.S. Congressman Edward Koch, who led the movement to ban U.S. military aid to Uruguay. The Koch amendment was one of the earliest country-specific cut-offs of military aid motivated by human rights concerns. Early U.S. human rights policy toward Uruguay sent mixed messages because of differences between Congress and the executive branch, but between 1977 and 1980 under the Carter administration U.S. human rights policy toward Uruguay was one of the most coherent and consistent of all the bilateral human rights policies. In 1977 Secretary of State Cyrus Vance announced that the United States would reduce economic aid to Uruguay, making it, along with Argentina and Ethiopia, a test case of the new administration's commitment to take human rights into consideration when granting economic aid. The United States also opposed twelve out of thirteen loan requests made by Uruguay to international financial institutions between 1977 and 1980.[41]

The Uruguayan military government was divided between soft-liners and hard-liners who disagreed about the necessary level of repression and the desirable time-table for a return of democracy.[42] International legal and political human rights pressures had the effect of strengthening the position of the soft-liners against their domestic opponents. The leader of the soft-line faction, General Alvarez, believed that progress on the human rights front could help him in his internal power struggles with other members of the military and with his future presidential ambitions. International pressure reinforced the soft-liner's preference for a plebiscite on a new constitution. Given the opportunity in 1980 to vote for the first time since the coup, the Uruguayan public defeated the military government's proposed constitution, starting the country on the path toward the return to democracy in 1985 and the eventual improvement of human rights practices. Torture is no longer systematically practiced in Uruguay, but neither have the torturers of the past been brought to justice. An amnesty law, and the public's reaffirmation of that law through a referendum, effectively blocked holding torturers legally accountable for their acts.[43]

The Uruguayan case is one in which a highly legalized international norm with a high degree of domestic popular acceptance, obligation, and delegation was successfully reinforced through persistent international enforcement pressure directed at a violating government. International human rights pressures did not function independently, but rather interacted with both strong public support for a return to democracy and the positions of soft-liners with the military regime.

In contrast to Uruguay, Paraguay's prohibition against torture was not highly legalized. Paraguay had not ratified any of the human rights treaties prohibiting torture,

41. Schoultz 1981, 295.
42. Gillespie 1991, 109–110.
43. Barahona de Brito 1997.

nor had it ratified the Optional Protocol or accepted the jurisdiction of the Inter-American Court of Human Rights. There was no form of international delegation for victims of torture in Paraguay.

Although Paraguay under Stroessner had been engaging in human rights violations since 1954, international attention to human rights violations in Paraguay began at about the same time as attention to Uruguay. Because of international neglect prior to that time, Paraguay's repressive regime had more than two decades to consolidate its power and co-opt or destroy all opposition.

Even though human rights norms were not legalized in Paraguay, there is substantial evidence that international human rights pressures contributed to stopping torture and other human rights abuses. For example, although Paraguay would not permit an on-site visit, the IACHR reported regularly on the human rights situation in Paraguay, both in the special country section of its annual reports and in two special country reports in 1978 and 1987. In its 1978 annual report the IACHR concluded that torture had declined considerably and all political prisoners had been released.[44]

It is difficult to separate the influence of the IACHR from the simultaneous pressures of the Carter administration, and it seems likely that both contributed to the enforcement of human rights norms. Reports by Amnesty International and Americas Watch found that human rights conditions in Paraguay improved after external political enforcement measures were brought to bear against it. Robert White, U.S. Ambassador to Paraguay during the Carter administration, was a vocal opponent of human rights violations in Paraguay. Americas Watch concluded that the number of political prisoners declined drastically when White raised the human rights issue there, and that many political exiles were permitted to return as a consequence of political pressure exerted by the new democratically elected government in neighboring Argentina.[45] Americas Watch attributed this improvement to both internal developments and external pressure. It emphasized the importance of political and economic uncertainty in an era when President Stroessner was seen to be failing as well as a willingness by the Catholic Church to abandon its neutrality toward the regime and replace it with a campaign that encouraged Paraguay's long-oppressed opposition. But it also noted that United States' abandonment of dictatorships throughout the world and increasing democratization throughout Latin America were important factors that pushed Paraguay toward rights improvements.[46]

Another, less appreciated aspect of the enforcement of international human rights law toward Paraguay took place through the U.S. judicial branch. In 1979 lawyers for a Paraguayan doctor, Jose Filártiga, and his daughter Dolly filed a lawsuit against Américo Peña Irala who was then in the United States. They accused Peña Irala, former police inspector of Asunción, with kidnapping and torturing to death Filártiga's teenage son, Joelito, in 1976 in Paraguay. The Filártiga family's lawyers in-

---

44. Inter-American Commission on Human Rights 1979. Because Paraguay had not ratified the International Covenant on Civil and Political Rights or its First Optional Protocol, the Human Rights Committee never had the opportunity to consider petition from Paraguayan victims of human rights violations.
45. Americas Watch 1995, 4.
46. Americas Watch 1986, 3. Also see Carter 1990.

voked the Alien Tort Claims Act of 1789, which grants federal courts jurisdiction in "any civil action by an alien for a tort only, committed in violation of the law of nations or a treaty of the United States," provided the court has personal jurisdiction over the alleged tortfeasor. The court's decision in the *Filártiga* case broke new ground because it held that in the 1970s the torturer now had a status in customary international law akin to that of the pirate and slave trader—"an enemy of all mankind."[47] A U.S. district court eventually awarded the Filártiga family $10 million in compensatory and punitive damages. In assigning punitive damages, the court declared: "Punitive damages are designed not merely to teach a defendant not to repeat his conduct but to deter others from following his example. To accomplish that purpose this court must make clear the depth of the international revulsion against torture and measure the award in accordance with the enormity of the offense. Thereby the judgement may perhaps have some deterrent effect."[48]

Since *Filártiga,* U.S. federal courts have adjudicated numerous cases involving human rights abuses in other countries under a variety of jurisdictional statutes. These include a groundbreaking case filed by the Letelier family against the Republic of Chile under the Foreign Sovereign Immunities Act for the car bomb murder of Orlando Letelier in the streets of Washington D.C.;[49] three cases against General Guillermo Suarez Mason, one of the more notorious perpetrators of disappearances during Argentina's "dirty war";[50] and a case against General Gramajo of Guatemala for torture and execution of peasants.[51] Courts in Spain and Italy have gone a step further in criminally indicting individuals responsible for violations of human rights in Latin America. The House of Lords decision in the Pinochet case demonstrates broadening international consensus that extranational criminal trials of rights violators should be allowed to proceed.

Despite the broadening trend to "borrow" the courts of other countries to seek justice, little is yet known about the impact of such cases on the government, police, and military officials in repressive countries. Anecdotal evidence suggests that foreign officials are aware of these cases and that they could have a chilling effect on repressive decisions. Former ambassador Robert White described an incident that occurred while he was ambassador to Paraguay: "After the case was decided in favor of Dr. Filártiga one of the people closest to General Stroessner told me that I just had to do everything possible to get this decision reversed. They don't really understand the independence of our court system here. And he stressed to me that no Paraguayan government figure would feel free to travel to the United States if this judgement was upheld because, you know, they would feel that they would be liable to arrest just being in any state in the United States."[52] Dr. Filártiga, however, has asserted that the

---

47. *Filártiga v. Pena-Irala,* 630 F.2d 876, 890 (2d Cir. 1980).
48. *Filártiga v. Peña-Irala,* 577 F. Supp. 860, 866 (S.D.N.Y. 1984).
49. *Letelier v. Republic of Chile,* 488 F. Supp. 665 (D.C.D.C. 1980).
50. *Forti v. Suarez Mason,* 672 F. Supp. 1531 (N.D. Cal. 1987), reconsidered, 697 F. Supp. 707 (N.D. Cal. 1988); *Martinez Baca v. Suarez Mason,* Civ. Action No. C-87–2057-SC (N.D. Cal. April 22, 1988); *Rapaport v. Suarez Mason,* Civ. Action No. C-87–2266-JPV (N.D. Cal., April 11, 1989).
51. *Xuncax v. Gramajo,* 886 F. Supp. 162 (D.C. Ma 1995).
52. As cited in Claude 1992, 336.

case made very little impact in Paraguay and did not lead to an improvement in the human rights situation there.[53]

The Stroessner regime was not as divided as the military regime in Uruguay. By the late 1980s, however, divisions were beginning to emerge within the ruling Colorado party and the military, especially about who would succeed the aging dictator. Colorado party officials were divided between those who supported the succession of Stroessner's son and those who opposed this "dynastic" model of succession. This conflict contributed to the coup in 1989, when Stroessner was deposed by his close associate General Rodriguez, who, to the surprise of many, oversaw a return to democratic rule. General Rodriguez, with nothing in his personal history to foreshadow his role as a champion of democracy, responded to a new international, regional, and domestic consensus in favor of democratic rule, and oversaw the most dramatic change in domestic structures in the last thirty-five years of Paraguayan history. Since that time, Paraguay has experienced some political turmoil; a coup attempt was resisted, and a president resigned after facing impeachment proceedings for being implicated in the murder of his vice president. Despite this turmoil, democracy has not been interrupted and systematic torture of political opponents is no longer practiced in Paraguay. Aside from four cases of alleged torture transmitted to the government in 1996, the UN Special Rapporteur on Torture made no mention of receiving cases of torture in Paraguay in his reports from 1992 to 1999.[54] After the transition, Paraguay ratified the American Convention on Human Rights, the Covenant on Civil and Political Rights, and both the UN and Inter-American Conventions Against Torture. In addition, in 1992 Paraguayans rewrote their constitution to include a list of human rights that widely conforms to international human rights instruments and establishes various institutions for protecting human rights. The human rights situation in Paraguay is still far from ideal, but significant improvement has occurred.

International law clearly contributed to reducing governmental use of torture in both Uruguay and Paraguay, though in neither case did it operate in isolation. By 1976, when the momentum of international support for international norms prohibiting torture was sufficiently advanced, organs of the UN and OAS, nongovernmental organizations, and other governments pressured both countries to abide by those norms. That pressure bore fruit when forces inside each nation's military determined that it was to their political advantage to yield. Their doing so cleared the path for greater civil society demand for human rights protections, which, in turn, led to an end to the use of torture and the restoration of democracy.

Case 2: Disappearances in Argentina and Honduras

Latin America helped introduce the term *disappearance* (translated from the Spanish word *desaparecido*) into the international human rights vocabulary. Although govern-

---

53. Interview with Dr. Joel Filártiga, Asuncion, Paraguay, 2 January 1996.
54. United Nations 1992–1999.

ments have long used "disappearances" to rid themselves of perceived opponents, international attention to this grave human rights abuse did not emerge until the 1970s, when repressive regimes in Latin America began to engage in it on a widespread and systematic basis.[55]

Argentina and Honduras differed in the extent to which they practiced disappearances and the degree of legalization of international human rights norms. In Argentina the official number of reported disappearances reached almost 9,000 between 1973 and 1983. In Honduras it is estimated that approximately 179 people disappeared between 1980 and 1992. In Argentina, the disappearances occurred during a brutal authoritarian government, and in Honduras they occurred after the country began a transition to a civilian democratic government with an election in 1981. Although neither country ratified the International Covenant on Civil and Political Rights prior to the period in which the disappearances occurred, Honduras had ratified the American Convention on Human Rights and accepted the compulsory jurisdiction of the Inter-American Court of Human Rights. This step provided delegation and opened the door for legal enforcement against Honduras that was not available with respect to Argentina.

Amnesty International and groups staffed by Argentine political exiles first brought the human rights situation in Argentina to world attention after the military coup in March 1976. Amnesty International estimated that between 2,000 and 10,000 persons had been abducted and presented evidence that the disappearances were part of a concerted government policy by which soldiers and the police kidnapped perceived opponents, took them to secret detention centers, tortured, interrogated, and killed them, and secretly disposed of their bodies.[56]

In response to increasing dissemination of information on human rights abuses in Argentina, the Carter administration, along with the French, Swedish, and other governments, denounced the rights violations of the Argentine junta. In 1977 the U.S. government reduced the planned level of military aid for Argentina on human rights grounds. The following year, Congress passed a bill eliminating all military assistance to Argentina.[57]

Although by the military's admission 90 percent of the armed opposition had been eliminated by April 1977, their defeat did not lead to an immediate change in human rights practices.[58] By 1978 the military was divided among different factions with different positions as to what the military government should do in the future. One faction was led by Admiral Massera, a right-wing populist; another by Generals Carlos Suarez Mason and Luciano Menendez, who supported indefinite military dictatorship and an unrelenting war against the left; and a third by Generals Videla and Viola, who hoped for eventual political liberalization under a military president. Over time, the Videla-Viola faction emerged supreme within the junta, and, by late

---

55. Amnesty International 1981, 1, 75.
56. Amnesty International 1977b.
57. U.S. Congressional Research Service 1979, 106.
58. *El Diario del Jucio*, No. 28, 3 December 1985, 5–8.

1978, Videla had gained more control over the Ministry of Foreign Affairs, which had previously been in the navy's sphere of influence.[59]

Within this new domestic context, the Videla-Viola faction decided to improve Argentina's international image and to restore military and economic aid flows.[60] This faction hoped it could use international human rights in its efforts to pursue a strategy of liberalization, which in turn would allow them to gain autonomy from the rest of the junta and improve Argentina's international image. This helps to explain Videla's willingness to permit the IACHR to conduct an on-site investigation in Argentina in December 1978 in exchange for a U.S. promise to unblock Export-Import Bank funds.[61] In the period that followed this invitation, the human rights situation in Argentina improved and the number of disappearances declined significantly.[62]

The IACHR's post-visit report was far more condemnatory of human rights practices than the Argentine military had anticipated. Argentine human rights groups smuggled the report into the country and made it available to key journalists, political figures, and opinion leaders, leading them to increasingly question official disclaimers of noninvolvement in the disappearances.[63]

Notwithstanding Argentina's prior unwillingness to formally ratify international human rights treaties and the fact that the norm against disappearance had not been codified per se, the Argentina case illustrates the effectiveness of informal enforcement measures in responding to violations of international human rights norms. Here no formal obligation, precision, or delegation existed. Even the IACHR's visit to and report on Argentina were exercises of its political function to investigate and document gross and systematic violations of human rights rather than exercises of juridical authority.[64] Nonetheless, the pressure worked and disappearances nearly stopped. It is unlikely that Argentina would have invited the IACHR to visit Argentina without strong international human rights pressures, including those of the U.S. government. The Argentine case is an example of bilateral and multilateral political enforcement working together to contribute to a decline in disappearances.

Pressure of another sort was brought to bear against Honduras. In April 1986 the IACHR submitted to the Inter-American Court of Human Rights three contentious cases involving 4 of some 140 cases submitted to the IACHR alleging disappearances in Honduras between 1981 and 1984. The IACHR, operating in its quasi-judicial capacity under the American Convention on Human Rights, found Honduras

59. Rock 1989, 370–71. This understanding of divisions within the military was reinforced during interviews with military officers and civilian policymakers of the Videla government, conducted in Buenos Aires in July–August 1990.

60. *Carta Política*, a news magazine considered to be very close to the military government, commented that international pressures on Argentina continued to increase and concluded that "the principal problem facing Argentine State has now become the international siege." Cuadro de Situación, *Carta Política* 57 (August 1978), 8.

61. Interviews with Walter Mondale, 20 June 1989, Minneapolis, Minn., and Robert Pastor, 28 June 1990, Wianno, Mass.

62. See Asamblea Permanente por los Derechos Humanos 1988, 26–31.

63. Mignone 1991, 56–57.

64. See Medina Quiroga 1990, 442–43.

responsible for violations of the American Convention based on Honduras' denial of any knowledge of the victims' whereabouts and its unwillingness to investigate.[65]

Since disappearances are not mentioned specifically in the American Convention, the IACHR asked the court to determine that Honduras had violated Articles 4, 5, and 7 of the convention, which guarantee the rights to life, humane treatment, personal liberty, and security. In its decision on the merits in the *Velásquez Rodríguez* case, the court concluded that these rights must be interpreted alongside Article 1(1) of the convention, which establishes the duty of governments to respect the human rights of individuals and to guarantee the enjoyment of the rights recognized in the convention. The court held that under Article 1(1) states have a duty to organize the governmental apparatus so that it is capable of juridically ensuring and actually ensures the free and full enjoyment of human rights.[66] As a consequence of this obligation, "states must prevent, investigate, and punish any violation of the rights recognized by the Convention."[67] Failure to do so may result in a finding that the state is liable for the alleged human rights violations because it failed to perform its duties under Article 1(1).[68]

In the course of testimony before the court, witnesses revealed that the Honduran army officers who carried out the abductions were first trained in the United States in 1980 and later received training in Honduras from Argentine and Chilean military instructors who had participated in the campaign of disappearances in their countries. During this period, the U.S. government increased foreign assistance to Honduras, helped train military and police officers, and failed to recognize and respond to credible reports of human rights violations. Argentine training of Honduran military personnel ended after the country's return to democracy in 1983, but U.S. training and support continued as part of the Reagan administration's program of support for the Nicaraguan contras operating out of Honduras.[69]

The court handed down its decisions in the three Honduras cases in 1988 and 1989. In the same years the Honduran government virtually stopped the practice of disappearances. Of the 175 documented cases of disappearances in Honduras, only 2 took place in 1989, and only 1 disappearance took place after 1989. The practice of disappearance in Honduras dropped from 26 cases in 1985 to 4 in 1986, the year the disappearance cases were submitted to the court, increased to 22 in 1987, then dropped to 10 in 1988, 2 in 1989, and none in 1990 and 1991.[70] In 1996 the UN Working Group on Disappearances recorded one case of disappearance in Honduras. In 1997 Honduras ratified the Inter-American Convention on the Forced Disappearance of

---

65. See Mendez and Vivanco 1990, 507, 535; *Velásquez Rodríguez* Case, Judgment, Inter-Am. Ct. H.R. (ser. C) No. 4 (1988); and the parallel *Godíñez Cruz* Case, Judgment, Inter-Am. Ct. H.R. (ser. C) No. 5 (1989). For convenience, this article will refer only to the *Velásquez Rodríguez* Case.

66. *Velásquez Rodríguez,* supra, n. 65, para. 166–67.

67. Ibid., para. 166.

68. Ibid., para. 182.

69. *New York Times,* 14 February 1986.

70. Yearly figures compiled from the "List of Disappeared in Honduras," Human Rights Watch/ Americas Watch 1994.

Persons, and in 1998 the U.S. State Department reported that there had been no reports of politically motivated disappearances in the previous year.[71]

It is not easy to isolate the role of the court's decision in this change because the 1988–89 period coincided with other political changes that affected Honduras. The regional peace process intensified after the 1987 Esquipulas meeting and the March 1988 cease-fire agreement between the Sandinistas and the Contras. When President George Bush took office in January 1989, he carried out a quiet but significant shift of U.S. policy toward Central America away from a military solution and toward a negotiated political solution. The end of the Cold War led to an expanded embrace of democracy both in the region and worldwide. In early 1990 a new government took office in Honduras; for the first time in fifty-seven years, power was peacefully transferred from one party to another, a transition often taken as an indicator of the consolidation of a new democracy.[72]

It is important to note, however, that the decline in disappearances in Honduras in 1988 preceded rather than followed many of the other developments. Thus the authoritative decision of a prestigious regional court must be seen as having contributed to a decline in the practice of disappearances. The decisions of the Inter-American Court of Human Rights in the Honduras cases appear to have been more influential domestically than the U.S. federal court decision in *Filártiga* was in Paraguay. This may be due to differences in the nature of the two kinds of cases. In the Honduran case, the court found the Honduran government itself responsible for the practice of disappearance, whereas in *Filártiga* an individual was found liable. The court's physical proximity (the Inter-American Court is located in Costa Rica) as well as the greater legitimacy of a truly regional court also may help to explain the different impacts of these two cases.

Case 3: Democracy in Uruguay and Guatemala

A discussion of the right to democracy further illustrates the interaction between strengthened legal norms and the application of political pressure to enforce those norms. Thomas Franck has argued that "democracy . . . is on the way to becoming a global entitlement, one that increasingly will be promoted and protected by collective international processes."[73]

In Latin America the strength of norms and legalization around the "right to democracy" has varied significantly over time. Prior to 1991, there was not a strong regional norm against military coups, which were considered part of the standard political repertoire in the region. Since then, prompt condemnation of any interruption of democracy in the region, backed by bilateral sanctions against the norm-violating state, is normal.

71. U.S. Department of State 1998.
72. Schulz and Sundloff Schulz 1994, 269.
73. Franck 1992, 46.

Comparing the international response to the coup in Uruguay in 1973 and the coup in Guatemala in 1993 illuminates the development and implementation of norms in favor of democracy in the region. The coup in Uruguay occurred well before the 1991 Santiago Declaration; the coup in Guatemala occurred after the Santiago Declaration, and that declaration was invoked to justify regional sanctions. Although the Santiago Declaration was not part of a treaty and did not have any of the dimensions of legalization, it nevertheless provided normative guidance for an effective regional response to the coup in Guatemala as well as to a similar coup in Peru in 1993.

In many ways the coups in Uruguay and Guatemala were similar. Both were "auto-golpes": when confronted by an armed guerrilla movement, the elected president, with the support of the military, undermined the constitutional order, closed Congress, censored the press, and arrested members of the political opposition.

The strength of the commitment to democracy and to international intervention on behalf of democracy in Uruguay was far stronger than in Guatemala. Uruguayan diplomats had supported early efforts in the 1940s in both the OAS and the UN to make democracy a condition for membership and to empower the institutions and their member states to sanction military coups. Even so, there was no initial international or regional response to the Uruguayan coup; it took over five years for international actors to develop the kinds of pressure that was applied immediately to Guatemala. Even when international pressure on Uruguay increased after 1976, almost all criticisms were directed against the human rights practices of the Uruguayan military regime, not against the interruption of democracy per se. Uruguay's democratic tradition was far stronger than almost any country in the region, but in the absence of a strong norm against interruptions of democracy, other countries failed to protest the coup.

In contrast, the international response to a coup attempt in Guatemala was rapid, clear, and forceful. When President Serrano carried out a "self-coup" in May 1993 by closing Congress and the judiciary and censoring the press, international pressures contributed to domestic efforts in Guatemala to force Serrano from power. In accordance with the Santiago Declaration, the OAS called an emergency meeting of foreign ministers of the region, which in turn called on member states to implement sanctions against the government. One of the most powerful sanctions was the threat by the United States to withdraw Guatemala's trade benefits under the General System of Preferences. It was this threat that apparently led business leaders to join other groups in civil society to pressure for Serrano's removal.[74]

International pressures did not work alone in the case of Guatemala, but operated in synergy with the domestic legal processes and domestic opposition. Unexpectedly, the judges of the recently formed Guatemalan Constitutional Court declared that the coup decree was unconstitutional and faxed their decision all over the world before the military shut the court down.[75] The court's pronouncement reinforced international pressure against the coup because external actors could say that they were

---

74. *New York Times*, 3 June 1993.
75. Interview with Judge Jorge Mario García Laguardia, Mexico City, 6 June 1996.

basing their actions both on international law and on a Guatemalan court order that declared the government action illegal. Encouraged by the actions of the court and by international condemnation, other sectors in civil society opposed the coup. Journalists ignored the censorship orders, and people poured into the streets to demonstrate in favor of democracy. Eventually the Guatemalan military responded to the pressure and ousted Serrano and his vice president.

Once Serrano was ousted, the reassembled members of Congress, under pressure from organized citizens in the streets, elected Ramiro de Leon Carpio, the former attorney general for human rights, as the new president of Guatemala. To most observers of Latin American politics, this scenario was surprising because for decades Guatemalan regimes had been among the region's most severe violators of human rights and were impervious to international human rights pressures. The Guatemalan case illustrates some of ways in which a society can move along the continuum from less democracy to more democracy; it also shows the role that international forces, including international norms, can play in that process. By 1999 the country had sustained its still fragile democracy, the UN had brokered a successful agreement between the government and the guerrillas to end the civil war, and two truth commissions, one sponsored by the UN and one by the Catholic Church, had produced definitive reports on human rights violations in the past. In 1998 the murder of Bishop Juan Gerardi, founder and director of the Archdiocesan Human Rights Office and director of the Catholic Church's *Nunca Más* (Never Again) project, suggested that the structures of power and impunity behind the human rights violations had not been fully dismantled,[76] but human rights monitors agreed that human rights violations had declined significantly.[77]

How can we explain the very different international responses to these comparable civilian-led coups in Latin America? Between 1990 and 1993, strong normative developments occurred in the region around the "right to democracy." At the OAS General Assembly meeting in Santiago in 1991, all thirty-five member states declared "their firm political commitment to the promotion and protection of human rights and representative democracy." The General Assembly unanimously approved Resolution 1080, which instructs the secretary general to convoke an emergency meeting of OAS foreign ministers to decide on a collective reaction "in the case of any event giving rise to the sudden or irregular interruption of a democratic government." This is a clear example of a norm event, not legalization, since the Santiago Declaration was not a treaty and lacked all aspects of legalization. Resolution 1080 does not constitute delegation, because the resolution specifies only that the foreign ministers "look into the events collectively and adopt any decisions deemed appropriate, in accordance with the Charter and international law." It has nevertheless proved to be an effective means of coordinating and legitimating political sanctions by member states.

76. Interviews with Helen Mack, Leila Lima, and Daniel Saxon, Guatemala City, 22, 23 May 1998.

77. Amnesty International listed neither reports of torture nor of new disappearances in Guatemala in 1998, though it expressed alarm over the continued high level of extra-judicial executions. Amnesty International 1999.

In 1992 the members of the OAS took this commitment to democracy further and amended the OAS Charter to include a new article (Article 9) giving the General Assembly the power to suspend from membership by two-thirds vote any government that overthrows a democratic regime. This amendment entered into force in 1997, and by late 1999 twenty-three member states had ratified this "Protocol of Washington." This significantly enhanced the level of obligation for the democracy norm in the Americas, particularly for the ratifying states. In addition, in 1990 the secretary general of the OAS set up a Unit for the Promotion of Democracy to provide advisory services and direct assistance, such as election monitoring and technical support, to member states.

The Santiago Declaration and Resolution 1080 provided the procedural means for the rapid regional response to the military coups in Guatemala (as well as in Peru, Haiti, and Ecuador) and put the OAS in the forefront of efforts by international organizations to promote democracy. The Protocol of Washington increases the legal obligation of the democracy norm, though levels of precision and delegation are still low. The Protocol of Washington has not yet served as a basis for any institutional response because no coup attempts have occurred in Latin America since it entered into force. Actions under the Santiago Declaration and the Protocol of Washington in response to military coups in the region are examples of political enforcement of regional norms on democracy.

The new norm of democracy and the accompanying institutional procedures were clearly important in restoring democracy in Haiti, Peru, Ecuador, and Guatemala. Both the Santiago Declaration and the Protocol of Washington were more significant in confirming rather than creating an emerging regional normative consensus, but they offered normative justification and institutional mechanisms for the OAS and member states to respond forcefully and immediately to military coups in the region, helping to prevent nascent dictatorships from becoming established. Before these norms existed, countries in the region failed to respond when the country with the longest democratic tradition—Uruguay—experienced a coup in 1973. After they existed, the OAS responded quickly to help sustain democracy in Guatemala, where it had less robust roots.

Conclusions

These cases suggest a process in which international human rights norms—some embedded in law and some not—were implemented through a wide range of judicial, quasi-judicial, and political channels. The enforcement of international norms through multiple legal and political mechanisms successfully influenced human rights behavior in Latin America.

The factors identified in the introduction to this special issue—degrees and combinations of legalization along the dimensions of obligation, precision, and delegation—turned out to be only partially helpful in explaining compliance with human rights norms in the countries examined here. The prohibition against torture was more legalized than norms about disappearances and democracy, but governments complied with all three norms, and torture is the issue-area in which change is occurring most slowly. Nor did some of the domestic factors we examined—severity of human rights violations and differences in domestic ratification of relevant treaties—explain the trends we saw. The countries differed significantly from each other with respect to all of these variables. Yet the most surprising findings were the convergences in expectations and in behavior among the countries.

International pressure was a crucial factor, but this pressure was exercised though diverse channels, and no single channel was more effective than another. The clearest variation in the amount of international pressure was not between countries or between issues but over time. Most of the kinds of pressures we describe did not occur before the 1973–76 period. By the 1980s, however, a "norms cascade"—a rapid shift toward new international human rights norms—impacted all three of the norms.[78] Before the norms cascade, the countries we considered violated human rights with impunity. Afterwards, each of the countries moved along a continuum toward greater compliance with international human rights norms.

Norms have a quality of "oughtness" that sets them apart from other kinds of rules. Norms involve standards of "appropriate" or "proper" behavior. We recognize norm-breaking behavior because it generates disapproval or stigma.[79] Many prohibitions are both norms and law. Almost all of the human rights norms in the region are embedded in both strong norms and international law, so it is difficult to distinguish what is driving behavior—norms or law. In the case of democracy we have a clear example of a norm at work (the Santiago Declaration) well before the law (the Protocol of Washington) went into effect. But even when they are embedded in law, not all human rights norms are equally legalized. Despite significant variation in legalization at both the regional level and the country level, behavior change occurred in all three issue-areas in all five countries.

Precise definitions and standard ways of showing the operation of a norms cascade do not yet exist.[80] Because most of the work on norms cascades has been done by legal theorists interested in domestic norms, there have not yet been efforts to model what an international norms cascade would look like. We suggest that norms cascades are collections of norm-affirming events. These events are discursive events— that is, they are verbal or written statements asserting the norm. Note that we are careful to define a norms cascade as something different from changes in actual behavior, because we are interested in exploring the effect of norms on behavioral change. Norm-affirming events can take various forms—they can be formal articulations of norms in declarations or treaties, they can be statements in speeches of

---

78. Sunstein 1997, 38.
79. See Elster 1989; and Sunstein 1997.
80. Sunstein, who invented the term, does not define it more precisely nor does he demonstrate its operation for purposes of research. Sunstein 1997. Picker presents a fascinating computer simulation model of norms cascades but also does not define or show how norms cascades operate in the real world. Picker 1997. Finnemore and Sikkink also do not show the operation of a norms cascade, although they suggest that where treaties exist on an issue, the entry into force of a treaty might be a useful proxy for the "tipping point" that begins a norms cascade. Finnemore and Sikkink 1998.

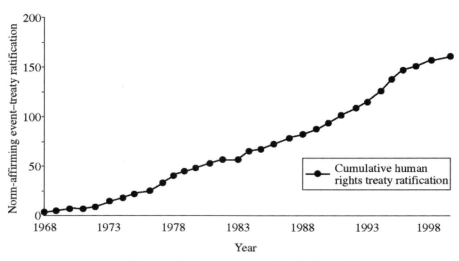

FIGURE 1. *Human rights norms cascade: OAS member states*

government officials, or they can be incorporated into domestic legislation that makes reference to international norms. Justifying norm breaking may also be a norm-affirming event, if in making the justification, the actor recognizes the existence of the norm and explains why it was not possible to abide by the norm in particular circumstances.[81]

While we support this broad definition of norm-affirming events, it would be impossible to document and record all such events for international human rights norms for all of Latin America over a thirty-year period. We map instead one piece of this broader set of norm events—formal government adhesion to an international or regional declaration or treaty affirming the norm.

International human rights norms often come clustered in declarations or treaties that bundle groups of norms with very different levels of legalization. Our regional norms cascade includes adherence to these general declarations and treaties as indicators of norm-affirming events. It also includes single-issue norm-affirming events, such as the ratification of issue-specific treaties. Figure 1 displays this illustrative mapping of cumulated major human rights norm-affirming events for the last three decades in Latin America. We think that this picture is a fair representation of the human rights norms cascade in the region. We believe that if we used a more expansive mapping of norm-affirming events, the number of events would be much greater but the pattern would be very similar. Figure 1 reveals that although the entire period from 1977 to the present could be considered a human rights norms cascade, the increase in norm-affirming events is particularly steep at two moments—from 1977 to 1981 and from 1990 to 1996.

81. Kratochwil and Ruggie 1986.

It is beyond the scope of this article to explain in detail what caused the norms cascade that occurred in Latin America during this period. Human rights norms first emerged in response to the dramatic violations during World War II, but in the Americas during the Cold War progress on human rights norms was stalled and subordinated to anti-communism and the logic of national security doctrines. The intense repression of the military dictatorships of the 1970s in Chile, Uruguay, and Argentina initiated a renewed concern with human rights throughout the region and contributed to the emergence of regional human rights networks, with active participation by exiles from repressive regimes. The efforts of these networks were reinforced by the human rights policies of the Carter administration. The resurgence of Cold War ideology under the Reagan administration temporarily dampened the norms cascade (but did not halt its progress), but with the end of the Cold War, U.S. support for newly authoritarian dictators waned. In the 1990s newly democratized regimes in Latin America, responding to both changed world conditions and strong domestic demand for democracy and an end to serious human rights abuses, embraced human rights norms. This response can be seen in the surge in norm-affirming events by Latin American governments.[82]

Whatever the cause, the evidence shows that once in motion the norms cascade developed a momentum of its own. The norms themselves, together with their accompanying domestic, regional, and international enforcement mechanisms intended to pressure countries to comply with them, caused regional political actors to transform their behavior. This change in behavior had the effect both of intensifying the norms cascade and transforming the political and human rights landscape across Latin America. We also suggest that decentralization of decision making helps explain variation in the impact that norms have on practices. Where decision making about norm implementation is more centralized, there is greater likelihood that norms cascades and norm enforcement mechanisms will have an impact. Because decisions about torture are more decentralized than decisions about disappearances or democracy, it is more difficult to change practice in this area.

Legalization is relevant to the outcomes here. Law has an important expressive function—it formally restates social values and norms. So even international human rights law that is not highly legalized may be important for expressing and communicating international norms.[83] Indeed, international law was essential for some, but not all, of the enforcement mechanisms we have discussed here. The extradition proceedings with respect to General Augusto Pinochet, for example, turned on arguments about what international human rights law requires. The British House of Lords concluded, consistent with our argument, that the issue-area of torture was more legalized and, as such, provided the only grounds upon which General Pinochet could be extradited to Spain to stand trial. What message will dictators elsewhere in the world take from the Pinochet case? Will they decide that they cannot torture because that realm is sufficiently legalized to put them at risk of extradition, but that

---

82. See Schoultz 1981; Forsythe 1989; Lauren 1998; Donnelly 1989; and Sikkink 1993.
83. Sunstein 1997, 36.

they can disappear, arbitrarily imprison, or carry out genocide, because the British House of Lords dismissed those accusations against Pinochet? We doubt it. But there are indications that current and past repressors of various sorts are limiting their international travel in fear that they, too, will face international arrest.[84]

In Latin America legalization increased the number of pathways (or "toolkits," as Judith Goldstein has argued) by multiplying the arenas within which human rights issues could be raised.[85] Legalization led to the creation of the Inter-American Court of Human Rights and to the UN Human Rights Committee's authority to hear individual complaints. But these legal channels were not the only, nor necessarily the most important, mechanisms through which human rights pressures were brought to bear. What was more important was how legal and political enforcement mechanisms reinforced each other as they underscored the increasing strength of the norm consensus.

The human rights norms also decreased the number of available political pathways. Military coups, for example, used to be acceptable behavior within the Latin American political game. This changed in the 1980s, when military coups were removed from the list of acceptable political action paths. Indeed, there have been no successful military coups in the region since 1982. The remaining puzzle is why repressive governments would respond at all to such international norms and pressures. Even at their most forceful, the sanctions imposed were not crippling. Military and economic aid was cut, as were certain trade credits or preferences, but trade and investment continued. Part of the answer is that the influence of international human rights law in Latin America occurred incrementally and was not intended by the target states. Authoritarian states agreed to certain international human rights norms, often because they hoped to reap the benefits of participation in an international and regional legal order and believed they could avoid any costs. Because international law is perceived as not having any enforcement mechanisms, states may have believed that they could selectively and instrumentally partake in it. But international human rights law was capable of imposing more costs than they originally anticipated because it was enforceable not only directly, but also indirectly through a wider range of political channels. These diverse channels eventually imposed more costs or required more compliance than state actors originally thought possible, but by the time this became apparent, states could not readily disentangle themselves from their legal obligations. Certainly, when Pinochet agreed to allow Chile to ratify the Convention Against Torture in 1988, he had no idea that the words of the convention would justify his arrest in the United Kingdom ten years later.

But the answer is more complex than just saying that these governments somehow made a mistake and were then caught in a web of their own making. We cannot understand the reactions of Latin American governments to international, regional, and domestic human rights norms and pressures without confronting the issue of

---

84. *New York Times*, 29 November 1998. The *International Herald Tribune*, 24 August 1999, mentions a "Pinochet Syndrome" humbling dictators of the world.
85. Goldstein et al., this issue.

legitimacy and esteem. Leaders of authoritarian governments sometimes responded to these pressures because as members of an international or regional society of states they had been "socialized" to care about what other states think of them.[86] Scholars have long understood that collective legitimation has become one of the major functions of international organizations.[87] Leaders increasingly seek or care about international legitimation because it can help to enhance or to undermine the domestic legitimacy and survival of their regime. But the reasons go even deeper than the need for domestic legitimacy. Human rights pressures operate not only at the pragmatic level by imposing material costs or jeopardizing domestic legitimacy but also at the social level by creating ostracized "out-groups" of norm breakers.

These social processes may have been especially effective in Latin America because they resonate with a tradition of commitment to international law and human rights norms. These norms are embedded in the belief systems of influential individuals and sectors of civil society and are articulated in positive law. Latin American dictators could not, as much as they tried, successfully sustain the story that human rights was simply "cultural imperialism." Because of this preexisting, well-established normative framework, international enforcement pressures resonated domestically as external pressures reinforced domestic values. As international human rights norms were increasingly articulated and clarified, individuals in Latin America demanded that their governments live up to these norms and welcomed external pressure to do so.

After re-democratization in the region, the effectiveness of past international human rights pressures reinforced the confidence of newly democratic governments in the efficacy of international legal institutions. Some of these governments have become enthusiastic supporters of efforts to further develop international and regional human rights law and institutions. The Argentine government, for example, helped draft and facilitate the final agreement on the UN Convention Against Torture in 1984. At the Vienna World Conference on Human Rights in 1993, when China and other Asian nations tried to organize nonaligned countries to fight against the notion of the universality of human rights, Latin American countries were conspicuously absent and instead joined forces with the Western countries of Europe and the United States.

Serious problems involving compliance with international human rights law continue to plague Latin America. But very diverse Latin American states have increasingly complied with prohibitions against torture, disappearance, and military coups over the last two decades. International norms and international law, implemented and enforced through the widest range of channels, are important parts of the explanation for these changes.

---

86. See Finnemore 1996; and Risse, Ropp, and Sikkink 1999.
87. Claude 1966.

Conclusion: The Causes and Consequences of Legalization

Miles Kahler

Legalization in contemporary world politics is a complex and varied mosaic rather than a universal and irreversible trend. Regional islands of high legalization, such as Europe, coexist with other regions that have largely rejected legalized institutions. Variation occurs across issue-areas as well as time. An increase in legalization in the global trade regime was capped by the establishment of the World Trade Organization (WTO) in the 1990s. At the same time, exchange-rate commitments under the International Monetary Fund (IMF) failed to return to the levels of obligation and precision they had displayed three decades ago. Regional security regimes display soft legalization for the most part, but certain global arms control agreements are precise, legally binding, and incorporate moderate levels of delegation.

Underlying variation in legalization and shaping its future trajectory is a close connection between law and politics—a connection endorsed by each of the contributors to this special issue, whether lawyer or political scientist. In this reforging and reexamining of the link between law and politics, the authors echo E. H. Carr, often taken as a paragon of realism, who asserted that "politics and law are indissolubly intertwined . . . . Law, like politics, is a meeting place for ethics and power."[1] Legalization, in creating new institutional forms, mobilizes different political actors and shapes their behavior in particular ways.

Politics is a meeting place for two questions that were posed in the introduction and receive tentative answers from these authors. First, why, among the variety of institutional forms available to governments, are legalized institutions—those displaying the three characteristics of heightened obligation, greater precision in rules, and delegation of rule interpretation and enforcement to third parties—preferred in some contexts and not in others? Second, what are the consequences of legalization? Although the authors are primarily interested in international outcomes, those outcomes are often related to an intervening effect that legalization has on domestic

I thank Karen Alter, Robert O. Keohane, Richard Steinberg, the editors of *International Organization*, and an anonymous reviewer for helpful comments on an earlier draft of this article. Pablo Pinto provided excellent research assistance.

1. Carr 1946, 177–78.

International Organization 54, 3, Summer 2000, pp. 277–299

politics, creating changes that reinforce or undermine legalized agreements and institutions. Explanations for legalization are joined to its consequences by reflexive
processes: domestic politics propels or inhibits legalization, and legalization, in turn,
shapes domestic political institutions and empowers domestic actors.

A final commonality among these authors should be noted. Although all adopt the
definition of legalization presented in "The Concept of Legalization,"[2] legalization
itself becomes more complex in the course of their investigations. The dimensions of
obligation, precision, and delegation co-vary in some cases; in other instances, an
increase in one dimension appears to substitute for low levels in another. In some
institutional settings precision implies authoritative interpretation that requires delegation to a third party. In other cases precision permits governments to avoid delegation by negotiating more complete contracts. Skewed patterns of legalization can
therefore emerge. A first look at legalization based on these cases finds a widespread
increase in precision—the voluminous size of the North American Free Trade Agreement (NAFTA) is only one example—but less clear-cut increases in obligation and
delegation. Robert Keohane, Andrew Moravcsik, and Anne-Marie Slaughter further
refine the dimensions of delegation to explain contrasting patterns of stasis and deepening.[3] They contrast transnational dispute resolution, characterized by relatively
high levels of autonomy, access, and embeddedness, with interstate dispute resolution. Their identification of new variants of legalization is one example of the ways in
which our understanding of legalization can change with additional investigation.

Explaining Legalization

Common explanations are assumed for movement from any point on the legalization
spectrum to any other point: from institutionalization to soft law and from softer to
harder forms of legalization described by Kenneth Abbott and Duncan Snidal.[4] Governments may opt for institutions that are not legalized, as they often have in certain
regions (such as Asia) and in certain issue-areas (such as economic policy coordination in the G-7). Institutionalization can increase without legalization: the Association of Southeast Asian Nations (ASEAN) has supported certain norms of behavior
through a panoply of transgovernmental institutions that are not highly legalized.
Central banks in the industrialized countries have developed understandings on regulatory oversight and commitments on capital adequacy, but collaboration is not based
on legalized institutions. As Abbott and Snidal point out, soft law need not be super-
seded by hard law. Actors may determine that soft law (or no law) serves their purposes.

Functionalist Explanations

The vocabulary used here—governments may opt for, actors may determine—
reflects one explanation for legalization that is familiar from the study of interna-

---

2. Abbott et al., this issue.
3. Keohane, Moravcsik, and Slaughter, this issue.
4. Abbott and Snidal, this issue.

tional institutions. In this broadly functionalist approach, governments choose legalized institutions because they solve particular problems of commitment or collective action, increasing the prospective benefits from cooperation. At the same time, governments must weigh the costs imposed by legalization. Legalized agreements and institutions will be selected when they provide superior net benefits when compared to nonlegalized (or less legalized) alternatives.

Abbott and Snidal outline some of the benefits that greater (harder) legalization provides. Government commitments are more credible under precise agreements of high obligation; delegated authority to interpret those commitments may also strengthen compliance. Legalization may be particularly important in providing an institutional solution to commitments fulfilled over an extended period of time. NAFTA's precision, for example, was part of the Mexican government's strategy to bind successor governments to its policies of economic openness. As the large literature on central bank independence suggests, delegation to a relatively autonomous agency may also serve to reduce time-inconsistency problems. Judicial or quasi-judicial agencies in legalized regimes may serve similar purposes by restricting future freedom of action by politicians.

The effects of legalization on transaction costs are more evenly balanced. Negotiating costs—*ex ante* transaction costs—are likely to be higher with hard legalization, as Abbott and Snidal point out, given increased levels of obligation and precision in such agreements. *Ex post* costs, however, may decline with legalization as costs associated with implementing incomplete contracts decline. Precision implies more complete contracts; delegation and adjudication can ease the costs of renegotiation associated with incompleteness. Frederick Abbott's account of NAFTA illustrates a choice between these two strategies: conflict reduction was sought largely through specificity of commitments and a precise plan of implementation rather than through increased delegation.[5] In the European Union (EU) and other regimes of enhanced delegation, judicial institutions such as the European Court of Justice (ECJ) have reduced implementation costs by using "the potential to set in motion a distinctive dynamic built on precedent."[6] Precedents permit governance by analogy: the efficient processing of a multitude of disputes on the basis of a relatively small number of earlier decisions.

Many international institutions display decentralized enforcement. In such an enforcement environment, legalization may increase capabilities for monitoring compliance and imposing sanctions. Higher levels of obligation and more precise rules reduce the costs of monitoring and lower the bar for enforcement actions; third-party or delegated dispute-resolution mechanisms clarify rules and their breach and may in some cases authorize sanctions. The contribution of legalization to levels of compliance, and even its net benefits, however, are questioned by some of the authors in this issue.[7]

---

5. F. Abbott, this issue.
6. Keohane, Moravcsik, and Slaughter, this issue.
7. See Lutz and Sikkink; Goldstein and Martin; and Alter, all in this issue.

Gains from cooperation that can be attributed to increased legalization may be more than offset by costs to governments in certain issue-areas. Abbott and Snidal point to two major categories of costs, what might be labeled unintended (if not unanticipated) consequences of legalization.[8] The first category, sovereignty costs, includes outcomes inferior to those that might be obtained in the absence of legalization, constraints that legalization imposes on policymaking autonomy, and "more fundamental encroachments on state sovereignty." Sovereignty costs are highest in this last category, when legalized institutions "impinge on the relations between a state and its citizens or territory."[9]

Resistance to legalization seems at times to represent an assessment of sovereignty costs rooted in ideological or normative resistance to external oversight or constraint. Beth Simmons, for example, finds a surprising willingness to accept legalization (and the sovereignty costs it entails) in order to avoid higher sovereignty costs from another source.[10] Before 1977, governments could commit to ending restrictions on current account transactions and thereby avoid multilateral surveillance by the IMF. When IMF surveillance was extended to all members, governments were much less likely to accept the legalized commitment to liberalization. (Governments that did not submit to IMF surveillance may also have gained higher international status.) Sovereignty costs may also have figured in resistance to further legalization of human rights provisions in the UN Charter and the failure of the United States to ratify the Genocide Convention after World War II. Since that resistance came from liberal democratic as well as authoritarian states, normative disagreement about human rights was not at the root of the resistance. Instead, concerns over an erosion of domestic jurisdiction appear to have been paramount.[11]

Sovereignty costs are not immutable, however, and careful measurement requires that they cannot be used automatically to account for unexplained resistance to legalization. National currencies are often assumed to be at the core of sovereignty. In recent years, however, currency boards (severely constraining if not eliminating national monetary authority) and support for dollarization suggest an overestimation in the past of sovereignty costs associated with curbs on national monetary autonomy. In many cases what appear to be sovereignty costs are in fact the second category of legalization costs described by Abbott and Snidal: those based on future uncertainty. Legalization's value as a commitment device implies that future changes in policy will be more costly; given the possibility of unexpected shocks and overall environmental uncertainty (particularly high in certain issue-areas), governments may view legalization as too risky, despite its substantial benefits. Resistance to the Comprehensive Test Ban Treaty (and other legalized arms control measures) in the United States derived in part from concerns over an uncertain future military environment. Na-

---

8. For the distinction between unintended and unanticipated consequences in functionalist analysis, see Martin and Simmons 1998, 749–50.

9. Abbott and Snidal, this issue.

10. Simmons, this issue.

11. Keck and Sikkink 1998, 86.

tional commitments to forgo restrictions on current account transactions (Article VIII of the IMF Articles of Agreement) also display clear evidence of concern over costs associated with uncertainty. Those states with a relatively high susceptibility to balance-of-payments crises display a significantly lower likelihood of assuming the commitment than states with a relatively low susceptibility to this type of crisis.[12]

Legalization in the international monetary regime reflects a clear trade-off between the benefits of commitment and the concomitant costs of inflexibility. When environmental volatility rose in the 1970s, legal obligations to fixed parties were broken, a breach ultimately legitimated by the Second Amendment to the IMF Articles of Agreement. When considering exchange-rate arrangements, contemporary developing countries face increasingly stark choices between currency boards (domestic legalization) or currency union (regional legalization) and a more flexible exchange-rate regime that permits governments to respond to shocks through discretionary changes in their exchange rates.[13] Judith Goldstein and Lisa Martin criticize greater precision and delegation under the WTO for eliminating a necessary degree of flexibility in trade rules in the face of international economic uncertainty.[14] In these issue-areas, as well as others, governments face a recurrent trade-off between credible commitments and discretion in dealing with future uncertainty. Legalization provides a means of commitment through hardened constraints on policy choice. At the same time, legalization may ensure higher costs when governments are forced to deal with unexpected shocks or domestic political change. As Abbott and Snidal describe, the assessment of sovereignty and uncertainty costs point not only to harder or softer legalization, but also to different forms of legalized institutions. They hypothesize that a combination of high uncertainty and low sovereignty costs will lead to institutions with lower precision coupled with higher obligation and moderate delegation. High sovereignty costs and lower uncertainty are likely to produce greater precision and obligation with less delegation.[15]

Asymmetries in Power and Legalization

If functionalist arguments suggest why states might choose legalized institutions as an efficient route toward the Pareto frontier, power asymmetries and distributional concerns explain the choice of legalization in other circumstances. One conventional hypothesis associates state preferences for legalized dispute resolution with lower bargaining power (measured in resources or size). More powerful states in this view will avoid more legalized institutions, since they can often obtain positive outcomes through ad hoc bargaining. This effect seems particularly clear with regard to delegation to third parties in dispute resolution. Among a large sample of regional trade agreements, James McCall Smith finds that those agreements with high economic

---

12. Simmons, this issue.
13. Eichengreen 1999, 105.
14. Goldstein and Martin, this issue.
15. Abbott and Snidal, this issue.

asymmetry among members do not have highly legalized dispute settlement proce-dures.[16] Simmons echoes this finding in her investigation of territorial disputes in Latin America: asymmetry in power means less likelihood of delegation to third-party dispute resolution.[17] Less powerful states in the European Union are the major internal lobby for maintaining existing levels of legalization in the face of large state unhappiness with an expansion of ECJ powers.[18]

This simple association between power asymmetry and preferences for legaliza-tion must be heavily qualified, however. The most powerful actors in the interna-tional system—the United States and the European Union—are among the strongest proponents of legalization (although to varying degrees across issue-areas). Abbott and Snidal suggest that more powerful states will value soft legalization, and particu-larly binding and precise rules, since any reduction in bargaining power in particular cases will be offset by a reduction in bargaining costs in the long run.[19] Stronger states will be much more skeptical of delegation, as confirmed in the results de-scribed earlier.

The preferences of states can also be explained by asymmetry in capabilities of a different kind: asymmetry in the legal resources that governments can mobilize. To fully explain state preferences over legalization, one must incorporate not only bargaining power in the issue-area in question but also access to legal resources and the preferences of domestic actors (considered in the next section). Small Euro-pean states are strong proponents of legalization, not only because they wish to constrain the behavior of their more powerful neighbors, but also because they possess legal resources out of proportion to their other capabilities. Developing coun-tries often lack highly developed legal systems and the resources that accrue to such systems and are therefore more skeptical of or even hostile to legalization. (Their colonial histories may also raise sovereignty costs.) The resistance of Asian govern-ments to legalization within regional economic organizations is puzzling given that legalization should serve to increase their ability to limit U.S. and Japanese latitude in bargaining over economic disputes. However, the imbalance of legal re-sources available to the United States within such a regime and the demonstrated willingness of the United States to serve as judge, jury, and policeman in trade dis-putes (a unilateralism applauded by some as filling gaps within the trade regime) has had the opposite effect. Most Asian states have been unwilling to incur stronger or more precise legal obligations within the Asia-Pacific Economic Cooperation forum, and they have resisted the creation of dispute-settlement mechanisms as well. In other settings that display more symmetry in capabilities, legalization has been more acceptable.[20]

16. Smith 2000.
17. Simmons 2000b.
18. Alter 1998b, 137.
19. Abbott and Snidal, this issue.
20. Kahler, this issue. For a positive reading of what some have called "aggressive unilateralism" in U.S. trade policy, see Downs, Rocke, and Barsoom 1996, 395.

Domestic Politics and Legalization

Legalization provides a rich arena for examining the domestic political underpinnings of international institutions, a much-debated subject and a much-lamented shortcoming in existing analysis.[21] The contributors to this special issue pay close attention to the effects that domestic politics has on choices for or against legalized institutions.

Domestic politics complements the preceding functionalist explanations for legalization by supplying an explanation for government preferences. Government preferences may not mirror those of their societies as a whole. Instead, domestic groups will typically have different preferences over legalization because of its effects on international outcomes, and political institutions will award some of those groups more influence over national policy than others. As Karen Alter makes clear, the simple availability of legalized institutions, particularly those that grant access to nonstate actors, does not mean that all groups will make effective use of those institutions.[22]

Several groups stand out as particularly powerful constituencies for legalization. The legal profession has played a prominent role in many international legalization efforts. Legalized international institutions reflect the professional norms of lawyers, magnify the influence of lawyers on policy, and increase the demand for legal services. Lawyers have been major proponents of the international legalization of human rights during this century, beginning in the 1920s when they replaced groups that had been motivated primarily by religion.[23] Their role has been supplemented since 1945 by a much wider transnational network of nongovernmental organizations that have embraced the cause of legalization.[24] Legalization of the General Agreement on Tariffs and Trade (GATT) and the World Trade Organization (WTO) has also received strong intellectual support from international trade lawyers.

National judiciaries, a key part of the legal community, have demonstrated more ambivalence toward international legalization. Their differentiated stance reflects the possibility that legalized international institutions might substitute for rather than complement domestic legal institutions.[25] Although the alignment of the ECJ with national judiciaries is an oft-told story, Alter points out that the attitudes of national judiciaries toward the expansion of European law and their contributions to that expansion have varied both within and across countries.[26]

A second constituency that is central to legalization in the late twentieth century is businesses engaged in the rapid expansion of international trade and investment. The emphasis on international economic agreements in this special issue is not accidental: legalization has achieved some of its most dramatic advances in this realm. The bulk of EU law, for example, has been directed toward creating the rights of eco-

21. Martin and Simmons 1998, 747.
22. Alter, this issue.
23. Keck and Sikkink 1998, 81.
24. Ibid., 85.
25. Martin and Simmons 1998, 747.
26. Alter, this issue.

nomic citizenship, not building precedents in social or civil rights.[27] International economic agreements increasingly reflect the concerns of those with specific assets in the member states. Traders and investors demand a stable policy environment, guaranteed by legalized commitments, and prefer predictable dispute-settlement procedures over intergovernmental bargaining. Investors, in particular, often seek legalized international agreements as a compensation or substitute for shaky legal systems in host countries. In ASEAN, business exerted pressure to obtain a dispute-settlement mechanism in the barely legalized free trade agreement, even though they would not be granted direct access to the dispute-settlement mechanism.

A second domestic political explanation for legalization places its emphasis, not on interest groups and their influence, but on the agency of national politicians. Recalling neofunctionalist analysis, these models portray legalization as a means of political problem solving for vote-maximizing politicians (or, in the case of authoritarian polities, leaders maximizing the support of a defined selectorate).[28] In this type of analysis the international equilibrium analysis of functionalism is replaced by the search for an efficient domestic political equilibrium (or, as in a two-level game, the first equilibrium must be squared with the second). The benefits and costs in this transformed functionalist analysis are no longer international benefits and costs but domestic political ones. Sovereignty costs are calculated as loss of support among particular constituencies that may value policy autonomy highly, such as nationalist parties, the military, the national security bureaucracy, or nationally based manufacturing. Benefits from international cooperation under legalized institutions are calibrated in terms of domestic political gains from a larger surplus or the gains to domestic supporters from redistribution at the expense of other states.[29] The costs of uncertainty become political costs if a politician constrained by legalized institutions is unable to compensate those interest groups affected by unexpected shocks.[30]

Domestic political problem solving may produce outcomes in which the international consequences of legalization, central to functionalist analysis, play little role. Legalization may provide symbolic or other political benefits and yield relatively few short-term gains at the international level. Such political motivations for legalization were central to the negotiation and ratification of the Kellogg-Briand Pact in 1928. Although this advance in legalization—branding as illegal the use of force as an instrument of national policy—did ultimately have consequences in the Nuremberg Tribunal and its punishment of the crime of aggression, most accounts of the pact see it as a fruitless and utopian gesture. The politics that lay behind the pact, however, had little to do with calculations of the international effects of legalization. Frank B. Kellogg, the U.S. secretary of state, was no friend of the American peace and pro-League of Nations movements that pushed the cause of outlawing war, although there is evidence that he became a believer in the pact as it was negotiated. The Harding and Coolidge administrations were forced, however, to take measures

27. See ibid.; and Shaw 1998.
28. For an example of this kind of explanation, see Richards 1999.
29. Richards 1999.
30. Downs and Rocke 1995, 87–91.

throughout the 1920s that would placate this powerful domestic constituency. The Kellogg-Briand Pact was the latest of these efforts to win the support of an important domestic constituency with minimal international commitments.[31]

The French foreign minister, Aristide Briand, played an even more intricate domestic game. Like most French politicians, he had little time for legalized instruments such as the pact; his first priority was pulling the politically constrained United States toward greater involvement in European security. His initial negotiating proposal of a bilateral pact to outlaw war with the United States was in effect a "negative military alliance" that would have ensured U.S. neutrality in a future conflict. Since neither this bilateral pact nor a formal alliance nor membership in the League of Nations were politically feasible in the United States, the multilateral, soft law approach of the Kellogg-Briand Pact to U.S. engagement was preferable to no engagement at all.[32] Essentially, Briand manipulated a powerful political coalition in the United States to prod a reluctant Coolidge administration toward the multilateral option.

Henry Stimson, secretary of state during the Hoover administration, followed a similar political logic. Hardly a proponent of legalization or the peace movement, Stimson claimed that the Kellogg-Briand Pact had changed international law and created, not legal obligations, but "moral obligations to cooperate with signatories in event an aggressor violated it."[33] Once again, legalization, which mobilized one constituency (the peace movement) and disarmed another (the isolationists) was a politically feasible avenue to wider diplomatic goals that had little to do with the international consequences of legalization.

A third explanation of legalization that is common to many of the cases in this special issue lies in the domestic political effects of legalization. Legalized international institutions, in contrast to other international institutions, are often based in the substance of domestic legal orders, which, in turn, contain commitments by governments to their own citizens that constrain government behavior. The first model of domestic politics explains preferences over legalization on the basis of domestic groups and desired international outcomes. The second explains legalization through the international payoffs that it provides to political entrepreneurs in winning domestic political support. This final, and most distinctive, link between domestic politics and legalization explains legalization through the prospective consequences of *international* legalization for *domestic* political outcomes. In other words, groups—and governments themselves—choose legalized international institutions to bind governments to particular domestic policies.

This linkage is readily apparent in the sphere of human rights, in which international legalization has committed governments to maintaining international standards of human rights in their domestic governance. Authoritarian regimes in Latin America accepted legalized obligations to respect human rights at home. Why they

---

31. For an account of the pact and its political underpinnings, see Ferrell 1952.
32. Ibid., 73, 99.
33. DeBoe 1974, 34–35.

accepted such potentially risky commitments is less clear. Ellen Lutz and Kathryn Sikkink suggest that membership in a high-status club and evidence of participation in the international legal order more than outweighed the low probability of enforcement that these governments expected under international conventions.[34]

In other instances governments were clearly aware that accepting legalized institutions would limit their domestic freedom of action. Goldstein describes the deployment of legalization by one branch of the government to undermine the influence of other political actors. The U.S. executive, with preferences that pointed toward liberalized trade, constructed binding arbitration arrangements under the Canada–U.S. Free Trade Agreement (later reproduced in NAFTA) in order to restrain more protectionist forces in Congress, the national trade bureaucracy, and among interest groups. Executive branch powers remained unaffected. Legalization imposed differential domestic effects in this instance that biased policy in particular directions favored by the U.S. executive.[35] NAFTA side agreements on labor and the environment had less significant domestic consequences, but they serve to reinforce commitments already made by governments to their own citizens through national legislation. The implementation of those commitments is strengthened by their transformation into international obligations. As Frederick Abbott describes, many of the benefits that governments saw in the legalized NAFTA agreement were not those of governments to other governments, but commitments that would serve to strengthen the confidence of investors. The heightened level of obligation and precision contained in NAFTA served to bind governments—and their successors—to economic openness and transparency, both substantial benefits to economic interests operating across national borders.[36]

In each of these issue-areas, but particularly in the governance of monetary, trade, and investment policies, international legalization can be seen as a substitute or reinforcement for domestic legal and constitutional restraints on government action. The substitution effect is clearest in the case of international monetary commitments. The pre-1914 gold standard was legalized, but the legal commitments were embodied in domestic legislation, commitments by governments (or their central banks) to the holders of their currencies. Democratization and the pressures that it placed on these commitments led eventually to international legalization under the Bretton Woods agreements. Today, currency boards (embedded in domestic legislation) compete with regional currency arrangements (international legalization) as different instruments for demonstrating the credibility of monetary commitments.

Explanations for Legalization

Explanations for variation in legalization are directed to both the supply of legalized institutions and the demand for those institutions. The supply of legalized institutions

---

34. Lutz and Sikkink, this issue.
35. Goldstein 1996.
36. F. Abbott, this issue.

is highly dependent on the preferences of the most powerful states in a given region or issue-area and on unanticipated domestic political dynamics, considered later, that may lead to the expansion of legalization. The United States and the principal states of Europe have played the largest role in shaping the character of global institutions and the institutions of their own regions. As more powerful actors that possess large legal resources in addition to their other capabilities, they may well prefer binding and precise agreements, but they may also be wary of high levels of delegation. In the face of these preferences, the construction of the highly legalized European Union poses an interesting counterfactual: if Germany had behaved as a "normal" great power, would legalization in the European Union have reached such high levels? Since 1945, Germany has had both domestic and international reasons for binding itself into a legalized international order. Its credibility as a law-abiding international actor—in its neighbors' eyes and in its own citizens' eyes—seemed to require the support of international legalization.

The preferences of the most influential states are also influenced by domestic political demands for legalized institutions. The most important environmental change that has increased that demand is growing global and regional economic integration. Many of the examples in this special issue are drawn from regional arrangements or the global trade institutions of GATT/WTO. Regional economic agreements in the 1990s promoted a new agenda of integration that includes liberalization of investment and the removal or modification of domestic policies that limit international exchange. The costs of opportunism have increased sharply, and the need for monitoring of often opaque practices is greater. These changes often require more precise and binding commitments by governments as well as at least a modest increase in delegation. James McCall Smith finds that, controlling for relative size and bargaining leverage of the parties, trade agreements that aim at ambitious levels of integration are more likely to have more legalistic dispute-settlement mechanisms.[37] Domestically, the constituencies that benefit from integration—particularly internationalized business—often lobby for a more stable and rule-governed economic environment.

A second global change—democratization—has had more ambiguous effects on legalization. On the one hand, democratization gives institutional voice to pro-legalization interests. Those interests fall into two groups. The first, primarily business groups, endorses legalization as contract (to use Abbott and Snidal's term). The second set of interests promotes legalization as normative covenant—human rights groups, for example. Among the industrialized democracies, law occupies a central institutional place, and these pro-legalization normative lobbies are powerful. On the other hand, democracy implies periodic political change and heightened levels of uncertainty that may argue for softer rather than harder legalized arrangements.

Outside the industrialized democracies, the intersection of legalization's supply and demand is often very different. Regional economic integration in some regions remains relatively low, removing a major source of demand for legalization. In the absence of interest group pressure, government attitudes toward international eco-

---

37. Smith 2000.

nomic integration are central in determining acceptance of international legalization. For economies that have witnessed wide fluctuations in policies (Latin America) or that have recently emerged from socialist regimes (the former Soviet Union or East Europe), legalized international institutions provide a useful means of quickly building policy credibility. Hence the eagerness of many transitional economies in Europe to join the European Union and the interest of some Latin American governments in NAFTA.

In other developing country cases, sovereignty costs will make participation in legalized institutions difficult or impossible. Etel Solingen's contrasting coalitions—internationalist and statist-nationalist—parallel likely positions toward legalization, particularly in regional institutions, throughout the nonindustrialized world.[38] Internationalist coalitions, interested in secure access to foreign markets and investment, are more likely to pursue legalization as a means to regional stability. Statist-nationalist coalitions, on the other hand, place a high value on national autonomy and stress local security threats. They are far more likely to assess both sovereignty and uncertainty costs as high. Rule-of-law societies are unlikely to be deeply rooted in either case; normative constituencies for legalization will therefore be weak. At the same time, democracy may be of the plebiscitary variety, raising levels of future uncertainty and reducing the demand for legalization. Liberalizing governments may attempt to bind their successors using legalization, but acceptable levels of legalization, given domestic constituencies skeptical or opposed to that institutional course, may not be high enough to constrain future behavior.

The supply of legalized institutions at the global and regional level is important. In some parts of the developing world that supply may be low or nonexistent. For societies that are candidates for membership in the European Union, an external strategy that awards a central place to international legalization is far more feasible than it is in other regions. For those governments whose regional supply of legalized institutions is low, membership in global institutions, such as the WTO, may provide an alternative means of obtaining policy credibility.

Consequences of Legalization

The authors of this special issue examine three important consequences of legalization. The most intensively argued in international relations, although often on grounds both narrow and ill-defined, are the effects of legalization on state behavior, particularly government compliance with international agreements. Does legalization add measurably to levels of compliance above what would be expected with agreements and institutions that embody less obligation, less precision, and less delegation? Realist critics have typically argued that legalization changes very little about state behavior, except, perhaps, when a legalized regime is imposed by a more powerful state on the less powerful. The authors in this special issue emphasize the contin-

---

38. Solingen 1998.

gency of legalization's effects on compliance. Once again, domestic political links are central to compliance effects.

The effects of legalization on the evolution of international norms has also been a subject of disagreement, in particular whether legalization has powerful independent effects over and above the dynamic of norm adoption. From a very different vantage point than the realists, constructivist skeptics take the view that normative effects dominate the institutional effects of legalization. Here, to the degree that the authors address this issue, they discern a clear positive interaction between norms and legalized institutions.

Finally, given its historical and spatial distribution, under what conditions will legalization harden and spread? Legalized institutions demonstrate regional concentration (Europe and North America); within those regions, they appear to have become more common over the past two decades. Elsewhere and at the global level, legalization demonstrates a pattern of both reinforcement and retrenchment over time. A partial explanation of these patterns appears to rest on the presence of unanticipated consequences of legalization that are grounded primarily in the connections between legalized international institutions and domestic politics.

Legalization and International Outcomes:
Cooperation and Compliance

Legalization contains an implicit promise: compared with institutions that do not share the characteristics of obligation, precision, and delegation, greater cooperative gains will be reaped by resolving collective action problems more efficiently. Distributional claims may also be dealt with in a less conflictual and more equitable way. (Of course, less conflict and more equity may not coincide in the same set of institutions.) States will not only move closer to the Pareto frontier, they will also deal more effectively with distributional disputes over the gains from cooperation.

These hypotheses are based on assumptions about compliance: the negotiating costs for legalized agreements (possibly greater than those in less-legalized settings) are more than offset by the higher levels of compliance with agreements that are reached. As George W. Downs, David M. Rocke, and Peter N. Barsoom have pointed out, however, studies that demonstrate high levels of compliance may well suffer from a selection bias: following functionalist logic, governments will only negotiate agreements and establish institutional rules that they fully intended to follow in any case. An apparently high level of compliance could result from the fact that legalization has not altered government behavior in the slightest.[39] In his evaluation of NAFTA, for example, Frederick Abbott argues that a more demanding test of its good compliance record awaits a change that alters political incentives in one or more of the partners.[40]

---

39. Downs, Rocke, and Barsoom 1996, 383.
40. F. Abbott, this issue.

Simmons confronts this methodological issue in her investigation of compliance with obligations to avoid current account restrictions under Article VIII of the IMF's Articles of Agreement. She controls for economic conditions that are likely to induce a government to apply current account restrictions (as well as political conditions such as democracy). Legalized commitments still have a positive effect on compliance: "an Article VIII country is some 60 percent less likely to turn to restrictions than are countries that continue to live under the 'transitional' Article XIV regime."[41] In this case legalization appears to have an independent and significant positive effect on the likelihood of compliance.

Political regime is often assumed to affect compliance with legalized institutional rules. Simmons disaggregates the "liberal democracy" variable that has often been associated with both the choice of legalization and higher rates of compliance with legalized commitments. Democracy—defined as a more competitive political system—has a negative effect on compliance. Although greater influence awarded to actors with preferences for legalization may be one effect of democracy, Simmons's result tracks a different consequence of democratic governance: "rules and popular pressures can and apparently sometimes do pull in opposite directions when it comes to international law compliance."[42] Economic variables that have the greatest effect on compliance with IMF commitments are not those measuring differences in economic structure. Politically significant variables—terms of trade volatility and slower growth—appear to have the greatest influence on government compliance. As described earlier, democratic governance is likely to place more pressure on compliance with legal obligations in plebiscitary democracies outside the industrialized world, polities that may lack both a strong attachment to domestic legal institutions and powerful, internationalized economic interest groups.

Democracy and its demands may not support compliance with international legal commitments. However, Simmons does discover a strong and significant relationship between compliance with legal commitments and regimes based on the rule of law. These regimes are defined by the willingness of their citizens to employ peaceful means of dispute resolution and by key institutions, such as a strong court system.[43] Contributors to this special issue point to several avenues of compliance that rule-of-law societies construct. Each of these avenues links domestic politics and legal systems to compliance with international legal commitments. The most direct and effective connection is the incorporation of international legal commitments into domestic law, lending them the weight of national enforcement powers. Such incorporation, however, is often resisted by national politicians favoring greater policymaking autonomy. Even in the highly legalized European Union setting, the ECJ doctrines of

---

41. Simmons, this issue.

42. Evidence on territorial disputes in Latin America also failed to find a "democratic effect" with respect to compliance, although the results were complicated by the small number of regimes that met contemporary standards of liberal democracy. Simmons 2000, 16. Simmons also finds that change of government is linked to noncompliance: an effect that is not specific to democracies but occurs on a regular basis in democratic regimes.

43. See Simmons's definition in this issue.

supremacy of EU law and direct effect (that individuals could use EC law directly in national courts to challenge national law and policy) remain controversial. The European Council has declined to acknowledge these claims through treaty revision or to grant such a role formally to national courts.[44] In the case of NAFTA, the U.S. Congress acted to preclude private-party reliance on NAFTA in court proceedings, excluding members of the national judiciary from larger roles in interpretation and implementation of the agreement.[45]

Under a rule-of-law regime, domestic "compliance constituencies" will often increase the probability of government compliance and encourage imposition of sanctions on other governments that violate legal commitments. These constituencies may intersect substantially with the pro-legalization groups mentioned earlier, but some groups may become compliance constituencies even though they were not original proponents of legalization.

Transnational dispute resolution empowers compliance constituencies in two ways. It grants access to nonstate actors, expanding the pool of those who may attempt to obtain compliance. These litigants will not be as constrained by concerns about reciprocity as other national governments. Increasing the embeddedness of legalized institutions allows these compliance constituencies to use domestic courts for enforcement, rather than relying solely upon influence with the national executive or legislature. Governments that do not comply face a new calculus: in addition to the international costs of breaching a legalized commitment, they must now face the much more serious reputational and political costs of breaching legal commitments before their own citizens. The costs of noncompliance should increase at higher levels of embeddedness.[46]

Even in systems of transnational dispute settlement, however, law-abiding governments may face significant domestic counterpressures to avoid policy change. In order to translate a legal victory into policy change, a compliance constituency must have a second, political, strategy, one that raises the prospective costs to any government that balks at the required change.[47] Even in less transnational systems with very circumscribed delegation, the precision of legal commitments may produce a focal point around which mobilized compliance constituencies can organize. This may be the principal effect of the environmental and labor side agreements under NAFTA. Under these agreements as well as regional human rights conventions, legalization strengthened transnational networks that mobilized in support of domestic compliance constituencies.[48]

In a democratic political setting, legalization may also have unexpected effects that undermine the domestic political balance between compliance constituencies and those who contest international commitments. Goldstein and Martin argue that legalization under the WTO may have exceeded its optimal level, given that member

---

44. Alter 1998b, 128.
45. F. Abbott, this issue.
46. Keohane, Slaughter, and Moravcsik, this issue.
47. See Alter, this issue; and Alter and Vargas 2000.
48. See F. Abbott, this issue; and Lutz and Sikkink, this issue.

governments must manage the demands of import-competing and exporting industries.[49] Increasing precision under the WTO offers more information to contending domestic interest groups. In some cases additional information may serve to strengthen protectionist (import-competing) interests, particularly in the negotiation stage of trade agreements. Exporters, the key compliance constituency, may gain greater political weight during the compliance phase of trade agreements, particularly if strategies of retaliation are carefully designed. In any case domestic free-trade coalitions may become more unpredictable and volatile. Goldstein and Martin also argue that a more legalized trade regime may change the "tool kit of policy options" available to elected officials who wish to make side payments to affected economic interests. Overall, they suggest a more contentious politics of compliance as one result of legalization. The prospective international gains that governments project from legalization may be offset by these domestic political consequences.

A final domestic consequence of international legalization may also affect compliance: shifts in decision-making authority that derive from a legalized agreement. One easy conclusion has too often been drawn from the European Union: legalized agreements improve compliance in rule-of-law societies through a shift in authority toward the judiciary. The European experience described by Alter, however, can hardly be viewed as a simple story of national courts as institutional compliance constituencies for European law. National courts have varied considerably in their willingness to collaborate with the ECJ by making references to the ECJ and enforcing European law. In particular, lower level courts and courts that are less entangled in national politics are more likely to refer a case or apply EU law. National courts may sometimes be barriers to effective compliance, in part because legalized international agreements may serve to marginalize them. NAFTA's panel procedures (together with the congressional actions already mentioned) served to substitute for parts of the national judiciary rather than deploying the judiciary to enforce the new trade rules. National courts may thwart international compliance by compelling litigation over enforcement measures. Less legalized administrative and market-based strategies may provide more effective enforcement results in such circumstances.[50]

Compliance with the international rules governing warfare demonstrates a complicated pattern that has depended on legalization's domestic consequences. Jeffrey Legro argues that the most complete explanation for compliance or noncompliance during World War II is the culture of military organizations, which predisposed them for or against the use of particular weapons.[51] Defining compliance as the avoidance by combatants of particular weapons during World War II narrows the explanation of compliance, however.[52]

---

49. Goldstein and Martin, this issue.

50. Mitchell's account of the discharge subregime in controlling oil pollution suggests that courts were reluctant to impose fines that would effectively deter illegal discharges; under the equipment subregime, administrative sanctions "skirted both flag state and port state legal systems—and the associated sensitivities regarding legal sovereignty." Mitchell 1994, 451.

51. Legro examines submarine warfare, strategic bombing, and chemical weapons. Legro 1995.

52. Although Legro's measurement of institutionalization differs from the concept of legalization used in this issue, his rankings of international restraints are roughly the same. Legro's claim regarding the

Organization of compliance constituencies for the rules of war is hampered by widespread deference to military expertise in waging war and by acceptance of the military monopoly on the use of force. Nevertheless, constraints on military force or weapons systems in World War II were shaped in part by anticipated political reactions to their development and use. The significant compliance constituencies were domestic publics (particularly in the United States and Britain) as well as the publics of key neutral states. For Britain and Germany, the key neutral state before December 1941 was the United States. Because of concern over American reaction to violations of rules on the use of particular weapons, some measure of American legalism was exported to the combatants.[53]

By discouraging development of certain weapons systems (particularly chemical weapons, where the ban on use was close to absolute), legalization served to shape organizational culture—why invest resources and craft doctrine for a weapon that was unlikely to be used? By inhibiting the development of capabilities, legal restraints served, in turn, to inhibit the use of certain weapons in wartime by creating concerns over relative preparedness and capabilities as compared to military foes.[54] Although restraints on the use of weapons systems during total war is perhaps the hardest case for legalization, compliance constituencies did have an impact, even in this harsh environment.

Norms and Legalization

The laws of war are one arena of legalization in which the interaction of norms and legal evolution is central. Lutz and Sikkink propose human rights and democracy in the Americas as another issue-area in which norms exhibit their own dynamic and influence on policy change. At first glance, growing respect for human rights in Latin America does not seem to be closely associated with the evolution of legal regimes. On the one hand, Latin American governments adopted legal commitments under UN and OAS human rights conventions just before authoritarian regimes took power in the 1970s and committed widespread human rights violations. On the other hand, contemporary patterns of compliance under democratic regimes fail to support a close relationship with legalization: although the prohibition against torture is the most legalized, with no derogations permitted under either customary international law or international covenants, torture persists (at reduced levels). Disappearances, the subject of much more recent legalized agreements, had virtually ended before legalization took place. Democracy, a barely legalized commitment, is, with the exception of Cuba, universal in the hemisphere.

---

superiority of an explanation based on organizational culture relies heavily on his coding of the chemical weapons ban, which he regards as less institutionalized than rules against unrestricted submarine warfare. If norms regarding chemical warfare are taken as stronger than Legro allows (predicting adherence), the superiority of the organizational culture explanation is greatly diminished. Using our definition of legalization, the two regimes appear very similar.

53. Even a politician such as Churchill, notably disdainful of restraints on warfare, noted the pressures from British public opinion. Legro 1995, 157–58.

54. See Price 1997, 109–11, 128; and Legro 1997, 53.

An alternative explanation for this pattern, advanced by Lutz and Sikkink, is a rapidly evolving regional and international normative consensus that was reinforced through both legal and nonlegal channels. This explanation has its own shortcomings, however. Most notably, the existence of a normative consensus is difficult to test outside the behavioral changes that are attributed to that emerging consensus. Few norms cascades in international relations are complete; nearly every widespread norm remains contested somewhere in the system. Although normative analysis identifies actors and processes, explanation too often appears to be post hoc. As norms become more deep-seated, the empirical difficulties do not end, since those norms are precisely the ones that are least likely to be explicitly invoked.[55]

In fact, the evolution of human rights practices in Latin America demonstrates an interaction between a building normative consensus, expressed by transnational human rights networks and enforced by powerful states, and legal commitments by states that were exploited strategically by other actors. One reason that legalization appears weaker in this story than in others is the rudimentary character of transnational dispute resolution in this issue-area. Although individuals (or groups) were the targets of human rights abuses, their access to legalized international institutions with delegated authority was highly restricted. In Latin America individuals has limited access to such institutions, but, in contrast to Western Europe, those institutions granting access had no enforcement powers against states. The Inter-American Court of Human Rights did possess such enforcement powers, but individuals could only seek redress through a lengthy process of petition; they had no standing before the court. This separation of access and enforcement in the legal regime prevented the development of powerful compliance constituencies within states, an unlikely possibility under repressive regimes in any case. Nevertheless, in the case of Uruguay, a citizenry schooled in the rule of law was able to publicize human rights violations through petitions to international institutions. In Honduras cases brought before the Inter-American Court of Human Rights reinforced the decline of disappearances. Compliance constituencies were necessarily external in large measure: transnational human rights networks that could supply publicity, resources, and pressure for enforcement through multilateral and bilateral channels.

Development of the ban on chemical weapons in this century demonstrates a similar evolution in which the uncertain status of an ultimately powerful norm was confirmed and reinforced by legalization. Richard Price notes the peculiarity of this norm: its absolute character and wide scope at an early stage.[56] It failed to prevent massive use of poison gas in World War I, however, and steps were taken toward legalization in the 1920s, rendering the ban more obligatory and precise. The power of the underlying norm overrode evidence from World War I that poison gas was not likely to be used against civilian populations as well as arguments that chemical weapons were more humane than many other military technologies.[57]

---

55. Price 1997, 104.
56. The following account is drawn from ibid.
57. Ibid., 96.

The norm against the use of chemical weapons shaped the content of legalized conventions, but neither norm nor conventions were able to ensure compliance. Throughout the century, sporadic violations (by Italy in the 1930s and Iraq in the 1980s) were met with minimal sanctions. Nevertheless, the absolute character of the ban was not contested, and legalization increased. Chemical weapons were never "conventionalized" in the preparations of any military force; instead, their possible use was seen as a "threshold of desperation."[58] The entry into force of the Chemical Weapons Convention in 1997 marked a significant increase in legalization of the ban, increasing both obligation and precision and delegating surveillance and enforcement to international agencies. Future violations of that convention will provide a test of the independent effects of legalization on compliance with a powerful international norm.

The cases of human rights and chemical weapons demonstrate the mutually reinforcing role that normative evolution and legalization can play. They intersect, as Abbott and Snidal suggest, in the realm of soft law, which often documents the status of an international norm at a particular point in time. Without at least modest legalization and the precision that it contributes, the content of norms is likely to remain contested for a longer period of time. In a large universe of state behaviors that might be subject to normative disapproval, legalization and its elevated obligation also helps to establish hierarchy, by highlighting those normative prohibitions that are regarded as particularly serious. Legalization also serves to attach the identity of "law abiding" (more valued in some societies than others) to those who observe particular norms.

Precision also can serve political purposes in mobilizing some who might be unconvinced by a purely normative argument. These compliance constituencies may extend beyond the usual legalization advocates. Particularly in societies comfortable with rule-of-law discourse, legalization serves to separate particular behaviors from "just politics." Victims of human rights abuses can be certified against accusations that they are "terrorists"; war criminals are designated as such, not simply as military men making tough decisions under fire. Those legalized designations and their precision carry political weight.

Finally, legalization serves to backstop normative evolution against retrogression. Norm cascades do not run in only one direction, as the uncertain history of both free trade and democracy in this century demonstrate. Norms that are encased in the heightened precision, obligation, and delegation associated with legalization are more likely to be secured. It seems unlikely, given the pressures of total war over the last century, that the chemical weapons ban could have survived and moved to its current level of legal development in the absence of earlier, oft-violated legal half-steps.

The interaction of international norms and legalization poses a dilemma for the normative or legal entrepreneur, however. One strategy reinforces a norm through harder legalization among a club of governments that share a normative consensus. A second strategy uses soft law to cast the normative net more widely, building as

58. Ibid., 136, 139–41.

broad a coalition as possible. Strengthening the normative consensus and possibly (but only possibly) the hardening of legal commitments is left to a more gradual process of learning. This dilemma resembles the competing paths to multilateralism described by Downs, Rocke, and Barsoom. They argue for the first strategy—one that builds deeper cooperation among a smaller group of countries first, and only then accepts new members.[59] Their logic may overlook the "network externalities" of norms, however, in which the value and strength of norms may grow with the numbers endorsing them.

Legalization: Spread and Retrenchment

Legalization may spread and harden or recede and soften over time for several reasons: a change in the resources or calculus of key actors, a change in the availability of institutional substitutes, the acceptance of legalized commitments by other governments, or an internal dynamic based on unanticipated consequences. Legalized institutions cannot be designed to encompass all future political circumstances. Institutions that were originally available to one set of actors with the required resources will later be open to other actors who avail themselves of the same resources. The United States and the European Union can now benefit disproportionately from legalized institutions because of their large legal resources. Over time, other governments are likely to use those institutions successfully, producing outcomes that may be less to the liking of the dominant powers. In legalized institutions with transnational dispute resolution, shifts in resources among domestic actors may have the same consequences.

The calculus of actors and their attitude toward legalization may change over time because of changes in the international environment and the perceived distributional consequences of legalization. If uncertainty raises the estimated costs of choosing legalized institutions, legalization may over time lower levels of perceived uncertainty, increasing the willingness to accept harder legal commitments. Legalization of the international trade regime has clearly lowered the probability of widespread trade wars, increasing the willingness of governments to accept additional constraints on their behavior.

Perceived distributional effects may reinforce or undermine legalization. Goldstein and Martin argue that distributional consequences of the trade regime become clearer as the regime becomes more legalized, creating domestic political reaction against liberalization. More directly, legalized systems may be seen as benefiting particular domestic and international interests and disadvantaging others, in part because of the availability of legal resources. As Alter points out, many of the benefits of contemporary legalization have flowed to those actors who support and benefit from international and regional economic integration.[60] For those who see the benefits of that integration as spread very widely, legalization is well worth any costs that

---

59. Downs, Rocke, and Barsoom 1998.
60. Alter, this issue.

it may impose on member governments. Much of the recent hostility toward legalized institutions such as the WTO is based on an alternative perception, however, that those benefits have been radically skewed, disadvantaging labor and environmental interests. Legalization under those circumstances simply confirms a bad distributional bargain.

International legalization is also subject to fluctuating demand based on the supply of institutional substitutes. Those substitutes may be domestic. Government credibility can be reinforced through domestic institutions (such as an independent judiciary or central bank) as well as through international means. The gold standard flourished without binding international obligations because domestic commitments were regarded as credible. In Asia, the availability of a legalized global trade institution, the WTO, has probably reduced demand for legalization at the regional level.

Governments appear to accept legalized commitments if other governments do so as well. In choosing to accept Article VIII obligations on current account transactions and in later compliance with those obligations, government actions are strongly influenced by the number of other states globally and regionally that have undertaken the same commitment and are complying with it.[61] Simmons suggests that this effect could be based on competition (an unwillingness to be disadvantaged in attracting trade and investment) or on socialization within a particular region. Whatever the explanation, this effect suggests a cascade similar to that posited for normative evolution, in which the probabilities for legalized commitments and compliance with them increase as numbers in the legalized club increase.

Many of the accounts of legalization in this special issue point to unanticipated domestic political consequences as an important dynamic in the expansion of legalization.[62] In certain cases governments choose legalized institutions in order to bind themselves or their successors. In other cases, however, governments have not foreseen the consequences of links between their own domestic politics and legalized international institutions. Authoritarian governments in Latin America, confident of their traditional role as gatekeeper between their societies and the international environment, were unprepared for a novel alignment between their own citizens, equipped with resources from transnational networks, and nascent legalized human rights institutions supported by foreign governments. The surprising (to European member governments) expansion of ECJ authority was based on the court's alignment with both national judiciaries and a "constituency of litigants" who valued the rulings of the ECJ and their access to those rulings.[63]

As Keohane, Moravcsik, and Slaughter argue, unanticipated political consequences are most likely when legalization is accompanied by high levels of delegation and, in particular, by transnational dispute resolution, which offers access to nonstate actors and drives litigation in unexpected directions. The inhibitions that states display in hardening and expanding legalization are not felt by individuals and

---

61. Simmons, this issue.

62. On the problems that unanticipated consequences pose for rational choice explanations, see Martin and Simmons 1998, 750–51.

63. Keohane, Moravcsik, and Slaughter, this issue.

corporations; the cases that individuals bring before the courts provide capital for those in the judiciary seeking to increase their influence.[64] High levels of embeddedness, in which means of enforcement are not in the hands of governments, make it much more difficult for governments to retreat from their legalized commitments when the consequences become clear.

The transnational dispute resolution model of reinforced legalization is far from automatic or irreversible, however. Many of the prerequisites for its expansion that can be found in the European legal system are unlikely to appear elsewhere. The preliminary ruling mechanism under Article 177 of the Treaty of Rome is a principal means for linking national courts with the ECJ. No other regional economic agreement has constructed such an institutional connection.[65] The U.S. Congress explicitly denied direct effect to NAFTA because of concerns over unanticipated legal consequences.[66] Alter describes the negative interactions that may arrest or halt legal expansion within this system of transnational dispute resolution. In a backlash against ECJ activism in the 1990s national governments used protocols and legislation to circumscribe ECJ rulings and explicitly excluded the ECJ from new areas of European Union power.[67] As Alter contends, "The ECJ's intermediaries are often fair weather friends," and they have also become open critics of the court.[68] Alter's account calls into question claims that transnational dispute resolution has "an inherently expansionary character."[69]

The Open Future of Legalization

The authors in this special issue demonstrate that legalization is an important feature of international collaboration at the century's end. Many of the contributors examine legalization's role in economic arrangements that proliferated and deepened in the 1980s and 1990s. Legalization has not been excluded from the domain of high politics, however. The Chemical Weapons Convention is a highly legalized treaty that attempts to prohibit a class of weapons that are among the most difficult to monitor. In contrast to the primarily intergovernmental character of the Chemical Weapons Convention process, the International Campaign to Ban Landmines produced an international convention banning another class of weapons through a radically transnational process in which national governments were relative latecomers. The establishment of international war crimes tribunals fifty years after the Nuremberg and Tokyo Tribunals is another sign of legalization in a sphere that had until recently been without significant delegation from states.

These striking examples should not obscure the ebb and flow of legalization over time, however, or the strong variation across issue-areas and regions that remains.

---

64. Ibid.
65. Alter 1998b, 145.
66. F. Abbott, this issue.
67. Alter, this issue.
68. Ibid.
69. Keohane, Moravcsik, and Slaughter, this issue.

Although economic integration in the past three decades has produced legalization in some issue-areas, the international monetary regime is less legalized than it was in 1970. Another global trend, democratization, has had mixed effects: empowering those who aim at greater international legalization across issue-areas but also creating hesitation in the face of the need to deal with political uncertainty in a flexible way. Demands for greater legalization from civil society conflict with the political need to retain policymaking discretion. Important regional variation in legalization remains: Europe and North America demonstrate the highest levels of international legalization with Latin America possibly taking a similar course. NAFTA and other regional free trade agreements show few signs of approaching the level of legalization incorporated in the European Union, however. Although access may grow for individuals and corporations in future economic agreements, there are few signs outside Europe of increased delegation or transnational dispute resolution in human rights or other important non-economic issue-areas.

The significance of legalization lies neither in its inevitability nor in its desirability in every international context. It remains but one institutional choice in world politics that a growing number of actors have grasped to advance their goals at the turn of the century. The authors of this special issue demonstrate that a rich research agenda surrounds that institutional choice. The agenda centers on the particular marriage of law and politics that legalization represents. The deeply political character of legalized institutions is powerfully and paradoxically reinforced in this special issue. Far from removing the politics from world politics, legalization embeds the relations between states in a particular political dynamic that is both international and domestic. To paraphrase E. H. Carr, legalized institutions offer a new meeting place for ethics and power among, as well as within, societies.

References

Abbott, Frederick M. 1990. GATT and the European Community: A Formula for Peaceful Coexistence. *Michigan Journal of International Law* 12 (1):1–58.

———. 1992a. Integration Without Institutions: The NAFTA Mutation of the EC Model and the Future of the GATT Regime. *American Journal of Comparative Law* 40:917–48.

———. 1992b. Regional Integration and the Environment: The Evolution of Legal Regimes. *Chicago-Kent Law Review* 68:173–201.

———. 1993a. NAFTA and the Future of United States—European Community Trade Relations: The Consequences of Asymmetry in an Emerging Era of Regionalism. *Hastings International and Comparative Law Review* 16: 489–526.

———. 1993b. Regional Integration Mechanisms in the Law of the United States: Starting Over. *Indiana Journal of Global Legal Studies* 1:155–184.

———. 1995a. *Law and Policy of Regional Integration: The NAFTA and Western Hemispheric Integration in the World Trade Organization System.* Dordrecht: Martinus Nijhoff/Kluwer.

———. 1995b. The Maastricht Judgment, the Democracy Principle, and U.S. Participation in Western Hemispheric Integration. In *German Yearbook of International Law 1994*, 137–61. Berlin: Duncker and Humbolt.

———. 1997a. The Intersection of Law and Trade in the WTO System: Economics and the Transition to a Hard Law System. In *Understanding Technical Barriers to Agricultural Trade*, edited by David Orden and Donna Roberts, 33–48. Minneapolis, Minn.: International Agricultural Trade Research Consortium.

———. 1997b. Foundation Building for Western Hemispheric Integration. *Northwestern Journal of International Law and Business* 17: 900–46.

———. 2000. The North American Integration Regime and Its Implications for the World Trading System. In *The EU, the WTO, and the NAFTA,* edited by J. H. H. Weiler, 171–99. Collected Courses of the Academy of European Law, vol. 10, bk. 2. Oxford: Oxford University Press.

Abbott, Kenneth W., and Duncan Snidal. 1997. The Many Faces of Legalization. Paper presented at the Conference on International Law and Domestic Politics, 4–7 June, St. Helena, Calif.

———. 1998. Why States Use Formal International Organizations. *Journal of Conflict Resolution* 42 (1):3–32.

———. 2000. International Standards and International Governance. Unpublished manuscript, University of Chicago, Chicago, Illinois.

Acharya, Amitav. 1998. Collective Identity and Conflict Management in Southeast Asia. In *Security Communities*, edited by Emanuel Adler and Michael Barnett, 198–227. Cambridge: Cambridge University Press.

———. 1999. Realism, Insitutionalism, and the Asian Economic Crisis. *Contemporary Southeast Asia* 21 (1):1–29.

Aggarwal, Vinod, Robert O. Keohane, and David Yoffie. 1987. The Dynamics of Negotiated Protection. *American Political Science Review* 81:345–66.

Alt, James, Jeffry Frieden, Michael Gilligan, Dani Rodrik, and Ronald Rogowski. 1996. The Political Economy of International Trade: Enduring Puzzles and an Agenda for Inquiry. *Comparative Political Studies* 29 (6):689–717.

Alter, Karen J. 1996a. The European Court's Political Power. *West European Politics* 19 (3):458–87.

———. 1996b. The Making of a Rule of Law: The European Court and the National Judiciaries. Ph.D. diss., Massachusetts Institute of Technology.

———. 1998a. Explaining National Court Acceptance of European Court Jurisprudence: A Critical Evaluation of Theories of Legal Integration. In *The European Court and National Court—Doctrine and Jurisprudence: Legal Change in Its Social Context*, edited by Anne-Marie Slaughter, Alec Stone Sweet, and J. H. H. Weiler, 227–52. Oxford: Hart Publishing.

———. 1998b. Who Are the Masters of the Treaty? European Governments and the European Court of Justice. *International Organization* 52 (1):121–47.

————. 2000. Regime Design Matters: Designing International Legal Systems for Maximum or Minimum Effectiveness. Paper presented at the 41st International Studies Association Conference, Los Angeles.

————. Forthcoming. *The Making of an International Rule of Law in Europe: The European Court of Justice and the National Judiciaries.* Oxford: Oxford University Press.

Alter, Karen J., and Jeannette Vargas. 2000. Explaining Variation in the Use of European Litigation Strategies: EC Law and UK Gender Equality Policy. *Comparative Political Studies* 33 (4):316–46.

Alvarez, Alejandro. 1943. *La Reconstrucción del Derecho de Gentes.* Santiago, Chile: Editorial Nascimento.

Americas Watch. 1986. *Paraguay: Latin America's Oldest Dictatorship Under Pressure.* New York: Americas Watch.

————. 1995. *Rule by Fear: Paraguay After Thirty Years Under Stroessner.* New York: Americas Watch.

Amnesty International. 1975. *Report on Torture.* New York: Farrar, Straus, and Giroux.

————. 1977a. *Deaths Under Torture and Disappearance of Political Prisoners in Paraguay.* New York: Amnesty International.

————. 1977b *Report of an Amnesty International Mission to Argentina.* London: Amnesty International.

————. 1981. *"Disappearances": A Workbook.* New York: AIUSA.

————. 1984. *Torture in the Eighties.* London: Amnesty International.

————. 1999. *Annual Report 1999.* London: Amnesty International.

APEC. 1998. Convenor's Summary Report on Dispute Mediation. Singapore: Asia-Pacific Economic Cooperation Secretariat. Available at <www.apecsec.org.sg/cti/cti98rpt2mins98a1_10.html>.

APEC Eminent Persons Group. 1993. A Vision for APEC: Towards An Asia Pacific Economic Community. Report of the Eminent Persons Group to APEC Ministers. Singapore: Asia-Pacific Economic Cooperation Secretariat.

————. 1994. Achieving the APEC Vision: Free and Open Trade in the Asia Pacific. Singapore: Asia-Pacific Economic Cooperation Secretariat.

————. 1995. Implementing the APEC Vision. Singapore: Asia-Pacific Economic Cooperation Secretariat.

Asamblea Permanente por los Derechos Humanos. 1988. Las Cifras de la Guerra Sucia. Buenos Aires: Asamblea Permanente por los Derechos Humanos.

ASEAN Regional Forum. 1999. Chaiman's Statement. The Sixth Meeting of the ASEAN Regional Forum. Singapore 26 July 1999. Available at <www.dfat.gov.au/arf/990799_arf_chairman.html>.

ASEAN Secretariat. 1997. *ASEAN Economic Co-operation: Transition and Transformation.* Singapore: Institute of Southeast Asian Studies.

Bailey, Michael, Judith Goldstein, and Barry Weingast. 1997. The Institutional Roots of American Trade Policy: Politics, Coalitions, and International Trade. *World Politics* 49 (3):309–38.

Baldwin, Robert. 1998. Imposing Multilateral Discipline on Administered Protection. In *The WTO as an International Organization,* edited by Anne Krueger, 297–327. Chicago: University of Chicago Press.

Ball, Carlos. 1996. The Making of a Transnational Capitalist Society: The Court of Justice, Social Policy, and Individual Rights Under the European Community's Legal Order. *Harvard International Law Journal* 37 (2):307–88.

Barahona de Brito, Alexandra. 1997. *Human Rights and Democratization in Latin America: Uruguay and Chile.* Oxford: Oxford University Press.

Barlow, Maude, and Bruce Campbell. 1993. *Take Back the Nation: Meeting the Threat of NAFTA.* Rev. ed. Toronto: Key Porter Books.

Barnard, Catherine. 1995. A European Litigation Strategy: The Case of the Equal Opportunities Commission. In *New Legal Dynamics of European Union,* edited by J. Shaw and G. More, 254–72. Oxford: Claredon Press.

Bass, Gary Jonathan. 1998. Judging War: The Politics of International War Crimes Tribunals. Ph.D. diss., Harvard. University.

Bassiouni, M. Cherif, compiler. 1998. *The Statute of the International Criminal Court: A Documentary History.* New York: Transnational Publishers.

Bassiouni, M. Cherif, ed. 1999. *International Criminal Law, Vols. I–III.* 2d ed. New York: Transnational Publishers.

Baxter, R. R. 1980. International Law in Her Infinite Variety. *International and Comparative Law Quarterly* 29:549–66.

Bebr, Gerard. 1981. *Development of Judicial Control of the European Communities*. The Hague: Martinus Nijhoff.

————. 1983. The Rambling Ghost of Cohn-Bendit: Acte Clair and the Court of Justice. *Common Market Law Reviews* 20:439–72.

Beck, Nathaniel, Jonathan Katz, and Richard Tucker. 1998. Taking Time Seriously: Time-Series Cross-Section Analysis with a Binary Dependent Variable. *American Journal of Political Science* 42 (4): 1260–88.

Bello, Judith Hippler. 1996. The WTO Dispute Settlement Understanding: Less Is More. *American Journal of International Law* 90: 416–18.

Bergsten, C. Fred. 1994. Sunrise in Seattle. *International Economic Insights* 5 (January–February):18–20.

Bermann, George A. 1998. Constitutional Implications of U.S. Participation in Regional Integration. *American Journal of Comparative Law* 46:463–79.

Bernard, Nicolas. 1996. The Future of European Economic Law in the Light of the Principle of Subsidiarity. *Common Market Law Review* 33:633–66.

Bernhardt, Rudolf. 1994. Human Rights and Judicial Review: The European Court of Human Rights. In *Human Rights and Judicial Review: A Comparative Perspective*, edited by David M. Beatty, 297–319. Dordrecht: Martinus Nijhoff.

Bilder, Richard B. 1981. *Managing the Risks of International Agreement*. Madison: University of Wisconsin Press.

Blankenburg, Erhard. 1996. Changes in Political Regimes and Continuity of the Rule of Law in Germany. In *Courts, Law, and Politics in Comparative Perspective*, edited by Herbert Jacob, Erhard Blankenburg, Herbert Kritzer, Doris Marie Provine, and Joseph Sanders, 249–316. New Haven, Conn.: Yale University Press.

Blom, Judith, Barry Fitzpatrick, Jeanne Gregory, Robert Knegt, and Ursula O'Hare. 1995. *The Utilisation of Sex Equality Litigation Procedures in the Member States of the European Community, a Comparative Study*. Brussels: Commission of the European Union, DG V.

Bodiguel, Jean-Luc. 1981. L'Ecole Nationale d'Administration et ses Implications sur la Haute Fonction Public. Ph.D. diss., Institute d'Etudes Politiques, Paris.

Boehlhoff, Klaus, and Axel Baumanns. 1989. Extra-Territorial Recognition of Exchange Control Regulations—A German Viewpoint. In *Adaptation and Renegotiation of Contracts in International Trade and Finance*, edited by Norbert Horn, 107–24. Boston: Kluwer.

Boisson de Chazournes, Laurence. 1998. Policy Guidance and Compliance Issues in Financial Activities: The World Bank Operational Standards. Paper prepared for meeting of American Society of International Law Project on Compliance with Soft Law, 8–10 October, Baltimore, Md.

Briggs, Herbert W. 1985. *Nicaragua v. United States:* Jurisdiction and Admissibility. *American Journal of International Law* 79:373–78.

Brownlie, Ian. 1984. The Expansion of International Society: The Consequences for the Law of Nations. In *The Expansion of International Society*, edited by Hedley Bull and Adam Watson, 357–70. Oxford: Clarendon Press.

Buira, Ariel. 1983. The Exchange Crisis and the Adjustment Program in Mexico. In *Prospects for Adjustment in Argentina, Brazil, and Mexico*, edited by John Williamson, 51–60. Washington, D.C.: Institute for International Economics.

Bull, Hedley. 1977. *The Anarchical Society: A Study of Order in World Politics*. New York: Columbia University Press.

Burley, Anne-Marie, and Walter Mattli. 1993. Europe Before the Court: A Political Theory of Legal Integration. *International Organization* 47 (1):41–76.

Buzan, Barry. 1993. From International System to International Society: Structural Realism and Regime Theory Meet the English School. *International Organization* 47:327–52.

Caporaso, James, and John Keeler. 1995. The European Union and Regional Integration Theory. In *The State of the European Union*, edited by Carolyn Rhodes and Sonia Mazey, 29–62. Boulder, Colo.: Lynne Rienner/Longmann.

Cappelletti, Mauro, and David Golay. 1986. The Judicial Branch in the Federal and Transnational Union: Its Impact on Integration. In *Methods, Tools, and Institutions: Political Organs, Integration Techniques, and Judicial Process*, edited by M. Cappelletti, M. Seccombe, and J. Weiler, 261–348. Berlin: Walter de Gruyter.

Carman, Gregory W. 1997. Resolution of Trade Disputes by Chapter 19 Panels: A Long-term Solution or Interim Procedure of Dubious Constitutionality. *Fordham International Law Journal* 21:1–11.

Carr, Edward Hallett. 1939. *The Twenty Years' Crisis 1919–1939*. London: The Macmillan Press, Ltd.

———. 1946. *The Twenty Years' Crisis, 1919–1939*. 2d ed. New York: Harper and Row.

Carter, Miguel. 1990. The Role of the Paraguayan Catholic Church in the Downfall of the Stroessner Regime. *Journal of Interamerican Studies and World Affairs* 32 (4):67–117.

Cassia, Paul, and Emmanuelle Saulnier. 1997. L'Imbroglio de la Banane. *Revue du Marché commun et de l'Union européene* (411):527–44.

Chalmers, Damian. 1997. Judicial Preferences and the Community Legal Order. *Modern Law Review* 60 (2):164–99.

———. 2000a. The Much Ado About Judicial Politics in the United Kingdom: A Statistical Analysis of Reported Decisions of United Kingdom Courts Invoking EU Law 1973–1998. Jean Monnet Working Paper. Cambridge, Mass.: Harvard University Law School.

———. 2000b. The Positioning of EU Judicial Politics Within the United Kingdom. *West European Politics* 23 (3).

Charney, Jonathan I. 1994. Progress in Maritime Boundary Delimitation Law. *American Journal of International Law* 88 (2):227–56.

———. 1999. The Impact on the International Legal System of the Growth of International Courts and Tribunals. *New York University Journal of International Law and Politics* 31 (4):697–708.

Chayes, Abram. 1965. A Common Lawyer Looks at International Law. *Harvard Law Review* 78 (7):1396–1413.

Chayes, Abram, and Antonia Handler Chayes. 1993. On Compliance. *International Organization* 47 (2):175–205.

———. 1995. *The New Sovereignty: Compliance with International Regulatory Agreements*. Cambridge, Mass.: Harvard University Press.

Cheng, Tun-jen. 1998. APEC and the Asian Financial Crisis: A Lost Opportunity for Institution-Building? *Asian Journal of Political Science* 6 (2):21–32.

Chia, Siow Yue. 1996. The Deepening and Widening of ASEAN. *Journal of the Asia Pacific Economy* 1 (1):59–78.

Chinkin, C. M. 1989. The Challenge of Soft Law: Development and Change in International Law. *International and Comparative Law Quarterly* 38:850–66.

Clark, Ann Marie. Forthcoming. *Diplomacy of Conscience: Amnesty International and Changing Human Rights Norms*. Princeton, N.J.: Princeton University Press.

Clarke, S. V. O. 1977. Exchange Stabilization in the Mid-1930s: Negotiating the Tripartite Agreement. Studies in International Finance, 41. Princeton, N.J.: International Financial Section, Princeton University.

Claude, Inis L. 1966. Collective Legitimation as a Political Function of the United Nations. *International Organization* 20 (3):367–79.

Claude, Richard P. 1992. The Case of Joelito Filártiga in the Courts. In *Human Rights in the World Community: Issues and Action*, 2d ed., edited by Richard Claude and Burns Weston, 328–39. Philadelphia: University of Pennsylvania Press.

Coase, Ronald. 1960. The Problem of Social Cost. *Journal of Law and Economics* 3:1–44.

Cohen, Benjamin J. 1998. *The Geography of Money*. Ithaca, N.Y.: Cornell University Press.

Colombatto, Enrico, and Jonathan R. Macey. 1996. A Public Choice Model of International Economic Cooperation and the Decline of the Nation State. *Cardozo Law Review* 18:925–56.

Conant, Lisa. 1998. Contained Justice: The Politics Behind Europe's Rule of Law. Ph.D. diss., University of Washington.

————. Forthcoming. Europeanization and the Courts: Variable Patterns of Adoption Among National Judiciaries. In *Europeanization and Domestic Structural Change*, edited by James Caporaso, Maria Green Cowles, and Thomas Risse. Ithaca, N.Y.: Cornell University Press.

Conseil d'Etat. 1992. Rapport Public.

Cottier, Thomas. 1992. Intellectual Property in International Trade Law and Policy: The GATT Connection. *Aussenwirtschaft* 1:79–105.

Covey, Russell Dean. 1996. Note: Adventures in the Zone of Twilight: Separation of Powers and National Economic Security in the Mexican Bailout. *Yale Law Journal* 105:1311–45.

Craig, P. P. 1998. Report on the United Kingdom: Constitutional Doctrine Within the United Kingdom: The Impact of the EC. In *The European Court and National Courts—Doctrine and Jurisprudence: Legal Change in Its Social Context*, edited by Anne-Marie Slaughter, Alec Stone Sweet, and J. H. H. Weiler, 195–224. Oxford: Hart Publishing.

Croome, John. 1995. *Reshaping the World Trading System: A History of the Uruguay Round*. Geneva: World Trade Organization.

Dam, Kenneth W. 1982. *The Rules of the Game*. Chicago: University of Chicago Press.

Dashwood, A., and A. Arnull. 1984. English Courts and Article 177 of the EEC Treaty. *Yearbook of European Law*:255–302.

Dashwood, Alan, and Robin White. 1989. Enforcement Actions Under Articles 169 and 170 EEC. *European Law Review* 14 (6):388–413.

Davey, William J. 1992. The Appointments Clause and International Dispute Settlement Mechanisms: A False Conflict. *Washington and Lee Law Review* 49:1315–28.

De Witte, Bruno. 1984. Retour à «Costa» La primauté du droit communautaire à la lumière du droit international. *Revue Trimestrielle du Droit Europèene* 20:425–54.

DeBoe, David C. 1974. Secretary Stimson and the Kellogg-Briand Pact. In *Essays on American Foreign Policy*, edited by Margaret F. Morris and Sandra L. Myres, 32–53. Austin: University of Texas Press.

Dehousse, Renaud. 1998. *The European Court of Justice*. New York: St. Martin's Press.

Denters, Erik. 1996. *Law and Policy of IMF Conditionality*. The Hague: Kluwer Law International.

Destler, I. M. 1995. *American Trade Politics*. 3d ed. Washington, D.C.: Institute for International Economics.

Destler, I. M., and John Odell. 1987. *Anti-Protection: Changing Forces in United States Trade Politics*. Washington, D.C.: Institute for International Economics.

Diebold, William Jr. 1952. The End of the ITO. Essays in International Finance, No. 16. Department of Economics and Social Institutions, Princeton University, Princeton, N.J.

Dixon, William J. 1993. Democracy and the Management of International Conflict. *Journal of Conflict Resolution* 37 (1):42–68.

Doner, Richard F. 1997. Japan in East Asia: Institutions and Regional Leadership. In *Network Power: Japan and Asia*, edited by Peter J. Katzenstein and Takashi Shiraishi, 197–233. Ithaca, N.Y.: Cornell University Press.

Donnelly, Jack. 1989. *Universal Human Rights in Theory and in Practice*. Ithaca, N.Y.: Cornell University Press.

Doremus, Paul. 1996. Externalization of Domestic Regulation: Intellectual Property Rights Reform in the Global Era. *Indiana Journal of Global Legal Studies* 3:341–74.

Downs, George W., and David M. Rocke. 1995. *Optimal Imperfection? Domestic Uncertainty and Institutions in International Relations*. Princeton, N.J.: Princeton University Press.

Downs, George W., David M. Rocke, and Peter N. Barsoom. 1996. Is the Good News About Compliance Good News About Cooperation? *International Organization* 50 (3):379–406.

————. 1998. Managing the Evolution of Multilateralism. *International Organization* 52 (2):397–419.

Doyle, Michael W. 1983a. Kant, Liberal Theories, and Foreign Affairs, Part 1. *Philosophy and Public Affairs* 12 (4):205–35.

————. 1983b. Kant, Liberal Theories, and Foreign Affairs, Part 2. *Philosophy and Public Affairs* 12 (4):323–53.

————. 1986. Liberalism and World Politics. *American Political Science Review* 80:1151–69.

Drzemczewski, Andrew Z. 1983. *European Human Rights Convention in Domestic Law: A Comparative Study*. Oxford: Oxford University Press.

Dursht, Kenneth A. 1997. From Containment to Cooperation: Collective Action and the Wassenaar Arrangement. *Cardozo Law Review* 19:1079–1123.

Edwards, Richard W., Jr. 1985. *International Monetary Collaboration*. Dobbs Ferry, N.Y.: Transnational Publishers.

Eichengreen, Barry. 1992. *Golden Fetters: The Gold Standard and the Great Depression, 1919–1939*. Oxford: Oxford University Press.

———. 1999. *Toward a New International Financial Architecture*. Washington, D.C.: Institute for International Economics.

Eichengreen, Barry, ed. 1985. *The Gold Standard in Theory and History*. New York: Methuen.

Eissa, Farouk Abu. 1998. Promotion of the Rule of Law in the Arab Region. *American Bar Association World Order Under Law Reporter* 5 (2):5.

Ellsberg, Daniel. 1963. Risk, Ambiguity, and the Savage Axioms. *Quarterly Journal of Economics* 75 (4):643–69.

Elster, Jon. 1989. Social Norms and Economic Theory. *Journal of Economic Perspectives* 3 (4):99–117.

Evans, John. 1971. *The Kennedy Round in American Trade Policy*. Cambridge, Mass.: Harvard University Press.

Everling, Ulrich. 1996. Will Europe Slip on Bananas? The Bananas Judgment of the European Court of Justice and National Courts. *Common Market Law Review* 33:401–37.

Farer, Tom J., ed. 1998. The Rise of the Inter-American Human Rights Regime: No Longer a Unicorn, Not Yet an Ox. In *The Inter-American System of Human Rights*, edited by David Harris and Stephen Livingstone, 31–64. Oxford: Clarendon.

Fasseur, Cornelis. 1992. Colonial Dilemma: Van Vollenhoven and the Struggle Between Adat Law and Western Law in Indonesia. In *European Expansion and Law*, edited by Wolfgang J. Mommsen and Jaap A. de Moor, 237–56. New York: Berg Publishers.

Fearon, James D. 1998. Bargaining, Enforcement, and International Cooperation. *International Organization* 52 (2):269–306.

Feldman, Mark B. 1986. Ted L. Stein on the Iran-U.S. Claims Tribunal—Scholarship Par Excellence. *Washington Law Review* 61 (3):997–1005.

Ferrell, Robert H. 1952. *Peace in Their Time: The Origins of the Kellogg-Briand Pact*. New Haven, Conn.: Yale University Press.

Finnemore, Martha. 1996. *National Interests in International Society*. Ithaca, N.Y.: Cornell University Press.

Finnemore, Martha, and Kathryn Sikkink. 1998. International Norm Dynamics and Political Change. *International Organization* 52 (4):887–917.

Fisher, Roger. 1981. *Improving Compliance with International Law*. Charlottesville: University of Virginia Press.

Fitzpatrick, Barry, Jeanne Gregory, and Erika Szyszczak. 1993. *Sex Equality Litigation in the Member States of the European Community: A Comparative Study*. Brussels: Commission of the European Union DG V.

Fix-Fierro, Hector, and Sergio Lopez-Ayllon. 1997. Communication Between Legal Cultures: The Case of NAFTA's Chapter 19 Binational Panels. Unpublished manuscript, Instituto de Investigaciones Juridicas de la Universidad Nacional Autonoma de Mexico, Mexico City.

Folsom, Ralph H. 1995. *European Union Law in a Nutshell*. 2d ed. St. Paul, Minn.: West Publishing.

Foot, Rosemary. 1998. China in the ASEAN Regional Forum. *Asian Survey* 38 (5):425–40.

Ford, A. G. 1985. Notes on the Working of the Gold Standard Before 1914. In *The Gold Standard in Theory and History*, edited by Barry Eichengreen, 141–65. New York: Methuen.

Forsythe, David. 1989. *Human Rights and World Politics*. 2d ed. Lincoln: University of Nebraska Press.

———. 1994. Politics and the International Tribunal for the Former Yugoslavia. *Criminal Law Forum* 5:401–22.

Franck, Thomas M. 1990. *Power of Legitimacy Among Nations*. New York: Oxford University Press.

————. 1992. The Emerging Right to Democratic Governance. *American Journal of International Law* 86:46–91.

————. 1995. *Fairness in International Law and Institutions.* New York: Oxford University Press.

Fried, Jonathan T. 1994. Two Paradigms for the Rule of International Trade Law. *Canada–U.S. Law Journal* 20: 39–56.

————. 1998. APEC as the Asia-Pacific Model for Regional Cooperation. In *China in the World Trade: Defining the Principles of Engagement,* edited by Frederick M. Abbott, 183–88. Cambridge, Mass.: Kluwer Law International.

Frieden, Jeffry A. 1991. Invested Interests: The Politics of National Economic Policies in a World of Global Finance. *International Organization* 45 (4):425–51.

Fuller, Lon L. 1964. *The Morality of Law.* New Haven, Conn.: Yale University Press.

Funabashi, Yoichi. 1995. *Asia Pacific Fusion: Japan's Role in APEC.* Washington, D.C.: Institute for International Economics.

Gal-Or, Noemi. 1998. Private Party Access: A Comparison of the NAFTA and EU Disciplines. *Boston College International and Comparative Law Review* 21:1–41.

Gamble, John King, Jr. 1985. The 1982 United Nations Convention on the Law of the Sea as Soft Law. *Houston Journal of International Law* 8:37–47.

Garofano, John. 1999. Flexibility or Irrelevance: Ways Forward for the ARF. *Contemporary Southeast Asia* 21 (1):74–94.

Garrett, Geoffrey. 1992. International Cooperation and Institutional Choice: The European Community's Internal Market. *International Organization* 46 (2):533–60.

————. 1995. The Politics of Legal Integration in the European Union. *International Organization* 49 (1):171–81.

Garrett, Geoffrey, and Barry Weingast. 1993. Ideas, Interests, and Institutions: Constructing the EC's Internal Market. In *Ideas and Foreign Policy: Beliefs, Institutions, and Political Change,* edited by Judith Goldstein and Robert O. Keohane, 173–206. Ithaca, N.Y.: Cornell University Press.

Garrett, Geoffrey, R. Daniel Kelemen, and Heiner Schulz. 1998. The European Court of Justice, National Governments, and Legal Integration in the European Union. *International Organization* 52 (1): 149–76.

Genevois, Bruno. 1989. Note. *Revue français du Droit administratif* 5 (5):824–33.

Gesser, Avi. 1998. Why NAFTA Violates the Canadian Constitution. *Denver Journal of International Law and Policy* 27:121–50.

Gillespie, Charles. 1991. *Negotiating Democracy: Politicians and Generals in Uruguay.* Cambridge: Cambridge University Press.

Gilligan, Michael J. 1997. *Empowering Exporters: Reciprocity, Delegation, and Collective Action in American Trade Policy.* Ann Arbor: University of Michigan Press.

Glendon, Mary Ann. 1991. *Rights Talk: The Impoverishment of Political Discourse.* New York: Free Press.

Glick, Leslie A. 1984. *Multilateral Trade Negotiations: World Trade After the Tokyo Round.* Totowa, N.J.: Rowman and Allanheld.

Gold, Joseph. 1965. *The International Monetary Fund and Private Business Transactions: Some Legal Effects of the Articles of Agreement.* Washington, D.C.: IMF.

————. 1979. *Legal and Institutional Aspects of the International Monetary System: Selected Essays.* Washington, D.C.: IMF.

————. 1980. The Rule of Law in the International Monetary Fund. IMF Pamphlet Series, 32. Washington, D.C.: IMF.

————. 1983. Strengthening the Soft International Law of Exchange Arrangements. *American Journal of International Law* 77:443–89.

————. 1984a. Public International Law in the International Monetary System. *Southwestern Law Journal* 38 (September):799–852.

————. 1984b. Legal Models for the International Regulation of Exchange Rates. *Michigan Law Review* 82 (April/May):1533–54.

————. 1988. *Exchange Rates in international Law and Organization.* Washington, D.C.: American Bar Association.

————. 1989. Article VIII, Section 2 (b) of the IMF Articles in Its International Setting. In *Adaptation and Renegotiation of Contracts in International Trade and Finance,* edited by Norbert Horn, 65–106. Boston: Kluwer.

Goldstein, Judith. 1993. *Ideas, Interests, and American Trade Policy.* Ithaca, N.Y.: Cornell University Press.

————. 1996. International Law and Domestic Institutions: Reconciling North American 'Unfair' Trade Laws. *International Organization* 50 (4):541–64.

Golub, Jonathan. 1996. The Politics of Judicial Discretion: Rethinking the Interaction Between National Courts and the European Court of Justice. *West European Politics* 19 (2):360–85.

Gong, Gerrit W. 1984. China's Entry into International Society. In *The Expansion of International Society,* edited by Hedley Bull and Adam Watson, 171–84. Oxford: Clarendon Press.

Goodman, John, Debra Spar, and David Yoffie. 1996. Foreign Direct Investment and the Demand for Protection in the United States. *International Organization* 50:565–91.

Green, Carl J. 1995. APEC and Trans-Pacific Dispute Management. *Law and Policy in International Business* 26 (3):719–34.

Gruchalla-Wesierski, Tadeusz. 1984. A Framework for Understanding Soft Law. *McGill Law Journal* 30:37–88.

Haas, Ernst B. 1958. *The Uniting of Europe: Political, Social, and Economic Forces, 1950–1957.* Stanford, Calif.: Stanford University Press.

————. 1975. *The Obsolescence of Regional Integration Theory.* Berkeley, Calif.: Institute of International Studies, University of California.

Haas, Peter M., ed. 1992. Knowledge, Power, and International Policy Coordination. *International Organization* 46 (1). Special issue.

Harding, Christopher. 1992. Who Goes to Court in Europe: An Analysis of Litigation Against the European Community. *European Law Review* 71(2):104–25.

Harlow, Carol. 1992. Toward a Theory of Access for the European Court of Justice. *Yearbook of European Law* 12:213–48.

————. 1996. "Francovich" and the Problem of the Disobedient State. EU Working Paper RSC 96/62. Robert Shuman Centre, European University Institute, Fiesole, Italy.

Harlow, Carol, and Richard Rawlings. 1992. *Pressure Through Law.* New York: Routledge.

Harris, Stuart. 1999. The Regional Response in Asia-Pacific and its Global Implications. Paper presented at the conference After the Global Crises: What Next for Regionalism, Warwick University, September.

Hart, H. L. A. 1961. *The Concept of Law.* Oxford: Clarendon Press.

Hart, Oliver. 1995. *Firms, Contracts, and Financial Structure.* Oxford: Oxford University Press.

Hartley, Trevor. 1994. *The Foundations of European Community Law.* 4th ed. Oxford: Clarendon Press.

Helfer, Laurence R. 1998. Adjudicating Copyright Claims Under the TRIPs Agreement: The Case for a European Human Rights Analogy. *Harvard International Law Journal* 39 (2):357–441.

Helfer, Laurence, and Anne-Marie Slaughter. 1997. Toward a Theory of Effective Supranational Adjudication. *Yale Law Journal* 107 (2):273–391.

Henkin, Louis. 1979. *How Nations Behave: Law and Foreign Policy.* 2d ed. New York: Council on Foreign Relations.

————. 1996. *Foreign Affairs and the United States Constitution.* 2d ed. Oxford: Oxford University Press.

Henkin, Louis, Gerald L. Neuman, Diane F. Orentlicher, and David W. Leebron. 1999. *Human Rights.* New York: Foundation Press.

Henkin, Louis, Richard Crawford Pugh, Oscar Schachter, and Hans Smit. 1993. *International Law.* 3d ed. St. Paul, Minn.: West Publishing.

Hillman, Jimmye S. 1997. Nontariff Agricultural Barriers Revisited. In *Understanding Technical Barriers to Agricultural Trade,* edited by David Orden and Donna Roberts, 1–32. Minneapolis, Minn.: International Agricultural Trade Research Consortium.

Hoang, Anh Tuan. 1996. ASEAN Dispute Management: Implications for Vietnam and an Expanded ASEAN. *Contemporary Southeast Asia* 18 (1):61–80.

Hobbs, Michael. 1990. Debt Policies for an Evolving Crisis. In *The Global Debt Crisis: Forecasting for the Future*, edited by Scott B. MacDonald, Margie Lindsay, and David L. Crum, 185–219. London: Pinter.

Hooker, M. B. 1978. *A Concise Legal History of South-East Asia*. Oxford: Clarendon Press.

Horn, Norbert. 1985. The Crisis of International Lending and Legal Aspects of Crisis Management. In *Adaptation and Renegotiation of Contracts in International Trade and Finance*, edited by Norbert Horn. Boston: Kluwer.

Horsefield, John Keith, and Margaret Garritsen de Vries. 1969. *The International Monetary Fund, 1945–1965: Twenty Years of International Monetary Cooperation*. 3 vol. Washington, D.C.: IMF.

Hudec, Robert E. 1992. The Judicialization of GATT Dispute Settlement. In *In Whose Interest? Due Process and Transparency in International Trade*, edited by Michael M. Hart and Debra P. Steger, 9–43. Ottowa, Ont.: The Centre for Trade Policy and Law.

———. 1993. *Enforcing International Trade Law: The Evolution of the Modern GATT Legal System*. Salem, N.H.: Butterworth Legal Publishers.

———. 1999. The New WTO Dispute Settlement Procedure. *Minnesota Journal of Global Trade* 8 (1): 1–53.

Hufbauer, Gary Clyde, and Jeffrey J. Schott. 1993. *NAFTA: An Assessment*. Washington, D.C.: Institute for International Economics.

Human Rights Watch/Americas Watch. 1994. *The Facts Speak for Themselves: The Preliminary Report on Disappearances of the National Commissioner for the Protection of Human Rights in Honduras*. English trans. by Human Rights Watch/Americas and the Center for Justice and International Law. Washington, D.C. Human Rights Watch/Americas Watch.

Hurrell, Andrew. 1993. International Society and the Study of Regimes: A Reflective Approach. In *Regime Theory and International Relations*, edited by Volker Rittberger, 49–72. Oxford: Oxford University Press.

Hurtig, Mel 1992. *The Betrayal of Canada*. 2d ed. Toronto: Stoddart.

Inter-American Commission on Human Rights. 1978. Report on the Situation of Human Rights in Uruguay. OEA/Ser.L/Z/II.43. Washington, D.C.: OAS.

———. 1979. Annual Report of the Inter-American Commission on Human Rights 1978. OEA/Ser.L/V/II.47, Doc. 13, Rev. 1. Washington, D.C.: OAS.

International Country Risk Guide. Database. Available at <http://prsgroup.com/.crg/icrg.html>.

International Monetary Fund (IMF). Various years. *Exchange Arrangements and Restrictions*. Washington, D.C.: IMF.

———. 1974. *Annual Report*. Washington D.C.: IMF.

Jackson, John H. 1989. *The World Trading System*. Cambridge, Mass.: MIT Press.

———. 1992. The Status of International Treaties in Domestic Legal Systems: A Policy Analysis. *American Journal of International Law* 86 (2):310–29.

———. 1997. Editorial Comment: The WTO Dispute Settlement Understanding—Misunderstandings on the Nature of Legal Obligation. *American Journal of International Law* 91: 60–64.

———. 1998. *The World Trade Organization: Constitution and Jurisprudence*. London: Royal Institute for International Affairs.

Jackson, John H., and William J. Davey. 1986. Legal Rules or Government Discretion—Which Rule Is Best? In *Legal Problems of International Economic Relations*, edited by John H. Jackson and William J. Davey, 1220–41. St. Paul, Minn.: West Publishing.

Jackson, John H., Jean-Victor Louis, and Mitsuo Matsushita. 1984. *Implementing the Tokyo Round: National Constitutions and International Economic Rules*. Ann Arbor: University of Michigan Press.

Jaggers, Keith, and Ted Robert Gurr. 1995. Tracking Democracy's Third Wave with the Polity III Data. *Journal of Peace Research* 32 (4):469–82.

James, Harold. 1995. The Historical Development of the Principle of Surveillance. *International Monetary Fund Staff Papers* 42 (4):762–91.

Janow, Merit E. 1996/1997. Assessing APEC's Role in Economic Integration in the Asia-Pacific Region. *Northwestern Journal of International Law and Business* 17 (2–3):947–1013.

Jarmul, Holly Dawn. 1996. Effects of Decisions of Regional Human Rights Tribunals on National Courts. In *International Law Decisions in National Courts,* edited by Thomas M. Franck and Gregory H. Fox, 247–84. Irvington-on-Hudson, N.Y.: Transnational Publishers.

Johnson, Kevin R. 1994. Free Trade and Closed Borders: NAFTA and Mexican Immigration to the United States. *University of California at Davis Law Review* 27: 937–78.

Johnston, Alastair Iain. 1999. The Myth of the ASEAN Way? Explaining the Evolution of the ASEAN Regional Forum. In *Imperfect Unions: Security Institutions over Time and Space,* edited by Helga Haftendorn, Robert O. Keohane, and Celeste A. Wallander, 287–324. Oxford: Oxford University Press.

Josling, Tim. 1999. The Agricultural Negotiations: An Overflowing Agenda. Paper prepared for the 24th Annual Economic Policy Conference of the Federal Reserve Bank of St. Louis, "Multilateral Trade Negotiations: Issues for the Millennium Round," St. Louis, 21–22 October.

Kahler, Miles. 1988. Organizing the Pacific. In *Pacific-Asian Economic Policies and Regional Interdependence,* edited by Robert A. Scalapino, Seizaburo Sato, Jusuf Wanandi, and Sung-joo Han, 329–50. Berkeley: Institute of East Asian Studies.

Kaplan, Morton A. 1957. *System and Process in International Politics.* New York: Wiley.

Katzenstein, Peter J. 1997. Introduction: Asian Regionalism in Comparative Perspective. In *Network Power: Japan and Asia,* edited by Peter J. Katzenstein and Takashi Shiraishi, 1–46. Ithaca, N.Y.: Cornell University Press.

Katzenstein, Peter J., Robert O. Keohane, and Stephen D. Krasner. 1998. International Organization and the Study of World Politics. *International Organization* 52 (4):645–86.

Keck, Margaret E., and Kathryn Sikkink. 1998. *Activists Beyond Borders: Advocacy Networks in International Politics.* Ithaca, N.Y.: Cornell University Press.

Keech, William R. 1995. *Economic Politics: The Costs of Democracy.* Cambridge: Cambridge University Press.

Keesing, Donald B. 1998. *Improving Trade Policy Reviews in the World Trade Organization.* Washington, D.C.: Institute for International Economics.

Kegley, C. W., Jr., and Gregory Raymond. 1981. International Legal Norms and the Preservation of Peace, 1820–1964: Some Evidence and Bi-Variate Relationships. *International Interactions* 8 (3):171–87.

Kellermann, A. E., W. M. Levelt-Overmars, and F. H. M. Posser. 1990. Primus Inter Pares: The European Court and National Courts: The Follow-up by National Courts of Preliminary Ruling ex. Art. 177 of the Treaty of Rome: A Report on the Situation in the Netherlands. European University Working Paper. Fiesole: European University Institute.

Kellman, Barry. 1998. Protection of Nuclear Materials. Paper prepared for meeting of American Society of Law Project on Compliance with Soft Law, 8–10 October, Baltimore, Md.

Kennan, George F. 1984. *Diplomacy in the Modern World.* Chicago: University of Chicago Press.

Kennedy, Duncan. 1976. Form and Substance in Private Law Adjudication. *Harvard Law Review* 89:1685–1778.

Kennish, Tim. 1995. NAFTA and Investment—A Canadian Perspective. In *NAFTA and Investment,* edited by Seymour J. Rubin and Dean C. Alexander, 1–35. The Hague: Kluwer Law International.

Keohane, Robert O. 1984. *After Hegemony: Cooperation and Discord in the World Political Economy.* Princeton, N.J.: Princeton University Press.

———. 1986. Reciprocity in International Relations. *International Organization* 40 (1):1–27.

———. 1988. International Institutions: Two Approaches. *International Studies Quarterly* 32:379–96.

———. 1995. Contested Commitments and Commitment Pathways: United States Foreign Policy, 1783–1989. Paper presented at annual meeting of International Studies Association, 21–25 February, Chicago.

Keohane, Robert O., and Lisa L. Martin. 1999. Institutional Theory, Endogeneity, and Delegation. Working Paper Series 99–07. Cambridge, Mass.: Weatherhead Center for International Affairs, Harvard University.

Keohane, Robert O., and Joseph S. Nye, Jr. 1977. *Power and Interdependence: World Politics in Transition.* Boston: Little, Brown.

Keohane, Robert O., Andrew Moravcsik, and Anne-Marie Slaughter. 1997. Toward a Theory of Legalization. Paper presented at the Conference on International Law and Domestic Politics, 4–7 June, St. Helena, Calif.

Keohane, Robert O., and Stanley Hoffmann, eds. 1991. *The New European Community: Decision-Making and Institutional Change.* Boulder, Colo.: Westview Press.

Kessler, Marie-Christine. 1986. *Le Grand Cour d'Etat.* Paris: Presses de la Fondation Nationale des Sciences Politique.

Khong, Yuen Foong. 1997. Making Bricks Without Straw in the Asia Pacific? *The Pacific Review* 10 (2):289–300.

———. 1998. ASEAN and the Southeast Asian Security Complex. In *Regional Orders: Building Security in a New World,* edited by David A. Lake and Patrick M. Morgan, 318–42. University Park: Pennsylvania State University Press.

Kindleberger, Charles P. 1986. *The World in Depression, 1929–1939.* Rev. ed. Berkeley: University of California Press.

Klotz, Audie. 1995. *Norms in International Relations: The Struggle Against Apartheid.* Ithaca, N.Y.: Cornell University Press.

Knack, Stephen, and Philip Keefer. 1995. Institutions and Economic Performance: Cross Country Tests Using Alternative Institutional Measures. *Economics and Politics* 7 (3):207–27.

Knight, Frank H. 1921. *Risk, Uncertainty, and Profit.* Boston: Houghton Mifflin.

Knox, John H. 1999. Finding a Role for Supranational Adjudication in International Environmental Law: The Submissions Procedure of the Commission for Environmental Cooperation. Unpublished manuscript, Dickenson School of Law, Pennsylvania State University, Carlisle, Pa.

Koh, Harold Hongju. 1996. Transnational Legal Process. *Nebraska Law Review* 75:181–207.

———. 1997. Why Do Nations Obey International Law? *Yale Law Journal* 106:2598–2659.

———. 1998. Bringing International Law Home. *Houston Law Review* 35 (3):623–82.

Kokott, Juliane. 1998. Report on Germany. In *The European Courts and National Courts,* edited by Anne-Marie Slaughter, Alec Stone-Sweet, and J. H. H. Weiler, 77–131. Cambridge, Mass.: Hart Publishing.

Koremenos, Barbara. 1999. On the Duration and Renegotiation of International Agreements. Ph.D. diss., University of Chicago.

Koskenniemi, Martti. 1999. Letter to the Editors of the Symposium (Symposium on Method in International Law). *American Journal of International Law* 93:351–61.

Krasner, Stephen D. 1999. *Sovereignty: Organized Hypocrisy.* Princeton, N.J.: Princeton University Press.

Krasner, Stephen D., ed. 1983. *International Regimes.* Ithaca, N.Y.: Cornell University Press.

Kratochwil, Friedrich V. 1989. *Rules, Norms, and Decisions.* Cambridge: Cambridge University Press.

Kratochwil, Friedrich V, and John Gerard Ruggie. 1986. International Organization: A State of the Art on an Art of State. *International Organization* 40 (4):753–75.

Krause, Lawrence B. 1994. The Pacific Century: Myth or Reality? The 1994 Panglaykim Memorial Lecture, 29 September, Jakarta.

———. 1997. The Progress to Date and Agenda for the Future: A Summary. In *Whither APEC? The Progress to Date and Agenda for the Future,* edited by C. Fred Bergsten, 241–46. Washington, D. C.: Institute for International Economics.

Krueger, Anne. 1998. *The WTO as an International Organization.* Chicago: University of Chicago Press.

Lauren, Paul Gordon. 1998. *The Evolution of International Human Rights: Visions Seen.* Philadelphia: University of Pennsylvania Press.

Legro, Jeffrey W. 1995. *Cooperation Under Fire: Anglo-German Restraint During World War II.* Ithaca, N.Y.: Cornell University Press.

———. 1997. Which Norms Matter? Revisiting the 'Failure' of Internationalism. *International Organization* 51 (1):31–63.

Leifer, Michael. 1989. *ASEAN and the Security of Southeast Asia.* London: Routledge.

———. 1996. *The ASEAN Regional Forum: Extending ASEAN's Model of Regional Security.* London: International Institute of Strategic Studies.

Lessig, Lawrence. 1995. The Regulation of Social Meaning. *University of Chicago Law Review* 62 (3): 968–73.

Lev, Daniel S. 1972. *Islamic Courts in Indonesia: A Study in the Political Bases of Legal Institutions.* Berkeley: University of California Press.

Levi, Margaret. 1997. *Consent, Dissent, and Patriotism.* Cambridge: Cambridge University Press.

Levi, Werner. 1976. *Law and Politics in the International Society.* Beverly Hills, Calif.: Sage Publications.

Lillich, Richard B., and Charles N. Brower, eds. 1994. *International Arbitration in the 21st Century: Toward Judicalization and Uniformity?* New York: Transaction Publishers.

Lindblom, Charles E. 1977. *Politics and Markets: The World's Political-Economic Systems.* New York: Basic Books.

Lipson, Charles. 1991. Why Are Some International Agreements Informal? *International Organization* 45 (4):495–538.

Lohmann, Susanne, and Sharyn O'Halloran. 1994. Divided Government and U.S. Trade Policy: Theory and Evidence. *International Organization* 48 (4):595–632.

Long, Olivier. 1985. *Law and Its Limitations in the GATT Multilateral Trading System.* Dordrecht: Martinus Nijhoff.

Loschak, Daniele. 1972. *Le role politique du judge administratif Français.* Paris: Librarie générale de droit et de jurisprudence.

Lowenfeld, Andreas F. 1996. Agora: The Cuban Liberty and Democratic Solidarity (Libertad) Act, Congress, and Cuba: The Helms-Burton Act. *American Journal of International Law* 90: 419–34.

Luchaire, François. 1991. Le Conseil constitutionnel et la souveraineté nationale. *Revue du droit public* II:1449–1513.

Lumsdaine, David Halloran. 1993. *Moral Vision in International Politics: The Foreign Aid Regime, 1949–1989.* Princeton, N.J.: Princeton University Press.

Lutz, Robert E., and Russell C. Trice. 1998. NAFTA at Five and the Loewen Case: Is NAFTA the Blood Relative of Lady Justice or the Angel of Death for State Sovereignty? *Translex* 2:1–5.

Macdermot, Niall. 1981. Uruguay in the International Organizations for the Protection of Human Rights. Colloquium on the Policy of Institutionalization of the State of Exception and Its Rejection by the Uruguayan People. Geneva.

Magee, Stephen P., William A. Brock, and Leslie Young. 1989. *Black Hole Tariffs and Endogenous Policy Theory.* New York: Cambridge University Press.

Mancini, Federico, and David Keeling. 1992. From CILFIT to ERT: The Constitutional Challenge Facing the European Court. *Yearbook of European Law* 11:1–13.

Maresca, John J. 1985. *To Helsinki: The Conference on Security and Cooperation in Europe 1973–75.* Durham, N.C.: Duke University Press.

Marreese, Michael. 1986. CMEA: Effective but Cumbersome Political Economy. *International Organization* 40 (2):287–328.

Martin, Lisa L., and Beth A. Simmons. 1998. Theories and Empirical Studies of International Institutions. *International Organization* 52 (4):729–57.

Mattli, Walter, and Anne-Marie Slaughter. 1995. Law and Politics in the European Union: A Reply to Garrett. *International Organization* 49 (1):183–90.

———. 1998a. The Role of National Courts in the Process of European Integration: Accounting for Judicial Preferences and Constraints. *The European Court and National Courts—Doctrine and Jurisprudence: Legal Change in Its Social Context*, edited by Anne-Marie Slaughter, Alec Stone Sweet, and J. H. H. Weiler, 77–131. Oxford: Hart Publishing.

———. 1998b. Revisiting the European Court of Justice. *International Organization* 52 (1):177–209.

Maupain, Francis. 1998. Compliance with International Human Rights Soft Law: The Case of International Labour Recommendations and Similar Instruments. Paper prepared for meeting of American Society of International Law Project on Compliance with Soft Law, 8–10 October, Baltimore, Md.

Mayer, Wolfgang. 1984. Endogenous Tariff Formation. *American Economic Review* 74:970–85.

Mazey, Sonia. 1998. The European Union and Women's Rights: From the Europeanization of National Agendas to the Nationalization of a European Agenda? *Journal of European Public Policy* 5 (1): 131–52.

McCann, Michael. 1994. *Rights at Work: Pay Equity Reform and the Politics of Legal Mobilization.* Chicago: University of Chicago Press.

McGivern, Brendan P. 1996. The WTO and Developing Asian Economies: Special Provisions for Dispute Resolution and Emerging Paradigms Within APEC. In *The Asia-Pacific Region and the Expanding Borders of the WTO: Implications, Challenges, and Opportunities*, edited by Mark A. Buchanan, 94–107. Victoria, B.C.: Centre for Asia-Pacific Initiatives.

McKeown, Timothy J. 1984. Firms and Tariff Regime Change: Explaining the Demand for Protection. *World Politics* 36:215–33.

Medina Quiroga, Cecilia. 1990. The Inter-American Commission on Human Rights and the Inter-American Court of Human Rights: Reflections on a Joint Venture. *Human Rights Quarterly* 12 (4): 439–64.

Meier, Gert. 1994. Der Streit um die Umsatzausgleichsteuer aus integrationspolitischer Sicht. *Recht der Internationalen Wirtschaft* 3/94.

Mekouar, Mohamed Ali. 1998. FAO/UNEP Non-Legally-Binding Instruments on Pesticides and Chemicals: The Requirement of Prior Informed Consent. Draft paper prepared for meeting of American Society of International Law Project on Compliance with Soft Law, 8–10 October, Baltimore, Md.

Mendez, Juan E., and Jose Miguel Vivanco. 1990. Disappearances and the Inter-American Court: Reflections on a Litigation Experience. *Hamline Law Review* 13: 507–77.

Mignone, Emilio F. 1991. *Derechos Humanos y Sociedad: El Caso Argentino.* Buenos Aires: Centro de Estudios Legales y Sociales y Ediciones del Pensamiento Nacional.

Milner, Helen V. 1988. *Resisting Protectionism: Global Industries and the Politics of International Trade.* Princeton, N.J.: Princeton University Press.

Mitchell, Ronald B. 1994. Regime Design Matters: Intentional Oil Pollution and Treaty Compliance. *International Organization* 48 (3):425–58.

Morales, Isidro. 1997. Confidence Building and Dispute Resolution under NAFTA. Assessing the Impact of Trade Regimes in the Deepening of Integration. Unpublished manuscript, University of the Americas, Puebla.

Moravcsik, Andrew. 1995. Explaining International Human Rights Regimes: Liberal Theory and Western Europe. *European Journal of International Relations* 1 (2):157–89.

———. 1997. Taking Preferences Seriously: A Liberal Theory of International Politics. *International Organization* 51 (4):513–53.

———. 2000. The Origin of International Human Rights Regimes: Democratic Delegation in Postwar Europe. *International Organization* 54 (2): 217–52.

Morris, Virginia, and Michael P. Scharf. 1995. *An Insider's Guide to the International Criminal Tribunal for the Former Yugoslavia: A Documentary History and Analysis.* Irvington-on-Hudson, U.K.: Transnational Publishers.

———. 1998. *The International Criminal Tribunal for Rwanda.* Irvington-on-Hudson, U.K.: Transnational Publishers.

Morrow, James D. 1994. Modeling the Forms of International Cooperation: Distribution Versus Information. *International Organization* 48 (3):387–423.

———. 1997. The Laws of War as an International Institution. Paper presented at Program on International Politics, Economics, and Security, February, University of Chicago.

———. 1998. The Institutional Features of the Prisoner of War Treaties. Paper presented at the Conference on Rational International Institutions, April, University of Chicago.

Mukerji, Sujoy. 1998. Ambiguity Aversion and the Incompleteness of Contractual Form. *American Economic Review* 88 (5):1207–31.

Nadal, Alejandro. 1997. Mexico: Open Economy, Closed Options: The Making of a Vulnerable Economy. In *Joining Together, Standing Apart: National Identities After NAFTA*, edited by Dorinda G. Dallmeyer, 35–62. The Hague: Kluwer Law International.

Noyes, John E. 1998. The International Tribunal for the Law of the Sea. *Cornell International Law Review* 32:109–82.

Ostry, Sylvia. 1998. APEC and Regime Creation in the Asia-Pacific: The OECD Model? In *Asia-Pacific Crossroads: Regime Creation and the Future of APEC*, edited by Vinod K. Aggarwal and Charles E. Morrison, 317–50. New York: St. Martin's.

Palmer, David Scott. 1996. Collectively Defending Democracy in the Western Hemisphere. In *Beyond Sovereignty: Collectively Defending Democracy in the Americas*, edited by Tom Farer. Baltimore, Md.: Johns Hopkins University Press.

Palmer, Geoffrey. 1992. New Ways to Make International Environmental Law. *American Journal of International Law* 86:259–83.

Pan, Eric J. 1999. Assessing the NAFTA Chapter 19 Binational Panel System: An Experiment in International Adjudication. *Harvard International Law Journal* 40 (2):379–449.

Pellet, Alain. 1998. The Conseil Constitutionnel, la souveraineté et les traités. *Cahier de Conseil Constitutionnel* 4 (second semester).

Pescatore, Pierre. 1981. Les Travaux du <Groupe Juridique> Dans la négociation des Traités de Rome. *Studia Diplomatica (Chronique de Politique Etrangère)* 34 (1–4):159–78.

Petersmann, Ernst-Ulrich. 1991. *Constitutional Functions and Constitutional Problems of International Economic Law*. London: Kluwer Law International.

Petersmann, Ernst-Ulrich, and Meinhard Hilf, eds. 1988. *The New GATT Round of Multilateral Trade Negotiations*. London: Kluwer Law International.

Petri, Peter A. 1997. Measuring and Comparing Progress in APEC. In *Whither APEC? The Progress to Date and Agenda for the Future*, edited by C. Fred Bergsten, 41–59. Washington, D.C.: Institute for International Economics.

Philip, George. 1985. Mexico: Learning to Live with the Crisis. In *Latin America and the World Recession*, edited by Esperanza Durán, 81. Cambridge: Cambridge University Press.

Picker, Randal. 1997. Simple Games in a Complex World: A Generative Approach to the Adoption of Norms. *University of Chicago Law Review* 64:1225–88.

Plötner, Jens. 1998. Report on France: The Reception of the Direct Effect and Supremacy Doctrine by the French Supreme Courts. In *The European Court and National Courts—Doctrine and Jurisprudence: Legal Change in Its Social Context*, edited by Anne-Marie Slaughter, Alec Stone Sweet, and J. H. H. Weiler, 41–75. Oxford: Hart Publishing.

Plummer, Michael G. 1998. ASEAN and Institutional Nesting in the Asia-Pacific: Leading from Behind in APEC. In *Asia-Pacific Crossroads: Regime Creation and the Future of APEC*, edited by Vinod K. Aggarwal and Charles E. Morrison, 279–316. New York: St. Martin's.

Pollack, Mark. 1997. Delegation, Agency, and Agenda Setting in the European Community. *International Organization* 51: (1):99–134.

Price, Richard M. 1997. *The Chemical Weapons Taboo*. Ithaca, N.Y.: Cornell University Press.

Ramos Uriarte, Jorge Luis. 1995. Foreign Investment in Mexico Under NAFTA. In *NAFTA and Investment*, edited by Seymour J. Rubin and Dean C. Alexander, 85–110. The Hague: Kluwer Law International.

Ramseyer, J. Mark, and Frances McCall Rosenbluth. 1997. *Japan's Political Marketplace*. Cambridge, Mass.: Harvard University Press.

Rasmussen, Hjalte. 1986. *On Law and Policy in the European Court of Justice*. Dordrecht: Martinus Nijhoff.

Ratner, Steven R. 2000. Does International Law Matter in Preventing Ethnic Conflict? *New York University Journal of International Law and Politics* 32:591–698.

Ratner, Steven R., and Jason S. Abrams. 1997. *Accountability for Human Rights Atrocities in International Law: Beyond the Nuremberg Legacy*. Oxford: Clarendon Press.

Raustiala, Kal. 1996. International Enforcement of Enforcement Under the North American Agreement on Environmental Cooperation. *Virginia Journal of International Law* 36 (3):721–63.

———. 1997. The Participatory Revolution in International Environmental Law. *Harvard Environmental Law Review* 21:537–86.

Ravenhill, John. 1995. Economic Cooperation in Southeast Asia: Changing Incentives. *Asian Survey* 25 (9):850–66.

————. 1998. Australia and APEC. In *Asia-Pacific Crossroads: Regime Creation and the Future of APEC*, edited by Vinod K. Aggarwal and Charles E. Morrison, 143–64. New York: St. Martin's.

Raymond, Gregory. 1994. Democracies, Disputes, and Third-Party Intermediaries. *Journal of Conflict Resolution* 38 (1):24–42.

Reich, Norbert. 1996. Judge-Made "Europe a la carte": Some Remarks on Recent Conflicts Between European and German Constitutional Law Provoked by the Banana Litigation. *European Journal of International Law* 7:103–11.

Reinhardt, Eric. 1995. Efficiency and Distribution in GATT Dispute Outcomes: A Statistical Study. Paper presented at the Annual Meeting of the American Political Science Association, Chicago, 31 August–3 September.

Reisman, W. Michael. 1988. Remarks. *Proceedings of the 82nd Annual Meeting of the American Society of International Law* 82:373–377.

Richards, John E. 1999. Toward a Positive Theory of International Institutions: Regulating International Aviation Markets. *International Organization* 53 (1):1–37.

Riesenfeld, Stefan A. 1974. Legal Systems of Regional Economic Integration. *American Journal of Comparative Law* 22:415–43.

Riesenfeld, Stefan A., and Frederick M. Abbott. 1994a. Foreword. In *Parliamentary Participation in the Making and Operation of Treaties: A Comparative Study*, edited by Stefan A. Riesenfeld and Frederick M. Abbott, 1–18. Dordrecht: Martinus Nijhoff.

————. 1994b. The Scope of U.S. Senate Control over the Conclusion and Operation of Treaties. In *Parliamentary Participation in the Making and Operation of Treaties*, edited by Stefan A. Riesenfeld and Frederick M. Abbott, 261–327. Dordrecht: Martinus Nijhoff.

Risse, Thomas, Stephen Ropp, and Kathryn Sikkink, eds. 1999. *The Power of Human Rights: International Norms and Domestic Change*. Cambridge: Cambridge University Press.

Risse-Kappen, Thomas 1995a. *Bringing Transnational Relations Back In: Non-State Actors, Domestic Structures, and International Institutions*. Cambridge: Cambridge University Press.

————. 1995b. *Cooperation Among Democracies: The European Influence on U.S. Foreign Policy*. Princeton, N.J.: Princeton University Press.

Robertson, A. H. 1966. *European Institutions—Cooperation: Integration: Unification*. 2d ed. New York: Frederick A. Praeger.

Rock, David. 1989. *Argentina 1516–1987: From Spanish Colonization to Alfonsin*. Berkeley: University of California Press.

Roessler, Friederich, Warren F. Schwartz, and Alan Sykes. 1997. Understanding Dispute Resolution in the WTO/GATT System. Unpublished manuscript, Georgetown University Law Center, Washington, D.C.

Rogowski, Ronald. 1989. *Commerce and Coalitions*. Princeton, N.J.: Princeton University Press.

Romano, Cesare. 1999. The Proliferation of International Judicial Bodies: The Pieces of the Puzzle. *New York University Journal of International Law and Politics* 31 (4):709–51.

Rosenne, Shabtai. 1995. *The World Court: What It Is and How It Works*. 5th ed. Dordrecht: Martinus Nijhoff.

Sands, Philippe, Ruth Mackenzie, and Yuval Shany, eds. 1999. *Manual on International Courts and Tribunals*. London: Butterworths.

Sauvy, Alfred. 1967. *Histoire Économique de la France entre les Deux Guerres*. Vol. 2. Paris: Fayard.

Scammell, W. M. 1985. The Working of the Gold Standard. In *The Gold Standard in Theory and History*, edited by Barry Eichengreen, 103–19. New York: Methuen.

Schachter, Oscar. 1977. The Twilight Existence of Nonbinding International Agreements. *American Journal of International Law* 71:296–304.

————. 1991. *International Law in Theory and Practice*. Dordrecht: Martinus Nijhoff.

Schattschneider, E. E. 1935. *Politics, Pressures, and the Tariff*. New York: Prentice Hall.

Schauer, Frederick, and Virginia J. Wise. 1997. Legal Positivism as Legal Information. *Cornell Law Review* 82 (5):1080–1110.

Schepel, Harm. 1998. The Mobilisation of European Community Law. In *Soziologie des Rechts*, edited by J. Brand and D. Strempel, 443–56. Baden-Baden: Nomos.

Schoenbaum, Thomas. 1998. APEC and Dispute Settlement. In *China in the World Trade: Defining the Principles of Engagement*, edited by Frederick M. Abbott, 189–96. Cambridge, Mass.: Kluwer Law International.

Schoultz, Lars. 1981. *Human Rights and United States Policy Toward Latin America*. Princeton, N.J.: Princeton University Press.

Schulz, Donald E., and Deborah Sundloff Schulz. 1994. *The United States, Honduras, and the Crisis in Central America*. Boulder, Colo.: Westview Press.

Schwartz, Jürgen. 1988. *Die Befolgung von Vorabentscheidungen des Europäischen Gerichtshofs durch deutsche Gerichte*. Baden-Baden: Nomos.

Schwebel, Stephen M. 1996. The Performance and Prospects of the International Court of Justice. In *Perspectives of Air Law, Space Law, and International Business Law for the Next Century*, edited by Karl-Heinz Bockstiegel, 291–98. Köln: Carl Heymanns Verlag.

Secchi, Carlo 1997. The Political Economy of the Uruguay Round: Groups, Strategies, Interests, and Results. In *Multilateralism and Regionalism After the Uruguay Round*, edited by R. Faini and E. Grilli, 61–111. London: Macmillan Press.

Seidel, Martin. 1987. Article 177 EEC: Experiences and Problems—Germany as a Member State. In *Asser Institute Colloquium on European Law Session XV*, edited by H. Schermers, C. Timmermans, A. Kellermann, and W. J Stewart, 239–58. Amsterdam: Elsevier Science.

Servicio Paz y Justicia Uruguay. 1992. *Uruguay Nunca Más: Human Rights Violations 1972–1985*. Philadelphia: Temple University Press.

Setear, John K. 1999. Whaling and Legalization. Unpublished manuscript. University of Virginia, Charlottesville, Virginia.

Sevilla, Christina R. 1997. A Political Economy Model of GATT/WTO Trade Complaints. Jean Monnet Working Paper 5/97. Cambridge, Mass.: Harvard University Law School.

———. 1998. The Politics of Enforcing GATT and WTO Rules. Ph.D. diss., Harvard University, Cambridge, Mass.

Shapiro, Martin. 1981. *Courts: A Comparative and Political Analysis*. Chicago: University of Chicago Press.

Shaw, Jo. 1998. Constitutional Settlements and the Citizen After the Treaty of Amsterdam. Jean Monnet Working Paper 7/98. Cambridge, Mass.: Harvard University Law School.

Shihata, Ibrahim F. I. 1994. *The World Bank Inspection Panel*. New York: Oxford University Press for the World Bank.

Shonfield, Andrew. 1976. *Politics and Trade*. London: Oxford University Press.

Sikkink, Kathryn. 1993. Human Rights, Principled Issue-Networks, and Sovereignty in Latin America. *International Organization* 47 (3):411–42.

———. 1996. The Emergence, Evolution, and Effectiveness of the Latin American Human Rights Network. In *Constructing Democracy: Human Rights, Citizenship, and Society in Latin America*, edited by Elizabeth Jelin and Eric Hershberg, 59–84. Boulder, Colo.: Westview Press.

———. 1997. Reconceptualizing Sovereignty in the Americas: Historical Precursors and Current Practices. *Houston Journal of International Law* 19 (3):705–29.

Simma, Bruno, and Andreas L. Paulus. 1999. The Responsibility of Individuals for Human Rights Abuses in Internal Conflicts: A Positivist View. *The American Journal of International Law* 93:302–16.

Simmons, Beth A. 1993. Why Innovate? Founding the Bank for International Settlements, 1929–30. *World Politics*. 45 (3):361–405.

———. 1994. *Who Adjusts? Domestic Sources of Foreign Economic Policy During the Interwar Years*. Princeton, N.J.: Princeton University Press.

———. 1997. Capacity, Commitment, and Compliance: International Law and the Settlement of Territorial Disputes. Paper presented at the Annual Meeting of the American Political Science Association, Washington, D.C., 28 August.

———. 1998. Compliance with International Agreements. In *Annual Review of Political Science, Vol. 1*, edited by Nelson W. Polsby, 75–94. Palo Alto, Calif.: Annual Reviews, Inc.

———. 2000a. Soft Law Compliance: The Case of Money Laundering. In *Commitment and Compliance: The Role of Non-binding Norms in the International Legal System,* edited by Dinah Shelton. Oxford: Oxford University Press.

———. 2000b. Capacity, Commitment, and Compliance: International Institutions and Territorial Disputes. Unpublished manuscript, Department of Political Science, University of California, Berkeley.

Simon, Jose Luis. 1990. *La Dictadura de Stroessner y Los Derechos Humanos.* Asuncion, Paraguay: Comite de Iglesias.

Skiles, Marilyn E. 1991. Stabilization and Financial Sector Reform in Mexico. Research Paper No. 9125. New York: Federal Reserve Bank.

Slaughter, Anne-Marie. 1995a. International Law in a World of Liberal States. *European Journal of International Law* 6:503–38.

———. 1995b. The Liberal Agenda for Peace: International Relations Theory and the Future of the United Nations. *Transnational Law and Contemporary Problems* 4:377–419.

———. 1997a. Busting Out All Over: The Proliferation of Actors in the International System. Unpublished manuscript prepared for the Conference on New Challenges for the Rule of Law: Lawyers, Internationalization, and the Social Construction of Legal Rules, 7–9 November, Santa Barbara, Calif.

———. 1997b. The Real New World Order. *Foreign Affairs* 76 (5):183–97.

———. 2000. Governing the Global Economy Through Government Networks. In *The Role of Law in International Politics*, edited by Michael Byers, 177–205. Oxford: Oxford University Press.

Slaughter, Anne-Marie, Alec Stone Sweet, and Joseph H. H. Weiler, eds. 1998. *The European Court and National Courts—Doctrine and Jurisprudence: Legal Change in Its Social Context.* Oxford: Hart Publishing.

Smith, James McCall. 2000. The Politics of Dispute Settlement Design: Explaining Legalism in Regional Trade Pacts. *International Organization* 54 (1):137–80.

Soesastro, Hadi. 1994. The Institutional Framework for APEC: An ASEAN Perspective. In *APEC: Challenges and Opportunities*, edited by Chia Siow Yue, 38–53. Singapore: Institute of Southeast Asian Studies.

Solingen, Etel. 1998. *Regional Orders at Century's Dawn: Global and Domestic Influences on Grand Strategy.* Princeton, N.J.: Princeton University Press.

Stein, Eric. 1981. Lawyers, Judges, and the Making of a Transnational Constitution. *American Journal of International Law* 75:1–27.

Stewart, Terence, ed. 1993–1999. *I–IV GATT Uruguay Round: A Negotiating History 1986–1994.* Hague: Kluwer Law International.

Stone Sweet, Alec. 1998. Constitutional Dialogues in the European Community. In *The European Court and National Courts—Doctrine and Jurisprudence: Legal Change in Its Social Context*, edited by Anne-Marie Slaughter, Alec Stone Sweet, and J. H. H. Weiler, 305–30. Oxford: Hart Publishing.

———. 1999. Judicialization and the Construction of Governance. *Comparative Political Studies* 32 (2):147–84.

———. 2000. *Governing with Judges: Constitutional Politics in Europe.* Oxford: Oxford University Press.

Stone Sweet, Alec, and Thomas Brunell. 1998a. The European Court and the National Courts: A Statistical Analysis of Preliminary References, 1961–95. *Journal of Public European Policy* 5 (1):66–97.

———. 1998b. Constructing a Supranational Constitution: Dispute Resolution and Governance in the European Community. *American Political Science Review* 92 (1):63–80.

Suleiman, Ezra. 1995. Is Democratic Supranationalism a Danger? In *Nationalism and Nationalities in the New Europe*, edited by C. Kupchan, 66–84. Ithaca, N.Y.: Cornell University Press.

Sunstein, Cass R. 1986. Legal Interference with Private Preferences. *University of Chicago Law Review* 53:1129–74.

———. 1996. *Legal Reasoning and Political Conflict.* New York: Oxford University Press.

———. 1997. *Free Markets and Social Justice.* New York: Oxford University Press.

Sykes, Alan O. 1991. Protectionism as a "Safeguard": A Positive Analysis of the GATT "Escape Clause" with Normative Speculations. *University of Chicago Law Review* 58:255–305.

————. 1992. Constructive Unilateral Threats in International Commercial Relations: The Limited Case for Section 301. *Law and Policy in International Business* 23 (2/3):263–330.

Tallberg, Jonas. 1999. Making States Comply: The European Commission, the European Court of Justice, and the Enforcement of the Internal Market. Ph.D. diss., Lund University, Lund, Sweden.

Teubner, Gunther. 1987. Juridification—Concepts, Aspects, Limits, Solutions. In *Juridification of Social Spheres: A Comparative Analysis in the Areas of Labor, Corporate, Antitrust, and Social Welfare Law*, edited by Gunther Teubner, 3–48. New York: DeGruyter.

Thambipillai, Pushpa, and Johan Saravanamuttu. 1985. *ASEAN Negotiations: Two Insights*. Singapore: Institute of Southeast Asian Studies.

Touffait, Adolphe. 1975. Les jurisdictions judiciares françaises devant l'interprétation et l'application du droit communautaire. In *La France et les Communautés Européenes*, edited by J. Rideau, P. Gerbet, M. Torrelli, and R. M. Chevallier. Paris: Librairie Générale de droit et de jurisprudence.

Trimble, Philip. 1985. International Trade and the "Rule of Law." *Michigan Law Review* 83 (February): 1016–32.

Tsebelis, George. 1994. The Power of the European Parliament as a Conditional Agenda-Setter. *American Political Science Review* 88 (1):128–42.

Tsebelis, George, and Geoffrey Garrett. n.d. The Institutional Determinants of Supranationalism in the European Union. Unpublished manuscript, Yale University, New Haven, Conn.

Tyler, Tom R. 1990. *Why People Obey the Law*. New Haven, Conn. and London: Yale University Press.

U.S. Congressional Research Service. 1979. *Human Rights and U.S. Foreign Assistance: Experiences and Issues in Policy Implementation (1977–1978)*. Report Prepared for U.S. Senate Committee on Foreign Relations. Washington, D.C.: U.S. Government Printing Office.

U.S. Department of State. 1998. Honduras Report on Human Rights Practices for 1997. Available at <www.global/human_rights/1997_hrp_report/honduras.html>.

U.S. Executive Branch. 1997. Study on the Operation and Effect of the North American Free Trade Agreement (NAFTA). Available at <www.ustreas.gov>.

United Nations. 1991. Commission on Human Rights. Report of the United Nations Working Group on Enforced or Involuntary Disappearances. New York: UN.

————. 1992–1999. Reports of the Special Rapporteur on Torture, Sir Nigel Rodley. New York: UN.

————. 1998. Report of the United Nations Working Group on Enforced or Involuntary Disappearances. New York: UN.

Upham, Frank K. 1987. *Law and Social Change in Postwar Japan*. Cambridge, Mass.: Harvard University Press.

Urata, Shujiro. 1998. Foreign Direct Investment and APEC. In *Asia-Pacific Crossroads: Regime Creation and the Future of APEC*, edited by Vinod K. Aggarwal and Charles E. Morrison, 87–188. New York: St. Martin's.

Vaky, Viron, and Heraldo Munoz. 1993. *The Future of the Organization of American States*. New York: Twentieth Century Fund.

Vedel, Georges. 1987. L'attitude des jurisdictions françaises envers les traités européens. Working Paper. Saarbrücken: Europa-Institut der Universität des Saarlands.

Verdier, Daniel. 1994. *Democracy and International Trade: Britain, France, and the United States, 1860–1990*. Princeton, N.J.: Princeton University Press.

Victor, David G. 1998. The Operation and Effectiveness of the Montreal Protocol's Non-compliance Procedure. In *The Implementation and Effectiveness of International Environmental Commitments*, edited by David G. Victor, Kal Raustiala, and Eugene B. Skolnikoff, 137–76. Cambridge: MIT Press.

Victor, David G., Kal Raustalia, and Eugene B. Skolnikoff. 1998. *The Implementation and Effectiveness of International Environmental Commitments: Theory and Practice*. Cambridge, Mass.: MIT Press.

Weatherhill, Steven. 1997. Reflections on EC Law's Implementation Imbalance in Light of the Ruling in *Heley Lomas*. In *Law and Diffuse Interests in the European Legal Order*, edited by Ludwig Kramer, Hans W. Micklitz, and Klaus Tonner, 31–53. Baden-Baden: Nomos.

Weil, Prosper. 1972. Preface. In *Le role politique du judge administratif Français*, edited by Daniele Lorschak. Paris: Librarie générale de droit et de jurisprudence.

————. 1983. Towards Relative Normativity in International Law? *American Journal of International Law* 77:413–42.

Weiler, J. H. H. 1991. The Transformation of Europe. *Yale Law Journal* 100:2403–83.

————. 1994. A Quiet Revolution: The European Court of Justice and Its Interlocutors. *Comparative Political Studies* 26 (4):510–34.

————. 1995. The State Über Alles: Demos, Telos, and the German Maastricht Decision. European University Institute Working Paper. Fiesole: European University Institute.

————. 1998. Epilogue: The European Courts of Justice: Beyond Doctrine or the Legitimacy Crisis of European Constitutionalism. In *The European Court and National Courts—Doctrine and Jurisprudence: Legal Change in Its Social Context*, edited by Anne-Marie Slaughter, Alec Stone Sweet, and J. H. H. Weiler, 365–91. Oxford: Hart Publishing.

————. 1999. *The Constitution of Europe: Do the New Clothes Have an Emperor? And Other Essays on European Integration*. Cambridge: Cambridge University Press.

Welch, Claude E., Jr. 1992. The African Commission on Human and People's Rights: A Five-Year Report and Assessment. *Human Rights Quarterly* 14:43–57.

Wesley, Michael. 1999. The Asian Crisis and the Adequacy of Regional Institutions. *Contemporary Southeast Asia* 21 (1):54–73.

White, James Boyd. 1990. *Justice as Translation: An Essay in Cultural and Legal Criticism*. Chicago: University of Chicago Press.

Wight, Martin. 1977. *Systems of States*. Leicester: Leicester University Press.

Williamson, Oliver. 1989. Transaction Cost Economics. In *Handbook of Industrial Organization*, edited by R. Schmalensee and R. D. Willig, 135–182. Amsterdam: North Holland.

Wils, G. 1993. *Prejudiciële vragen van Belgische rechters en hun gevolgen*. Pradvies. Belgium: Tjeenk Willink.

Winham, Gilbert. 1986. *International Trade and the Tokyo Round Negotiation*. Princeton, N.J.: Princeton University Press.

————. 1998. NAFTA Chapter 19 and the Development of International Administrative Law—Applications in Antidumping and Competition Law. *Journal of World Trade* 32 (1):65–84.

Wirth, David A. 1994. Reexamining Decision-Making Processes in International Environmental Law. *Iowa Law Review* 79:769–802.

World Bank. 1995. World Data. CD-ROM, STARS retrieval system. Washington, D.C.: World Bank.

————. 1998. World Development Indicators database. Washington, D.C.: World Bank.

World Trade Organization. 1995. *The Results of the Uruguay Round of Multilateral Trade Negotiations*. Geneva: WTO.

Yamakage, Susumu. 1997. Japan's National Security and Asia-Pacific's Regional Institutions in the Post–Cold War Era. In *Network Power: Japan and Asia,* edited by Peter J. Katzenstein and Takashi Shiraishi, 275–305. Ithaca, N.Y.: Cornell University Press.

Yamazawa, Ippei. 1992. On Pacific Economic Integration. *Economic Journal* 102 (November):1519–29.

Yarbrough, Beth, and Robert M. Yarbrough. 1992. *Cooperation and Governance in International Trade: The Strategic Organizational Approach*. Princeton, N.J.: Princeton University Press.

Young, Oran R. 1979. *Compliance with Public Authority*. Baltimore, Md.: Johns Hopkins University Press.

————. 1989. The Politics of International Regime Formation: Managing Natural Resources and the Environment. *International Organization* 43 (3):349–75.

Zaring, David. 1998. International Law by Other Means: The Twilight Existence of International Financial Regulatory Organizations. *Texas International Law Journal* 33:218–330.

Zhang, Yunling. 1998. China and APEC. In *Asia-Pacific Crossroads: Regime Creation and the Future of APEC*, edited by Vinod K. Aggarwal and Charles E. Morrison, 213–34. New York: St. Martin's.

Zoller, Elisabeth. 1992. *Droit des relations extérieures*. Paris: Presses Universitaires de Paris.

Zuleeg, Manfred. 1993. Bundesfinanzhof und Gemeinschaftsrecht. In *75 Jahre Reichsfinanzhof-Bundesfinanzhof,* edited by Prasident der Bundesfinanzhof, 115–30. Bonn: Stollfuß Verlag.